MORE
THAN
CHATTEL

Blacks in the Diaspora

Darlene Clark Hine,
John McCluskey, Jr.,
and David Barry Gaspar

General Editors

Rita, a celebrated black beauty at Rio de Janeiro ca. 1822 by Augustus Earle (1793–1838), watercolor: 20 x 28.9 cm. Rex Nan Kinell Collection, the National Library of Australia.

MORE THAN CHATTEL

BLACK WOMEN AND SLAVERY IN THE AMERICAS

Edited by

David Barry Gaspar and Darlene Clark Hine

Indiana University Press • Bloomington and Indianapolis

The paper used in this publication meets the minimum requirements of American
National Standard for Information Sciences—Permanence of Paper for Printed
Library Materials, ANSI Z39.48-1984.

Manufactured in the United States of America

Library of Congress Cataloging-in-Publication Data

More than chattel : black women and slavery in the Americas / edited
   by David Barry Gaspar and Darlene Clark Hine.
      p.   cm. — (Blacks in the diaspora)
   Includes bibliographical references (p.   ) and index.
   ISBN 0-253-33017-3 (cloth: alk. paper). — ISBN 0-253-21043-7
(pbk. : alk. paper)
      1. Slavery—America.   2. Women slaves—America—Social conditions.
   3. Women, Black—America—Social conditions.   4. Antislavery movements—
   America.   I. Gaspar, David Barry.   II. Hine, Darlene Clark.   III. Series.
   HT1049.M62   1996
   306.3'62'082—dc20   95-36096

1 2 3 4 5 01 00 99 98 97 96

To the memory of two black
mothers and teachers

Anne-Marie Felina Gaspar Nicklette
Lottie Mae Thompson Clark

CONTENTS

PREFACE

The idea for this book originated in several conversations between the editors about scholarly works on slavery, slave societies, and women's history. Recent scholarship indicated that there was a lively interest in these fields, but we wondered to what extent scholars actually engaged in intellectual exchange across them, or how work in each may have affected the other. Areas of inquiry may initially develop independently, but later on their connections may become clearer and more integrated work can emerge. Has this occurred in the study of slavery and women's history? As interesting as this question obviously is, we thought that an initial stage in developing or finding a satisfactory answer would be to ask what work was being done on black women and slavery in the Americas. We were particularly interested in themes and conceptual frames. A call for papers produced an interesting set of clusters of themes, and these have shaped the organization of this volume, which, it is clear, does not have a comprehensive geographical or regional coverage within the Americas.

The contributors to this volume, focusing on the lives, situations, and experiences of slave and free black women, explore diverse dimensions of slavery and the related forces that shaped slave society to show that one of the most decisive of these forces was gender, however it may have been constructed in particular societies or applied in particular situations. To explore slavery and slave society through the prism of the lives of black women is to come to a better understanding of how much scholars have missed or misconstrued when they have used the term *slave* without due regard to gender, or with reference specifically to slave men. Gendered relations and expectations within the slave societies of the Americas constituted a powerful force that shaped the lives of slaves in such a way that slave women experienced slavery quite differently from slave men, although it is difficult to identify a strong sense of such differentiation in the slave laws. These laws lump the slave population of both sexes together in the interest of social control, presenting a homogenized image that conceals more than it reveals about the realities of slave life. The study of slave women through other kinds of sources, including plantation records and other accounts of their responses to slavery, help to reveal a more richly differentiated picture of slavery.

Black women were exploited as slaves in regard to both their productive and their reproductive capacities. Their resistance to slavery was rooted in a deep sense of the oppressive weight of this double burden which they were forced to carry and to endure. If slave women did not figure prominently in the organization of collective resistance such as revolt, it was not because they lacked the will but because, as mothers of children and nurturers of their families, they engaged in less confrontational or nonviolent forms of resistance that emphasized the need for creative struggle to survive dehumanization and abuse. In this they set an example for their children and menfolk. The chapters in this volume reflect these concerns about the value of the study of black women and slavery in the Americas. Together they help to present a sharper image of the forces of slavery against which black women fought for survival and for dignity, for themselves, for their families, for their children's children, because they saw themselves as more than chattel, more than the personal property of another.

The materials discussed in the fifteen chapters facilitate the organization into three parts: "Africa and the Americas," "Life and Labor," and "Slavery, Resistance, and Freedom." If part of the main concern of this collection of essays is captured in the subtitle, "Black Women and Slavery in the Americas," then the African background context of the cultures and societies from which the slaves came to the Americas and the circumstances under which they were uprooted and transported through forced migration become matters of major concern. The first chapter, by Claire Robertson, in the part entitled "Africa and the Americas," deals with that context and serves as an introduction to the book. Robertson's deeply probing essay, focusing primarily on the issues of family and the sexual division of labor, suggests a number of ways to answer basic questions about what must be taken into account about African society and culture in order to interpret the experiences of black women under slavery in the Americas.

The eight chapters in the part entitled "Life and Labor" emphasize that black women in slave societies of the Americas were valued primarily because of their productive capacities as workers in a wide range of environments. Their primary involvement in commodity production and the supply of other labor services may have dominated the thinking of slaveowners, but black women struggled against enduring lives overwhelmingly devoted to work for their masters' benefit. Within the interstices of the various slave systems of the Americas, black women opened up enough space for the realization of some autonomy. Richard H. Steckel, Cheryll Ann Cody, Mary Karasch, Robert A. Olwell, Hilary Beckles, Robert W. Slenes, Wilma King, and Brenda E. Stevenson focus on a wide range of issues within this thematic frame, including the health of slave women, their socialization, childbearing and rearing, motherhood, domestic work, life on the frontier, commercial employment and autonomy, and the significance of the black family.

Although scholarship about slavery in the Americas has expanded topically in recent years, slave resistance remains of major interest, partly because the nature of slavery invests the phenomenon with an enduring significance that is also related to the larger human struggle against oppression in its various forms. It is also partly because the growing interest in the history of black women in slavery raises new questions about resistance, or forces a reformulation of old questions that were perhaps once thought to have been addressed adequately. Building upon much wider contexts of slave life and labor, three of the chapters in the part entitled "Slavery, Resistance, and Freedom" focus on slave resistance to show that women were much involved in this complex response to slavery based demonstrably on their consciousness that they were more than chattel. Barbara

Bush, David Barry Gaspar and Bernard Moitt explore the individual and collective efforts of slave women to challenge the forces of dehumanization and destruction inherent in slavery.

Collective slave resistance in the form of revolt was often aimed at the attainment of freedom ultimately, that is to say, freedom from white ownership and rule, but many slave women were able to obtain their individual freedom through other means. The origins of most of these women within slavery and the dominant impact of slavery as a shaper of relations in slave society meant in the end that freedom was always limited. In the last three chapters of this volume, David P. Geggus, Susan M. Socolow, and L. Virginia Gould explore dimensions of the worlds of free black/colored women and show that the study of the lives and circumstances of this section of slave society in the Americas, which was neither slave nor fully free, offers insights into the character of slave society. In slavery and in freedom, gender factors shaped the lives of black women in significant ways. Much work remains to be done, of course, on all of the issues raised in this volume; we hope that the work presented here will stimulate research into other questions that will ultimately lead to a better understanding of the different roads that black women in the Americas have traveled in their quest for true emancipation.

We would like to thank all of the contributors for their patience and support in the completion of this project. To Joan Catapano, Assistant Director of Indiana University Press, we offer special thanks for believing that no obstacle was too difficult to overcome. Thanks are also due to Connie Blackmore, Dot Sapp, Thelma Kithcart, Jenna Golnik, and Jane Twigg for typing the manuscript. Connie Blackmore and Jenna Golnik especially always seemed to make problems fade away with ease.

Finally, we acknowledge with gratitude the contribution of Celia E. Naylor-Ojurongbe, who graciously took time off from her own scholarly pursuits to work on the selected bibliography.

THE EDITORS

AFRICA
AND THE
AMERICAS

1

AFRICA INTO THE AMERICAS?
SLAVERY AND WOMEN,
THE FAMILY, AND THE
GENDER DIVISION OF LABOR

Claire Robertson

Among the many forms of socioeconomic deprivation, African slavery on both sides of the Atlantic has probably provoked the most historical debate, and recent contributors to it have focused on women slaves. Still, there has been little cross-fertilization of ideas between Africanists and New World specialists. It is time to remedy this situation. In the 1990s we need to look at our African heritage and the various sorts of issues that muddy the waters. The study of gender issues in particular provides an excellent lens for new analyses, while use of comparative method can clarify much about socioeconomic structure.

This chapter attempts to place New World African slavery as it related to women into the context of African slavery and culture, and by so doing illuminate both. It draws on my own and others' African research and on recent research on gender with respect to New World slavery, especially the other essays in this volume. I will try to identify the parameters of some of the crucial issues and to widen the debate where appropriate, while acknowledging that there is a pressing need for more research. These issues include the definition of types of slavery and status deprivation; the matrifocal family debate, especially as it pertains to possible African retentions; and labor use with regard to gender, sometimes termed the gender division of labor, with particular attention to fertility issues as they relate to class.

This analysis is possible only because of the opening up of research on African slavery in the 1970s and 1980s that followed several decades in which the subject was almost entirely ignored in the explosion of African nationalism and pan-Africanism surrounding independence for most countries on the continent.[1] African and African-American nationalists often agreed that white rule had damaged male control over females. African men cited colonial laws that prohibited wife beating, while women were gaining economic autonomy, if not usually prosperity. African-American men felt that slavery had removed their authority to control their families—wives and children alike—and their power to protect them against white atrocities. Any attempt to consider women's rights was seen as divisive and irrelevant; race oppression was the central issue.

We have now moved into a more radical phase of scholarly analysis. In it no one is exempt; everyone is equal. This equality assumes not only that humans are entitled to equality of rights but also that they have equality in human potential—that men, women, children, Africans, Europeans, African-Americans, and European-Americans alike share the complexity that makes human nature so endlessly fascinating. This means, however, that if virtue, intelligence, and altruism can be found universally, so can ambition, greed, and violence. In every group there are victims and oppressors and, especially in many cases of African slavery, it was possible to be simultaneously both slave and slaveowner. The determinants of the nature of oppression are not to be found in any essential human nature but in economic systems. If there is a universal human need, it is to maximize survival by maximizing gain, and most civilizations have employed slavery at one time or another to do so. At issue here is how African slavery in its cultural context relates to African-American slavery in the New World, especially with regard to women.

Types of Slavery and Status Deprivation

Slavery was universal in highly differentiated societies in the ancient world, including those in Africa. But its form varied radically in accordance with the economic needs of a society, which could change over time. Sub-Saharan Africa was an ancient source of slaves, albeit on a relatively small scale, supplying North Africa, the Middle East, and the Persian Gulf area. A few African slaves even trickled into underdeveloped northern Europe, but they were more curiosities than economic necessities in medieval times. It was only with the worldwide expansion of the European economy in the seventeenth and eighteenth centuries that the European-American demand for African slaves assumed large proportions. An enabling factor in the development of this trade was the existence in Africa of an internal and an export slave trade. The export trade, however, seems to have been much smaller than the ultimate size of the New World trade.[2] In European eyes Africans made desirable slaves because they were accustomed to agricultural labor—most were sedentary horticulturalists—and they were able to endure harsh labor in the tropical West Indies. The epidemiological factor worked in Africans' favor and against Native Americans, who died in droves from exposure to European-borne diseases. Africans also died in large numbers under the notorious conditions of the Middle Passage and from harsh treatment and hard labor in the West Indies, in particular; but ultimately they survived their masters and mistresses.

Those were not, however, the main reasons Africans were enslaved; nor was their race.[3] They became slaves primarily as a result of the economic needs of Africa and the Americas. In both areas, wealth was to a large extent dependent on labor recruitment because ownership of land was useless without labor to work it. According to Mary Karasch (chapter 4 in this volume), frontier areas of Brazil in the early nineteenth century absorbed most of the slaves, drawing them away from older settled areas in a pattern similar to the large-scale sale of slaves away from Virginia to newer areas of settlement in North America. Richard Roberts and Suzanne Miers noted that expanding African states were often both the greatest suppliers (they sold their prisoners of war) and the greatest users of slaves.[4] However, one should not push this analogy too far. There were major differences between sub-Saharan Africa, where most land was controlled but not owned by lineages,[5] and the southern United States, for instance, where private land ownership eventually triumphed as the westward movement of European-Americans drove out Native Americans, whose concepts of landholding were more akin to those of Africans. Nonetheless, it is well to recognize that without a West African slave trade that took advantage of extensive interior trade networks, there would have been very little export slave trade because of the incapacity and ignorance of European-Americans regarding Africa and the ability of Africans to control trade and keep out foreigners. As Walter Rodney observed, the African ruling class enabled, assisted, and benefited from the slave trade.[6] Thus Africa and the Americas have been inextricably linked by a trade that most scholars agree exploited more Africans than it benefited.

Large areas of precolonial Africa were underpopulated, hence the need for slavery, which served as a means both to recruit much-needed labor and to increase population. The export slave trade, of course, only magnified the need for slavery within certain African societies by depopulating some areas. Igor Kopytoff and Suzanne Miers pointed out that slavery in Africa entailed a continuum all the way from relatively mild forms of clientage and pawnship to chattel slavery similar to the European-American form prevalent in the United States and the West Indies.[7] There were areas in Africa where European chattel-type slavery existed owing to extensive European settlement, as in South Africa.[8] This chapter, however, is particularly concerned with forms of slavery used by Africans. These forms were far more complex and varied than chattel slavery as it evolved in the United States. They were also usually less onerous. The variations can be explained by the tremendous cultural differences within Africa, the world's second largest continent with thousands of languages and cultures, and by contrasting economic conditions. Mercantile rather than industrial capitalism characterized most eighteenth- and nineteenth-century West African economies; large areas paid tribute and had a fair degree of local economic autonomy. In the late-eighteenth and nineteenth centuries, however, the United States and the West Indies were required to meet the needs of industrial capitalist development in Europe and the northeastern United States. The routinization of slave labor in their economies was driven by the needs of the industrializing world, which forced

ever-greater rates of exploitation in a foretaste of the relationship of the twentieth century "developed" world to the "developing" world, where mechanization
in the center and partial mechanization at the periphery increased the rate of
exploitation of manual labor. The cotton gin and the steam-driven sugar mill
created a need for more slave labor in the nineteenth-century South and the Caribbean,[9] just as the twentieth-century introduction of the plow to reduce men's
labor in breaking ground in sub-Saharan Africa greatly intensified women's labor
of cultivation. Similarly, the increasing involvement of West Africa in the "legitimate" export trade (not the "illegitimate" slave trade) in commodities needed
for European industrial use, such as palm oil, increased the internal demand for
slaves in the late nineteenth century.[10]

Despite vast variations in African forms of slavery, it is possible to make some
generalizatic f the first striking characteristic about African slavery is its variability—fr   nild debt servitude to harsh plantation slavery—the second is its
malleabi   Even under harsh chattel slavery in Africa (usually called Islamic or
market-based), manumission was possible for significant numbers of slaves. In
the nineteenth-century Sahel, where a close analogue to southern United States
chattel slavery existed, "because so many slaves were women, one feature of
slavery . . . was the assimilation of females through concubinage and marriage
and the *automatic emancipation* of children by slave women, if the master accepted paternity."[11] In fact, multiple modes of emancipation were a common
feature of African slavery. Most slaves kept in Africa were women who, if they
bore free children to their masters, could often be freed themselves. Moreover,
male and female slaves usually had the right to keep any monetary earnings and
so could buy their freedom more easily than was the case in the United States, although some owners did hire out slaves and keep most of their earnings, as in
the United States.[12]

But most African slavery was not chattel slavery, even though most large-scale
slavery was. More common was what has variously been termed lineage, kin-
based, or absorptionist slavery, which was used primarily to increase labor but
had as an essential feature the eventual assimilation of the slave into society.
Two-generation slavery was therefore uncommon.[13] The fact that most slaves
were women aided this absorption, as did polygyny when women became junior
wives to free men. In Islamized societies where free women were secluded, slave
women performed, as they did in other African societies, most of the field labor.
Pawnship was very common; most pawns were girls whose labor paid the interest on their fathers' or other male relatives' debts. If they were seduced by a male
member of the creditor's lineage, they would be married to him, with cancella-
tion of the debt serving as bridewealth to legitimate the marriage. In such cases
the status of pawn merged invisibly with the status of woman; both were disad-
vantaged.[14] Such arrangements were particularly common in mercantile West
African coastal society.

Less severe than pawnship was clientage, in which slaves had autonomy over
most aspects of their lives but by law "belonged" to free persons or lineages and

owed them a share of their crops, cash, or labor each year, as well as political loyalty. Such retainers were typical of African societal organization into lineage families, clans which recruited by birth, marriage, slavery, and free clientage.[15] The distance between clientage and chattel slavery was great; one ultimate goal of clientage was to increase the free population (a comparison with the situation of Indian slave women in Brazil as mentioned by Karasch in chapter 4 is worth attention). While in most African societies slave ancestry carried a stigma, it could also be hidden because it was not usually associated with a caste bearing visible markers. In Africa, with the abolition of slavery ex-slaves usually became clients and beneficiaries of a certain patronage from former owners, whereas in the United States South this was far less common because racism, as well as continued efforts by whites to subordinate as laborers African-Americans who tried to evade that control, inhibited the development of clientage.[16]

However, slavery in Africa was not a benign institution. It was, as in the Americas, concerned above all with the extraction of maximum profit from the slave's labor. To do so it relied on force. Claude Meillassoux's description of Sahelian slavery could just as well apply to the United States plantation South: "Desocialized, depersonalized, desexualized, slaves are susceptible to a severe exploitation not tempered by any concern about preserving their physical and social capacities of reproduction." In another telling description equally applicable to southern slaveowners, Meillassoux said that "the [slaveholding] aristocracy must be a repressive class, armed, turned as much against the [free] people as against the slave class."[17] The element of force was, of course, essential to the creation and perpetuation of slave systems, but even in this aspect Africans had many varieties of enslavement. A majority of slaves were probably prisoners of war, but kidnapping and judicial processes also accounted for substantial numbers, as well as the innumerable small transactions involved in pawning. The methods used varied in incidence over time and from place to place.[18] In times of famine people sometimes sold their children to wealthier buyers or to passing slavers.[19]

There were also more means of escape in Africa than in the United States or the West Indies. If slaves were, by definition, strangers in their owners' societies, in Africa some had the possibility of returning home, although if they had been very young when enslaved they often no longer knew their original homes or had lost rights in their natal societies.[20] Nonetheless, fleeing a cruel owner was more likely to be possible where there were fewer means of enforcement—no patrols to stop runaways—and societies nearby that did *not* practice slavery. Because of the kinship organization of the vast majority of societies, the slave or ex-slave might always be a stranger to some extent, but there were numerous methods for creating fictive kinship ties. There were also usually means for improving one's status within slavery. In nineteenth-century equatorial Africa, for example, some male slaves became heads of free lineages.[21] This was not a unique situation for precolonial Africa. It is therefore not surprising that given the vulnerability of kinless persons in many African societies (flight was more likely to bring reenslavement elsewhere than liberation, for instance), some male slaves preferred to buy slave women as wives for themselves than to buy their own freedom. There were also slave women who owned slaves.[22] "Those who have people are wealthier than those with money" is an old Igbo saying.[23]

To turn to slavery in the United States South is to narrow the definition of slavery considerably, despite the attempts at ameliorative views. Of course, slavery there did not begin as the relatively rigid institution it later became. In the early days of white settlement there was a continuum from white and black indentured servants to chattel slavery, but as the desire to increase the rate of exploitation arose with the development of industrial capitalism, slavery evolved in a segregated, castelike direction, with fewer opportunities for manumission.[24] Frederick Cooper noted that "racial distinctiveness is a particular form of the more universal condition of the slave . . . being an outsider."[25] As the nineteenth century wore on, southern slaves had only those rights their owners chose to give them, which meant that they were completely subject to the arbitrary whims of those who profited from their labor. Even freed blacks in the South were constantly threatened with re-enslavement, and in the North they were subject to restrictions on mobility (many states had constitutional provisions prohibiting freed blacks from entry), education, occupations, meetings, and a variety of other activities.[26] Meanwhile, forms of debt servitude in which whites had participated mostly disappeared and were made illegal by the end of the nineteenth century.[27] In the West Indies they had disappeared by 1700.[28]

Slavery elsewhere in the Americas—in the dependencies of countries which had not yet developed industrialized economies—could display all the African virtuosity in variations. Stanley Elkins was apparently confused and dismayed by Latin American slavery, which he found exhibited, in legal terms, "a comparative lack of precision and logic . . . , an exasperating dimness of line between the slave and free portions of society, a multiplicity of points of contact between the two, a confusing promiscuity of color, such as would never have been thinkable in our country [the United States]." Manumission and miscegenation were common, and emancipation was accomplished smoothly,[29] with constant reminders of African forms of slavery. Freedpersons in Brazil filled essential economic slots, and many slaves bought their own freedom.[30]

Nowhere is the distance between Africa and the southern United States more striking than in Cooper's East African example of the use of slaves by owners as armed soldiers,[31] also common in West Africa. While a random sample of Work Projects Administration (WPA) slave narratives yielded an example of a slave being used to replace his conscripted southern master as a soldier in the United States Civil War,[32] it stood out for its uniqueness. United States slaves were allowed to bear arms for the Confederacy only as a result of increasingly dire conditions after March 1865.[33] If more prosperous freed blacks in the United States and the West Indies routinely owned and even traded slaves (see Susan M. Socolow, chapter 14 this volume),[34] there is little evidence that slaves themselves owned slaves (Hilary Beckles, chapter 6 in this volume, gives one example from Barbados). The conclusion is inescapable. Despite all the evidence adduced by

Eugene Genovese, Herbert Gutman, Angela Davis,[35] and others regarding United States slaves' refusal to be victims and their participation in making their own world, the fact remains that the definition of slavery as it evolved in the southern United States and the West Indies was much narrower than in Africa, the continuum truncated, and race used as a caste marker.

Marriage and the Family: The Matrifocal Debate and the African Heritage

Among students of slavery in the United States, no area has provoked so much controversy as slavery's impact on African-American marriage and the family, probably because of the contemporary implications for welfare policy. The debate has centered mainly on the issue of matrifocality, defined as family disorganization, some scholars and policymakers claiming that both were a legacy of slavery,[36] others that neither occurred.[37] In this debate the use of African evidence has been problematical: dismissing African variability as proscribing any generalizations; describing United States slavery as so disruptive as to destroy any African cultural heritage; or, conversely, claiming that the African cultural heritage, in particular the matrifocal family model, prepared African-Americans in useful ways for their experience under slavery. Furthermore, lack of attention to African materials has led scholars to compare the status of free and slave males without considering women, as well as to ignore African accommodations to slavery in seeking to explain African-American accommodations to it. The comparison is always to free Africans, usually male. Most scholars demonstrate only a passing knowledge of African historical sources, which is understandable given its formidable variety and quantity. Here I will suggest insights on this debate that have occurred to me as an Africanist with a passing knowledge of the American historical literature. The comparison will be based mainly on analysis of precolonial nineteenth-century West African society and of United States slavery from the 1820s to the Civil War as found in ex-slave narratives (collected in the 1930s by the United States government's Work Projects Administration) and in selected secondary sources. Owing to the nature of the sources it is not possible to give exact dates for most of the incidents mentioned.

The argument over African-American families has centered to a great extent on the nature of women as matriarchs, a debate reflected in the various views about African women. It is widely recognized that there are African societies where matrilinearity, female economic independence, or both gave (and give) African women more autonomy and precolonial political power than European-American women can claim historically or in the present. Most spouses in Africa did not and do not practice community of property. In many societies women have historically had the right to own and convey property without male permission. Coastal West Africa in particular has been a locus for extensive involvement of women in trade, with consequences that sometimes involved women having political and economic power. Many African societies had separate male and female structures that involved independent female political action; in southeastern Nigeria women's collective action forced chiefs to abdicate and the British to change their form of colonial rule in the 1920s and 1930s.[38] There is, then, an argument to be made that African cultural forms that survived slavery might include wider and more authoritative roles for women than European-Americans generally recognized.

Indeed, the temptation to see Africa in the Americas is overwhelming, especially when analyzing the lives of slaves held in the United States. The Georgia Sea Islands supply images of women wielding long pestles threshing rice in huge mortars, wearing African-style headscarves or straw hats.[39] Karasch (chapter 4) mentions something similar in Brazil. In many places women carried babies on their backs as they toiled in the fields, slipping them around to nurse.[40] They carried water on their heads, walking gracefully along (Beckles, chapter 6). A striking example was the action of the Virginia slave Sukie, who, in disgust at male behavior while she was on the auction block, raised her dress to expose her genitals to potential buyers as a form of ridicule,[41] an old accepted means for African women to protest against men's actions. (To appreciate one of the profound cultural differences involved, it is only necessary to note that male exposure of genitalia is used in the United States to try to intimidate women.) And then there is, of course, the manifold evidence of African influence present in religious, linguistic, dance,[42] and musical forms.[43] Given no cultural context for all of this, any African or Africanist would still have no problem in identifying, at the very least, strong African influence.

It does not necessarily follow, however, that relatively strong African female autonomy translated itself into African-American matriarchal women. Not only does female autonomy usually mean poverty rather than power, but also the issue of matriarchy is problematic both conceptually and in its use of African evidence. Suzanne Lebsock spotted the conceptual problem accurately; it has everything to do with American patriarchal notions and nothing to do with African evidence for matrifocality. Women are called matriarchs, Lebsock stated,

> when the power they exercise relative to men of their own group is in some respect greater than that defined as appropriate by the dominant culture. Given this standard, women need not be the equals of men, much less men's superiors, in order to qualify as matriarchs. . . . The woman who had no vote, no money, and no protection under the law was nonetheless a "matriarch," so long as she also had no husband present to compete with her for authority over her children.[44]

What about African evidence regarding matriarchy? The fact remains that we have no historical record anywhere of a matriarchal society in a sense equivalent to patriarchal, that is, where women held most positions of power and authority and dominated the society's economic and ideological structure. Matrilinearity, common in Africa, is simply a way of tracing descent or inheritance through the female line from mother's brother to sister's son, not from mother to daughter in an analogue to patrilinearity.[45] Some analogous de facto (because not legal) matri*laterality* (mother-to-daughter succession) occurred in Africa but was not dominant and coexisted with patrilinearity in the same society.[46]

Matrifocality is a different phenomenon again. Contemporary sociologists and anthropologists have begun defining the basic building block of all societies as the unit of mother and children because the father's degree of participation cross-culturally is so variable that hypothesizing the universal existence of the Western-type nuclear family imposes a false assumption. Because of the strong mother-child unit and variable male participation created by polygyny, one might claim some validity for a matrifocal African cultural heritage. However, polygyny was class-related and associated with wealth, and therefore with the kinds of people who were less likely to fall prey to the slave trade. Many slaves came from decentralized societies, which had difficulty defending themselves from the armies of centralized monarchies and were less likely to have large-scale wealth and polygyny. Poor populations were more vulnerable to slavery incurred by reason of debt and to the vagaries of their wealthy patrons. The slave trade absorbed mainly those who were less likely to practice polygyny. In fact, it is almost impossible to distinguish any specific matrifocal African influence in view of the probably stronger influence exerted by the economic constraints imposed on slave families (and free black families, for that matter) by a racist capitalist society. Poverty seems to have had a similar impact on Africans and African-Americans.

Most saliently missing from much of the discussion of "matrifocal" black families in the United States is class and gender analysis,[47] which is shunned by those who profit from black poverty while reinforcing it, and by some African-Americans who perceive the stressing of class and gender differences within the community to be divisive. The focus is therefore on race, which as an analytical (not a political) category contains no methods for finding solutions to problems, since this category invented by the oppressors disregards cultural, geographical, and class differences so completely as to be useless except in relationship to "white" oppression because anyone "black" is defined as "other."[48] This is not to deny that race and racism have taken on a life of their own to force otherwise disparate groups to weld together for political purposes, but caste systems have real economic underpinnings, as does patriarchal and racist ideology, and can only be changed by attacking their economic foundations. To believe that the roots of oppression lie in seeking economic gain is to connect it to the universal need of humans to survive, not to instinct, which is biologically based and therefore immutable. Methods used by the dominant classes to maximize gain in order to ensure their dominance have changed and will continue to do so. Slavery was, above all, an economic system which displayed many variations and changes in order to maximize profit in a context of changing economic systems.[49]

To carry out an analysis of possible African underpinnings of the "matrifocal" family, it is first necessary to define matrifocality. A matrifocal family is one in which the mother plays a substantial role in providing subsistence and making decisions. The father may or may not be present, and there is nothing necessarily unhealthy about it. According to this definition, many precolonial West African families were at least partially matrifocal, especially if they were polygynous. Each wife normally had a hut of her own in a common compound, the children staying with the mother until mostly grown, when males would join their fathers or have separate huts. Most West African women, whether polygynous or not, were (and are) expected to grow or buy the food for their families. If free women were secluded, slave women would grow or buy food for them under the supervision of their mistresses. Thus in the sense of supplying subsistence needs, African families were normally matrifocal. This aspect of African socioeconomic structure carried over into the New World and was reinforced by slavery. As Nancy Tanner put it, "Black women have always been socialized to be strong and resourceful and to know that motherhood . . . is not mutually exclusive to working outside the home."[50]

Decision making is another issue, however. In Africa even daily subsistence decisions—when to plant, what to plant, how much grain or other staple to dole out—were often controlled by men, although the division into "women's" crops and "men's" crops sometimes mitigated that control. Patriarchal rather than matriarchal authority was the dominant norm. So much was this the case that customary etiquette concerning eating in most societies involved separate dining, with men and older boys going first and therefore taking the major share of the protein, while women and children got the leftovers.[51] Access to nutritious food was therefore status-related, and slave diet was often poor, consisting mainly of starchy staples. There were even social norms prohibiting women cooks from snitching from the pot in some societies, or making certain particularly nutritious foods (eggs, meat) taboo for women.[52] Patriarchal ideology that stigmatized women as "other"—left, bad, awkward, wrong, stupid, and so on—was widespread in Africa and still has currency there, as elsewhere. We have had to discard romantic notions of egalitarian precolonial Africa, even while recognizing that colonialism created or vastly exacerbated existing economic inequalities in African societies.

It is very difficult, then, to make an argument supporting matriarchy, or even matrifocality, as dominant in most African societies. Rather, patriarchal authority dominated most facets of life even if women often had substantial economic responsibilities and autonomy. The problem is that too often women's economic autonomy is assumed to entail economic and political power in both Africa and the United States. This has facilitated in Africa the scapegoating of women for social and economic problems (the ideal scapegoat has the image of power while in reality she is powerless to defend herself from victimization)[53] and in the United States the blaming of black families, women members in particular, for African-American problems created by the dominant sector of society. Thus on both sides of the Atlantic patriarchal ideology has contributed to blaming women for socioeconomic problems created by exploitation from the upper classes, with the added oppression in the United States of caste creation according to race and in Africa of the stigma associated with slavery and gender (all slaves' work was stigmatized as being "women's work").[54]

Patriarchal ideology has been abundantly evident in attacks by both white and black scholars on matriarchal or matrifocal slave family structure. There is prima facie evidence that many forces worked against male authority within United States slave households. The argument against the existence of male authority rests on two premises—that conditions under slavery were simply not conducive to the maintenance of family life and that male slave authority was undermined and the integrity of slave families therefore destroyed. Lack of male authority was equated with deformed or nonexistent families. W. E. B. Du Bois stated the case, supported later by others, when he cited such contributory conditions as squalid living, absence or lack of paternal authority, absence of working mothers, and poverty encouraging theft. "Such a family was not an organism at best; and, in its worst aspect, it was a fortuitous agglomeration of atoms," Du Bois observed.[55] Richard O. Wade stated the case forcefully in his work on urban slavery: "the bonds of slavery were a good deal stronger than the bonds of matrimony" because children went with their mothers, who had only shallow affection for them; people had lots of temporary attachments; and women slaves outnumbered men in town.[56]

Among the chief culprits reducing the stability of slave marriages was forced separation. Sale, inheritance of slaves, and the mobility of slaveowners broke up many families. In a sample of 499 ex-slave narratives, Paul Escott found that sale was the primary cause of separation of family members; 58.5 percent of the separations came from sale as compared with 9.4 percent from gift, the closest competitor.[57] Lorenzo Ivy's mother's master caught "cotton fever" and moved south from Virginia, breaking up seven slave families.[58] There are many harrowing tales of family separations.[59] A common, perhaps apocryphal, tale indicates the extreme anxiety among slaves regarding the evil effects of being sold—a mother and her small son, sold separately, meet again years later and get married, only to discover to their horror their true relationship.[60] There is some evidence that women may have been sold more frequently than men, despite assumptions in the literature that men were sold more frequently and willingly by masters because they were more valuable than women and masters did not want to separate mothers and children. The random sample of ex-slave narratives included ninety-six women and eighty-two men drawn from George P. Rawick, *The American Slave: A Composite Autobiography*, and Charles L. Perdue, Jr., et al., *Weevils in the Wheat*.[61] In the narratives frequent mention was made of separation of mothers and babies by sale. Women were more likely than men to be sold (23.4 percent to 20.4 percent) and much more likely to be sold repeatedly (there were six accounts of women being sold several times versus two for men). It makes sense that owners would retain men, who were more valuable in their eyes, and sell women, the obverse of the situation in Africa, where women were more valued and retained and men were more likely to be sold. The preferential sale of women might have militated against the existence of stable families, unless the women sold were mostly childless.

The counterarguments employed to prove the strength, stability, and existence of slave families have by now been generally accepted. Most United States slaves lived in families which were relatively stable. Promoting their stability was in the interests of slaveowners, but families were also a means of resistance for slaves. Cooper noted that everywhere slaveowners relied on a combination of force, economic dependence, and social constraints to keep control over slave populations.[62] Robert Fogel and Stanley Engerman listed the three main functions of a slave family from the slaveowner's point of view as to be an economic unit performing social reproductive functions such as cooking and handing out rations, an instrument for maintaining social control (reducing runaways and pacifying workers), and a means for promoting increase in the slave population. Owners employed a number of incentives to promote marriage, such as giving feasts or holidays, garden plots, and houses, and punishments for divorce or adultery.[63] The arguments for the stability of slave marriage also tend to promote the strong role of the male within the slave family. John Blassingame provides the best example of this, although Gutman and Fogel and Engerman also appear to believe that female-headed households are by nature aberrant and unstable.[64] Blassingame goes so far as to approve some of the more noxious aspects of patriarchal authority within families when he says, "Many [male] slaves were lucky enough to have masters who refused to intercede in family affairs" and allowed bondmen to punish children and beat their wives.[65] In fact, the situation of women slaves showed ample evidence of the exercise of patriarchal authority by both husbands and masters. Masters had to approve slave marriages but often did so at the instigation of male slaves. The prospective brides were not necessarily consulted (see Brenda E. Stevenson, chapter 9 in this volume).[66]

There is a Mongo (Central African) saying, "Don't lose contact with your family if you don't want to become a slave of your husband,"[67] that refers to women's vulnerable position in marriage when their natal family members are not nearby to protect them should their husbands abuse them. Many United States slave women were powerless in this regard. If the routine sale of slaves put all slaves at the mercy of their masters and mistresses, women slaves sold away from their families of origin not only were unlikely to be heads of "matrifocal" families if separated from them but also were in double jeopardy with no natal family to protect them against abusive husbands, although fictive kin might have performed this function. Katie Johnson, an ex-slave from Virginia, said that some "good" masters punished slaves who mistreated their wives, but others did not.[68] One slave was hanged for killing his wife.[69] On occasion bondman and master could unite in fraternal solidarity against a woman. Perdue gave an extraordinary account in which a mistress wanted William Lee whipped for throwing her down on the ground. He and the master went to the barn and staged an elaborate fake whipping out of her sight but not sound, then got drunk together.[70] In an early nineteenth-century West Indian example, Mary Prince helped her master's daughter evade further beating by her drunken father.[71] I found no parallel example of cross-class, cross-race female solidarity when a mistress did the same to protect a bondwoman.[72]

In the West Indies there is evidence suggestive of more patriarchal relations among slaves indicating that male owners and slaves had a common interest in keeping slave women subordinate in order to profit from their labor (see David P. Geggus, chapter 13, and Bernard Moitt, chapter 12, this volume).[73] David Barry Gaspar (chapter 11) found in seventeenth-century Antiguan records six cases of slave men who had killed slave women but none of the opposite. A high male-to-female ratio may have exacerbated rivalries over women. B. W. Higman found that in the British West Indies in the eighteenth century, male slaves had greater social and economic status than female slaves and received more rations, clothing, and utensils from the master. They headed most slave households and held more skilled jobs than women did.[74] Patriarchal ideology and the allowing of privileges to male slaves may in fact have been occasionally successful devices used by slaveowners to divide and conquer the slaves whereby masters traded off authority over slave women to slave men in exchange for acquiescence to masters' authority by the men. Miriam Tlali, a prominent South African author, suggested that white South Africans employed this tactic with some success in their attempts to control Africans.[75]

It is possible, then, that in the desire to combat "matriarchal" ideas scholars have sometimes been blinded to the existence of slave patriarchy. It is true that slave women, owing to their economic roles and residential separation from spouses (which occurred frequently from residence on different plantations as well as from sale), had a fair amount of autonomy. Also, unlike free men, United States and West Indian slave men in the nineteenth century could not legally own their wives and children. All of these factors probably made for a more egalitarian spousal relationship than prevailed in white society at the time.[76] But one must beware of the masking of inequality by the use of relational terms; "social intimacy did not negate economic exploitation: both were part of a highly authoritarian structure couched in a familial ideology," Cooper stated.[77] The institution of slavery was constructed upon and through patriarchal ideology; it reinforced rather than undermined it when reinforcing it suited its own economic interests. In a percipient analysis, Jacqueline Jones stated that

> black women and men in the long run paid a high price for their allegiance to patriarchal family structure and it is important not to romanticize this arrangement as it affected the status and opportunities of women, even within the confines of black community life. . . . Former slaves were "free" only in the sense that they created their own forms of masculine authority as a counter to poverty and racism.[78]

In fact, by vilifying female-headed households patriarchal ideology facilitates class oppression of black families. Here caste creation by race is particularly salient. Black families (here and earlier I use the term *black* intentionally to emphasize the racial category imposed by "whites") have been the victims of conscious attacks by whites, especially under "freedom" in the United States and apartheid

in South Africa. The main vehicle of this attack has been the deprivation of economic opportunities and imposition of poverty. Until relatively recently, blacks
in the United States were barred from serving apprenticeships and joining unions
and were discriminated against in wholesale fashion.[79] Only in the last few years
in South Africa were they allowed to form unions or apprentice for highly
paid jobs (such "job reservation" laws were forced to bend under the pressure of
economic efficiency considerations). Poverty is a great disintegrator of male-
headed families when societal norms enjoin that the male be the chief provider.
To be female-headed is to be poor—because of discrimination against women
expressed in access to education and jobs, disproportionately lower pay, and the
assignment of all the domestic work and most of the child rearing to women.

Some middle-class feminist scholars have given so much primacy to the patriarchal ideology within households, which places an uneven burden of work on
women, that they blame men for women's oppression, which they locate primarily within the household. But a class perspective gives a truer view—that
when the dominant classes find lower-class families to be possible obstacles to
their complete dominance, they will have no compunction about attempting to
destroy them, the first step being to remove men from the household. Employers
prefer to deal with individuals rather than collectively organized workers; families, as well as unions, may provide organization. The destruction of families particularly applies when race is at issue, as racism facilitates the dehumanizing of the
oppressed. African-American scholars, then, are absolutely correct in viewing the
black family as demonstrating strength under adversity, as forming a bulwark
against dehumanization, and as constituting a vehicle for resistance (see Stevenson, chapter 9),[80] while South Africanists have made similar arguments regarding
African families there.[81]

It may be suggested, in fact, that since "free" United States black families no
longer served the function of social control for slaveowners, they then became a
threat and therefore were to be destroyed, or at least not fostered. Lebsock
found that families of freedpersons in antebellum Petersburg, Virginia, suffered: "For free black women, the high rate of gainful employment and the high
incidence of female-headed households were symptoms of oppression . . .
products of a shortage of men and of chronic economic deprivation."[82] When
Frank F. Furstenberg and colleagues controlled for income level in a comparison
of female-headedness by ethnicity in Philadelphia from 1850 to 1880, however,
they found that most of the significant differences between African-Americans
and others disappeared, while the remainder could be accounted for by the
higher incidence of widowhood among African-Americans due to lesser access to
health care and more poverty.[83] Gutman, in his extensive comparisons of various
communities of African- and European-Americans in 1880, 1905, and 1925,
found far more similarities than differences in regard to female-headedness.
Given the demographics of the situation, he expected to find a greater disparity
and fewer males present than he did.[84]

Progressive exclusion from skilled work helped to reduce blacks' upward mobility after 1885, but when class level is considered, black families were not no-

ticeably female-headed in comparison with white families until quite recently.[85] Engerman traced a large differential in the development of female-headed African- and European-American families to the 1930s, but without controlling for income levels. Even so he found less difference than he expected (note the expectations of a high incidence of female-headedness among several scholars here).[86] La Frances Rodgers-Rose analyzed census data from 1960 and 1973 and found a dramatic increase in female-headedness among African-American families that was due more to an increase in the number of unwed mothers than to divorce or desertion by men (family disintegration). She showed a direct correlation between female-headedness and poverty for both whites and blacks, especially associated with the presence of children in the households. Federal government policies in the 1960s for the first time in United States history redistributed income somewhat and allowed more unwed mothers to set up households that were independent of those of their parents, accounting for some of the phenomenon.[87] Welfare laws in many states until recently did not permit aid to families with adult males present. For the poor, an "intact" family was often an unaffordable luxury. Because far more African- than European-American families are poor, more of their children live in female-headed families. Hence, neither the African-influenced subculture nor the legacy-of-slavery arguments explains the high incidence of female-headedness among contemporary African-American families; an economic explanation has more validity. In the words of one analyst,

> in attempting to separate racial from economic inequality and blaming family pathology for black people's condition, current ideology obscures the system's inability to provide jobs, decent wages, and adequate public services for the black poor. And in a racist-patriarchal society, the effects of the system's weaknesses fall most heavily on black women and children. Just as black family life has always been a barometer of racial and economic injustice and at the same time a means of transcending and surviving those injustices, black families headed by women reflect the strength and difficulty of black life in the 80s.[88]

To end this section on the family, let me return for a bit to the original argument regarding African cultural influences. If slaveowners reinforced patriarchal African ideology (and extended male privilege European-style), which affected slave families, there were also more positive cultural adaptations that served African-American families well as survival tactics, as Christie Farnham argued.[89] For instance, the forced breakup of families and the throwing together of strangers in one hut as spouses or work partners were ameliorated within the slave quarters by the development of African-style fictive kin networks. In a situation where having a baby could be a form of self-assertion and resistance, premarital sex and children who were illegitimate by European-American law (slaves were not allowed legal marriages but viewed customary forms as binding) were accepted. Premarital sex was also common in West Africa (and in Europe among the working classes) in the nineteenth century; it was viewed as a way of determining whether or not a prospective wife was fertile. In Africa, marriage was not normally arranged by the partners but by lineage elders to meet socioeconomic and political needs, often in consultation with the prospective groom; sometimes prospective brides exercised influence over choice of spouse and sometimes not. The function of marriage as an economic partnership was paramount not only in Africa but also in Europe until the rise of Western industrialization with its concomitant romantic ideology that justified housewifery (a middle-class wife should devote herself to domestic affairs for her husband and children because she loves them; working-class women must work outside the home as always and so are to be despised). Under slavery, marriage was also an economic affair in which slave women performed a service not only for their masters but also for their families by providing the reproductive labor enabling them to survive. And parenting in Africa often involved diffuse responsibility for child rearing among various generations in the compound and several wives; in the Americas, slavery and the masters' arrangements did not permit the slave mother to pursue the middle-class ideal of devoting exclusive attention to her children.[90] Perforce other members of the slave community played a role. Mothers' heavy agricultural labor responsibilities in both Africa and the Americas meant that child rearing could not be their central activity most of the time.[91]

It is clear, then, that the economic conditions of slavery reinforced the utility of certain African practices: fictive kin networks, premarital or bridal pregnancy, marriage as a predominantly economic arrangement, diffuse responsibility for parenting, and women performing much of the agricultural labor. However, to view these practices as isolated incidentals is to begin in the wrong place when trying to understand the great changes that took place when Africans came to the New World. We need rather to *begin* with African family structure in a more holistic fashion, then move to the experience in the Americas without the distortions imposed by the sexist and racist assumptions involved in the matrifocal/matriarchal arguments.

The predominant family form in West African precolonial cultures was the lineage family—extended clans tracing their ancestry in common. Individuals were usually given clan names prescribed by gender and birth order, and sometimes day names. The repetitiveness of naming often led to extensive creative use of nicknames which distinguished individuals from each other by emphasizing character traits. Clan members, or members of component lineages within clans, usually shared use rights in a defined portion of land which the elders allocated. Those elders were predominantly male but could also often be female. They arranged the marriages of junior members; to legitimize a marriage and its offspring, bridewealth was paid in kind or in money. Getting married was often a gradual process involving progressive exchanges of labor and goods between lineages. Blood ties were often stronger than conjugal ties, and ceremonies celebrating birth and death more important than those connected to marriage. A relatively few wealthy men practiced polygyny; most polygynous men had no more than two wives. Women's labor was a chief source of wealth in creating surplus crops and in adding more people to lineages, so that polygyny maximized male gain. Fertility was highly valued, infertility often automatic grounds for divorcing a woman (it was assumed to be a female failing). Child-rearing practices involved extended breastfeeding (which improved infants' survival chances), indulgence of small children, and strict discipline for older children to instill respect for their elders. Age rather than gender was often the primary characteristic determining authority, but gender was also salient in many ways, and patriarchal ideology and practices widespread. Many of these characteristics were adaptations to a situation of labor scarcity and land surplus that was exacerbated by the export slave trade.

Uprooting Africans to the Americas removed them from kin ties. Higman found that first-generation African immigrants in Trinidad were usually "isolated from any formal family system." Only in certain instances did the favorable conditions of a low sex ratio (relatively even numbers of women and men) and a high concentration on large stable plantations of persons from one African culture allow substantial retentions of particular familial forms. When these conditions did not prevail, there was extensive interethnic marriage and a loss of particular ethnic identity; most creole families were quite different from African families as a consequence. Large creole extended families were rare; nuclear families were most common in rural areas and mother-child units in towns.[92]

Many slaves arrived in the United States from the West Indies, not from Africa. They often had been born or had spent some years in the Caribbean. They were usually acquired by small-scale owners; the average owner had fewer than five slaves.[93] These conditions were not usually conducive to retention of a particular African ethnicity, although there were exceptions.[94] Neither did the conditions of slavery permit perpetuation of many African customs. The corporate features of the lineage family mainly disappeared: property holding, ancestral shrines (see Robert W. Slenes, chapter 7 in this volume), arranged marriages,[95] and bridewealth. Polygyny became economically dysfunctional.[96] Prolonged breastfeeding was discouraged by slaveowners for economic reasons, especially in the United States.[97] Thus we are left with more diffuse African-influenced familial characteristics retained in a drastically transformed social situation. Creative naming continued, perhaps reinforced by the imposition of foreign names. Respect for the elders was maintained in a context of expanded fictive kinship ties, but their power was greatly diminished. Wide kin networks were impeded by slavery's disruptive effects but were actively sought after emancipation and became a key ingredient in survival. Patriarchal authority continued in reduced form under slavery and strengthened again after emancipation.

The changes that occurred during slavery must be reevaluated, but in ways that neither privilege the African heritage unduly nor suffer from overpreoccupation with categories ultimately derived from racist views. Some of the critical questions to be answered are these: Why did conjugal ties apparently strengthen under slavery in the Americas compared with Africa? Was it a reaction to weakened lineage ties? Or is the impression of stability among slave marriages too strong owing to bias in the data toward large plantations? Slenes (chapter 7) tells us that in Brazil there was more marital instability on small holdings. In this connection we need to know more about the transition among many

African-Americans to a Western-type, ego-centered family where kinship is defined not by inheritance of clan membership, as in lineage families, but by a circle of relatives around a particular individual. Stevenson's contribution to this volume raises further questions along this line. For instance, what role did the imparting of European notions of housewifery, including extensive skills in areas like fancy sewing and the culinary arts, play in changing African notions regarding domestic work? In a related area, Robert Olwell (chapter 5 in this volume) draws attention to the fact that some women slaves acted as traders and to the question of how that affected the family economy. Evidence that has not been sufficiently analyzed points to the widespread persistence of African-style markets and women's trade in the Americas, but few attempts have been made to assess the implications of these phenomena for women's status.[98] Now that we know that slaves sometimes did earn money and could own property, we need to examine how women's earnings affected their families' welfare and power relations within families. Why were the traders women, as in West Africa? Olwell suggests that it may have been because women's autonomy was not perceived as threatening by their owners, but it seems equally probable that African women simply carried on what they had been doing in Africa. These are the kinds of issues and questions that need to be raised about the relation between African-American families and an African heritage; we need no further tracking of the red herrings of "matrifocality" and "matriarchy."[99]

In sum, common socioeconomic conditions in Africa and the Americas reinforced certain cultural retentions from Africa, but these do not include matriarchy and matrifocality. The causes of matrifocality are found in recent American history. Patriarchal ideology and practice, which was functional as a means of social control for slaveowners, dominated slave and free families, although slave men were hindered in asserting absolute authority. Lineage families as residential groupings, which in Africa were associated more with prosperity and long-settled residence, disappeared under slavery. Poverty rather than custom was the biggest enforcer of matrifocality, serving both as cause and effect, while matrifocality characterizes contemporary African-American families more than it did slave ones. Rather than persist in a defensive focus on matrifocality, researchers would do better to grapple with historical changes that, if understood, would allow them to define African-American families as different from African families, although related and equally valuable. Stevenson's suggestion in this volume about a negotiated African-American reality which combined European-American and Native American influences with African fundamentals into new and distinctive forms is worth further examination.

The Gender Division of Labor

Having emphasized the slave family as a vehicle for resistance with adaptive mechanisms drawn from African practices, to complete a class analysis with integrity one must still debunk further the claim of absolute equality within slave families by considering the gender division of labor. The evidence clearly shows that whether in Africa or the Americas, women slaves added the considerable burden of exclusive responsibility for domestic work to their already crushing burden of "outside" labor. In the United States, communal laundry and cooking facilities were available only on large plantations, which were in the minority.[100] To say that women did housework for "love"[101] is not to mitigate its severity but to paper it over with romantic ideology. Insofar as this gender division of labor prevailed, as it still does for most women in the world, the slave family was not an instrument of equality, as Genovese, Blassingame, and White would have it,[102] but of inequality.[103] Jones noted that the more autonomy slave families had, the stricter was the gender division of labor,[104] which one would expect, given an often strict African gender division of labor.[105] After emancipation the work of women and men became even more segregated.[106]

Angela Davis noted that "traditionally the labor of females, domestic work, is supposed to complement and confirm their inferiority." She then went on, however, to assume that because slave women also labored overwhelmingly at fieldwork, designated by the upper classes in free United States society as men's work, that this released them "from the chains of the myth of femininity."[107] Here she may have succumbed to Western patriarchal mythology, which defines women's work as domestic despite women's historical and present productive work outside the home. This class-biased view of women's work exclusively as housewifery is also reflected when some assume that when women work outside the home, especially if it is work usually defined as "men's," they are liberated. But spending twelve to eighteen hours a day in dreadful manual labor, using rudimentary tools (in this aspect the United States South emulated the generally low level of technology prevalent in Africa at the time),[108] spinning and weaving for the owners, and doing housework, is not liberation. Furthermore, patriarchal notions dictated that women slaves were overrepresented in fieldwork compared with men, who were disproportionately selected for skilled occupations such as artisans, drivers (overseers), and coachmen.[109] In the field no work was reserved exclusively for males, although in theory clearing the land was (as in Africa); women did whatever work was necessary. A Mississippi ex-slave, Hattie Jefferson, commented that her mother helped to do "everything that was to be done," while in Virginia, Amelia Walker echoed Sojourner Truth's most famous speech in saying that she watched her mother plow using three horses and "thought women was 'sposed to work 'long with men, I did."[110]

If women slaves were at least equal to men in performing hard labor, they also shared equally in punishment for not working hard enough, in the field or the house. In fact, domestic servitude with its increased contact with mistresses may have made bondwomen more vulnerable than men to whippings. In Georgia, Campbell Davis's sister was whipped as much for not spinning enough as his uncle was for not picking enough cotton, while in Virginia young Henrietta King's face was crushed by a rocker as her mistress beat her for stealing a piece of candy she had left out in order to tempt the child.[111] Cruelty was not limited by gender identity.[112] Stevenson (in this volume) says that women fieldworkers were treated more abusively than men, and Jones suggested that women may have been whipped more often than men.[113] Elizabeth Fox-Genovese suggested that mistresses were often "more crudely racist than their men"[114] in relation to the treatment of house servants. Of course, sometimes a bondwoman might use muscles developed by hard work to prevent beatings by her mistress, as Lucy Delaney did. But in that case her mistress told her master to beat her.[115]

Anyone familiar with African history will not be surprised by all this; African women did (and do) most of the agricultural work in a gender division of labor very similar to that under slavery in the Americas. Despite the relative paucity of slave women in the West Indies, this division of labor still prevailed there, and it became even more distinct as the sex ratio became more equal (see Geggus and Moitt, chapters 13 and 12).[116] According to Barbara Bush (chapter 10), "The sole reason for the existence of black women in the Caribbean was their labor value." Stevenson (chapter 9) and Betty Wood both concur that women slaves were primarily valued as laborers.[117] Beckles (chapter 6) notes that women field slaves brought higher prices than house slaves. However, the fact that African women did most of the field labor does not explain why slave women in the Americas did more fieldwork. That explanation is related to European-American patriarchal notions blended with the exigencies of slavery as a system of forcibly extracted labor. Most of the slaves kept in Africa were women, primarily because of their labor value.[118] In the Americas more African men than women were imported, primarily because Africans exported more men than women by a ratio of about two to one.[119] A secondary reason for importing more male slaves was the European belief that field labor was men's work and men were stronger than women. The irony of this perception is that while men may be more muscular than women, in Africa it was the women who did and do most of the routine heavy hauling. Another irony is that once slavery was established in the Americas, patriarchal notions intervened to give skilled artisanal work mostly to slave men, as well as any positions of authority allowed to slaves.[120] Thus United States male slaves usually brought a higher price than women slaves,[121] and women's field labor was arbitrarily assigned a lower value than men's, regardless of actual productivity.[122] Accordingly, it was easier for male slaves to buy their freedom because they had more earning opportunities. It was also easier for men to escape because their occupations allowed off-plantation work, customs allowed them to visit women on other plantations, and they did not need to take small children along.[123] Although there were more freedwomen than men in southern towns, this discrepancy was made up for by the excess of freedmen over women in northern cities; men were more likely to move north.[124] There were even cases during the Civil War, or when masters were incompetent, in which male slaves ran plantations.[125]

But what about domestic work done for slaveowners? It has been widely noted that most adult slaves did both "big house" chores and fieldwork because most slaveowners did not have big plantations that entailed much specialization of tasks.[126] However, more domestic work did fall to women, young girls, and the relatively few mature women who specialized as cooks. The position of "big house" cook was a relatively privileged one that some older women seem to have worked into and ex-slaves referred to with pride. Its high status may account for its being the most common occupation held by female relatives mentioned by both sexes in ex-slave narratives (29 percent), but fieldwork was a close second (21 percent). Fieldwork was often mentioned as an underlying assumption, as if everyone did it.[127] Petty housework—dusting, sweeping, scullery— seems to have been done mainly by girls. The women in the sample were almost all girls at the time of emancipation and did such work as their most common occupation under slavery. But among the occupations of mature women mentioned by the whole sample, it was relatively minor (9 percent). A typical work profile of a female slave included daily fieldwork, spinning and weaving three or four hours in the evening under a quota system, and her family's cooking, cleaning, laundry, and child rearing—a heavy load indeed. Fieldwork often began before dawn and lasted until after dark.[128] Children started working at age six to eight (see Cheryll Ann Cody, chapter 3 in this volume). Older women beyond prime fieldwork years often performed some semispecialized functions in social reproduction of the slave family such as midwifery and collective child care, along with the customary fieldwork when necessary and spinning and weaving (see Stevenson, chapter 9). Child care, however, was more likely to be the responsibility of slightly older children, who were sometimes male (see King and Stevenson).[129]

In this context it does not make a lot of sense to follow a common 1970s feminist approach of separating analyses of the domestic and public spheres, as women's work in both was mainly for the profit of the master. From an Africanist perspective, one of the most striking aspects of United States and Caribbean plantations is the subsistence activities; while slaves produced cash crops that were exported in large quantities, they also maximized profits by manufacturing or producing most of their own subsistence needs.[130] The superexploitation of slave women's labor in subsistence activities such as spinning and weaving and in domestic work for their own families was one of its most salient characteristics, as was the work's routine undervaluation.

A last point worth mentioning about the gender division of labor is the tendency to blame the work that slave women did for their "outcast" status.[131] Obviously, this work involved behavior considered unacceptable for free white middle- and upper-class women. One ex-slave mentioned that she and her coworkers had to pin up their dresses around their necks in order to pick tobacco,[132] and owners did not routinely issue underwear to slaves. It was not the work itself but rather the slaves' status that allowed them to be put to any task whatsoever, regardless of gender or age;[133] notions of appropriate behavior by gender were class-related. Poor white women and servants did the same sort of work slaves did, but not as intensively (see Stevenson).[134] It is the lower-class and inappropriate-work-for-women stigma that has caused black women to be accused of usurping men's roles, putting these women in a position, as Deborah Gray White says, of having to "prove their womanhood . . . as Sojourner Truth did in 1858."[135]

Regarding women slaves, the issue of so-called domestic work, however, is also related to the subjects of sexual harassment and slave breeding. These are, or should be seen as, two different issues, but they have sometimes been conflated in the literature.[136] Sexual harassment is concerned with power. It is a means for men or persons in positions of power to assert social control over women or other powerless people.[137] Adolescent girls who did much of the housework were particularly subject to sexual harassment.[138] According to the ex-slave Reverend Massie, masters or members of their families routinely harassed female house servants, an assertion reinforced by numerous examples from the slave narratives (see the contributions by Stevenson, Bush, and Geggus in this volume).[139] Perhaps the most satisfying example because of her resistance was the cook Sukie, who, when approached by the master for sex in the kitchen, refused, struggled with him, and pushed him rear end first into a pot of boiling lye. Since he did not want to reveal to his wife what had happened, he got revenge by selling rather than whipping Sukie. Still, the incident permanently broke his habit of "bothering" slave women.[140]

For slave women, sexual harassment was the ultimate oppression; it has been variously termed "a psycho-physical dimension [of oppression] that male slaves did not experience" (see Geggus in chapter 13), a threat to women's "self-respect and their emotional autonomy."[141] and a means of "bestializing her and breaking her resistance, violating her only area of possible autonomy."[142] While sexual harassment was also an attack on slave men's property rights in women, to view it solely as that is to take an unpardonably narrow and sexist approach.[143] To go further and blame slave women for this harassment is to concur with racist approaches which view dark-skinned people as incurably promiscuous. Psychological projection, as in this case where the lust of the owning class is projected onto its victims, is a common mechanism permitting oppressive behavior to continue.[144]

Sexual harassment is intimately linked to the institution of concubinage, widely recognized as one of the few means that some slave women might use to better their status and achieve manumission, or at least favored treatment. In the United States it was most common in urban areas (see L. Virginia Gould, chapter 15 in this volume) and resulted in the freeing of a number of women slaves.[145] In the West Indies it may have been a more successful method of manumission owing to the scarcity of women in both free and slave populations (see Geggus, Beckles, and Susan M. Socolow in this volume).[146] In Africa concubinage not only often produced free children by customary law, but in many cases also entailed freeing the mother.[147] In certain towns in Africa, Brazil, and the United States there was a market for beautiful slave women intended for use as prostitutes or concubines (see Stevenson, Karasch, and Gould in this volume).[148]

As White stated, however, it was "risky to expect liberation from one's enslavers."[149] Most concubinage was probably the end result of sexual harassment in which slave women had no choice, and it did not necessarily lead to manumission.[150] The slave narratives do not support the contention that many bondwomen obtained manumission successfully through concubinage. Sella Martin was the child of a slave woman and the overseer, who was the nephew of the mistress. The mistress handpicked Sella's mother as a concubine for her nephew and gave her favored treatment through a reduced workload and better food. But when the mistress felt that her nephew was delaying marriage because he was too attached to his concubine, she surreptitiously sold Sella's mother and the two children of the union.[151] In any contest between a mistress and a bondwoman, the mistress held the power and could usually, even if the master objected, see to it that the slave was punished or sold.[152] At the very least, she could make life extremely unpleasant for a house slave. It was probably the potential for sexual rivalry (mistresses worried about de facto polygyny as well as class and caste differences), as well as concern about overturning labor discipline, which made slave-mistress female solidarity seemingly nonexistent. Catherine Clinton noted that mistresses' cruelty to female slaves was often prompted by misdirected anger caused by their husbands' sexual liaisons with slaves.[153] The case of Jacqueline Lemelle, presented so convincingly by Gould (chapter 15), seems to be exceptional in that the master had no free wife, left property to Jacqueline and their children, and freed them. He did not, however, free Jacqueline's daughter by another man. Judith K. Schafer has shown that in law cases involving privileged quadroon mistresses in New Orleans, who were freed and left property by their masters in the securest way possible, these rights were not usually upheld by the Louisiana Supreme Court.[154] So, while the sexual desirability of some slaves may have driven up their price, it did not often benefit the women involved and may even have worsened their situation in some cases. Harriet Jacobs (Linda Brent), in a novel incorporating her own experiences of slavery, wrote, "If God has bestowed beauty upon her, it will prove her greatest curse. That which commands admiration in the white woman only hastens the degradation of the female slave." She made sexual harassment of her slave woman heroine by her hypocritical master a key element of the plot.[155]

Slave breeding is a separate issue because it concerns forced or planned intraslave unions and economics. Sexual harassment was more likely to be economically dysfunctional in that it interfered with productivity both physically (Sukie was making soap when the master tried to rape her) and psychologically. Slave breeding involved the selection of "prime stock" to breed, regardless of the will of the participants, with the chief aim of producing superior children for purposes of sale or labor. The evidence for slave breeding anywhere is scant, as many have noted (see King, chapter 8) and as the sample of ex-slave narratives used here shows.[156] The ex-slave Katie Darling stated in 1937, "Niggers didn't court like they do now, Master would pick out a po'tly man, and a po'tly gal and jist 'put 'em together.' What they wanted was the stock."[157] Two men mentioned masters' concern for breeding superior stock, one saying that he knew a big male slave who did no work but was used exclusively for breeding, the other that he was refused a pass to visit a woman on a neighboring plantation because the master did not want him breeding her due to his small size.[158] Annie Burton said that if a woman proved infertile after a year or so of marriage she would be sold.[159] Jennings, who made the most extensive compilation of data from Rawick on slave breeding, noted that 4.8 percent of the women and 10.3 percent of the men refer to it, many with eugenic implications. Pointing the other direction, however, is Jennings' equally important data showing maltreatment of pregnant women.[160] Escott found that slave breeding was rare, usually carried out when the master arranged pairings on his own plantation.[161] The lack of data showing widespread slave breeding in the United States and the British Caribbean indicates that production rather than reproduction was the planters' chief concern.[162]

More convincing would be more generalized proof that changes in planters' policies toward encouraging childbirth resulted in higher slave fertility. The problem with this search is that in the United States the slave trade was outlawed in 1807, well after the slave sex ratio had evened out from 1730 to 1750.[163] A relatively even sex ratio is a necessary precondition for creating stable unions and therefore high fertility (shifting liaisons increase the possibility of venereal disease and an unfavorable environment for raising children). United States slave fertility from 1750 on was relatively high.[164] Among the sixty-five ex-slaves in the sample who gave the number of children in their natal families, the average was 7.4, probably higher than for their African counterparts at that time.[165] But does this mean that slaveowners carried out slave breeding?

The fact that prices for United States women slaves were normally lower than for men slaves (see Bush, this volume), except in the often-mentioned cases where women were going to be used as concubines or prostitutes (Socolow, this volume),[166] would seem to indicate that their reproductive capacity was not valued highly.[167] Labor considerations seem usually to have outweighed those of fertility, and yet women's labor was routinely undervalued. The only direct evidence in the sample of slave narratives that incentives were used to encourage reproduction was provided by Rhoda Hunt's mother, whose owner told her that she would be freed when she had her *twelfth* child (she died a month before the child appeared and so the promise was never fulfilled).[168]

More evidence puts United States women slaves in a position analogous to that of African women in Sahelian slavery described by Meillassoux:

> She was not recruited in order to procreate but to work . . . , if she coupled she was not married; if she gave birth she was reduced to the role of genetrix, her children belonging to the master and constantly threatened with being removed from her; when she got old, no right or recognized link permitted her to hope that her children would see to her needs.[169]

In one narrative, slave women, shipped south and trudging along the road in "coffles," abandoned their babies in exhaustion at the side of the road. Poor whites then picked them up and eventually used them as a cheap source of slave labor. In another, slave traders forced young women slaves being shipped south by train to abandon babies beside the tracks because they wanted the girls for labor in the cotton fields.[170] According to Jones, masters warned prospective slave mothers that they wanted neither "runts" nor girls born on their plantations.[171] Stories of pregnant women enduring beatings are common.[172] Some overseers would not let women nurse babies while at work in the fields.[173] Most owners denied all responsibility for slave offspring, which meant that they might have sold their own children with impunity, despite their "superior" breeding in racist terms. Ira Berlin noted a tendency for slaveowners to emancipate mulattos more frequently than other slaves and attributed it to their desire to privilege their offspring,[174] but it might equally h. been due to embarrassment and the tendency to view "white" blood and hard l. as being incompatible.

In general, slave childbearing and rearing were not among slaveowners' top priorities, it seems. Although slave women died less often in childbirth than did their mistresses (white women's lack of exercise and corsets were factors here), slave infant mortality was higher.[175] While slave women's deliveries were usually handled by slave midwives, their mistresses were attended by male doctors, showing that masters placed higher priority on free births.[176] The age at first birth for slave women was usually nineteen or twenty,[177] or approximately five years after reaching puberty. This means both that masters were more interested in young women's labor than in their fertility and that promiscuity among young slave women was uncommon.

If childbearing had low priority with owners, child rearing seems to have fared little better, as the high infant mortality rate shows. The low life-expectancy rate for slaves[178] was traceable mainly to the circumstance that most children did not survive childhood, a fate they had in common with their African counterparts. Despite laws prohibiting the practice, children too young to care for themselves were sometimes sold away from their families (see King, chapter 8). James Lucas's mother bore him in a cotton field, then got up and kept working.[179] Whatever the slaves' own inclinations, they had to spend most of their time in the fields working; they had little time to spend with their children, a phenomenon noted by both Booker T. Washington and Frederick Douglass.[180]

What accounts under these conditions, then, for higher slave than white fertility? Producers, that is, slave workers, and especially the men, got relatively superior diets. Most men and women in the sample reported that their diets had been good under slavery. Meals included meat, dairy products, greens, root crops, and cereals.[181] However, far more women than men (37.8 percent versus 28.6 percent) reported poor or mediocre diets. Nonetheless, the diets of United States slaves, probably because they consumed wild game and sweet potatoes,[182] were far superior to West African and West Indian slave diets in general, and disease was less prevalent. Even if most owners seem not to have been particularly concerned about childbearing, they did sometimes pay attention to labor stabilization (stable slave families) and often to labor productivity through the provision of nutritious diets. Both are conducive to high fertility. Even though whipping was freely employed for both sexes, it apparently did not disrupt the slave population physically enough to reduce fertility substantially. Nor did frequent childbearing impede slave women's labor value; they gave a rate of return on investment approximately equal to that of male slaves,[183] which is, in the end, probably why most slaveowners were relatively neutral toward slave childbearing. It neither boosted nor diminished profits to a significant extent, but child rearing could diminish profits and was hindered substantially.

Fertility and Economics: Class Implications

Fertility is directly connected to class status. Historically and worldwide, fertility usually falls when the economic status of a population rises, meaning that the upper classes try to perpetuate their class status by having fewer but better-provided-for children. The nineteenth-century United States white population followed a common European pattern of progressively lower fertility,[184] but slaves would not have had the same incentives. As in Africa today, where no social security in old age is provided by wealth or the state, populations involved in labor-intensive work in which more hands mean a lighter workload generally maintain maximum fertility unless they are at the very edge of subsistence or are severely disrupted. From 1880 to 1920, African-American fertility declined as income rose in keeping with the pattern of European-American fertility and for some of the same reasons: increased urbanization and education and reduced involvement in agriculture.[185]

If slave fertility in the United States was high, in the Caribbean it was not. Extensive legal measures and both positive and negative incentives to raise fertility after the slave trade ended did not succeed (see the chapters by Bush and Geggus in this volume). The Caribbean experience points again to the critical role of economic and environmental factors: the uneven sex ratio, in which men usually greatly outnumbered women, impeded stable liaisons; abortion and infanticide were used as forms of resistance in what was probably the most brutal slave regime in the world (the labor imperatives of sugar cane cultivation, in particular);[186] nutrition was poor and no allowances were made for pregnancy in either diet, punishments, or labor requirements;[187] and there were negative climatic and epidemiological factors (see Bush, this volume).[188] Steckel (this volume) notes that Caribbean slave children's diets were very poor because they were not workers, that their weight resembled that of modern slum dwellers in Lagos and Bangladesh, and that infant mortality rates were double the rates of the free population. These Caribbean populations were obviously both closer to subsistence level and more disrupted than slaves in the United States.

Significantly, after emancipation the Caribbean birthrate rose (see Bush, this volume), while in the United States it remained stable. The ex-slaves in the sample, most of whom were born in the 1850s, had an average of 7.4 children per family, most of them born after the Civil War, an identical fertility rate to that of their parents. Life expectancy, diet, and skills for blacks all declined as whites took measures to force blacks into a caste by keeping them out of skilled jobs and in sharecropping arrangements, which for employers had an advantage over slavery in that they did not need to provide subsistence for tenants.[189] "We jist changed a marster for a boss," one ex-slave said; another observed, "Dem share-croppuhs is jes like slaves. . . ."[190] The major change in work organization was that most ex-slaves worked in family groups rather than in gangs, which was certainly less onerous.[191] There was a widely noted "withdrawal" of female ex-slave labor from the "public" work force, but this does not necessarily mean that these women were out of agricultural labor. They were doing unpaid "family" labor instead, which was also more reflective of African patterns, where patriarchal authority largely controlled the disposition of agricultural labor. Ex-slave women were often mainly responsible for provisioning their families.[192] Mann maintains that the labor arrangements of sharecropper families were strongly patriarchal, with male heads of families allocating members' labor inputs and disposing of profits.[193]

Many United States ex-slaves stayed put after emancipation, not for love of the owner but because they were not told they were free[194] or had nowhere to go and nothing with which to establish themselves. Other slaves were thrown off plantations with nothing;[195] President Abraham Lincoln's reputed promise of forty acres and a mule was not honored. In only one slave narrative in the sample did an ex-master leave a male ex-slave the wherewithal to become economically independent.[196] Sallie Hafford, known as the oldest woman in the United States before she died in 1912 at the age of 116, had managed her late master's plantation in Kentucky for his young son in exchange for a promise of five acres, a horse, and a cow. Instead, when the son grew up, he sold her possessions and kept the money.[197] After the war the streets of Norfolk, Virginia, were thronged with indigent ex-slaves, mostly women and children, while in Louisiana and Mississippi ex-slaves were put into stockades and died in hordes from disease and malnutrition.[198]

> Taxation and fiscal policies were used to transfer income from blacks to whites, perhaps more effectively . . . than had been possible under slavery. . . . Time on the cross did not come to an end for American blacks with the downfall of the peculiar institution.[199]

"Emancipation" of slaves in equatorial African society came with the imposition of colonial rule; one African described it as follows: "Then the whites came and subjected us all to their laws. Now all blacks are slaves of the whites."[200] In order not to disrupt African labor relations in Malawi and Zambia, the British "emancipated" slaves in this manner:

> The former [African] masters were then given a steadily increasing role in defining the laws governing these relationships and in administering it in the villages, and the spirit in which it was done was not one of egalitarian reconciliation.[201]

For women in Africa, "slavery and slavedealing often continued for many years [after emancipation] under the guise of marriage," according to Roberts and Miers.[202] Women's labor remained too valuable to relinquish readily, especially in areas where labor-intensive agriculture continued. Since such labor is still needed in much of sub-Saharan Africa, men have found it necessary to devise new forms of subordination. In a few countries slavery for women continues despite its illegality.

Class relations, expressed in fertility rates and other indicators, do not disappear with the wave of a legal wand. If class status is somewhat malleable for exceptional individuals by socioeconomic mobility, caste status is inescapable, and violations of caste are severely punished, often by violence. This is one reason why Gutman concluded that because of a lack of opportunities for occupational organizing and social mobility, "the family system *may* have been more important in giving cohesion to the black than to the white lower-class community." However, "both the caste system and the class system are changing through time; both are responsive to shifts in the economy. . . ."[203]

In moving from forms of slavery in Africa to the development of the United States caste system, this chapter has demonstrated that slavery on both sides of the Atlantic represented a continuum in which the status of slaves varied to a certain extent. For African and African-American women the continuum from free to slave was always narrower than for men because all women were subject to economic oppression in the name of patriarchal ideology. Jones could be describing African rather than United States ex-slave women in this comment:

> For most women, the rigors of childbearing and rearing, household chores and outside employment represented a continuum from slavery to freedom, unbroken by schooling or other opportunities to expand their horizons beyond [their homes].[204]

The unifying theme here is that economics rather than custom seems to be the chief motor for change and that gender considerations are also impelled by economics. If capitalism (or socialism, for that matter) requires it, working-class women will be put to whatever work the dominant classes require, without amelioration by cross-class female solidarity. Culture can facilitate adaptations. It can create an ideology out of race, for instance, as well as familial forms which moderate or intensify oppression. But it does not determine the direction of economic change; the causal direction is rather the reverse. But economies can be changed to ameliorate exploitation. Oppression by gender and race can be divisive, but out of it should emerge enough strength to get rid of it. This will mean, however, undermining the economic forms that profit by it. The ex-slave Susan Jones said, "We didn't expect so much from freedom but anything was better than what we had."[205] We should not be satisfied with half-measures; we need the energizing force of the abolition of debilitating socioeconomic divisions.

Ultimately, the issues of freedom and labor are the same for women.[206] To modify a statement by Gerda Lerner, the *economic* subordination of women "provided the model out of which slavery developed as a social institution."[207] We do well to remember, as Angela Davis said, that "the strength and efficacy of social struggles . . . bear an immediate relationship to the range and quality of female participation."[208] There will be no liberation without women's liberation; there is no such thing as partial equality. What did African women bring to the Americas? A legacy of autonomy and strength, even under adversity. With that strength as a model we can rebuild—more strongly because we will be united in our diversity.

Notes

1. As Martin Chanock writes, "For the first decades of the rewriting of African history [away from being the story and justification of European colonialism], slavery in African societies was not a fashionable subject of study. The particular sensitivities of African studies were such that slavery 'as a term was reserved for something done by whites to Africans and the anger and outrage aroused by this part of the African historical experience [the export slave trade] obscured the existence of slavery in pre-colonial African societies." Chanock, *Law, Custom and Social Order* (London: Cambridge University Press, 1985), p. 160.

2. There are no reliable estimates of the total magnitude of the internal African slave trade, nor would the state of the data permit anything but some regional analyses.

3. Deborah Gray White sees race as a *cause* for enslavement, whereas it seems rather to have functioned as a post hoc ideological *justification* for enslavement. See White, *Ar'n't I a Woman? Female Slaves in the Plantation South* (New York: Norton, 1985), p. 162.

4. Richard Roberts and Suzanne Miers, Introduction, in *The End of Slavery in Africa*, ed. Roberts and Miers (Madison: University of Wisconsin Press, 1988), p. 6.

5. The most striking exception was in Ethiopia, where feudal monarchy and Christianity combined to enforce private land ownership. Economic conditions also promoted privatization of land ownership in a few areas of long European contact along the West African coast, for instance.

6. Walter Rodney, *A History of the Upper Guinea Coast 1545–1800* (Oxford: Clarendon Press, 1970), p. 253.

7. Igor Kopytoff and Suzanne Miers, "African Slavery as an Institution of Marginality," in *Slavery in Africa*, ed. Miers and Kopytoff (Madison: University of Wisconsin Press, 1977).

8. Robert Ross, "Oppression, Sexuality and Slavery at the Cape of Good Hope," *Historical Reflections* 6 (1979): 421–33.

9. Marietta Morrissey, *Slave Women in the New World* (Lawrence: University Press of Kansas, 1989), p. 27.

10. Roberts and Miers, Introduction, in *The End of Slavery in Africa*, p. 26.

11. Paul Lovejoy, *Transformations in Slavery* (Cambridge: Cambridge University Press, 1983), p. 214, emphasis mine.

12. Frederick Cooper, *Plantation Slavery on the East Coast of Africa* (New Haven: Yale University Press, 1977), p. 187; Patricia Romero Curtin, "Laboratory for the Oral

History of Slavery: The Island of Lamu on the Kenya Coast," *American Historical Review* 88 (1983): 862.

13. Patrick Manning, "Contours of Slavery and Social Change in Africa," *American Historical Review* 88 (1983): 847–48.

14. Claire C. Robertson, *Sharing the Same Bowl* (Ann Arbor: University of Michigan Press, 1990), p. 226.

15. This situation was particularly common in towns along the east coast of Africa, where, according to Curtin, "Laboratory for the Oral History of Slavery," p. 859, it continued even up to Kenyan independence in 1963. See also Cooper, *Plantation Slavery*, pp. 162–94.

16. Gerald Jaynes, *Branches without Roots* (New York: Oxford University Press, 1986), pp. 237, 249, 315.

17. Claude Meillassoux, *Anthropologie de l'esclavage* (Paris: Presses Universitaires de France, 1986), pp. 89, 93, translation mine. Meillassoux used *social reproduction* here in the Marxian sense of total reproduction of the conditions for perpetuating the society, which includes domestic labor and child care as well as subsistence agriculture. In the United States South, poor whites also sometimes needed passes to move around and could be regarded with contempt by slaves: "Po' whites was just like stray goats." See Charles L. Perdue, Jr., T. E. Barden, and R. K. Phillips, eds., *Weevils in the Wheat* (Bloomington: Indiana University Press, 1980), pp. 78, 326.

18. Manning, "Contours of Slavery and Social Change," p. 846.

19. See Edward Alpers, "The Story of Swema: Female Vulnerability in Nineteenth-Century East Africa," in *Women and Slavery in Africa*, ed. C. Robertson and M. Klein (Madison: University of Wisconsin Press, 1983), p. 200.

20. Claire Robertson, "Post-Proclamation Slavery in Accra: A Female Affair?" in *Women and Slavery in Africa*, ed. Robertson and Klein, pp. 220–45; Joseph C. Miller, *Way of Death: Merchant Capitalism and the Angolan Slave Trade 1730–1830* (Madison: University of Wisconsin Press, 1988), p. 162.

21. Bogumil Jewsiewicki and Mumbanza Mwa Bawele, "The Social Context of Slavery in Equatorial Africa during the Nineteenth and Twentieth Centuries," in *The Ideology of Slavery in Africa*, ed. P. Lovejoy (Beverly Hills: Sage, 1981), p. 88.

22. Claire Robertson and Martin Klein, "Women's Importance in African Slave Systems," in *Women and Slavery in Africa*, ed. Robertson and Klein, pp. 14–15.

23. Buchi Emecheta, *The Slave Girl* (New York: Braziller, 1977), p. 151.

24. W. E. B. Du Bois, *The Negro American Family* (1908; reprint, Westport: Negro Universities Press, 1971), p. 46.

25. Cooper, *Plantation Slavery*, p. 266.

26. Ira Berlin, *Slaves without Masters* (New York: Pantheon, 1974), chap. 10; Leon Litwack, *North of Slavery* (Chicago: University of Chicago Press, 1961), pp. 51–53, 153 ff.

27. The United States Constitution does not proscribe debt servitude, but most states do. Guy Loftman, attorney, personal communication, July 2, 1989.

28. Barbara Bush, *Slave Women in Caribbean Society 1650–1838* (Bloomington: Indiana University Press, 1990), pp. 12–13.

29. Stanley Elkins, *Slavery, a Problem in American Institutional and Intellectual Life*, 2d ed. (Chicago: University of Chicago Press, 1968), pp. 63, 78–80. As others have after him, Elkins identified the squalor in Latin America as evolving from the class system not a color barrier, mistakenly abandoning any appreciation of the relationship of the development of capitalism to the evolution of United States slavery.

30. Carl Degler, *Neither Black nor White* (Madison: University of Wisconsin Press, 1971), pp. 43–45.

31. Cooper, *Plantation Slavery*, p. 194.

32. George P. Rawick, ed., *The American Slave: A Composite Autobiography*, Supp. Series 1 (Westport: Greenwood, 1977), vol. 8; f. 918.

33. Allan Millett, personal communication, January 18, 1990.

34. Suzanne Lebsock, "Free Black Women and the Question of Matriarchy: Petersburg, Virginia, 1784–1820," *Feminist Studies* 8 (1982): 271–92.

35. Eugene Genovese, *Roll, Jordan, Roll: The World the Slaves Made* (New York: Vintage, 1972); Herbert G. Gutman, *The Black Family in Slavery and Freedom, 1750–1925* (New York: Pantheon, 1976); Angela Davis, "Reflections on the Black Woman's Role in the Community of Slaves," *Black Scholar* 3 (1971): 2–15.

36. E. Franklin Frazier, "Family Disorganization among Negroes," *Opportunity* 9 (1931): 204; D. P. Moynihan, "The Negro Family: The Case for National Action," United States Department of Labor, Office of Policy Planning and Research Report (March 1965).

37. Herbert Gutman, "Persistent Myths about the Afro-American Family," *Journal of Interdisciplinary History* 6 (1975): 181–210; Christie Farnham, "Sapphire? The Issue of Dominance in the Slave Family, 1830–1865," in *"To Toil the Livelong Day,"* ed. Carol Groneman and Mary Beth Norton (Ithaca: Cornell University Press, 1987), pp. 68–83; Davis, "Reflections"; Jacqueline Jones, "'My Mother Was Much of a Woman': Black Women, Work and the Family under Slavery," *Feminist Studies* 8, no. 2 (1982): 235–69; and *Labor of Love, Labor of Sorrow* (New York: Basic, 1985).

38. Kamene Okonjo, "The Dual Sex Political System in Operation: Igbo Women and Community Politics in Midwestern Nigeria," in *Women in Africa*, ed. Nancy J. Hafkin and Edna G. Bay (Stanford: Stanford University Press, 1976), pp. 45–58; Judith Van Allen, "'Aba Riots' or Igbo 'Women's War'? Ideology, Stratification and the Invisibility of Women, in *Women in Africa*, ed. Hafkin and Bay, pp. 58–86; Cheryl Johnson-Odim, "Class and Gender: A Consideration of Yoruba Women during the Colonial Period," in *Women and Class in Africa*, ed. Claire C. Robertson and Iris Berger (New York: Holmes and Meier, 1986), pp. 237–54.

39. Elizabeth Fox-Genovese, *Within the Plantation Household* (Chapel Hill: University of North Carolina Press, 1988), p. 310.

40. Jones, "'My Mother Was Much of a Woman,'" p. 238.

41. "She pult up her dress an' tole de nigger traders to look an' see if dey could fin' any teef down dere." Perdue et al., *Weevils in the Wheat*, pp. 48–49.

42. For a description of African dance forms used among United States slaves, see Perdue et al., *Weevils in the Wheat*, pp. 49–50.

43. Sterling Stuckey, *Slave Culture: Nationalist Theory and the Foundations of Black America* (New York: Oxford University Press, 1987), p. 79 ff.; Peter H. Wood, *Black Majority: Negroes in Colonial South Carolina from 1670 through the Stono Rebellion* (New York: Knopf, 1974), chap. 6; Lawrence W. Levine, *Black Culture and Black Consciousness: Afro-American Folk Thought from Slavery to Freedom* (New York: Oxford University Press, 1977), p. 19 ff.

44. Lebsock, "Free Black Women," pp. 272–73.

45. Susan Mann, "Slavery, Sharecropping, and Sexual Inequality," *Signs* 14 (1989): 787, confuses matrilinearity with matrilaterality, while Bush, *Slave Women in Caribbean Society*, p. 93, assumes matrifocality to accompany African matrilinearity.

46. Robertson, *Sharing the Same Bowl*, gives one example.

47. In pursuing class analysis I follow Robert Staples' pioneering critique of the Moynihan Report in "Towards a Sociology of the Black Family," *Journal of Marriage and the Family* 33 (1971): 126, where he states, "By disregarding the socioeconomic situation of black families, the primary variable that causes the differentiation of black family behavior is not taken into account."

48. South African whites most minutely defined racial categories in elaborating on the United States model, with an opportunistic flair shown in their treatment of Japanese businessmen.

49. There are some interesting studies of changes in African slave systems; see, for instance, Lovejoy, *Ideology of Slavery in Africa* and *Transformations in Slavery*, and Roberts and Miers, *The End of Slavery in Africa*.

50. Nancy Tanner, "Matrifocality in Indonesia and Africa and among Black Americans," in *Woman, Culture and Society*, ed. Michelle Z. Rosaldo and Louise Lamphere (Stanford: Stanford University Press, 1974), p. 154.

51. Du Bois, *Negro American Family*, p. 19, gives a West Indian example of this practice.

52. Claire Robertson, "Food Distribution and Gender in Africa," *TransAfrica Forum* 4, no. 3 (1987): 27–29.

53. Claire Robertson, "The Death of Makola and Other Tragedies: Male Strategies against a Female-Dominated System," *Canadian Journal of African Studies* 17, no. 3 (1983).

54. Robertson and Klein, "Women's Importance," p. 10.

55. Du Bois, *Negro American Family*, pp. 48–49.

56. Richard Wade, *Slavery in the Cities: The South, 1820–1860* (New York: Oxford University Press, 1964), pp. 119–21. See also Frazier, "Family Disorganization among Negroes."

57. Paul Escott, *Slavery Remembered: A Record of Twentieth-Century Slave Narratives* (Chapel Hill: University of North Carolina Press, 1979), p. 48.

58. Charles L. Perdue, Jr., in Perdue et al., *Weevils in the Wheat*, p. 152.

59. Rawick, *American Slave*, vol. 4, p. 1022, and vol. 11, p. 52; Perdue in Perdue et al., *Weevils in the Wheat*, pp. 42, 71, 258.

60. Perdue et al., *Weevils in the Wheat*, pp. 106, 160.

61. The sample included one out of every four narratives, omitting accounts that were too fragmentary to answer any of my questions, and as wide a geographic spread as possible. The Rawick volumes used were series 1, vols. 1 (Alabama), 4 (Georgia), 5 (Indiana/Ohio), 8 (Mississippi), and 11 (North and South Carolina). Perdue et al. includes only Virginia narratives. Since regional differences are not a chief issue here, I refer to a slave's location only when necessary. In any case, the ex-slave was often not living in the same place when interviewed as when in slavery.

62. Cooper, *Plantation Slavery*, p. 255.

63. Robert Fogel and Stanley Engerman, *Time on the Cross: The Economics of American Negro Slavery* (Boston: Little, Brown, 1974), vol. 1, pp. 127–28.

64. Gutman, "Persistent Myths," p. 193; Fogel and Engerman, *Time on the Cross*, pp. 133–42.

65. John Blassingame, *The Slave Community: Plantation Life in the Antebellum South* (New York: Oxford University Press, 1972), p. 92.

66. Thelma Jennings, "Us Colored Women Had to Go Through a Plenty,'" *Journal of Women's History* 1, no. 3 (Winter 1990): 45–74; Perdue in Perdue et al., *Weevils in the Wheat*, pp. 89, 94.

67. Jewsiewicki and Mumbanza, "The Social Context of Slavery," p. 74.

68. Perdue in Perdue et al., *Weevils in the Wheat*, p. 161.

69. Rawick, *American Slave*, vol. 4, p. 1004.

70. Perdue in Perdue et al., *Weevils in the Wheat*, p. 195.

71. William Andrews, ed., *Six Women's Slave Narratives* (New York: Oxford University Press, 1988), p. 13 of Prince narrative.

72. Catherine Clinton, *The Plantation Mistress: Woman's World in the Old South* (New York: Pantheon, 1982), p. 190, claimed that female solidarity "could and sometimes did cement relationships between owner and owned" but at the same time acknowledged that the "vast majority of [white] women were more concerned with the practicalities of the system . . . than with humanitarian ideology."

73. Du Bois, *Negro American Family*, p. 19.

74. B. W. Higman, "The Slave Family and Household in the British West Indies," *Journal of Interdisciplinary History* 6 (Autumn 1975): 284–85.

75. Personal communication, May 19, 1989.

76. White, *Ar'n't I a Woman?*, pp. 142, 160.

77. Cooper, *Plantation Slavery*, p. 227. Jacqueline Jones, "One Big Happy Family?" *Women's Review of Books* 6 (1989), also pointed this out in her critique of Fox-Genovese, *Plantation Household*.

78. Jones, "'My Mother Was Much of a Woman,'" p. 261.

79. Philip Foner, *Organized Labor and the Black Worker, 1619–1973* (New York: Praeger, 1974).

80. Blassingame, *Slave Community*, p. 103; Jones, "'My Mother Was Much of a Woman,'" p. 261; Davis, "Reflections," p. 4.

81. Deborah Gaitskell, "Housewives, Maids or Mothers: Some Contradictions of Domesticity for Christian Women in Johannesburg, 1903–1939," *Journal of African History* 24 (1983): 241–56.

82. Lebsock, "Free Black Women," p. 287.

83. Frank F. Furstenberg, Jr., T. Hershberg, and J. Modell, "The Origins of the Female-Headed Black Family: The Impact of the Urban Experience," *Journal of Interdisciplinary History* 6 (1975): 224–26. Darrel E. Bigham's results from southern Indiana in 1880 confirm this finding; "The Black Family in Evansville and Vanderburgh County, Indiana, in 1880," *Indiana Magazine of History* 75 (1979): 134.

84. Gutman, *Black Family*, pp. 443–47, 454–55, 526.

85. Allison Davis, B. B. Gardner, and M. R. Gardner, *Deep South* (Chicago: University of Chicago Press, 1941), p. 299; Gutman, "Persistent Myths," p. 205.

86. Stanley Engerman, "Black Fertility and Family Structure in the United States, 1880–1940," *Journal of Family History* 2 (1977): 134–35.

87. La Frances Rodgers-Rose, "Some Demographic Characteristics of the Black Woman: 1940 to 1975," in *Black Woman*, ed. Rodgers-Rose (Beverly Hills: Sage, 1980), pp. 37–39.

88. Barbara Ommolade, "It's a Family Affair: The Real Lives of Black Single Mothers," *Village Voice*, July 15, 1986.

89. Farnham, "Sapphire?" pp. 72–82.

90. White, *Ar'n't I a Woman?*, pp. 127–28.

91. White, *Ar'n't I a Woman?*, p. 66, misled in stressing that African women's dominant role was as mother. Certainly strong ideology supported African motherhood, but in terms of time allocation, subsistence work outside the home always has had to come first for most women, children accompanying their mothers where possible. Indeed, as I have argued elsewhere (*"Trouble Showed Me the Way": Women, Men, and Trade in the Nairobi Area, 1890–1990*, Berkeley: University of California Press, forthcoming), motherhood was and is largely constructed in terms of the work that women do, an aspect also present in African-American culture (see Toni Morrison, *Sula*, New York: Knopf, 1977).

92. Higman's contrasting examples of the experiences of the Igbo and Mandinke ethnic groups are convincing. See B. W. Higman, "African and Creole Family Patterns in Trinidad," *Journal of Family History* 3 (1978): 174–77.

93. Gutman, *Black Family*, pp. 328, 103; John B. Boles, *Black Southerners, 1619–1869* (Lexington: University Press of Kentucky, 1984), p. 107.

94. See, for example, Margaret Washington Creel, *"A Peculiar People": Slave Religion and Community-Culture among the Gullahs* (New York: New York University Press, 1988).

95. There is contradictory evidence regarding the existence of preferential mate selection among relatives in African-influenced unions in the West Indies, according to Higman, "African and Creole Family Patterns," p. 175. The reasons are that West African cultures differed greatly, both in allowance of the practice and in the matter of which relatives were supposed to marry (cross-cousins, parallel cousins, etc.). Matrilinearity or patrilinearity influenced the choice as well as differing definitions of incest.

96. For polygyny in the United States, see Perdue et al., *Weevils in the Wheat*, p. 209. It is worth noting a contrary case showing that when escaped slaves could determine their own socioeconomic organization, polygyny could survive very well in the New World. It is widely practiced to the present by communities of Maroon descent in Suriname who have identifiable strong roots in Gold Coast cultures and whose contemporary marital practices bear a striking resemblance to those in present-day coastal areas of Ghana. See Sally Price, *Co-wives and Calabashes* (Ann Arbor: University of Michigan Press, 1984).

97. B. W. Higman, *Slave Populations of the British Caribbean 1807–1834* (Baltimore: Johns Hopkins University Press, 1984), pp. 352–54.

98. Morrissey, *Slave Women in the New World*, pp. 53–55, 164; Bush, *Slave Women in Caribbean Society*, pp. 49–50, 60, 164.

99. I am partially indebted for this argument to Niara Sudarkasa's pioneering contribution on the subject of African-American families' African inheritance in "Interpreting the African Heritage in Afro-American Family Organization," in *Black Families*, ed. H. P. McAdoo (Beverly Hills: Sage, 1981), pp. 37–53.

100. Mann, "Slavery, Sharecropping, and Sexual Inequality," pp. 781–82. However, in the antebellum period a steadily increasing proportion of slaves lived on plantations with twenty slaves or more; see Boles, *Black Southerners*, p. 107.

101. Fox-Genovese, *Plantation Household*, p. 33.

102. Farnham, "Sapphire?" p. 78; White, *Ar'n't I a Woman?*, p. 159.

103. Jones, "'My Mother Was Much of a Woman,'" p. 236; Farnham, "Sapphire?" p. 80.

104. Jones, *Labor of Love*, p. 38.

105. Africans frequently had, however, flexible notions of the construction of gender, including the practice of woman-marriage; see Ifi Amadiume, *Male Daughters, Female Sons: Gender and Sex in African Society* (London: Zed, 1987).

106. Mann, "Slavery, Sharecropping, and Sexual Inequality," p. 785. Morrissey, *Slave Women in the New World*, p. 155, noted that Maroon women in the West Indies followed the dominant African pattern of doing almost all the agricultural work.

107. Davis, "Reflections," p. 7.

108. Hierarchical labor systems seem to foster lack of concern with labor-saving devices. Women probably invented horticulture and did much of the labor until technological improvements made it less labor-intensive, more profitable, and more attractive to men. See Ester Boserup, *Woman's Role in Economic Development* (New York: St. Martin's Press, 1970).

109. Fogel and Engerman, *Time on the Cross*, pp. 141, 219; Herbert S. Klein, "African Women in the Atlantic Slave Trade," in Robertson and Klein, *Women and Slavery*, p. 35.

110. Rawick, *American Slave*, vol. 8, p. 1131; Perdue et al., *Weevils in the Wheat*, p. 292. White cites Sojourner Truth, *Ar'n't I a Woman?*, p. 14. See also Wilma King, chapter 8 in this volume.

111. Rawick, *American Slave*, vol. 4, p. 1064; Perdue et al., *Weevils in the Wheat*, p. 191.

112. Rawick, *American Slave*, vol. 8, p. 1217; Perdue et al., *Weevils in the Wheat*, p. 259.

113. Jones, *Labor of Love*, pp. 20–21.

114. Fox-Genovese, *Plantation Household*, p. 35.

115. Andrews, *Six Women*, p. 27 of Delaney narrative; see also C. W. Larison, *Sylvia Dubois: Biography of the Slave Who Whipt Her Mistres and Gand Her Fredom* (1883; reprint, New York: Oxford University Press, 1988).

116. Higman, *Slave Populations*, pp. 189–91.

117. Betty Wood, "Some Aspects of Female Resistance to Chattel Slavery in Low Country Georgia, 1763–1815," *Historical Journal* 30 (1987): 608.

118. Robertson and Klein, "Importance."

119. Manning, "Contours of Slavery and Social Change," p. 839; Miller, *Way of Death*, p. 130; Klein, "African Women," p. 35.

120. Higman, *Slave Populations*, pp. 190–91.

121. Fogel and Engerman, *Time on the Cross*, p. 75.

122. Mann, "Slavery, Sharecropping, and Sexual Inequality," p. 780; John Campbell, "Work, Pregnancy, and Infant Mortality among Southern Slaves," *Journal of Interdisciplinary History* 14 (Spring, 1984): 797–98.

123. White, *Ar'n't I a Woman?*, p. 75. African women slaves also had more difficulty in escaping or buying their own freedom for the same reasons; see Roberts and Miers, Introduction, p. 39.

124. Berlin, *Slaves without Masters*, p. 177.

125. Blassingame, *Slave Community*, p. 203.

126. A major fault of Fogel and Engerman's *Time on the Cross* is that it relies too heavily on a few sets of meticulously kept records from large plantations, as does Campbell, "Work."

127. This sample also came disproportionately from large plantations averaging 181 slaves per holding.

128. Rawick, *American Slave*, vol. 4, p. 1049; vol. 8, p. 1039; vol. 11, pp. 131–32.

129. Rawick, *American Slave*, vol. 4, p. 1343.

130. Fogel and Engerman, *Time on the Cross*, p. 154, reduced the rate of exploitation of slaves by deducting the cost to masters of supporting slave children by doing such things as buying their clothing. This is outrageous in light of the amount of work put in by slaves in producing clothing, shoes, and food and in hunting or fishing for food. It resembles most closely the colonialists' insistence on charging Africans for all administrative costs while systematically exporting the profits from plantations and mines. One ex-slave commented, "White folks is too greedy." Perdue et al., *Weevils in the Wheat*, p. 54.

131. White, *Ar'n't I a Woman?*, p. 162.

132. Perdue et al., *Weevils in the Wheat*, p. 224.

133. Meillassoux, *Anthropologie de l'esclavage*, p. 100.

134. Fox-Genovese, *Plantation Household*, pp. 193, 202.

135. White, *Ar'n't I a Woman?*, p. 167.

136. White, *Ar'n't I a Woman?*, pp. 34–38; see also Stevenson and King (chapters 9 and 8 in this volume).

137. Davis, "Reflections," p. 13.

138. White, *Ar'n't I a Woman?*, pp. 49–50.

139. Perdue et al., *Weevils in the Wheat*, p. 207.

140. Rawick, *American Slave*, vol. 4, p. 1344; Perdue et al., *Weevils in the Wheat*, p. 257; White, *Ar'n't I a Woman?*, p. 89. Catherine Clinton, "Caught in the Web of the Big House: Women and Slavery," in *The Web of Southern Social Relations*, ed. Walter J. Raser, Jr., Frank Saunders, Jr., and Jon L. Wakelyn (Athens: University of Georgia Press, 1985), pp. 19–34, has an extensive discussion of sexual harassment.

141. Perdue et al., *Weevils in the Wheat*, pp. 48–49.

142. Mary Ellison, "Resistance to Oppression: Black Women's Response to Slavery in the United States," *Slavery and Abolition* 4 (1983): 56.

143. Davis, "Reflections," p. 13.

144. Clinton, in *Plantation Mistress*, p. 201, wrote, "To argue that the master's . . . sexual aggression was equally painful to the husband who was being humiliated and to the wife who was being violated is sexist and irresponsible."

145. Davis et al., *Deep South*, p. 297; Wade, *Slavery in the Cities*; Lebsock, "Free Black Women."

146. Bush, *Slave Women in Caribbean Society*, pp. 12–13.

147. Curtin, "Laboratory," pp. 859–60; Cooper, *Plantation Slavery*, p. 195, to cite only two examples out of many.

148. White, *Ar'n't I a Woman?*, pp. 37–38, Curtin, "Laboratory," p. 874, mentions that young boys were also used this way on the East African coast.

149. White, *Ar'n't I a Woman?*, p. 34.

150. See Perdue et al., *Weevils in the Wheat*, pp. 86, 117, for examples.

151. Blassingame, *Slave Community*, p. 702.

152. Perdue et al., *Weevils in the Wheat*, p. 190; Jones, "'My Mother Was Much of a Woman,'" p. 248.

153. Clinton, *Plantation Mistress*, p. 188.

154. Judith K. Schafer, "'Open and Notorious Concubinage': The Emancipation of Slave Mistresses by Wills and the Supreme Court in Antebellum Louisiana," *Louisiana History* 28 (1987): 165–82.

155. Harriet A. Jacobs, *Incidents in the Life of a Slave Girl* (1861; reprint, Cambridge: Harvard University Press, 1987), p. 46.

156. Fogel and Engerman, *Time on the Cross,* p. 83; Du Bois, *Negro American Family,* p. 26. In *Ain't I a Woman?* (Boston: South End Press, 1981), p. 39 ff., bell hooks probably makes the strongest argument for the practice of slave breeding; but her evidence also includes owners' negligence of child rearing, so the implications are inconsistent. Bush, *Slave Women in Caribbean Society,* p. 128, says there is "no hard evidence" for slave breeding in the West Indies.

157. Rawick, *American Slave,* vol. 4, p. 1050.

158. Perdue et al., *Weevils in the Wheat,* pp. 291, 300.

159. Andrews, *Six Women,* p. 5 of Burton narrative.

160. Jennings, "'Us Colored Women,'" pp. 49–51.

161. Escott, *Slavery Remembered,* p. 45.

162. Higman, *Slave Populations,* p. 349.

163. White, *Ar'n't I a Woman?,* p. 67.

164. White, *Ar'n't I a Woman?,* p. 87; Blassingame, *Slave Community,* p. 214.

165. John Thornton, "Sexual Demography: The Impact of the Slave Trade on Family Structure," in Robertson and Klein, *Women and Slavery in Africa,* pp. 39–48.

166. Rawick, *American Slave,* vol. 11, p. 133.

167. There is, however, some contrary evidence that good "breeders" brought high prices. See Rawick, *American Slave,* vol. 8, p. 1241; vol. 11, p. 300; vol. 4, p. 1203; Perdue et al., *Weevils in the Wheat,* p. 160. We need more data on prices.

168. Rawick, *American Slave,* vol. 8, p. 1075.

169. Meillassoux, *Anthropologie de l'esclavage,* p. 113.

170. Perdue et al., *Weevils in the Wheat,* pp. 292, 33.

171. Jones, "'My Mother Was Much of a Woman,'" p. 238.

172. See Perdue et al., *Weevils in the Wheat,* p. 190, for instance.

173. Rawick, *American Slave,* vol. 8, pp. 899–900.

174. Berlin, *Slaves without Masters,* pp. 178–79.

175. Fogel and Engerman, *Time on the Cross,* p. 123; Blassingame, *Slave Community,* p. 94.

176. White, *Ar'n't I a Woman?,* p. 124; Rawick, *American Slave,* vol. 11, p. 136.

177. White, *Ar'n't I a Woman?,* p. 104.

178. In Louisiana in 1850 the life-expectancy rate was twenty-nine years for male and thirty-four years for female slaves; see White, *Ar'n't I a Woman?,* p. 84.

179. Rawick, *American Slave,* vol. 8, p. 1330.

180. Frederick Douglass, *Narrative of Frederick Douglass, an American Slave, Written by Himself* (Boston: Anti-Slavery Office, 1845), p. 3; Booker T. Washington, *Up from Slavery* (New York: A. L. Burt, 1901), p. 4. See also Rawick, *American Slave,* vol. 8, p. 1215.

181. It is important to remember, however, that the ex-slaves were speaking in the context of the 1930s Depression, when all were elderly and many experienced severe deprivation. Escott, *Slavery Remembered,* p. 10, noted that ex-slaves interviewed by whites recalled having had much better diets under slavery than ex-slaves interviewed by African-Americans.

182. Fogel and Engerman, *Time on the Cross,* pp. 113–15.

183. Fogel and Engerman, *Time on the Cross,* p. 70.

184. White, *Ar'n't I a Woman?*, p. 87.

185. Engerman, "Black Fertility and Family Structure," p. 129.

186. Higman, *Slave Populations*, p. 328; Bush, *Slave Women in Caribbean Society*, pp. 138–40.

187. Morrissey, *Slave Women in the New World*, pp. 106, 114–15, 122, 130. Amenorrhea is associated with very low proportions of body fat because of poor nutrition, strenuous labor, and/or strenuous exercise.

188. Fogel and Engerman, *Time on the Cross*, p. 156.

189. Fogel and Engerman, *Time on the Cross*, p. 261; Gutman, "Persistent Myths," pp. 205–8; Davis et al., *Deep South*, pp. 289–91.

190. Rawick, *American Slave*, vol. 8, p. 1343; Perdue et al., *Weevils in the Wheat*, p. 53.

191. Jones, *Labor of Love*, p. 60.

192. Jones, *Labor of Love*, p. 67.

193. Mann, "Slavery, Sharecropping and Sexual Inequality."

194. Rawick, *American Slave*, vol. 8, p. 1155; Perdue et al., *Weevils in the Wheat*, pp. 3, 53.

195. Rawick, *American Slave*, vol. 4, p. 1105; vol. 8, p. 1343.

196. Perdue et al., *Weevils in the Wheat*, p. 195. Jefferson Davis sold a plantation to ex-slaves but got it back as they had no capital to keep it running; Rawick, *American Slave*, vol. 8, pp. 994–95.

197. *Herald-Times*, Bloomington, Ind., July 29, 1989.

198. Rawick, *American Slave*, vol. 8, p. 1343; Perdue et al., *Weevils in the Wheat*, p. 118.

199. Fogel and Engerman, *Time on the Cross*, p. 171.

200. Jewsiewicki and Mumbanza, "Social Context of Slavery," p. 96.

201. Chanock, *Law, Custom and Social Order*, p. 171.

202. Roberts and Miers, Introduction, in *The End of Slavery in Africa*, p. 40.

203. Gutman, "Persistent Myths," p. 208; Davis et al., *Deep South*, pp. 9, 538–39.

204. Jones, *Labor of Love*, p. 77.

205. Rawick, *American Slave*, vol. 8, p. 1257.

206. Seymour Drescher, *Capitalism and Anti-Slavery: British Mobilization in Comparative Perspective* (New York: Oxford University Press, 1987), p. 135, described abolitionists as being primarily concerned with freedom, slaveowners with labor.

207. Gerda Lerner, "Women and Slavery," *Slavery and Abolition* 4 (1983): 193. Lerner uses "domestic" where I have placed "economic." Meillassoux, *Anthropologie de l'esclavage*, p. 283, is incorrect in stating that the "slave represents the first historical form of property being used for a means of production." Women, as Engels recognized, formed the first human population used as a means of production.

208. Davis, "Reflections," pp. 14–15.

LIFE
AND
LABOR

2

WOMEN, WORK, AND HEALTH
UNDER PLANTATION SLAVERY
IN THE UNITED STATES

Richard H. Steckel

The large number of programs in black studies and in women's studies created within the past two decades establish these areas as growth industries of academics. Accompanying this expansion has been a burgeoning literature on the involvement of these groups in the economy, society, and politics of the past. The role of women in economic history has attracted much attention and scholars have examined labor force participation rates of women by age and marital status, the degree of occupational segregation, and the nature of work in the home.[1] Within the field of black history, participants have hotly contested issues in slavery, such as the profitability and relative efficiency of slave labor, the nature of the interregional and African slave trades, and demographic features of the slave system.[2]

Despite the popularity of research on women and blacks in general and interest in slavery and economic issues in particular, the overlap of these research areas is surprisingly small. Study of slave women has claimed little attention.[3] Although the rationale for this neglect is elusive, an explanation might note that much of the agenda of current research on slavery was forged before the modern rise of women's studies. The present generation of scholars is still grappling with issues, such as diet, disease, and the family, that were defined in the antebellum debate over abolition. Progress has been marked more by the assimilation of new data sources and techniques of analysis than by the formulation of new questions. On the other hand, many subjects in the spotlight of women's studies, including labor force participation rates, pay scales, and political activity, hold little interest in the context of slavery. Yet women under slavery is a topic worthy of study in its own right, for learning, among other things, about performance under adversity and conditions that shaped life after emancipation.

Whatever the explanation for the lack of research about slave women, this chapter takes a step toward redressing the balance, using the concept of the life cycle to examine the course of work and health from childhood to old age in the United States. Particular attention is given to the health of pregnant women and to conditions on cotton plantations. The main sources of information include slave manifests, plantation records, slave narratives, probate records, and the census.

Diverse sources of evidence indicate that work was a central aspect of slave life. Virtually all studies that address the subject show that the initiation process began in childhood or early adolescence and, with the exception of infirmity and periods of illness or injury, slaves worked throughout their life span. The slave narratives indicate that few slaves escaped work in childhood: 48 percent of those who discussed the subject began working before age seven, 84 percent before age eleven, and only 7 percent reported that no work occurred before age fourteen.[4] Child labor had a niche within the wide–ranging tasks required on a large farm. Young slaves picked cotton, carried drinking water to the fields, picked up trash, helped in the kitchen, fed chickens and livestock, minded young children, pulled weeds, and gathered wood chips for fuel. Although it is difficult to establish the intensity, duration, and physical demands of these jobs, it seems clear that the tasks were part of a real work experience that prepared the way for regular adult labor.

According to the narratives, male and female children had substantially different work experiences. Girls began work at younger ages and were involved more with housework than with fieldwork. One-half of the males and 21 percent of the females who worked as children participated regularly in fieldwork. Nearly 53 percent of the girls, but only 44 percent of the boys, who ever worked as children were working by age seven, but by age ten the numbers working were approximately equal. Females also began their adult jobs at younger ages; 71 percent of the girls but only 63 percent of the boys who mentioned the topic were performing their adult jobs before age fourteen. Girls not only began work earlier but were more productive than boys at certain tasks, such as picking cotton.[5] This evidence is consistent with estimates of net earnings (value of labor minus maintenance costs) that show females were more productive than males before age seventeen.[6] Explanations of this pattern note that girls matured earlier than boys and that boys may have been held out of work until they were productive in the fields. These patterns of work during childhood and adolescence suggest that the transition to adult labor required greater reorientation of females than males. The typical girl began her working life entirely or partially in the house but ended up in the fields, while the typical male spent his working life as a field hand. Adaptation to labor in the fields after working in the surroundings of the big house was an additional challenge posed for females by adolescence.

Although the distribution of skills and occupational mobility are contentious issues in slavery research, all accounts agree that a large majority of slaves spent their prime working years as field hands. On one side of the debate in the recent literature on this issue, Robert Fogel and Stanley Engerman argued from probate records that only three–quarters of adult males were ordinary laborers and that the other slaves were skilled craftsmen, such as blacksmiths and carpenters; semi-skilled workers, such as gardeners and coachmen; or managers.[7] Semiskilled, and especially skilled, jobs were less available to women, 80 percent of whom labored in the fields. Most of the women not employed in fieldwork were servants, seam-stresses, or nurses. Using plantation records and probate records, Fogel and Engerman also reported that skilled slaves tended to be older than field hands; 75 percent of all artisans were aged thirty or above, but only 46 percent of the males aged fifteen and above were thirty years or older.[8] Fogel and Engerman used the information on the skill distribution by age and evidence on incentives to suggest that diligent slaves could have looked forward to upward mobility; masters reassigned slaves from fieldwork to one of the skilled or semiskilled crafts or household staff positions as a reward for diligent performance.

Herbert Gutman and Richard Sutch disputed the Fogel-Engerman account of upward mobility by challenging the representativeness of their sources, by offering alternative explanations, and by examining other sources of evidence.[9] They pointed out that the probate records in question were atypical because the region of the sample (southern Louisiana) produced sugar, the holdings were large, and the age distribution was skewed toward males over fourteen years of age. It was also possible, they noted, that slaves too old or incapable of heavy work were transferred into less physically demanding jobs. Gutman emphasized that fewer than 3 percent of the troops from Kentucky who served in the Union Army reported their occupation as other than farmer or laborer.[10] In pursuit of issues raised in the debate, Michael Johnson examined the distribution of skills reported on the mortality schedule of the 1860 census for certain counties in Georgia, Mississippi, and South Carolina. After adjustments for the age distri-bution of deaths, these data suggest that 77 to 91 percent of the males and 63 to 77 percent of the females were field hands. The percentages for women are below those reported by Fogel and Engerman, while the percentages for men were only moderately higher, which casts doubt on the Gutman-Sutch objec-tions that the Fogel-Engerman sample is atypical. Of course, defenders of Fogel and Engerman would point out that the critics' sources also have limitations. The Union Army records may undercount skilled slaves and servants because they were loyal to the system and had lower rates of enlistment, while skilled and semiskilled slaves may have had mortality rates below those of field hands. Longitudinal data (records that track characteristics of the same individuals over time) are needed to resolve questions about mobility. Patient sifting through a succession of plantation inventory lists that included names and occupations would provide valuable insights into the incentive structure. The evidence ex-amined to date suggests that a modest minority of all slaves could look forward to regular adult labor in a skilled or semiskilled position, but whether women had relatively more of these positions than men remains an open question.

Whatever the distribution of skills and rewards, several sources confirm that slaves often worked hard at physically demanding tasks. The modern conveniences of home and workplace make it difficult for our generation to comprehend the rigors of slave labor. Yet the tools and methods typical of the era—hoes powered by human muscle and plows drawn by oxen, mules, or horses but guided by people—establish that fieldwork was demanding. The strains of physical exertion were relatively greater in farming, where workers were driven in gangs by overseers or drivers who could apply force. This style of work performance was frequently used in plowing, planting, or hoeing operations on large farms (roughly ten or more workers) that raised cotton or sugar. Work was probably less strenuous, but nonetheless demanding, on small farms, where slaves often worked with and were paced by the owner; on tobacco farms, where demands were more evenly spread throughout the year; and on rice farms, where the task system, which allowed workers some freedom to pace individual effort, was often used. The frequency and the detail of reports about slave labor from narratives and observers confirm the general high level of toil.[11] Consistent with rigorous work, Fogel and Engerman estimated that slaves produced approximately 35 percent more output per year than free farmers.[12] While there is disagreement over the size and meaning of their estimate, a good case could be made that the intensity of gang labor was an important source of the greater output.[13]

Although firm evidence is lacking about the ages at which older slaves were transferred from the most demanding fieldwork to less rigorous tasks, the process was probably under way as early as in the mid- to late thirties. Men and women once suitable for the plow gangs were moved to hoe gangs and, after further decline, to the lighter work of trash gangs. Movement out of regular fieldwork to positions of unpaced labor, such as weaver, seamstress, gardener, and stock minder, probably accelerated after slaves reached their late forties or early fifties. The age profile of net earnings mirrors the changing capacity for work. Annual net earnings reached a peak while slaves were in their early to mid-thirties.[14] The maximum occurred approximately three to five years earlier among women than among men. As late as age fifty, however, net earnings were as large as 50 percent (women) to 70 percent (men) of the maximum. The gradual nature of the decline suggests that strength and endurance, while valuable, were not all that was required of a slave to make an important contribution to plantation operations. Farms made good use of a labor force that was diverse in capacity for work by allocating slaves to appropriate tasks. Remarkably, the net earnings of slaves as old as age seventy were, on average, greater than zero.[15] Because fewer than 1.5 percent of all slaves above age nine were aged seventy or more, planters profitably employed nearly all slaves who were beyond the age of late childhood.

The labor demands of slavery inevitably affected other aspects of slave life, such as health, family interaction, recreation, and opportunities for personal reflection. Slaves tired from work in the fields must have had little enthusiasm for games and amusements and little time to spend with their children. There were slack periods, however, that occurred before and after the harvest, when celebrations and marriages often took place.[16] Nevertheless, the overwhelming majority of a slave's adult life was spent engaged in or recovering from toil.

Hard work had adverse consequences for slave health. This topic is probed extensively here because health is fundamental to well-being and because recently developed evidence and techniques have added new dimensions of understanding, particularly in regard to pregnant women and their newborn children. Fogel and Engerman, using the disappearance method to estimate food consumption for adults as the difference between food production and nonslave utilization on large southern farms, argued that the diet was substantial calorically and exceeded recommended levels of the chief nutrients. Critics examined every step of this procedure and raised questions about methods of food preservation and cooking, the adequacy of the diet for blacks, and whether the diet was sufficient for the work effort required of slaves. Richard Sutch found the estimates too generous, especially for important nutrients, but he concluded that the diet was sufficient to maintain the slave's body weight and general health.[17] Kenneth and Virginia Kiple argued that nutritional deficiencies were exacerbated by a biological heritage that was adapted to African conditions.[18] The material in the rest of this chapter reviews this debate in light of new evidence on heights from slave manifests and on mortality rates from plantation records. The discussion begins with background information on human growth.

Laboratory experiments on animals and observations of human populations under a variety of conditions have led physiologists, nutritionists, and human biologists to conclude that anthropometric measurements are reliable indicators of health. Specifically, stature during the growing years, the age at which adult height is reached, and final adult height "reflect accurately the state of a nation's public health and the average nutritional status of its citizens."[19] Average heights for a specific population can be gauged relative to well-defined patterns of human growth. Height velocity (the annual increase in height) is greatest during infancy, falls sharply before age three, then ordinarily declines irregularly through the preadolescent years. During adolescence velocity rises sharply to a peak that usually reaches approximately one-half of the velocity attained during infancy. Thereafter velocity falls sharply and reaches zero at maturity. In girls the onset of the adolescent growth spurt occurs about two years earlier, and the magnitude of the spurt is slightly smaller than in boys. Girls and boys are approximately the same height prior to the spurt, and the difference in adult size between men and women is due to the additional growth achieved by males during adolescence. The velocity profiles derived from longitudinal and cross-sectional data have the same basic shape, but there are important differences attributable to individual differences in the timing and intensity of the adolescent spurt.

The pattern of growth reflects the interaction of genetic and environmental factors. Although the relative importance of these factors and the nature of their interaction is a matter of debate, many well-nourished populations have approximately the same growth profile and final adult height. The average heights of West Europeans, North American whites, and North American blacks, for example, are nearly identical.[20] Therefore it seems likely that American slaves and North American whites of the nineteenth century had approximately the same growth potential.

Average stature is a measure of net nutrition, which depends upon diet, or the intake of nutrients, and claims on the diet made by work or physical activity, infections, and the efficiency with which the body converts nutrients into outputs. Malnutrition and illness may interact to produce an effect on growth larger than the separate effects of each in isolation. At the end of a period of slow growth due to illness or malnutrition, velocity may exceed the average for a given chronological age. Normal height may be restored through catch-up growth, but if conditions are unsatisfactory, growth may resume at only the normal rate. Approximately normal height may be achieved through extension of the growing period. Boys tend to be more severely retarded than girls by a given environmental insult.

Evidence on the stature of American slaves is abundant from slave manifests prepared after 1807 in accordance with the Bill for the Abolition of the Slave Trade.[21] As part of an identification scheme designed to prevent slave smuggling, the bill required ship captains to prepare duplicate manifests that described each slave by name, age, sex, height, and color. Comparison of individuals in the cargo at the port of destination with the manifest confirmed that the slaves originated within the United States. The discussion below is based on a sample of 10,562 manifests and 50,606 slaves transported primarily from Atlantic coast ports between 1820 and 1860.[22]

Table 1 lists the average heights of American slaves from childhood to maturity.[23] The estimated velocity profiles closely resemble those found in modern growth studies. The values declined uniformly for several years after age 4.5, reaching a preadolescent minimum around age 9.5 in females and age 10.5 in males. The adolescent spurt is clearly visible in both sexes. The age at the peaks of the adolescent growth spurt were 13.3 years for girls and 14.8 years for boys, which are 1 to 1.5 years later than found in well-nourished modern populations. In accordance with other growth studies, the girls matured more rapidly than the boys.

The columns labeled "Centile" show the average location of slaves at each age relative to modern height standards; the lower the centile, the smaller the children, relatively speaking. The most interesting aspects of these data are the low levels in childhood and the climb through the centiles that occurred during and after adolescence. The younger slave children were extraordinarily small, falling on average below the first or second centile of modern standards and below most of the average heights observed these days for children in the poorest populations of developing countries. The slums in Lagos, Nigeria, and urban areas of Bangladesh provided environments for growth superior to those faced by slave children.[24] The harshness of life registered in high mortality rates

TABLE 1. Height by Age of American Slaves, 1820–1860, with Estimated Velocity Compared (by Centile) with Modern Standards

		Females			Males	
Age	Height	Estimated Velocity*	Centile†	Height	Estimated Velocity	Centile
4.5	35.90	2.77	0.5	35.70	2.85	0.2
5.5	38.53	2.51	0.9	38.42	2.62	0.4
6.5	40.93	2.29	1.3	40.93	2.41	0.7
7.5	43.12	2.11	1.5	43.26	2.24	1.0
8.5	45.16	1.98	1.6	45.42	2.10	1.3
9.5	47.12	1.93	1.5	47.47	2.00	1.4
10.5	49.06	1.99	1.4	49.45	1.96	1.9
11.5	51.13	2.16	1.8	51.42	1.99	2.4
12.5	53.39	2.38	1.2	53.44	2.08	2.9
13.5	55.84	2.46	0.8	55.59	2.21	3.1
14.5	58.18	2.16	1.6	57.85	2.31	2.2
15.5	60.04	1.53	5.8	60.15	2.26	1.2
16.5	61.24	0.90	13.4	62.29	1.97	1.2
17.5	61.91	0.46	20.0	64.04	1.51	3.8
18.5	62.24	0.22	24.5	65.30	1.02	9.2
19.5	62.39	0.10	26.8	66.11	0.63	15.4
20.5	62.46	0.05	27.8	66.59	0.36	20.0
21.5	62.49	0.02	28.1	66.86	0.20	23.3
Adult	62.51		28.4	67.17		27.1

Source: Slave manifests. See Richard H. Steckel, "A Peculiar Population: The Nutrition, Health, and Mortality of American Slaves from Childhood to Maturity," *Journal of Economic History* 46 (September 1986): 724–725.

* Estimated velocity (i.e., Annual increase in height)=value of first derivative of Preece-Baines function at exact age shown.

† Centile=position within a modern height distribution, given as a percent; average or typical height is represented by the 50th percentile.

during infancy and childhood. Table 2 shows that slave losses before adolescence were roughly double those of the general population in the antebellum United States. Notably, the excess infant mortality rate for slaves was more than 15 percentage points.

The patterns of the centiles by age in table 1 show that females were relatively better off in childhood and as young adults, while males fared better as adolescents. Up to age 9.5 and beginning again at age 15.5, the centiles for females exceeded those for males, while at age 10.5 to 14.5 the centiles attained by males exceeded those reached by females. Although most of these differences were small, the patterns suggest that some systematic differences in health related to age existed between the sexes.

Comparisons with other populations demonstrate that the upward movement through the centiles, or "catch–up growth," that occurred following early ado-

**TABLE 2. Mortality Rates per Thousand for Slaves and for the
General U.S. Antebellum Population**

Age	Slaves	Entire United States
0	350	179
1–4	201	93
5–9	54	28
10–14	37	19
15–19	35	28
20–24	40	39

Source: Plantation records, with data calculated by indirect methods from cencus materials. See Richard H. Steckel, "A Dreadful Childhood: The Excess Mortality of American Slaves," *Social Science History* 10 (Winter 1986): 427–65; Michael R. Haines and Roger C. Avery, "The American Life Table of 1830–1860: An Evaluation," *Journal of Interdisciplinary History* 11 (Summer 1980): 73–95.

lescence was remarkable.[25] Evidence on growth patterns from European and American populations of the eighteenth and nineteenth centuries and from developing countries of the twentieth century suggests that at least under typical circumstances, most societies allocated resources which resulted in the attainment by children and adults of approximately equal ranking relative to modern standards. If the children were small, then the adults tended to be small; if the children were large, the adults were correspondingly taller. Therefore the growth recovery of American slaves was exceptional, if not unprecedented.

Why were the slave children so small and why was the recovery so large? The origins of poor health can be traced to difficult periods of fetal and infant growth, a topic explored below in the section on seasonal deprivation. Slave newborns probably weighed on average less than 5.5 pounds, or 2,500 grams, compared with modern standards of 3,450 grams.[26] Under conditions of breast-feeding, the situation may have improved temporarily for those who survived the first month of life, but health probably declined within three or four months after birth. Table 3 shows that the number of pounds of cotton picked by women slaves per day attained normal levels within three months after delivery, which suggests that one or more of the daytime breast-feedings were replaced by food supplements. Manual feeding introduced unsanitary implements and contaminated food, while the diet emphasized starch paps and gruels. This diet lacked sufficient protein and was probably deficient in iron and calcium. It is not surprising that the mortality of infants aged one to eleven months was as high as 162 per thousand in a sample of plantation records.[27] Moreover, the average rate of loss was nearly 50 percent higher in months one through four compared with months five through eight, which is consistent with the hypothesis that breast-feeding was attenuated in early infancy.

Heights are a measure of net nutrition, or the actual diet minus claims on the diet made by illness, physical effort, and maintenance. Although direct evidence on childhood illness is lacking, the downward trend in mortality rates by age re-

TABLE 3. Daily Cotton-Picking Rates of U.S. Women Slaves
before and after Giving Birth

Period	Rate (in pounds)	Percent of Normal
9–12 weeks before	73.2	83.4
5–8 weeks before	69.2	78.8
1–4 weeks before	67.0	76.3
Week of birth and week after	31.3	35.6
2–3 weeks after	8.6	9.8
4–7 weeks after	67.1	58.9
8–11 weeks after	80.6	91.8
Other weeks	87.8	100.0

Source: Plantation records. See Jacob Metzer, "Efficient Operation and Economies of Scale in the Antebullum Southern Plantation," mimeographed paper, 1974.

ported in table 2 suggests that sickness decreased during childhood. The discussion of childhood labor also suggests that work effort probably made no more than a small claim on the diet before early adolescence. If the judgments about the decline in sickness and the lack of work effort are correct, the conclusion has to be that the diet remained poor. Yet it is clear from the discussions of slaveowners among themselves about the care and feeding of slaves that they focused on working slaves. One planter stated that "a negro deprived of a meat diet is not able to endure the labor that those can perform who are liberally supplied with it."[28] Planters usually stated allowances of meat, corn, and other foods in terms of working or laboring hands. If children were mentioned at all, they usually received "proportionally less," presumably in relation to work effort. The descriptive literature also points to malnutrition among children. Slaveowners discussed the shiny bodies, plump bellies, and glistening ribs of their young slaves, which are signs of protein deficiency. Explanations for the different patterns of the centiles by sex and age, noted in connection with the discussion of table 1, should be sought in terms of the concept of net nutrition. It is likely, on biological grounds, that females adapted better than males to deprivation, which may explain why girls attained greater centiles than boys up to age 9.5. If this explanation is correct, however, it adds to the need for understanding the relative height disadvantage of adolescent girls at ages 10.5 to 14.5. Some of this disadvantage may be attributed to the earlier maturation of girls in the reference (modern) population. Part of the decline in the centiles of girls is simply an artifact of the result that girls began adolescence one to three years earlier than boys. Yet the period of time that girls were at a disadvantage is so long (five years), compared to the difference in ages of the onset of adolescence, that an additional explanation is required. One hypothesis would emphasize the stress encountered by many girls, but few boys, in adapting to the shift from housework to fieldwork.[29] If girls had a health disadvantage during adolescence, they recovered rapidly thereafter. Young women attained the twentieth centile of modern height standards by age 17.5, but the men did not do so until three years later. Moreover, women had a slight advantage over men in attained height relative to modern standards (centile 28.4 versus 27.1). While biological factors may have contributed to the postadolescent advantage of females, it is also likely that work routines tended to place men in the most strenuous positions, such as plowing.

The slow rate of growth recovery during childhood raises the question of motives. How did owners reach the decision to exclude meat from childrens' diets? Although scientific understanding of nutrition and health was primitive in the early nineteenth century, owners could have accumulated knowledge from a long process of trial and error. Planters had considerable experience with the feeding of slaves and livestock and had reasons to suspect a connection between diet and growth. Feeding meat to children was an investment in which the net income was negative during the early years because meat was costly and children did not work. But children, adequately fed, emerged taller and stronger when they entered the labor force. One can calculate the rate of return on this investment with the help of simplifying assumptions on ages of entry into the labor force, the extent of protein deficits, and the attainment of modern height standards.[30] It is plausible that annual outlays per child sufficient to cover protein deficits would have ranged from at least $3.80 at age one to $5.90 at age nine. Data on slave values by height assembled by the Union Army indicate that net earnings (relative to the mean) increased by 1.375 percent per inch of stature, which forms the basis for calculating the financial benefits of the improved diet. These sources and methods produce a negative rate of return (average for males and females), which means that the present value of expected outlays exceeded the present value of expected returns. Therefore it is likely that owners found it profitable to exclude meat from the diet of slave children.

Slave children realized some catch-up growth at ages when they entered the labor force. Other things being equal, net nutrition should have deteriorated because of the extra work effort. The point is that other things must not have been equal. The diet improved by more than enough to offset the additional demands of physical activity and to allow a small amount of catch-up growth. This growth pattern is consistent with the slaveowners' emphasis on meat for workers. The small delay in the age of peak velocity (1 to 1.5 years behind modern standards), the magnitude of the peak velocities (nearly as large as modern standards), and the continuation of growth after adolescence establish that slaves were, on average, well fed as workers. Deficiencies, no doubt, existed in the diets of some working slaves, but these were not widespread or severe enough to retard average growth for the workers as a whole.

While heights and mortality rates by age shown in tables 1 and 2 shed light on health over long periods, such as a year or more, significant seasonal variations in health also occurred. These short-term fluctuations in health were particularly important for pregnant women and their developing fetuses. Maternal carelessness and neglect have been recurrent themes in the literature on the health of infant slaves. Slaveowners blamed mothers for smothering infants by rolling on them while sleeping. Some observers attributed these deaths to infanticide, but the recent literature emphasizes sudden infant death syndrome (SIDS), which occurs often from one to six months after birth and has causes stemming from fetal deprivation.[31] Although there is now substantial agreement that SIDS was relevant, the recent literature also points to other causes of infant death. Fogel and Engerman emphasize that the quality of prenatal care was an important factor behind infant mortality rates that were only moderately high (about 18.3 percent) by nineteenth-century standards. In their view, "health care was at its best for pregnant women."[32] However, John Campbell casts doubt on the quality of prenatal care by linking higher infant mortality rates to work before birth.[33] Kenneth F. Kiple has placed slave infant mortality rates substantially above the level determined by Fogel and Engerman. His explanations are related to diet and climate ill-suited to persons of African descent.[34]

Seasonal patterns of work, diet, disease, and mortality shed light on alternative hypotheses about infant health. The neonatal (from birth to the end of the first month) mortality rate is particularly sensitive to the quality of health care for pregnant women. Table 4, which is based on data from three large cotton plantations in South Carolina and Alabama, shows that neonatal losses had a marked seasonal pattern.[35] A peak occurred in late winter and early spring, centered in March, and a second, smaller concentration of deaths existed for births from September through November. The average probability of death in February–April and in September–November was 40.6 percent, compared with 10.5 percent in other months. Newborn slaves had diverse prospects for survival depending upon month of birth.

Because neonatal survival rates are sensitive to birth weight, which is strongly influenced by prenatal conditions, one is led to the literature on maternal health for possible explanations of the seasonal patterns. Study of conditions in developing countries and of nutritional adversity in developed nations shows that the following factors are systematically associated with low birth weight: malnutrition of the mother, specific dietary deficiencies of the mother, maternal and fetal infections, work during pregnancy (especially effort that requires standing), ingestion of toxic substances (such as alcohol or tobacco), small stature of the mother, and possibly genetic factors.[36] It is unlikely that genetic conditions or conceptions by maternal stature varied importantly by season of the year. Descriptions of Christmas parties or other postharvest celebrations indicate that alcohol consumption may have peaked in December or January, but this phenomenon is an unlikely explanation of the bimodal nature of the seasonal mortality distribution. Moreover, heavy consumption of alcohol during pregnancy tends to stunt childrens' growth permanently, which is largely inconsistent with the growth recovery noted after age ten. The discussion below emphasizes instead seasonal fluctuations in work, diet, and disease.

Human growth occurs through increase in the number of cells and increase in the size of cells.[37] Proliferation of cells dominates early development, but during a second phase the growth in numbers slows down and cell size increases

TABLE 4. **Probability of Slave Infant Death within One**
        Calendar Month of Birth

Month of Birth	Probability
January	0.116
February	0.221
March	0.692
April	0.335
May and June	0.197
July and August	0.054
September	0.464
October	0.342
November	0.380
December	0.265

Source: Plantation records. See Steckel, "A Dreadful Childhood."

rapidly. In the third phase, there is almost no proliferation and cell size increases rapidly. If conditions are poor during the proliferation phase, the number of cells is restricted and cannot be increased by later feeding, but reversal of small cell size may be possible. Cell multiplication is largely responsible for the high growth rate of the fetus compared with the child. It is thought that few, if any, nerve cells and only a small proportion of new muscle cells, for example, appear more than twenty-eight weeks after fertilization has occurred. The growth process establishes that fetal conditions, especially those of the first phase, are critical to later development.

The Dutch hunger winter of 1944–45 created a natural laboratory for the study of fetal development.[38] Neonatal mortality rates, particularly for stillbirths, were highest among pregnancies conceived in the famine or exposed to the famine during the first trimester only. In contrast, undernutrition during the last trimester alone did not elevate stillbirths, but it reduced birth weight by about 300 grams and increased neonatal mortality. Because high rates of stillbirth signify deprivation at or near conception, comparisons of neonatal and stillbirth losses by month or season may clarify the seasonal timing and therefore the causes of insults during pregnancy.

On southern plantations, the work year in cotton cultivation began in January with a lay-by period. By this time the harvest was complete or nearly finished, the hours of daylight were near the minimum, and harsh weather may have prevented fieldwork. Preparation of the ground for the next crop began in late January or early February, and the plowing and planting seasons followed in March and April. These months were particularly strenuous for adults because the tasks were physically demanding and the young and the old were not able to contribute. Owners pressed work at an intense pace to meet planting deadlines, and cool weather meant that breaks for meals and rest could be short. Study of the work records on four plantations shows that the number of days actually worked in the fields as a share of the total days was highest in March, followed by April and February.[39] A brief lay-by period followed planting, and the hoeing season continued through June or early July. The next lay-by extended from the remainder of July until the harvest began in mid- or late August. The picking season involved long hours, but the work was less demanding and the pace was easier than plowing and planting, and the effort was distributed over more workers.

Plantation manuals, daily work records, and other sources show that women's work was arduous and that pregnant women had little or no reduction in work loads before the fifth month.[40] Table 3, discussed earlier, shows that women continued to work almost until delivery, at least during seasonal peaks in the demand for labor. Studies of modern data clearly show that mothers engaged in "hard" work have smaller newborns.[41] Birth weights in early twentieth-century Britain were about 350 grams lower among women who worked up to the day of confinement compared with mothers who spent more than ten days in a prematernity home.[42] Yet the physical efforts of these modern women must have been modest by the standards of American slaves, especially during seasonal peaks in the demand for labor, and therefore the effects of slave work were more severe. Low birth rates related to physical exertion are a familiar problem in developing countries, and many prenatal programs now stress the benefits of less work.[43]

Infections reduce appetite and lower nutrient absorption and utilization. Fetal infections are common and important causes of intrauterine malnutrition in developing countries.[44] Maternal illnesses, such as a gastrointestinal and respiratory infections and malaria, also retard intrauterine growth. African women infected with *Plasmodium falciparum* malaria, for example, had newborns who weighed about 263 grams below those of noninfected mothers.[45] The effects of infections are relevant for the seasonal pattern of neonatal mortality because illnesses in the antebellum South were concentrated in summer and early autumn. About 34.2 percent of all deaths of slaves aged fifteen to forty-nine occurred in June, July, and August, while nearly 49 percent of the deaths from fevers in New Orleans took place in August and September.[46]

Nominally, the slave diet was probably best from midsummer through early winter. By July fresh vegetables were available, and consumption of fresh meat increased with the slaughter season of late autumn and early winter. Fluctuations in the diet are unlikely to have been a major force in the seasonal pattern of neonatal losses because if they were important then the rates should have been greatest in the spring and approximately six to eight months thereafter. The pattern of relatively few deaths in December and January and in May and June creates difficulties for the dietary hypothesis.

The data in table 5 show that the highest rate of stillbirth loss on the three large plantations occurred in November and December, which is consistent with hard work and net nutritional deprivation during the preparation and planting season. The adverse effects of work during the harvest and diseases of the "sickly season" may have more than offset any improvements in the diet, because stillbirth rates were also high during late winter and early spring (February through April). The low incidence of stillbirths in August, September, and October and the high neonatal mortality rates during these months suggest that deprivation shortly before delivery at this time of the year was an important adverse ingredient in newborn health. Hard work shortly before delivery probably added to the high ratio of neonatal losses to stillbirths from February through April. The relative incidence of neonatal deaths and stillbirths and the finding that stillbirths were highest near the end of autumn indicate that the preparation and planting season was the time of greatest deprivation.

The evidence examined in this chapter establishes that American slave children had a dreadful childhood. These children attained levels of net nutrition that approached those of the slowest growing population ever studied by auxologists. But catch-up growth that was gradual in late childhood and rapid during and after adolescence brought slaves to approximately the twenty-eighth centile of modern height standards. This remarkable growth pattern, related information on mortality rates, and dietary recommendations of owners establish that slaves were poorly fed as children but well-fed as workers. The wide seasonal swings in newborn mortality and the extensive recovery from growth depression suggest that African adaptations played, at most, a supporting role in American slave health. Instead, seasonal deprivation of pregnant women arising mainly from hard work and infections, attenuated breast-feeding, and malnutrition in childhood stemming from inadequate protein and other nutrients were the major actors in their poor health. Adolescent girls, who were smaller than boys relative to modern height standards, may have encountered stress in adapting to the change from work in the house to work in the fields.

These findings suggest several directions for new research. The literature on slavery generally recognizes the effects of bondage on the acquisition of skills, while work on the postwar period incorporates discrimination, but neither focus of research develops the possible consequences of nutritional deprivation in childhood. Because recent studies suggest that chronic nutritional deprivation retards the acquisition of motor skills, stunts mental development, and induces apathy, nutritional conditions under slavery may have influenced personality development and could have impeded the economic progress of blacks after the war.

Investments in good nutrition for slave children had low rates of return, but free populations allocated relatively more resources toward children. Research should explore explanations for this contrast. It is possible, for example, that planters valued only the physical development of raw labor, whereas free populations valued mental development or were driven by an altruism toward their own children that planters did not have for slave children. Whatever the reasons, it is clear that certain conceptions of slave childhood should be redrawn.

TABLE 5. Slave Infant Stillbirth Rates and Mortality Rates per Thousand

| Month of Birth | Stillbirths | Mortalities—Days from Birth to Death | | | | Number of Stillbirths Plus Births |
		0–1	*2–6*	*7–29*	*0–29*	
January, May, June, July	0	8	21	24	52	387
February, March, April	18	36	19	43	95	224
August, September, October	3	10	23	36	67	314
November, December	21	21	16	11	48	194
All Months	10	17	21	30	64	1,119

Source: Plantation records. See Steckel, "A Dreadful Chilhood."

Eugene Genovese, for example, portrays these early ages as "protected years" that provided a "foundation of physical health," a "time to grow physically" and to "parry the most brutal features of [their] bondage."[47] Instead, poor nutrition restricted exploration and play and retarded growth. Slave children probably sought to escape their dreadful childhood and join the adult labor force because of the nutritional rewards.

Promotion of the work ethic through nutrition may have occurred at the expense of the slave family, at least as it influenced interaction between children and their parents. Workers generally ate breakfast and lunch in the fields and probably ate after the children in the evening. Because children were often fed separately, parents had little time to spend with their young children on a regular basis. Under these conditions, slaves too old to work in the fields probably socialized young slave children. After emancipation, black women withdrew substantially from field labor and spent more time in household activities, including child rearing. The women who spent most of their time in the fields may have lacked the experience to train their young children adequately.

The findings on attenuated breast-feeding are relevant for the debate over forces that shaped slave culture. A high volume of imports to the Caribbean constantly renewed African customs and, consistent with those customs, breast-feeding in the sugar colonies continued in some form for about two years after birth.[48] The available evidence shows that the duration was much shorter in the United States and was abbreviated compared with that of upper class southern whites.[49] Thus the goals were not to imbue black slaves with southern ideals, and clearly slaves were not the source of change. Instead, the example of breast-feeding indicates that owners reckoned with the high value of women's time in their formulation of rules and regulations that shaped cultural practices. This argument in no way suggests that slaves were creatures of profit and loss, devoid of their own identities. Owners had to contend with firmly established cultural traditions, but ultimately slaves relinquished or modified any customs that were costly to their owners. The extent to which slaves were able to impose costs and deny profits by successfully resisting changes desired by owners or by successfully initiating changes unwanted by owners is a measure of the autonomy of slave culture. Thus it would be interesting to know the extent to which breast-feeding in the sugar colonies was driven by an accommodation to prior beliefs or by a low value of women's time in sugar cultivation.

Notes

1. See, for example, Claudia Goldin, "Historians' Consensus on the Economic Role of Women in American History: A Review Essay," *Historical Methods* 16 (1983): 74–81 and references therein.

2. The debate over *Time on the Cross: The Economics of American Negro Slavery* by Robert William Fogel and Stanley L. Engerman (Boston: Little, Brown, 1974) typifies this line of research. See, for example, Paul A. David, Herbert G. Gutman, Richard Sutch, Peter Temin, and Gavin Wright, *Reckoning with Slavery* (New York: Oxford University Press, 1976).

3. Notable exceptions include Deborah Gray White, *Ar'n't I a Woman?: Female Slaves in the Plantation South* (New York: Norton, 1985); Jacqueline Jones, *Labor of Love, Labor of Sorrow: Black Women, Work, and the Family from Slavery to the Present* (New York: Basic, 1985).

4. The discussion of the narratives draws heavily upon Stephen C. Crawford, "Quantified Memory: A Study of the WPA and Fisk University Slave Narrative Collections," Ph.D. dissertation, University of Chicago, 1980.

5. Jacob Metzer, "Rational Management, Modern Business Practices, and Economies of Scale in the Ante-Bellum Southern Plantations," *Explorations in Economic History* 12 (1975): 123–50.

6. Fogel and Engerman, *Time on the Cross*, p. 76.

7. Fogel and Engerman, *Time on the Cross*, p. 39.

8. Fogel and Engerman, *Time on the Cross*, vol. 2, p. 117.

9. Herbert Gutman and Richard Sutch, "Sambo Makes Good, or Were Slaves Imbued with the Protestant Work Ethic?" in David et al., *Reckoning with Slavery*, pp. 55–93.

10. Herbert G. Gutman, *Slavery and the Numbers Game: A Criticism of Time on the Cross* (Urbana: University of Illinois Press, 1975), p. 73.

11. Former slave Hannah Davidson testified that she was so exhausted by work that "I was like an inchworm crawling along a roof. I worked until I thought another lick would kill me"; see George P. Rawick, ed., *The American Slave: A Composite Autobiography*, Series 1 (Westport: Greenwood, 1972), vol. 16 (Ohio). Frederick Law Olmstead observed slave women "who twitched their plows around on the headland, jerking their reins, and yelling to their mules, with apparent ease, energy, and rapidity." He saw no indication "that their sex unfitted them for the occupation." See Olmstead, *A Journey in the Back Country in the Winter of 1853–1854* (New York: Mason Brothers, 1860), p. 81. See Jones, *Labor of Love, Labor of Sorrow*, chap. 1, for additional examples of hard work.

12. Fogel and Engerman, *Time on the Cross*, p. 192.

13. The latest in a long list of articles on this question is Elizabeth B. Fields, "The Relative Efficiency of Slavery Revisited: A Translog Production Function Approach," *American Economic Review* 78 (June 1988): 543–49.

14. Fogel and Engerman, *Time on the Cross*, pp. 74–76.

15. Calculated from U.S. Census Office, *Population of the United States in 1860* (Washington, D.C.: Government Printing Office, 1864).

16. On the seasonal timing of marriages, see Richard H. Steckel, "Slave Marriage and the Family," *Journal of Family History* 5 (Winter 1980): 406–21.

17. Richard Sutch, "The Treatment Received by American Slaves: A Critical Review of the Evidence Presented in *Time on the Cross*," *Explorations in Economic History* 12 (1975): 335–438.

18. Kenneth F. Kiple and Virginia H. Kiple, "Slave Child Mortality: Some Nutritional Answers to a Perennial Puzzle," *Journal of Social History* 10 (March 1977): 284–309.

19. Phyllis B. Eveleth and James M. Tanner, *Worldwide Variation in Human Growth* (Cambridge: Cambridge University Press, 1976), p. 1. See also James M. Tanner, *Fetus into Man: Physical Growth from Conception to Maturity* (Cambridge: Harvard University Press, 1978).

20. Eveleth and Tanner, *Worldwide Variation*, chaps. 2–4.

21. Charles H. Wesley, "Manifests of Slave Shipments along the Waterways, 1808–1864," *Journal of Negro History* 27 (April 1942): 155–74.

22. The manifests are housed in Record Group 36 of the National Archives. Additional characteristics of the sample and methods of analysis are discussed in Richard H. Steckel, "A Peculiar Population: The Nutrition, Health, and Mortality of American Slaves from Childhood to Maturity," *Journal of Economic History* 46 (September 1986): 721–41.

23. Although the results have been smoothed to give a sharper picture of the growth profile, substantive conclusions are identical in the raw data.

24. Richard H. Steckel, "Birth Weights and Infant Mortality among American Slaves," *Explorations in Economic History* 23 (April 1986): 179.

25. For comparisons see Steckel, "A Peculiar Population," and Richard H. Steckel, "Growth Depression and Recovery: The Remarkable Case of American Slaves," *Annals of Human Biology* 14 (March–April 1987), 111–32.

26. Steckel, "Birth Weights."

27. Steckel, "Birth Weights."

28. Cited in James O. Breeden, ed., *Advice among Masters: The Ideal in Slave Management in the Old South* (Westport: Greenwood, 1980), p. 94.

29. For a discussion of stress and growth, see E. M. Widdowson, "Mental Contentment and Growth," *Lancet* 1 (1951): 1316–18.

30. Qualifications and details are discussed in Steckel, "A Peculiar Population," pp. 736–38.

31. See, for example, Todd L. Savitt, *Medicine and Slavery: The Diseases and Health Care of Blacks in Antebellum Virginia* (Urbana: University of Illinois Press, 1978); M. P. Johnson, "Smothered Slave Infants: Were Slave Mothers at Fault?" *Journal of Southern History* 47 (1981): 493–520; R. L. Naeye, "Sudden Infant Death," *Scientific American* 242 (1980): 56–62.

32. Fogel and Engerman, *Time on the Cross*, p. 122.

33. John Campbell, "Work, Pregnancy, and Infant Mortality among Southern Slaves," *Journal of Interdisciplinary History* 14 (1984): 793–812.

34. See, for example, Kenneth F. Kiple, *The Caribbean Slave: A Biological History* (Cambridge: Cambridge University Press, 1984).

35. For details and qualifications, see Richard H. Steckel, "A Dreadful Childhood: The Excess Mortality of American Slaves," *Social Science History* 10 (1986): 427–65. The results are similar if two additional plantations from South Carolina are included in the sample.

36. See, for example, F. E. Hytten and I. Leitch, *The Physiology of Human Pregnancy* (Oxford: Blackwell, 1971); W. M. O. Moore, "Prenatal Factors Influencing Intrauterine Growth: Clinical Implications," in R. Boyd and F. C. Battaglia, eds., *Perinatal Medicine* (London: Butterworths, 1983), pp. 245–63; and National Research Council, Committee on Maternal Nutrition/Food and Nutrition Board, *Maternal Nutrition and the Course of Pregnancy* (Washington, D.C.: National Academy of Sciences, 1970).

37. Tanner, *Fetus into Man*; L. S. Hurley, *Developmental Nutrition* (Englewood Cliffs: Prentice-Hall, 1980).

38. Moore, "Prenatal Factors."

39. John F. Olson, "Clock-Time vs. Real-Time: A Comparison of the Lengths of the Northern and Southern Agricultural Work Years," in Robert W. Fogel and Stanley L. Engerman, eds., *Without Consent or Contract: Technical Papers on Slavery* (New York: Norton, 1990).

40. Campbell, "Work, Pregnancy, and Infant Mortality."

41. Reductions of 210 grams for Ethiopian women were reported by N. Tafari, R. L. Naeye, and A. Gobezie, "Effects of Maternal Undernutrition and Heavy Physical Work during Pregnancy on Birth Weight," *British Journal of Obstetrics and Gynecology* 87 (1980): 222–26.

42. H. T. Ashby, *Infant Mortality* (Cambridge: Cambridge University Press, 1915).

43. Ann Ashworth, "International Differences in Infant Mortality and the Impact of Malnutrition: A Review," *Human Nutrition: Clinical Nutrition* 36c (1982): 7–23.

44. J. J. Urrutia, L. J. Mata, F. Trent, J. R. Cruz, E. Villatoro, and R. E. Alexander, "Infection and Low Birth Weight in a Developing Country: A Study of an Indian Village in Guatemala," *American Journal of Diseases in Childhood* 129 (1975): 558–61.

45. E. F. P. Jelliffe, "Low Birth-Weight and Malarial Infection of the Placenta," *Bulletin of the World Health Organization* 33 (1968): 69–78.

46. Richard H. Steckel, "Slave Mortality: Analysis of Evidence from Plantation Records," *Social Science History* 3 (1979): 86–114, and "A Dreadful Childhood," p. 442.

47. Eugene D. Genovese, *Roll, Jordan, Roll: The World the Slaves Made* (New York: Pantheon, 1974), pp. 504–5.

48. Herbert S. Klein and Stanley L. Engerman, "Fertility Differentials between Slaves in the United States and the British West Indies: A Note on Lactation Practices and Their Possible Implications," *William and Mary Quarterly*, 3d Series, 35 (1978): 357–74.

49. For a discussion of southern whites, see Sally McMillen, "Mothers' Sacred Duty: Breast-feeding Patterns among Middle- and Upper-Class Women in the Antebellum South," *Journal of Southern History* 60 (1985): 333–56.

3

CYCLES OF WORK AND OF CHILDBEARING
SEASONALITY IN WOMEN'S LIVES
ON LOW COUNTRY PLANTATIONS

Cheryll Ann Cody

Historians interested in the comparative study of New World slave populations have often relied upon demographic measures of fertility and mortality as indices of the quality of slave life. They have found that there were low levels of fertility among slave women on sugar plantations. Slave women in nonsugar areas, however, bore children in greater numbers, contributing, as in the case of the United States, to population growth. The explanation for low levels of fertility among sugar plantation women can be found in the labor requirements of sugar production and in the difficult climate of the tropics.[1] To a large degree this comparative analysis has shaped the way we look at the work of slave women in the United States. Perhaps because the slave population of the United States achieved growth through natural increase, little attention has been given to the tension between women's productive and reproductive functions. We know, however, that slave women in the United States endured frequent pregnancies and still often remained among the most productive workers in the fields.

When scholars examine the relation between women's work and childbearing, they focus on the outcome as measured by the frequency of infant and maternal mortality, not on the process of pregnancy itself, which played such an important role in the lives of plantation women. To a large degree the outcome approach mirrors the attitude of slaveowners, who strove to balance the immediate return realized by the labor of pregnant women in the field against the long-term benefits of the birth of a healthy infant.[2] Michael Johnson drew a connection between the hard physical labor required of pregnant slave women and the high incidence of infant death attributed to smothering, which, he argues persuasively, were cases of sudden infant death syndrome.[3] John Campbell, however, in his study of pregnant women on the Kollock cotton plantation in Chatham County, Georgia, found that they received a work release of about twenty-five days during pregnancy and that such release time, especially early in pregnancy, produced a higher survival rate for slave infants.[4] A more satisfactory approach for analysis of the relation between the productive and reproductive roles of slave women can be found in the life cycle. Deborah White found that pregnancy and motherhood brought a new status for slave women within the community and reinforced recognition of their reproductive value in the eyes of the owner. Initiation of this phase of the female life cycle created greater inter-dependence among women who shared knowledge about childbearing and worked together in the "trash" gang.[5]

Focusing on the reproductive careers of nearly a thousand slave women in South Carolina's low country, this chapter offers a somewhat different approach to the tensions between women's productive and reproductive roles. By analyz-ing the seasonality of labor in the fields and the seasonality of childbearing, it traces the complex relation between the annual cycles of crop production and pregnancies and births. The connection between physical labor and the timing of pregnancies is not simple. Two related factors must be considered. Because relief from hard labor coincided with the fall harvest of foodstuffs, the diet of slaves improved, perhaps affecting fecundity. A seasonal pattern of disease in the low country also may have influenced the timing of conceptions and affected miscarriages.

Two types of evidence are used to examine the seasons of life: demographic measures and planting calendars. Demographic evidence was derived from three sets of vital registers of slave populations at fifteen rice and short-staple cotton plantations to reconstruct the maternal histories of 928 plantation women. All plantations were in St. John's Berkeley Parish in low country South Carolina. The Ball family records were kept from 1735 to 1865, and they dealt with eleven rice-producing plantations located near the "T" of Cooper River. These documents are used to reconstruct 630 maternal histories and include mortality data for individuals born during the nineteenth century.[6] The business records of Peter Gaillard span his career (1783–1832) as a cotton planter at The Rocks, located in upper St. John's Berkeley, and were continued by his heir until 1847. From these records 127 maternal histories were reconstructed, and again mor-tality evidence was noted.[7] The Ravenal family records include birth registers for three plantations—Hanover, Wadboo, and Pooshee—which were also located in the upper portion of the parish and devoted to cotton. Considered together, the Ravenal plantation records span the years 1751 to 1867 and include the maternal histories of 171 slave women. The Ravenals did not systematically record deaths.[8] The maternal histories derived from these three sets of planta-tion records are used here to establish three demographic measures which are analyzed below: season of birth, intervals between births, and infant mortality rates by season of birth.

The second type of evidence—planting calendars—was gleaned from ac-counts of plantation work on the St. John's Berkeley holdings. These records vary greatly in the amount of detail they contain and entry consistency. Frequently planters began the crop year with good intentions and daily comments, only to abandon regular entry as plantation activity intensified. Nonetheless, an accurate description of plantation labor can be constructed.

The calendar of rice production at Comingtee plantation in 1849 is a good indicator of the seasonal demands placed on slave workers and the balance between staple crop and foodstuff production (see table 1, which gives notations from the original documents).[9] Slave laborers began planting in late March or early April and continued sowing the crop through June, when the more strenuous task of hoeing the fields started. Hoeing and weeding continued into early August, when fields were flooded for the last time and labor demands were temporarily reduced. Throughout the spring and summer, work in the rice fields accompanied planting, hoeing, and harvesting of subsistence crops. In 1849 slaves at Comingtee planted corn, oats, potatoes, and peas in the large fields. During the hiatus in rice production of the final "lay-by flow," adult male slaves (ages sixteen to fifty-four) worked on the maintenance of parish roads. If the designated work lay some distance from the home plantation, the men camped at a nearby site.[10] Plantation women and children remained at home and tended food crops. In late August slaves began cutting, thrashing, and pounding the rice. These activities, again interspersed with the harvest of foodstuffs, continued for six to eight weeks until the crops were harvested. Once the slaves pounded the season's rice crop, preparations began for the next spring's planting, with plantation workers devoting two to three months to repairing ditches and dikes.

Planting calendars for the cotton plantations also reveal an efficient mix of subsistence and cash crop production. Table 2 shows that at The Rocks (1811–1813) cotton planting was followed by seven full hoeings of the crop between April 11 and August 2.[11] Each hoeing of Gaillard's 270 acres under cotton consumed about two weeks. Some hoeing periods were consecutive, that is, one followed directly upon the other, while others were interspersed with weeks during which the slaves worked on raising potatoes, corn, peas, and yams. Only during the August lay-by, or break in the labor demands of cotton, was slave labor directed solely to the production of foodstuffs. The intense period of cotton picking began on September 6 and ended the first week of October. The break in the labor demands of cotton coincided with the rice hiatus when all of the parish's men served their required road duty.

The daily account of labor for the Ravenals' Pooshee plantation in 1847 (see table 3) adds further details to the annual cotton cycle and the production of foodstuffs.[12] Slaves prepared the cotton grounds and other fields in mid-February, interspersing outdoor labor with the indoor work of sorting and ginning cotton. The first seed was planted in early April, and by the final week of the month the cotton plants were big enough for the first hoeing to begin. As on the Gaillard plantation, each hoeing required about two weeks, and the daily labor routine was varied by work in the corn and potato fields. For about three weeks in late June and July slaves devoted their complete attention to provisions. Then followed a final surge of activity in the cotton fields before the plants were topped on August 20. The lay-by of the cotton crop lasted until

TABLE 1. Slave Work Calendar at Comingtee Plantation, 1849

		Rice Production	*Other Activities*
January		Hands turning rice land	Working on roads
		Raking trash to manure lands	Hauling manure on oats land
		Cleaning ditches	
February		Preparing land in swamp	
		Cleaning ditches and moving ditch dirt to low places	
		Hoeing off stubble	
March		Preparing land to plant	Four hands to weed churchyard
		Cleaning drains	Bedding up corn lands
	30	Commencing to plant rice	Planting corn lands
			Hoeing oats
April		Planting rice	Preparing land to plant balance of corn and to plant potatoes
			Planting potatoes and corn
May		Hoeing rice	Hoeing corn
	10	Finished planting rice	Chopping out grass
			Ploughing/hoeing corn
June		Hoeing rice	Planting peas
	21	Drawing reserves on the rice lands	Cutting oats
			Carrying in oats
			Listing in oat stubble
July		Hoeing rice	Preparing land for slips
	26	Stripping blands	Slip planting
			Hoeing peas
August		Making barrel staves	Hoeing peas
	13–25	Commenced rice harvest	
September 19		Thrashing rice	Working on roads
			Harvesting corn
			Picking peas
October		Gleaning rice fields	Picking peas
	18	Starting mill	
November		Finished harvest	Digging groundnuts
	7		Digging slips
December		Working on breach at Big Dam Reserve	

The hands all worked cheerfully and well to the end, average 11 hours per day

Source: Keating S. Ball, Comingtee Plantation Book, 1849–1852, vol. 5, Ball Family Papers, Southern Historical Collection, University of North Carolina, Chapel Hill.

TABLE 2. Composite Planting Calendar at The Rocks Plantation, 1811–1813

		Cotton Production		*Other Activities*
January			3–13	Oats
March	25–30	Planting cotton, 270 acres		
April			2–3	Planting potatoes, 18½ acres yellow and red
			4–5	Planting corn, 130 acres; also 25 acres oats, wheat, yams (slips), and pumpkins
	11–23	First hoeing of cotton		
	24–			
May	6	Second hoeing of cotton	7–10	Thin and manure corn
			11	First hoeing of potatoes
	13–22	Third hoeing of cotton	23–24	Second hoeing of corn
	26–			
June	5	Fourth hoeing of cotton	6	Third hoeing of potatoes
			7–12	Third hoeing of corn
			12	Cut wheat and planted pumpkins
	13–28	Fifth hoeing of cotton (partial gang)	13	Listing for slips (yams)
	17	First cotton blossoms	19	Planting slips
			20–21	Planting peas in the corn
			24	Cut oats
July			2	Fourth hoeing of corn
	13	Finished sixth hoeing of cotton, began seventh hoeing	17–18	Planting slips
			24-25	Planting slips
August	2	Finished seventh hoeing	3	Planting turnips
			7–20	Stripping blades off corn
			27	Hoeing peas
September			1	Making bricks
	6	Began picking cotton		
October			2	Began picking peas
			18	Began picking corn
November			7	Planting wheat

Source: Peter Gaillard Planting Book, 1803–1825, South Carolina Historical Society, Charleston, S.C.

mid-September, when slaves worked intensely picking the crop. For the next two months the slaves' labor varied from harvesting cotton to picking peas, digging yams, and clearing new ground. From December to mid-February, days of ginning and moting cotton were interspersed with outdoor labor as slaves planted winter crops, collected manure and tended to fences and fields.

**TABLE 3. Agricultural Work Calendar at Ravenal Family
Cotton Plantation, 1847**

		Cotton Production		*Other Activities*
January			1–2	Preparing oat fields
	4	Ginning cotton	5	Planting 10 acres oats
			6–7	Making fence around
	8–12	Sorting cotton		oat field
	13–22	Ginning cotton	23–28	Getting manure out of pond
	29	Moting and ginning		
	30	Sorting cotton		
February			1	Getting out pond manure
			2	Listing potato ground
	3	Ginning and moting	4	Finished listing potato field
			5–6	Getting out pond manure
			8–9	Cleaning ground
			10–12	Getting pond manure
	13–19	Listing cotton ground	20–26	Ditching and mending fences
	27	Moting and ginning		
March	1–3	Bedding cotton ground		
	4–6	Ginning and moting		
	8–9	Bedding cotton ground	10–11	Bedding potato ground
	12	Sorting and ginning		
	13	Listing cotton ground	15–16	Planting potatoes
	17	Listing cotton ground		
	18–25	Bedding cotton field		
	26	Cotton house work		
	27–31	Bedding cotton field		
April	1–3	Planting about 50 acres	5	Bedding potato field
		cotton	6–8	Picking joint grass
	9	Bedding cotton field	10	Planting rest of potato crop
	12–13	Bedding cotton ground		
	14	Planting rest of cotton	15	Working on road ditch
			16–17	Making fence
			19–20	Opening ditches in corn field
	21–30	Working cotton		
May	1–3	Working cotton	4	Listing corn field
	5–7	Finishing first working	8–13	Listing corn field
		of cotton	14	Planting 20 acres corn
			15	Working potatoes
	17–21	Working cotton	22	Working potatoes
	24–31	Working cotton		
June	1–10	Working cotton		
	11	Planting over rice		
	12	Supplying cotton field		
		in rice		
	14–17	Working cotton	18–21	Working potatoes

Month	Date	Activity	Date	Activity
	22	Working cotton	23	Planting slips
			24–30	Working corn
July			1–2	Working corn
			3	Planting slips
			5–9	Working corn
			10	Planting slips
			12	Finishing first working of corn
			13, 14	Planting peas in corn
	15	Working cotton	16	Shucking corn
			19	Planting slips
	20–21	Working cotton	22–23	Listing peas ground
			24	Planting 8 acres peas
	26–31	Working cotton		
August	2–12	Working cotton	13	Listing ground for early peas
			14	Planting early peas
			16–17	Working slips
			18–19	Working peas
	20	Topping cotton	21	Mending ditches and bank
			23–24	Stripping blades
			25–26	Working cornfield peas
			27	Stripping blades
			28–31	Working cornfield peas
September			1	Working peas
			2–3	Stripping blades
			4–8	Working cornfield peas
			9	Working early peas
			10–11	Preparing turnip patch
			13	Cleaning old ground
	14–15	Picking through cotton	16–22	Cleaning new ground
	23–28	Picking through cotton		
	29	Picking cotton, have in house 1200 lbs	30	Cleaning ground
October			1–4	Cleaning new ground
	5–14	Picked through cotton	15–16	Picking peas
	18–23	Picking cotton	18–23	Picking peas
			25–26	Breaking in corn
	27–30	Picking cotton		
November	1–6	Picking through cotton 4 times		
	8–9	Picking cotton	10–12	Digging in slips
	13	Picking cotton	15	Planting rye
	17–20	Picking cotton	22	Cleaning new ground
	23	Ginning	25–27	Bring rails out of swamp
	29–30	Ginning and moting		
December	1	Picking cotton		
	2–4	Ginning and moting	6–10	Listing in manure

TABLE 3. (*continued*)

Cotton Production	Other Activities
	11 Planting rye and oats
13 Moting and gining	14 Banking potaotes
	15 Bedding over potatoes in field
16–23 Moting and ginning	24 Making fence
29–31 Moting and ginning	

Source: Henry Ravenal, Ravenal Planting Book, 1845–1854, Ravenal Family Papers, South Carolina Historical Society, Charleston, S.C.

The planting calendars reveal four significant features of crop production at these St. John's Berkeley parish plantations. First, rice and cotton production required similar planting, hoeing, and harvesting cycles. In each instance the lay-by season lasted about a month and occurred in late August and early September. During the lay-by, male slaves served on the parish road crews, and unless the projects were nearby, they were absent from the plantations, at least during the week. Second, both rice and cotton required processing once harvested. During the winter months, slaves pounded rice and moted and ginned cotton, alternating these tasks with days of outdoor labor for cleaning dikes and ditches and preparing the fields. Slaves spent the "slack" months of labor, then, deeply involved in cash-crop production. Third, a variety of subsistence crops for consumption by people and animals were grown at each site. Slaves tended these crops throughout the year, interspersing labor on corn, potatoes, peas, oats, and yams with the cultivation of rice or cotton. Subsistence production brought variety to the slave labor regime and diet, as well as feed for the farm animals. Fourth, the work calendars do not provide significant evidence of a dual labor system in which male and female workers performed separate tasks. At the Ravenal cotton plantation, where daily accounts were maintained, the entire labor force clearly alternated activities. It was only in the legally mandated road duty that gender determined the labor required of slaves.

A second set of factors found in the annual cycles of morbidity and mortality experienced by low country slaves also influenced the timing of conceptions and births to slave women. One indicator of the cycle is the seasonal patterns of recorded deaths, both in plantation registers and the 1850 and 1860 Mortality Schedule of the census. As a general rule, infants and children died in greater numbers during the summer and fall (June through November) than during the winter and spring. For plantation adults, ailments in February and March proved most lethal. Nonetheless, the late summer months brought much ill health among African-Americans of the region, whose recognized "immunity" to malaria might spare them death but debilitated them in substantial numbers.[13] Sims

White, the 1850 census enumerator for St. John's Berkeley Parish, noted the causes of slave deaths and the seasonal pattern: "The diseases to which Negroes are generally liable amongst Children, [are] inflammation of the bowels caused by teething and worms and amongst Adults Pneumonia, dropsy and typhus fever—bilious fever [malaria] which is the disease of the climate [and] is seldom fatal to blacks."[14] Slaves on the tidal rice plantations may have suffered the ill effects of the low country disease environment more fully than those at the upper parish cotton plantations. The homes of rice workers were adjacent to the swampy fields, further exposing them to diseases such as malaria that were readily transmitted by insects.[15] In addition, some observers believed that the high incidence of respiratory ailments among African-Americans was an occupational hazard of rice production. According to the census enumerator, across the East Cooper River in St. Thomas and St. Dennis Parish, "Pneumonia prevails in the Parish during the Winter months from the necessary exposure of the Negroes in the rice levi."[16]

At each of the three plantation clusters—the Ball family rice plantations and the Gaillard and Ravenal cotton plantations—slave women gave birth in a strong seasonal pattern during the months of highest labor demand and greatest ill health. To analyze the significance of this pattern, the seasonal pattern of conceptions must be considered (see table 4). On the Ball rice plantations, one third of the children were born during three months—August, September, and October. Plantation women at the Ravenal sites bore their children in the same seasonal cycle: one in three infants was born during the late summer-fall months of August, September, and October. At The Rocks, the Gaillard cotton plantation, births to slave women were concentrated in July, August, and September in a somewhat weaker pattern, with about 30 percent of all births occurring in those months. If births were evenly distributed throughout the year, roughly one in four (or 25 percent) would occur in each seasonal grouping. On both the Ball and the Ravenal plantations, then, the frequency of late summer-fall births was about 30 percent greater than would be expected.

Historians traditionally interpret seasonal patterns of birth by focusing on the seasonal patterns of conceptions. In the case of these low country plantation women, about one third of the children were conceived during the late fall and winter months of November, December, and January. This seasonal pattern is consistent with the labor cycle and the food availability cycle of these agricultural populations. As labor requirements were reduced, plantation couples possessed both greater energy and time for their families.[17] Diet also improved with the fall harvest, perhaps increasing fecundity for slave women.[18] The relation between seasonality of conceptions and disease cycle is also intriguing. Not only did a greater number of conceptions occur after the malaria season, but the timing of the late fall-winter peak may be related to the ill effects of malaria during the summer months. *Falciparum malaria*, which was endemic in the low country, is known to cause fetal deaths during the early months of pregnancy in women who have the disease.[19] Because all evidence of conceptions

TABLE 4. Seasonality of Slave Births at Three Low Country Plantation Clusters, 1735–1865

Birth Month	Conception Month	Ball 1735–1865[a] (Rice)		Gaillard 1786–1847[b] (Cotton)		Ravenal 1748–1865[c] (Cotton)	
		N	Ratio	N	Ratio	N	Ratio
January	April	216	1.08	38	0.76	50	0.74
February	May	154	0.84	36	0.79	36	0.59
March	June	150	0.75	42	0.84	61	0.91
April	July	144	0.74	46	0.95	49	0.75
May	August	186	0.93	49	0.98	58	0.86
June	September	182	0.94	48	0.99	86	1.32
July	October	222	1.11	56	1.12	83	1.23
August	November	268	1.34	67	1.34	89	1.32
September	December	271	1.39	55	1.14	81	1.24
October	January	245	1.22	50	1.00	98	1.45
November	February	165	0.85	45	0.93	47	0.72
December	March	162	0.81	56	1.12	56	0.83
Total		2,365		588		794	
	Seasonality Coefficients[d]		0.54		0.40		0.62

[a] Ball Plantations $X^2 = 110.1$ df=11 P<.001.

[b] Gaillard Plantations $X^2 = 14.72$ df=11 P<.20.

[c] Ravenal Plantations $X^2 = 64.11$ df=11 P<.001.

[d] Seasonality coefficient computed as the difference between the mean of the ratios of the three highest consecutive months and the mean of the ratios of the three lowest consecutive months.

captures only those which resulted in a birth, the low number of conceptions in May, June, and July could reflect miscarriages in August and September, followed by a second conception in December or January.

Other scholars suggest that the seasonality of conception among plantation women reflects a slave marriage season that occurred during the autumn with the harvest festivals.[20] Were this the case, we could expect that first conceptions would occur in a seasonal pattern and that the timing of the conception of a second child might reflect an "echo effect" of this first seasonal pattern. Conceptions of subsequent children would be dispersed equally throughout the year. The seasonality of first births, second births, and third or higher parity births indicates that the seasonal pattern of conception remained consistent among all plantation women, whether it was their first pregnancy or their third. (See tables A–C in the appendix to this chapter.) Among the Ball slaves, where our population is largest, the pattern is consistent and statistically significant. Analysis of birth by parity for the cotton plantation is more problematic, largely due to the relatively small number of cases. Second and higher parity births among Gaillard plantation women appear to be more widely dispersed throughout the year, and our test of significance indicates that the pattern could be random. For slave women on the Ravenal cotton plantations, the seasonal patterns remained both consistent and strong, but for first and second births, they could also be the result of random factors. The persistence of the seasonal pattern beyond the second birth suggests that the seasonal effect is not a one-time development related to marriage but is related to other factors, such as cycles of labor, food supply, and diseases, that affect all women.

The seasonal pattern of conceptions and births among plantation women can be looked at in another way that focuses more directly on the interaction of women's productive and reproductive functions. Because the number of births peaked in the late summer, precisely when the women's labor was in greatest demand, a trimester approach to analysis of their pregnancies yields interesting results. Childbirth occurred at regular intervals for both rice and cotton plantation women. If the first child survived beyond nine months, the second child would follow about twenty months later—for a total birth interval of twenty-nine months. If the first child died in infancy, the interval between births was greatly reduced, to about eighteen months.[21] The regularity of childbearing, in combination with the strong seasonal patterns, meant that many women were in the last trimester of pregnancy during the season of highest labor demand and greatest illness. On the Ball rice plantation during the nineteenth century, two in five women of childbearing years were pregnant and nearly one in five of all childbearing women was in her final trimester, when hard physical labor was at its peak.

Some women bore their children in such a strong seasonal pattern that every second year they were in the final stages of pregnancy at harvest. The maternal history of the slave woman Cate, at the Ravenal cotton plantation, Pooshee, illustrates this point well. Born in 1829, Cate was nineteen years old when she gave birth to her first child, Phillip, in September 1848. Two years later, in August, a second child followed who died in early infancy, and the next August Cate gave birth to her third child. Between 1853 and 1865 Cate gave birth to six more children, each born between September and December. The slave woman Sue, at The Rocks, experienced a similar seasonal pattern of pregnancies. Her first child, Chance, was born in July 1806 and died five months later. In September 1807 she had a son. She gave birth to three more sons and two daughters who were born in June, July, or August. Again, the seasonal pattern of her births meant that Sue was in her last trimester during seasons of both hard labor and ill health.

What was the effect of the season of birth on the survival of slave infants? Because the number of births peaked during the characteristically hazardous months for slave infants and children, it would appear that seasonal cycles of conception and birth contributed to higher levels of mortality. The frequency of infant deaths and their rates by month and season of birth were computed for the two plantation clusters that kept detailed birth registers (see table 5). These patterns must be considered only as suggestive, because newborns were included only if complete birth date and death date information was available. Infants born to women on the Ball family rice plantations suffered a very high rate of death—460 deaths per 1,000 live births, with monthly mortality rates ranging from 339 to 571. Though the death rates fluctuated from month to month, the seasonal rates suggest that month of birth offered little improvement in survival prospects for infants. Children born in October, November, and December suffered a somewhat higher death rate than those born in other seasons. At the Gaillard cotton plantation, the rate of infant death (190) was less than half that on the rice plantations. Again, month by month figures varied, fluctuating from a low of 82 for October to a high of 306 for January. Children born in the fall months of October through December experienced the lowest level of infant mortality at 129 deaths per 1,000. Those born in the summer suffered the highest level of infant mortality.

The seasonal patterns of infant death suggest that at high mortality sites, such as the Ball rice plantations, season of birth had little influence on the survival rate of children. All children, regardless of when they were born, faced grim prospects of survival. On the Gaillard plantation the pattern is more complex. Children born during the summer, when their mother's labor was in highest demand, suffered nearly twice the level of infant mortality as those born after the harvest. This seasonal increase in infant mortality is consistent with the observations of census enumerators and others that the summer months were particularly arduous for plantation infants. Higher mortality during the winter months may reflect the special vulnerability of nursing infants to the ill health of their mothers.

For plantation women in South Carolina's low country, the agricultural cycle of production and biological cycle of reproduction were deeply intertwined. Although agricultural labor was required throughout the year, the spring planting months and the autumn harvesting months of September and October were the most demanding periods. For low country slaves, particularly those who worked in the rice fields, these months were also a time of exposure to the diseases of the region, particularly malaria. In late autumn, however, slaves could look forward to better days of reduced workload, enhanced diet, and improved disease environment. Proportionately large numbers of slave infants were conceived during this period. The pattern of late fall conceptions holds true for slave women on both rice and cotton plantations and at all stages in their maternal histories. Because about one–third of all children were conceived in the months after the harvest, many slave women faced the final trimester of pregnancy at a time when their labor would be of greatest value in the fields.

TABLE 5. Seasonal and Monthly Infant Mortality for the Ball Family Plantations, 1800–1864, and The Rocks (Gaillard Family Plantation), 1786–1847, by Month of Birth

Month		Ball			Gaillard		
	N	IMR[a]	Ratio[b]		N	IMR[a]	Ratio[b]
January	50	440	0.96		36	306	1.89
February	47	511	1.11		35	171	0.90
March	35	400	0.87		40	175	0.92
Seasonal	132	455	0.99		111	216	1.14
April	39	538	1.17		45	222	1.17
May	59	424	0.92		46	130	0.68
June	56	411	0.89		44	205	1.08
Seasonal	154	448	0.97		135	185	0.97
July	66	470	1.02		55	200	1.05
August	82	488	1.06		62	258	1.36
September	59	339	0.73		52	211	1.11
Seasonal	207	440	0.95		169	231	1.22
October	56	571	1.24		49	082	0.43
November	40	425	0.92		45	156	0.82
December	39	513	1.12		53	150	0.79
Seasonal	135	511	1.11		147	129	0.67
All	628	460			562	190	

[a] IMR=Infant mortality rate computed as number of deaths per 1,000 live births for individuals with full registration.

[b] Ratio=Monthly or seasonal infant mortality rate as a ratio of the total infant mortality rate.

Though a slave woman's advanced stage of pregnancy might encourage owners and overseers to lighten her work load, deliverance from the fields was no certainty. For women on the Ball rice plantations, all pregnancies must have been filled with worry for the health of the child. Since nearly half of all infants did not survive the first year, childbirth was just one step in the watch that was kept over the newborn—a watch that as often as not ended in great sadness. Plantation women on the Gaillard cotton plantation could regard the birth of their children with greater hope. The harvest season meant not only a reduction in labor, fresh food, and improved health, but also the prospect of the birth of a healthy child.

APPENDIX

Table A. Seasonality of Slave Births on the Ball Plantations,
by Parity, 1735–1865

Birth Month	Conception Month	First Births[a] N	Ratio	Second Births[b] N	Ratio	Third + Births[c] N	Ratio
January	April	47	1.08	37	1.10	132	1.07
February	May	30	0.75	22	0.72	102	0.90
March	June	30	0.69	17	0.51	103	0.83
April	July	29	0.69	30	0.92	85	0.71
May	August	43	0.99	28	0.83	115	0.96
June	September	43	1.02	31	0.95	108	0.87
July	October	48	1.10	48	1.43	126	1.02
August	November	58	1.33	49	1.46	161	1.30
September	December	57	1.35	42	1.29	172	1.44
October	January	53	1.22	46	1.37	146	1.18
November	February	35	0.83	22	0.68	108	0.90
December	March	40	0.92	24	0.71	98	0.79
Total		513		396		1,456	
Seasonality Coefficient[d]			0.59		0.67		0.56

[a] First Births $X^2 = 24.85$ df=11 P<.01.

[b] Second Births $X^2 = 45.87$ df=11 P<.001.

[c] Third and Higher Parity Births $X^2 = 63.06$ df=11 P<.001.

[d] Seasonality coefficient computed as the difference between the mean of the ratios of the three highest consecutive months and the mean of the ratios of the three lowest consecutive months.

Table B. Seasonality of Slave Births on the Gaillard Plantations, by Parity, 1786–1847

Birth Month	Conception Month	First Births[a]		Second Births[b]		Third + Births[c]	
		N	Ratio	N	Ratio	N	Ratio
January	April	7	0.81	2	0.30	29	0.84
February	May	4	0.51	4	0.66	27	0.86
March	June	5	0.58	8	1.19	29	0.84
April	July	9	1.06	8	1.23	29	0.87
May	August	7	0.81	8	1.19	34	0.99
June	September	6	0.71	5	0.77	37	1.11
July	October	15	1.73	6	0.90	35	1.02
August	November	11	1.30	8	1.19	48	1.40
September	December	15	1.77	6	0.92	34	1.02
October	January	11	1.27	11	1.64	28	0.81
November	February	3	0.35	6	0.92	36	1.05
December	March	10	1.15	7	1.04	38	1.10
	Total	103		79		404	
	Seasonality Coefficient[d]		0.97		0.59		0.30

[a] First Births X^2 =19.5 df=11 P<.10.

[b] Second Births X^2 =8.39 df=11 P>.50.

[c] Third and Higher Parity Births X^2 =10.5 df=11 P>.30.

[d] Seasonality coefficient computed as the difference of the mean of the ratios of the three highest consecutive months and the mean of the ratios of the three lowest consecutive months.

Table C. Seasonality of Slave Births on the Ravenal Plantations, by Parity, 1748–1865.

Birth Month	Conception Month	First Births[a]		Second Births[b]		Third + Births[c]	
		N	Ratio	N	Ratio	N	Ratio
January	April	10	0.67	11	0.89	29	0.74
February	May	12	0.82	5	0.44	19	0.53
March	June	14	0.87	11	0.89	36	0.92
April	July	13	0.83	7	0.58	29	0.76
May	August	11	0.68	15	1.22	32	0.82
June	September	20	1.28	18	1.50	48	1.26
July	October	24	1.49	12	0.98	47	1.20
August	November	21	1.30	15	1.22	53	1.35
September	December	17	1.09	15	1.25	49	1.29
October	January	22	1.37	17	1.38	59	1.51
November	February	10	0.64	9	0.75	28	0.74
December	March	13	0.81	10	0.81	33	0.84
	Total	187		145		462	
	Seasonality Coefficient[d]		0.67		0.64		0.65

[a] First Births X^2 =16.63 df=11 P<.20.
[b] Second Births X^2 =13.79 df=11 P<.30.
[c] Third and Higher Parity Births X^2 =40.05 df=11 P<.001.
[d] Seasonality coefficient computed as the difference between the mean of the ratios of the three highest consecutive months and the mean of the three lowest consecutive months.

Notes

1. Herbert S. Klein and Stanley L. Engerman, "Fertility Differentials between Slaves in the United States and the British West Indies: A Note on Lactation Practices and Their Possible Implications," *William and Mary Quarterly* 3d Series, 35 (April 1978): 357–75; Richard S. Dunn, "A Tale of Two Plantations: Slave Life at Mesopotamia in Jamaica and Mount Airy in Virginia, 1799–1828," *William and Mary Quarterly* 3d Series, 34 (January 1977): 32–65; Barry W. Higman, *Slave Population and Economy in Jamaica, 1807–1834* (Cambridge: Cambridge University Press, 1976); Michael Craton, "Hobbesian or Panglossian? The Two Extremes of Slave Conditions in the British Caribbean, 1781 to 1834," *William and Mary Quarterly* 3d series, 35 (1978): 324–56; Cheryll Ann Cody, "Age Specific Fertility Rates for Enslaved Populations: A Comparison of Low Country South Carolina and St. Ann's Parish, Jamaica," paper presented at the IUSSP Conference on the Peopling of the Americas, May 1992, Veracruz, Mexico.

2. Nebiat Tafari, Richard L. Naeye, and Abeba Gubezie, "Effects of Maternal Undernutrition and Heavy Physical Work during Pregnancy on Birth Weight" *British Journal of Obstetrics and Gynecology* 67 (March 1980): 222–26. For a summary of the

ongoing debate on the impact of pregnant women's work on infant survival, see M. J. Saurel-Cubizolles and M. Kaminski, "Work in Pregnancy: Its Evolving Relationship with Perinatal Outcome: A Review," *Social Science Medicine* 22 (1986): 431–42.

3. Michael P. Johnson, "Smothered Slave Infants: Were Slave Mothers at Fault?" *Journal of Southern History* 47 (November 1981): 493–520.

4. John Campbell, "Work, Pregnancy, and Infant Mortality among Southern Slaves," *Journal of Interdisciplinary History* 14 (Spring 1984): 793–812.

5. Deborah Gray White, *Ar'n't I a Woman? Female Slaves in the Plantation South* (New York: Norton, 1985), pp. 99–101, 109–11.

6. Ball Family Papers, 1631–1920, John Ball Plantation Account Book, 1812–1834, and John Ball Plantation Records, 1738–1895, South Carolina Historical Society, Charleston, S.C.; John and Keating S. Ball Plantation Books, vols 1–10, and William J. Ball Plantation Books, vols 1–2, Southern Historical Collection, University of North Carolina, Chapel Hill, N.C.; Ball Family Papers, 1696–1800, Keating S. Ball, Coming-tee Plantation Book, 1849–1896, South Caroliniana Library, University of South Carolina, Columbia, S.C.; Ball Family Papers, 1792–1834, Keating S. Ball Plantation Book, 1860–1867, William R. Perkins Library, Duke University, Durham, N.C.; Record Series: *Wills* Charleston District, *Inventories*, Charleston District, South Carolina Department of Archives and History, Columbia, S.C. For the full demographic reconstruction of slave life on the Ball plantations, see Cheryll Ann Cody, "Slave Demography and Family Formation: A Community Study of the Ball Family Plantations, 1720–1896," Ph.D. dissertation, University of Minnesota, 1982.

7. Peter Gaillard Plantation Accounts and Memoranda Book, 1783–1832; Gaillard Family Plantation Book, 1825–1847; Peter Gaillard Planting Book, 1803–1825; all at South Carolina Historical Society, Charleston, S.C. See also Cheryll Ann Cody, "Naming, Kinship, and Estate Dispersal: Notes on Slave Family Life on a South Carolina Plantation, 1786–1833," *William and Mary Quarterly* 3d Series, 39 (January 1982): 192–211.

8. "A List of Negroes born at Hanover, 1751–1801," "Births of Negroes belonging to Rene Ravenal (Wadboo), 1771–1824," and Slave Birth List, 1812–1867, by Henry Ravenal, untitled, Ravenal Family Records, South Carolina Historical Society, Charleston, S.C. Slaves were recorded from 1737 to 1801 at Hanover, 1771 to 1830 at Woodboo or Wadboo, and 1811 to 1867 at Pooshee. Though some slaves were moved between sites as a result of marriage gifts and generational transfer of property, most individuals were not. For the purposes of demographic calculations, individuals were removed from the population when the evidence from their plantation of residence ceased. On the demographic reconstruction, see Cheryll Ann Cody, "Marital Unions and Childbearing on the Ravenal Plantations: A Caribbean Pattern in the South Carolina Low Country?" paper presented at the annual meeting of the Association for Ethno-history, November 1988, Williamsburg, Va.

9. Keating S. Ball, Comingtee Plantation Book, 1849–1852, vol. 5, Ball Family Papers, Southern Historical Collection.

10. St. John's Berkeley Highroads Commission Records, South Carolina Historical Society.

11. Peter Gaillard Planting Book, 1803–1825, South Carolina Historical Society.

12. Henry Ravenal, Ravenal Planting Book, 1845–1854, South Carolina Historical Society.

13. Cody, "Slave Demography and Family Formation," chaps. 4 and 5. See also Todd Savitt, *Medicine and Slavery: The Diseases and Health Care of Blacks in Antebellum Virginia*

(Urbana: University of Illinois Press, 1978), and Kenneth F. Kiple and Virginia Himmel-steib King, *Another Dimension of the Black Diaspora: Diet, Disease and Racism* (New York: Cambridge University Press, 1981).

14. Sims White, enumerator, Manuscript Returns, *Seventh Census of the United States*, (1850) Mortality Schedules, St. Johns Berkeley Parish, Charleston, S.C.

15. Joseph Purcell, Survey taken May 1788, "A Plan of a Body of Land Situated on the East Branch of Cooper River . . . belonging to John Ball Esq," and Joseph Purcell, Survey taken March 1786, "A Plan Exhibiting the shape and form of a Body of land called Limerick," in Henry A. M. Smith Collection, South Carolina Historical Society.

16. Thomas Jememy, enumerator, Manuscript Returns, *Seventh Census of the United States* (1850) Mortality Schedules, St. Thomas and St. Dennis Parish, Charleston, S.C.

17. On decline in male libido due to undernutrition and overwork, see E. LeRoy Ladurie, "L'Aménorrhée de famine (xviiie–xxe siècles)," *Annales* 24 (November–December 1969): 1589–1601. Empirical data confirm a strong relationship between frequency of intercourse and probability of conception; see John C. Barrett and John Marshal, "The Risk of Conception on Different Days of the Menstrual Cycle," *Population Studies* 13 (November 1969): 455–61.

18. On this debate, see Rose Frisch, "Demographic Implications of the Biological Determinants of Female Fecundity," *Social Biology* 22 (1975): 17–22, and Jane Menken, James Trussell, and Susan Watkins, "The Nutrition Fertility Link: An Evaluation of the Evidence," *Journal of Interdisciplinary History* 11 (Winter 1981): 425–44.

19. Peter Wood, *Black Majority: Negroes in Colonial South Carolina from 1670 through the Stono Rebellion* (New York: Norton, 1974), p. 87; H. M. Giles et al., "Malaria, Anaemia and Pregnancy," *Annals of Tropical Medicine and Parasitology* 63 (1969): 245–63.

20. Robert Fogel and Stanley Engerman, *Time on the Cross: The Economics of American Negro Slavery* (New York: Little, Brown, 1974), pp. 139–41; Richard Steckel, "Slave Marriage and the Family," *Journal of Family History* 5 (Winter 1980): 406–21.

21. Cody, "Slave Demography and Family Formation," chaps. 4–5.

4

SLAVE WOMEN ON THE BRAZILIAN FRONTIER IN THE NINETEENTH CENTURY

Mary Karasch

In the interior of Brazil, between the Araguaia and the Tocantins rivers, there is a strangely beautiful land of low mountains, wide savannahs, and thorny vegetation. Six months of rain and six months of dry season twist vegetation into contorted shapes, while the spring months cover the trees with yellow, purple, and orange flowers. Besides the two great tributaries of the Amazon which flow to the north from central Brazil, a third river, the Paranaíba, demarcates the southern border of the region known in the eighteenth and nineteenth centuries as Goiás.

Into this forbidding terrain, once roamed by Gê–speaking populations, came explorers from São Paulo. They invaded, seeking new sources of Indian slaves to replace those who had died on the farms of São Paulo and the legendary gold and emerald mines of the interior. They found both slaves and gold in Goiás in the 1720s and put their Indian and African slaves to work in the mining camps. Portuguese and Spanish immigrants joined the gold rush with their slaves, and almost overnight the mining camps became towns with churches, stores, and small houses.

Early Goiás was a male–dominated world of owners and slaves, but occasionally an African or Indian woman accompanied her master into this remote frontier. As was usual in the boom phase of a mining frontier, women were uncommon until villages and towns were settled. By the time the mining boom had ended in the 1770s, whites and their slaves had created an "urban society" of small towns similar to many in the neighboring province of Minas Gerais, and by the end of the nineteenth century women of all colors lived throughout the region between the Araguaia and Tocantins.[1]

One might assume that little documentation survives for any of the region's population groups, much less for women of African ancestry, because the region was sparsely settled and reaching it required months of travel from the capital of Rio de Janeiro. Fortunately for the social historian, local archives in Goiás are unusually rich because of its numerous small towns that date back to the eighteenth century. Goiás also has two major repositories of documents: the old capital of the state, the City of Goiás (also known as Goiás Velho or Old Goiás), and the new capital of Goiânia. Documents that survive include parish registries of slave births, deaths, and marriages; notarial registries of slave manumissions; tax records and slave registries for 1872–1887; census data about slaves; and records of the black brotherhoods—to name but a few. Drawing on such records, this chapter represents a preliminary attempt to identify and describe many of the significant characteristics of the work and culture of women of African ancestry in the late colonial and early national periods in Goiás.

The Goiás documentation has an importance that goes beyond the mere survival of the kinds of documents that were ordered to be burned in Brazil[2] to providing data for useful comparative studies of the evolution of creole slave societies. With the creolization of the slave population, the proportion of female slaves increased. By the time of the abolition of slavery in Brazil in 1888, the region of Goiás had a predominantly creole, or Brazilian–born, slave population in which female slaves slightly outnumbered male slaves; in the towns female slaves almost always outnumbered male slaves. Along with the decline in the dominance of male slavery in Goiás, slavery as an institution clearly eroded in the nineteenth century, while the free population of color grew in size and, to a great extent, replaced slave labor. The slow transition from a society in which the majority of African-Brazilians were enslaved to one in which the majority of the people of color were free suggests a "natural" erosion of the institution of slavery. In 1804, 40 percent of the population had been enslaved, compared with less than 7 percent by 1872 (see the table).

The reason for the decline of slavery is tied closely to the broad socioeconomic transformations of nineteenth–century Goiás. Briefly stated, the collapse of the gold mining boom by the 1770s led many slaveowners to leave the mining towns and to take their male slaves with them or to sell them to other provinces. The initial exodus of slaves does not explain, however, the population growth of the early nineteenth century nor the continual entry of migrants from neighboring provinces. Slaves continued to be brought into Goiás by free immigrants from Maranhão, Bahia, Minas Gerais, and Mato Grosso who sought land, gold, or work on the frontier. As the new settlers drove the Indians from their ancestral lands, the most powerful landowners (*fazendeiros*) carved out landed empires and used their slaves and free men of color to herd cattle or plant coffee trees and sugar cane, while their women raised food crops and wove textiles. Other land–hungry immigrants took up squatting, renting, or sharecropping a small plot of land (*sitio*) on the *fazendas*. The ownership of slaves was widespread in Goiás. The fazendeiros owned as many as fifty slaves, while many renters and sharecroppers, often men and women of color, owned one, two, or three slaves. In the towns, the largest slaveowner might be the parish priest, especially

Slaves in the State of Goiás, 1804–1885

Census		Slave Population			Percentages	
Year	Total Population				Female	
		Male	Female	Total	Slaves	All Slaves[a]
1804	50,365	12,094	7,933	20,027	39.6	39.8
1825	62,478	7,329	6,046	13,375	45.2	21.4
1832	68,497	7,220	6,041	13,261	45.6	19.4
1848	79,339	5,681	5,275	10,956	48.2	13.8
1856	121,992	6,416	5,918	12,334	48.0	10.1
1861	133,565	5,787	5,661	11,448	49.5	8.6
1872	158,920[b]	5,337	5,211	10,548	49.4	6.6
1885[c]		2,857	2,961	5,818	50.9	

[a] Percentage of total population.
[b] The census records 158,920, but my calculations yield 158,929.
[c] Only the slave population was counted in 1885.

Sources: RJBN, 9,4,2, Goiás (Capitania), Correspondencia official de D. Francisco de Assis Mascarenhas . . . , "Estado da População da Capitania de Goiaz no anno de 1804; RJBN, 11,4,2, Estatistica de Província de Goiás . . . , 1825; RJAN, Cod. 808, vol.1, Censo da População da Provincia de Goyaz, 1832; ibid., Mappa estatisco [sic] da População da Provincia de Goiaz, 1848; RJAN, Relatorio Apresentado à Assemblea Legislativa Provincial de Goyaz na Sessão Ordinaria de 1858 pelo Exm. Presidente da Provincia Dr. Francisco Januario da Gama Cerqueira (Goyaz: Na Typ.ª [Typographia] Goyazense 1858); Brasília, Senate Library, Relatorio lido na abertura d'Assembléa Legislativa de Goyaz pelo Presidente da Provincia o exm.º sr. José Martins Pereira de Alencastre no dia 1º de Junho de 1862 (Goyaz: Typ.ª Provincial, 1862), pp. 125–26; RJAN, Relatorio Apresentado a' Assembléa Legislativa Provincial de Goyaz pelo Exm.º Sr. Dr. Antero Cicero de Assis Presidente da Provincia Em 1 de Junho de 1875 (Goyaz: Typª Provincial, 1875), pp. 43–44; and AHG, caixa 352, Quadro geral estatistico da população escrava dos Municipios da Provincia de Goyaz, até 30 de Junho do corrente anno, organisado a vista dos quadros parciaes, enviados pelo Thezouraria de Fazenda em officio de 1º deste mez, 9 December 1885.

if he came from an important white family in the region. Mulatto priests, however, served in Goiás, and they, too, owned slaves. Both urban and rural men and women of color, as well as the white minority, owned slaves.[3]

Migration to the frontier in the nineteenth century was tied to the transition of Goiás from a mining economy, which demanded intensive labor use and large numbers of male slaves, to a diversified agropastoral economy with some gold prospecting, which was not labor intensive and could utilize female as well as male labor. Furthermore, free labor could supplement slave labor, especially on the cattle ranches.

The economy of Goiás experienced deep recession in the early nineteenth century, but the region recovered and eventually experienced growth and development. While it did not share directly in the nineteenth-century export boom of the coffee economies of Rio de Janeiro, Minas Gerais, and São Paulo, the region diversified its exports to neighboring provinces and expanded its trade via the rivers to the north or by mule team to Minas Gerais, Rio de Janeiro, and São Paulo. Nineteenth-century exports from Goiás to Brazil's other provinces included gold, which was still mined and smuggled to Belém; tobacco and tropical forest products; coffee, which was shipped to São Paulo; sweet *marmelada*, made from quinces; cattle, which were herded overland to Bahia; and cheap cotton cloth, which was sold to the plantations of São Paulo. The diversity and volume of exports accounted for the economic development of Goiás, as well as for the continued use of slave labor. Slave and free labor was also used to raise food crops such as manioc, corn, rice, and beans for local consumption.[4]

If slave labor was in such demand, why did male slavery decline during the nineteenth century? The most important reason may have been that large slaveowners sold their young boys and teenagers to the coffee plantation regions. After the effective abolition of the African slave trade to Brazil in the early 1850s, slaveowners in Goiás responded to the market demand for slave labor for the coffee plantations of the southeast by selling their surplus males and some females. Not unusual was the case where a slaveowner in Bonfim sold Marianna's two legitimate children, Agostinho, age ten, and Benedicto, age six, to Minas Gerais. He also sold the parda Inacia, age sixteen, thus separating her from her mother, Anna. In part this process can be traced via the slave registries, known as *matriculas*, that record the destiny of slaves listed in 1872. "Sold to Minas" was a common explanation for the fate of young teenagers.[5] Government officials voiced concern at the drain of slaves from Goiás, but labor-hungry settlers merely continued to find new sources of slaves among the Indians. Census data (see the table) confirm the decline in the number of male and female slaves in the province. Over a period of eighty years the number of male slaves dropped from a high of 12,094 in 1804 to only 2,857 in 1885, while females declined more gradually from 7,933 to 2,961. While these statistics are probably inaccurate, they at least point to a general pattern of decline and to a more equitable proportion of male to female slaves by 1848. In contrast, only 20 percent of the slave population of one town in 1783 was female.[6]

The decline of male slavery and the concurrent rise of a creole slave population had a number of important consequences for the slave women of Goiás in terms of labor use and family life. Before turning to the specifics of female slavery in Goiás, however, we need to characterize the female population. The women of color who labored as slaves in Goiás were diverse in ethnic origin and color. We cannot describe them with a single term, such as African-Brazilian, Afro-Brazilian, or black, because such terms convey North American images of a social group that was far more complex. First, not all slave women in Goiás were of African origin, acquired by purchase or born of African mothers. Many were Indian women acquired by right of conquest, usually as a consequence of the frontier wars that white settlers fought with tribes such as the Xavante. The settlers often killed the men but kept the women and children and integrated them into their households. In parish baptismal and death registries, such as those of Nossa Senhora do Monte do Carmo in Natividade near the Tocantins River, priests recorded the Indian captives as slaves or *agregados* (household dependents).[7] Their descendants continued as slaves or free persons of color who entered consensual unions or married African-Brazilians as well as whites. In time, the descendants of Indian female slaves joined the majority of people, collectively called *gente de cor* (people of color) in Brazil. Although some were still enslaved, the majority were free by 1872; therefore it is often difficult to trace the Indian female slaves, although family traditions often identify eighteenth-century Indian women as ancestors of elite white families.[8] We also cannot establish the proportion of Indian women in the slave population of Goiás, because Indian slavery was customary, especially in northern Goiás, and many Indian women and their children were never identified as slaves in official records, although they were branded, bought, sold, traded, and treated as slaves.

African women are more easily traced. Scribes often identified the Africans by ethnic indicators, or at least by the Portuguese word *Africana*. Ethnic terminology for Africans is not as specific as it was at Rio de Janeiro or Salvador, Bahia, but ethnic terms survive in sales tax records of the early nineteenth century.[9] Sources that indicate port of origin in Africa, African nation, or ethnic groups in Africa reveal that Goiás drew on slaves imported through both Salvador, Bahia, and Rio de Janeiro. Therefore Goiás had a remarkably diverse African population, because Salvador tended to receive its slaves from the region of West Africa, while Rio imported Africans from West-Central and East Africa. The basic division between West African and Central African slaves was reflected in Goiás in the distinction made between Mina (originally a slave from the Costa da Mina, but later from all of West Africa) and Angola. Hence slave women of African origin were most likely to be known as Minas or Angolans, perhaps the two most common terms for Africans in the Goiás documents.

Many single white and black men migrated to Goiás in the eighteenth century, and racial intermixture began with the first expeditions that captured Indian women. Ultimately, many terms were used to describe the racially mixed people of Goiás, but most common were the following: *mestizo* and *caboclo* for the child of a European and an Indian; *cafuzo* or *cariboca* for the descendant of an Indian and an African; *mulato* or *pardo* for the mulatto; and *cabra* for the child of a black or African with some connotation of racial mixture. The terms for black women were *negra*, *preta*, or *crioula* (if born in Brazil), all of which might be used interchangeably for the same woman of dark color.[10]

In summary, the slave women of Goiás were likely to be Indians and Africans and their racially mixed descendants. By the late nineteenth century, the ethnic and color groups had blended so that it was often difficult to determine the precise ancestry of a woman on the basis of her physical appearance. Even "white" women, who formed a small minority of the population, often had an Indian or African ancestor, although they tended to stress their Spanish or Portuguese ancestry. These patterns of racial mixture, which led to different definitions of color based on hair texture, skin color, and physical features, are important in understanding how and why slave women would be incorporated into Luso-Brazilian families. Whether a woman was perceived as white, *parda*, or *preta* determined her destiny—her status in a household and her occupation as a slave woman. Those who most closely approached the white norms of physical beauty were most likely to be selected for domestic services, while those who were defined as black were more likely to labor in the fields.[11]

Why were so many nonwhite women enslaved in Goiás? Perhaps the most important reason was the shortage of women of any color, especially in the eighteenth century. The women who accompanied the explorers and adventurers from the coastal regions were slave women. They were forced to move with their owners. Because there were never enough slave women attached to the expeditions, the explorers captured Indian women to carry their loads, cook for them, and act as their sexual partners. Later these women became their mistresses, prostitutes, and, on occasion, legal wives. In remote mining camps or on large ranches, miners and fazendeiros lived openly with their slave women and mestizo children; these children, if not their Indian mothers, might escape slavery. Besides the white men, the black and Indian men who came with the expeditions from São Paulo also took Indian women as sexual partners and sometimes entered into long-term consensual unions with them. In other words, the racial mixture that occurred involved not just white men and Indian women; Indian women also fell victim to men of color from the coast. Their children, if dark in color, had fewer opportunities for upward social mobility, and many joined the slave populations of Goiás.

African women also met the sexual and familial needs of the frontiersmen. In the eighteenth century, one African woman frequently accompanied a Portuguese miner and his slave gang to a mining camp. In official records she was registered as the cook for the gang. In the early eighteenth century, gold miners in Minas Gerais and Goiás purchased Mina women to take with them to the gold fields as their companions and cooks. Other "entrepreneurs" acquired African women to profit from their earnings as prostitutes in the mining camps. Miners often formed stable consensual unions with African women, freed them, and even recognized their children. In some cases they married them in the churches. Catholic priests who were not celibate also recognized and freed their own mulatto children by slave women, although they could not marry them. One typical example of this pattern was that of the priest Marcelino Teixeira Chaves, who had a son by Joana, the slave of Antônio Severiano da Luz. Freed at baptism in 1855, the son, Monsenhor Bento Severiano da Luz, took his mother's master's surname and went on to become a priest and rector of his seminary in Cuiabá, Mato Grosso. He also earned a doctorate in philosophy and theology in Rome. As one of the best orators of his time, he was noted for his "great culture and extraordinary talent." His mother later joined him in Cuiabá, where he treated her "with special care." He died in 1917.[12]

During the early period of settlement, the newly rich and powerful monopolized the minority of slave women, whom they used to form temporary families until they returned to their legal wives in Portugal or São Paulo or other "civilized" areas of Brazil. Indian and African women had little choice in sexual or marriage partners, and they often had little opportunity to form a stable consensual union with men of their own nations. However, once they were abandoned by their white men, enslaved and freedwomen were more likely to marry men of their own nations, although many also continued to live in consensual unions with available free men.

Slave women performed many other functions besides the sexual and familial. While they bore and raised children, some also provided the food and clothing of the households, while others were forced to engage in agricultural labor. On at least one fazenda visited by an English traveler, its brown and black women did "the most work." There was usually a sharp division of labor by sex on the frontier. Men led exploration expeditions and mined for gold; they herded cattle, manned the boats on the great rivers, hunted and fished, engaged in long-distance trade via mule teams or riverboats, led religious rituals as Catholic priests, served as soldiers in frontier garrisons, and filled bureaucratic posts as governors, judges, mayors, and policemen. Although an exceptional woman might lead an expedition,[13] mine for gold, or manage a fazenda, the vast majority of women engaged in occupations defined by the culture as appropriate for women. Free women, freedwomen, and slave women often pursued the same occupations, and it was not uncommon for white women, other than upper-class women in larger towns, to work alongside their slave women in the households or fields. Besides child care, occupations specific to women included household service and food and clothing production. Slave women also might be expected to engage in cash crop production and sugar distilling.

One of the most important roles of women in Africa is "to enable the family to eat."[14] This tradition was just as important in Goiás. Almost any activity connected with food was the unique sphere of women, except for hunting, fishing, or the care of large animals (cattle, horses, mules), which men monopolized. Slaveowners required slave women to raise fruits and vegetables for the household and to process them along with game and fish; to carry water; to collect firewood and cook; and if there was a surplus, to sell fruits and vegetables. Elite women and their high-status slave women worked at food preparation while cloistered in the households; but the poor and the newly enslaved were more likely to engage in work that took them into the forests, fields, or streets, then considered the domain of men.[15]

Indian women knew the forests well. If they were trusted, their owners permitted them to gather herbs, spices, wild fruits, and forest products. One of their most arduous forest labors was to collect and transport firewood, which often involved the porterage of heavy loads. Some also had knowledge of how to manipulate natural poisons and narcotics. One wonders how much of this knowledge they passed on to the African women who became healers and *feiticeiras*, skilled in curing or causing illness with natural herbs or poisons. Both Indian and African women brought the skills of gatherers to their new lives. While some used these skills to feed their households, others used them to facilitate slave resistance and the murder of abusive owners.[16] However, gathering wild plants and fruits was only a small part of the food production activities of these women. They also raised fruits and vegetables on small garden plots attached to their owners' houses in the towns or on the small farms and fazendas in the rural areas. They not only planted, weeded, and harvested vegetables, but they also collected from the surrounding trees a large variety of tropical fruits. These slave women also cared for small animals such as chickens, pigs, and goats.[17]

Many fruits and vegetables in tropical Latin America require only peeling before they can be eaten or cooked, but there was one plant whose special characteristics significantly increased the work load of women. There are two principal varieties of manioc (also known as *mandioca* or *cassava*)—the sweet and the bitter. The sweet varieties have a shorter growing season and can be harvested in six to nine months, then simply peeled and cooked like any other vegetable. The bitter varieties, however, require twelve to eighteen months to mature and will not spoil if left unharvested for several months, so women can harvest them at their leisure. The disadvantage to the bitter varieties is that they may have high levels of prussic acid, which can be lethal if not removed properly. The manioc roots must be peeled, soaked in water, then placed in a *tipiti* (basket-press) to remove the liquid. Once reduced to a white pulp, manioc is processed further into a dry manioc meal (*farinha*) or made into a bread that can be stored for long periods. It can also be boiled into a mush, roasted, baked, even consumed as a pudding—what we know as tapioca. Today, as in the past, manioc cultivation and processing alone comprise much of an Indian woman's work load.[18] In Goiás, white settlers quickly adopted manioc because of its versatility. It became one of the food staples of the region. Slave women usually labored at one or all phases of the cultivation and processing of manioc, mastering the techniques involved, which were defined as woman's work. It was not, however, the only labor-intensive activity of slave women. Without mills to grind corn into corn meal, slave women had to stand for long hours at the *pilão* (the tall mortar and pestle made of wood) and pound the kernels into powder. In many parts of Brazil, the pilão is one of the powerful symbols of slavery, because of the arduous labor it required of slave women. A third important staple—rice—required harvesting, drying in the hot sun, and removal of the outer husk. Other food staples, such as beans, required less labor of slave women, but their cultivation and harvesting demanded additional labor.[19]

In the early nineteenth century, Goiás exported marmelada (the sweet of the *marmelo*, or quince fruit) to other provinces, and women commonly made and sold sugared fruit candies, as they still do. Although it is unclear whether slave women played any special role in the marmelada business, they did not escape the household production of the sugared delicacies. It is also uncertain whether they produced the sugar that went into the sweets, although some slave women made *rapadura* (bricks of sugar) and worked as *alambiqueiros*, distilling a white rum. Others were listed as agricultural laborers on the tax records of *engenhos* (sugar mills), but whether they actually cut the cane or fed it into the mills for crushing, as they did in Pernambuco, is unknown. In any case, only a small minority worked on small sugar plantations.[20] How many slave women worked in the production of cotton and coffee is also unknown. In most cases, we can only deduce that they performed agricultural labor when they appear on the tax records for the estates that produced such crops, or when they are listed as agricultural workers on the slave registries of the 1870s and 1880s.

Next to agricultural labor, one of the most common occupations of slave women in Goiás was cooking. The slave registries and tax records usually registered "*cozinheira*" (cook) as the occupation pursued by the majority of slave women. Unlike the system in the North American South, where slave women often prepared food for their own families, a common pattern in Brazil was the employment of one female or male cook to prepare food for the entire household, a mining crew, or a gang of plantation workers.[21] If the number of people to feed was large, then masters added more cooks. One suspects that the cultural pattern of one woman cooking for many men evolved in Brazil because male slaves usually outnumbered female slaves on sugar plantations; thus masters employed the smaller number of slave women in cooking for themselves, their male slaves, and their entire extended household.[22]

In addition to cooking, urban slave women in the small towns of Goiás sold prepared foods. Black women, including slaves and freedwomen, appeared in official records when they applied for licenses to sell foodstuffs, cooked foods, or drinks in market stalls, small shops, and taverns. In Minas Gerais such women did a brisk trade for gold with miners and their slaves, and no matter how much the Portuguese authorities tried to stop their profitable trade in food and liquor for gold, black women grew wealthy from the trade, usually buying their freedom and purchasing slaves, some of whom they later freed. Wills left by freedwomen in Goiás, as well as brotherhood records, testify to how much gold they acquired through their economic activities, including the retail trade in foods. A lengthy will left by Catarina Fernandes, a Mina freedwoman from the small village of Santa Luzia, declared that she had acquired her property by "my industry and my work." Since her husband had died and she had no children, she disposed of her property, which included fourteen slaves and some tiled-roofed houses. She also left money for prayers for the souls of her deceased slaves.[23]

Slave women in the mining areas of Brazil had access to such wealth in part because of the nature of social values in Brazil. Elite women (usually, but not always, white women) lived protected in the households; to enter the streets and engage in trade with men lowered a woman's status. At most, an impoverished widow in need of an income would sell food from her house or send her slave women hawking food they made at home. As male slaves were usually committed to the mining gangs, artisanal occupations, or later to agropastoral activities, slave women had the street trades open to them without competition from slave men or free women. Black women were not the only ones involved in retail trade, however; Portuguese merchants and peddlers also worked at buying and selling goods, although they were more likely to control the dry-goods business or to employ their slave women in the vending of food and liquor.[24]

Prostitution was another "vending business" monopolized by slave women in the early period of the mining boom. Slaveowners in Brazil, even women of respectable households, commonly required their slave women to earn money for them by selling themselves. The shortage of women on the frontier and the demand for prostitutes encouraged owners to exploit their slave women, who were paid for their "services" in gold. While the majority of prostitutes in the colonial period were women of color, a minority of poor white women also entered the business in the nineteenth century. Today, nonwhite women continue to be "recruited" into prostitution. While it is difficult to trace the slave prostitutes through the official documents, one wonders at the large number of single freedwomen in the death registries and in other documents.[25] Why were so many defined as beggars or poor when they died? Because they had once worked as prostitutes? Impoverishment is still a common fate for ex-prostitutes in modern Brazil.

Slaveowners of Goiás commonly employed slave women as domestic servants, but they were not as specialized in the variety of their jobs as slavewomen in the large and elegant households of Rio de Janeiro and Salvador, Bahia.[26] Although sources are lacking about the work of household slaves on the fazendas, the urban tax records permit a glance at the household occupations of slave women in the small towns of Goiás. Most households had only one or two slave women. The largest slaveowner in many small towns was the Catholic priest, who might have five or six slaves, including women and children. As noted, most urban slave women were cooks. An additional slave woman in a household was usually a laundress or seamstress. If the household had more women, they might work as starchers or ironers. A few younger women might be listed as spinners. Usually children completed the tax list, and young boys often served as pages. In general, the tax records suggest that the variety of occupations open to slave women was very restricted—as it was for most women in Goiás in that period.[27]

Located far from the coast and remote from sources of imported textiles and clothing, Goiás offered one other occupation to slave women, and that was textile production. The role of Indian women in making cloth using European looms and techniques went back at least to the Jesuit villages of Christian Indians (*aldeias*) established in Goiás in the eighteenth century. After the Jesuits were expelled in 1759, government officials continued the aldeia tradition and employed their Indian women in weaving cloth.[28] In the early nineteenth century, when Goiás struggled to escape its economic decline, bureaucratic planners sought a solution in the establishment of a textile factory in the City of Goiás.

Using male and female labor, the textile factory produced cheap cotton cloth for export to the plantations of São Paulo, where the cloth was used to make slave clothing. Textile making at the factory stimulated the production of cotton in Goiás, but by that time an indigenous textile tradition had also emerged in which rural women picked cotton, spun it into threads, and wove it into cloth. Slave women, therefore, appear in the documents as spinners, less often as weavers. Free women of all colors wove clothing and coverlets. The weaving of vegetable-dyed cotton coverlets in eighteenth-century patterns is still pursued in Goiás.[29] Two other craft occupations associated with women in Goiás, past and present, are basketry and ceramics for making household containers. Indian women continued to make pottery in their traditional styles, while slave women worked in unglazed *barro*. Baskets, of course, served for storing and carrying foodstuffs, while ceramic jars were useful as pots to carry water from the fountains and wells to fill the water jars kept in every household. The porterage of water was one of the most common daily tasks of slave women.[30] The records of Goiás refer to another category of slave women. In this group were many of the aged and infirm who begged for a living. Often freed before they died, these women lived in the streets and on church steps.[31]

Not all was misery or hard labor for the black women of Goiás. Other documents, principally those of the black brotherhoods, offer a glimpse of the black religious and social communities in which women participated. Unfortunately, their roles in African-derived religions are thus far unknown for Goiás, although some black women appear in the records as *curandeiras* (healers) and *feiticeiras* (a pejorative word meaning witches, but actually referring to women religious leaders within African traditions). Thus far we are limited to descriptions of the role of black women within the Catholic lay brotherhoods of Our Lady of the Rosary and St. Benedict (the black saint from sixteenth-century Sicily).[32]

In most of the small towns of Goiás that had a significant number of black slaves, there was a black brotherhood dedicated to Our Lady of the Rosary or St. Benedict. Most of them were founded by ex-slaves and slaves in the eighteenth century. Another lay brotherhood dedicated to Our Lady of the Good Death or to Our Lady of the [Immaculate] Conception was supported by the *pardos* (mulattoes), which included mulatto slaves and freedpersons. Whites maintained still other brotherhoods, which were the most numerous and wealthy in Goiás. As society was divided by color, so too were the brotherhoods, although there was no segregation in the churches; whites worshiped in the black churches and vice versa. Whatever the color of the lay brothers, each brotherhood erected its own churches. Built on the meager earnings of their slaves and freed members, the slave churches were usually the smallest and poorest. In remote areas of Goiás, the black brothers and their women associates governed the brotherhood and its church through the board (*mesa*) and seldom saw a priest, except once or twice a year to administer the sacraments. Other black churches in the largest towns had white or pardo priests to say

Mass and administer the sacraments. In many cases, black Catholics were able to raise money for only a small chapel, or to ornament an altar within another church that was dedicated to St. Benedict.[33]

Slaves made great sacrifices to build their own churches. They clearly valued this expression of their religious beliefs. One example is that of the unfinished church of Our Lady of the Rosary of Natividade. The German traveler Pohl reported in 1819 that it was designed to be the greatest church in the entire captaincy. Free blacks began its construction, but the church was never finished because the blacks were determined to build it themselves, and they lacked the financial resources to do so once revenue from the gold mines declined in the early nineteenth century. Natividade also had a small church dedicated to St. Benedict, which is now in ruins.[34]

Among the many reasons the black churches were important to slaves and freedpersons was that they served a traditional African function of a burial association. In the eighteenth and nineteenth centuries, the deceased were buried within the churches. The place of burial and the style of funeral usually reflected the deceased person's status in the community. Slaves who had no church were buried outside the churches or simply where they had died. To ensure proper burial as defined at that time, slaves had to erect their own churches so that their members could receive honored funerals and burials near the high altar within the church. Even whites who had a special devotion to Our Lady of the Rosary might be buried in the slave churches.[35] Another important function of the black brotherhoods was to give alms to their poor members and their families. They also raised money to assist their slave members in buying their freedom. In other parts of Brazil, brotherhoods were formed for the sole purpose of liberating their slave members.[36] In Goiás, the members of at least one brotherhood were notably successful in obtaining their liberty. In the early nineteenth century, most of the members of the board of the brotherhood of Our Lady of the Rosary were enslaved; by the 1860s, the majority had escaped slavery.[37] How so many won their freedom is not yet known, but it is probable that the brotherhood played a role, as brotherhoods did elsewhere in Brazil.

When brothers and their family members were sick or impoverished, the brotherhood also raised money to care for them. Much income came from the brotherhood's properties, such as houses or slaves donated by freedpersons when they died. Elderly freedwomen were especially generous in donations to the black brotherhoods of the Rosary. They often donated houses in exchange for care in their old age, funeral expenses, and prayers for their souls after death.[38] To those who lived in that period, the most valuable services of the black brotherhoods were to give praise to Our Lady, honor their patron saints, and console the brothers with essential religious rituals, especially prayers for the souls of the dead. That freedwomen valued these rituals can be traced through the amounts of gold they donated to the black brotherhoods for the purchase of wax for candles, masses, funerals, and prayers for the dead. The most important festivities the members financed were the procession and High

Mass for the feast days of Our Lady of the Rosary and St. Benedict. Much of their time was spent raising funds to import the necessary ritual goods, such as taffeta and candles, from Rio de Janeiro. Candles would display the wealth of the brotherhood and light up the festivities, while the imported cloth would clothe the image of Our Lady of the Rosary or the kings and queens.[39]

The brotherhoods also served as a foci for the social and political organization of the local communities. Every year the brotherhood elected a new king, queen, male judge, and female judge, as well as other officers, to lead the brotherhood for a year. Apparently, one of the criteria for selection was the ability to give donations in gold or wax to help pay for the costs of feast days, which were celebrated with novenas, solemn High Masses, sermons, processions with music, and fireworks. The long lists of slaves and freedwomen who served in the posts of queens, judges, and board members testify to the important role of black women in the brotherhoods, as well as to their financial resources.[40]

The extent of black women's power in the brotherhoods of Goiás remains uncertain,[41] but available sources suggest that the black brotherhood and the church it supported comprised the central socioreligious institution in the lives of African-Brazilian women in Goiás. They baptized their children in the church, married there, and received elaborate funerals (if wealthy enough to afford them) and prayers for their souls after death. If they became infirm or aged, their brothers and sisters cared for them until death, after which they donated their property to the brotherhood—usually a small house and one or more slaves.

This behavior, as revealed in the official brotherhood records, suggests that black women readily adopted the religion of their masters; but as in other parts of Brazil, the black brotherhoods also kept alive African religious traditions. Today, African drum music, dance steps, and dress styles play a part in the religious rituals with which blacks celebrate the feast of the Holy Spirit on Pentecost Sunday. The black kings dress in blue and lead a procession of dancers and musicians in satiny red clothing with sparkling mirrored images and Angolan-style headdresses. On the eve of Pentecost, they enact a drama in which they meet a queen with her separate retinue of dancers and musicians dressed in green.[42] Goiás is one place in Brazil where African-Brazilian traditions that have died out elsewhere on the coast still may be seen in performance.

Although the brotherhood records only hint at the cultural richness of the festivals, they provide more information on the formation of the slave families of Goiás, whether formed through a legal Catholic marriage or a consensual union. Baptismal records from Our Lady of the Rosary in various towns in Goiás[43] identify not only single mothers and their "natural" children but also slave couples with legitimate children, that is, those born into a family in which husband and wife had been married in the Catholic Church. The identification of godparents further clarifies other family ties because aunts and uncles of the child often served as godparents. Marriage records from other churches also document the marriages of slaves and thus the formation of "legitimate" Catholic families (in the views of the time). The most significant records for documenting the later slave family in Goiás, however, are the slave registries of the 1870s and 1880s (the matriculas).[44] They identify not only the mother but also the father (if known), and they list the children by name (thus sex), age, and legitimacy. One can, therefore, establish the number of children born legitimate or illegitimate. Although the data remains to be analyzed, one surprising pattern is already clear—that is, a tendency for African mothers to be recorded with a legal husband and legitimate children, while many *crioulas* with natural children were involved in consensual unions.[45] Where husband and wife lived together on the same fazenda, they often had four or more children. Only rarely did slave women have eight to ten children listed on a matricula. It was common for single women to have only one or two children. Many single men usually completed a fazenda's roster. Extended families, including godparents, parents, and grandchildren, also appear on the lists. Finally, the breakup of slave families, usually through the sale of one or more of the children, can be documented because the matriculas record the sales of slaves, as well as their deaths and manumissions. As in the rest of Brazil, the majority of slaves freed in Goiás were women.

Although research is still in progress, it is evident that the high quality of the surviving documentation in Goiás will permit historians much-needed insights into many important questions about Brazilian slavery—the nature and character of the slave family; the religious, cultural, and social significance of the black brotherhoods in the formation of African-Brazilian culture and community life; and the role of slave women in the slave society of Brazil. A focus on slave women and their incorporation into Luso-Brazilian families may also lead to a better understanding of the character of Brazilian race relations. Brazil was, and is, different from the United States in the character of its race relations. Perhaps one key to unlocking some of the features of the differences and their meaning lies in the place of the slave woman in both societies.

Notes

1. A general history of the early period in Goiás is Luiz Palacin, *Goiás 1722–1822: Estrutura e Conjuntura numa Capitania de Minas*, 2d ed. (Goiânia: Oriente, 1976).

2. On what was and was not burned in 1890–1891, see Robert W. Slenes, "O que Rui Barbosa não Queimou: Novas Frontes para o Estudo da Escravidão no Século XIX," *Estudos Econômicos* 13; no. 1 (January–April 1983): 117–49. The authorities in Goiás received the order to burn the documents, but as far as I was able to determine, they burned only a small number of documents in the governor's office.

3. Goiânia, Arquivo Histórico de Goiás (hereafter AHG), caixa 9, Relação dos Habitantes asituados no termo da Freguezia d'Nossa Senhora do Rozario, Minas d'Meiaponte, Comarca de Villa boa d'Goyaz, 1818. This document records the number of slaves owned by fazendeiros and small farmers on sitios. The number of individuals who owned but one

or two slaves, as well as those who had more than ten, also can be documented through the matriculas, where each slaveowner was registered with the number of slaves he or she owned. Each slave was identified by name, color or national origin if African, parentage (legitimate or illegitimate), and occupation, with additional information, if known, on date of death, sale, or manumission. City of Goiás, Arquivo do Museu das Bandeiras (henceforth AMB), nos. 705–42, Ministerio da Agricultura, Matriculas de Escravos, 1872–1887.

4. An economic history of Goiás is Paulo Bertran, *Formação Econômica de Goiás* (Goiânia: Oriente, 1978). On foodstuffs produced in Goiás, see Rio de Janeiro, Biblioteca Nacional (hereafter RJBN), I–32,14,13, Vallée, Presidios Coloniaes da Provincia de Goyaz, 1857; and Rio de Janeiro, Arquivo Nacional (hereafter RJAN), Cod. 807, vol. 10, Francisco Joze Roiz Barata, Memoria sobre a Agricultura e Commercio da Capitania de Goyaz, 1806, ff. 65–91.

5. AMB, no. 708, Matriculas, Bonfim, 1872–1873, records that João da Costa Ferreira sold two black boys, Agostinho, age ten, and Benedicto, age six, the legitimate children of Bonifacio and Marianna, to Minas Gerais. He also sold Ignacia, *parda*, age sixteen, the natural child of Anna.

6. In 1783 the Arrayal e Freguezia da Anta had 971 pardo and black male slaves but only 236 parda and black female slaves. There were also 201 white males, 139 white females, and 76 free males and 102 free females who were black and pardo. RJBN, 16,3,2, Notíca Geral da Capitania de Goiás, 1783.

7. City of Goiás, Biblioteca de Fundação Educacional da Cidade de Goiás (hereafter BFEG), Livro de Obitos, Natividade, 1809–1859. For example, Severino, infant, Indian of the Caráó nation, who had come from the backlands of Alcantara, was an agregado of Marcella da Cunha. He was buried in 1836.

8. Jarbas Jayme, *Famílias pirenopolinas (Ensaios genealógicos)*, 5 vols. (Pirenópolis: Estado de Goiás, 1973), is a detailed genealogical study of the major families of Pirenópolis (formerly Meiaponte), including those descended from Africans and Indians. Nineteenth–century photographs of African-Brazilian women are included.

9. Nagô slaves were sold in Crixás; in AMB, no 169, Escravos, "Siza dos Escravos ladinos," 1810–1821. In the nineteenth century the term Nagô was used for the Yoruba people of western Nigeria and Benin. See Mary C. Karasch, *Slave Life in Rio de Janeiro, 1808–1850* (Princeton: Princeton University Press, 1987), pp. 26–27. On the Minas, see C. R. Boxer, *The Golden Age of Brazil 1695–1750* (Berkeley: University of California Press, 1964), pp. 175–76.

10. Official documents, such as tax records, usually restricted themselves to a few color terms. In general, they used *preta* or *crioula*, *parda* or *mulata*, and *cabra*. For a more extended discussion of color terms, see my *Slave Life*, pp. 4–8; and Auguste de Saint-Hilaire, *Viagem à Província de Goiás*, trans. Regina Regis Junqueira (Belo Horizonte: Livraria Itatiaia, 1975), p. 129, n. 8.

11. See my discussion of status values in *Slave Life*, pp. 66–75, and Kathleen J. Higgins, "Masters and Slaves in a Mining Society: A Study of Eighteenth-Century Sabará, Minas Gerais," paper delivered at the 1987 annual meeting of the American Historical Association, Washington, D.C. One can document similar status values in Goiás through marriage patterns. See, for example, "Famílias de Origem Africana," in Jayme, *Famílias pirenopolinas*, vol. 5, pp. 393–447.

12. Higgins, "Masters and Slaves," pp. 9–11, and Boxer, *Golden Age*, pp. 174–75. A brief biography and photograph of Monsenhor Bento Severiano da Luz appears in Jayme, *Famílias pirenopolinas*, vol. 5, photograph section.

13. James W. Wells, *Exploring and Traveling Three Thousand Miles through Brazil* (Philadelphia: J. B. Lippincott, 1886), vol. 2, p. 187. Damiana da Cunha, a Caiapó (Kaiapó) Indian woman, received in 1819 a commission from the governor of Goiás to organize an expedition to pacify a group of her people. See my "Damiana da Cunha: Catechist and *Sertanista*," in *Struggle and Survival in Colonial America*, ed. David G. Sweet and Gary B. Nash (Berkeley: University of California Press, 1981), pp. 102–20.

14. Cynthia Brantley, "To Enable the Family to Eat: African Women and Food," paper delivered at the Sixth Berkshire Conference on the History of Women, Smith College, Northampton, Mass., June 3, 1984.

15. On the distinctions between the world of women (the house) and the domain of men (the street), see Sandra Lauderdale Graham, *House and Street: The Domestic World of Servants and Masters in Nineteenth-Century Rio de Janeiro* (Cambridge: Cambridge University Press, 1988), introduction and chap. 1. The cloistering of white women and high-status slave women was a common custom in colonial Brazil. See Karasch, *Slave Life*, pp. 71–73.

16. On the types of labor done by Indian women in the nineteenth century, see Saint-Hilaire, *Viagem*, p. 71. On African-Brazilian women as healers, see my *Slave Life*, pp. 263–64. One of the most famous women in Goiás, described as a "doctor, friend, and counselor" to the humble peasants of Goiás in the 1920s, was Benedita Cipriano Gomes, who was born of a peasant family near Pirenopólis. Her photograph is in Jayme, *Famílias pirenopolinas*, vol. 5, photograph section.

17. There are few descriptions of slave women actually engaged in these activities; one can only generalize about their work activities based on the number of slave women listed in the matriculas as engaged in agricultural labor in combination with the taxes on agricultural commodities produced on the estates. For the matriculas, see n. 3. The taxes on agricultural commodities may be found at the AHG in the unsorted *caixas* (boxes of documents) that are organized by year. They usually appear with packages of unsorted Fazenda documents. Caixa 28, for example, has the tax records for 1839 on sugar plantations, including their slaves.

18. Milton de Albuquerque, *A Mandioca na Amazônia* (Belém: Superintêndencia do Desenvolvimento da Amazônia, 1969), p. 12, cites various theories of origin of the domestication of manioc, including those that point to central Brazil, including Goiás. For a clear description of manioc as a plant, see William O. Jones, *Manioc in Africa* (Stanford: Stanford University Press, 1959), pp. 3–33.

19. See the photograph of two women working together at a large pilão in Stanley J. Stein, *Vassouras: A Brazilian Coffee Country, 1850–1890* (New York: Atheneum, 1970), facing p. 81. On foodstuffs raised, see RJAN, Cod. 807, vol. 10, Barata, Memoria, 1806, f. 70.

20. See n.17. Marivone Matos Chaim, *Sociedade Colonial Goiás—1749–1822*, 2d ed. (Brasília: Centro Gráfico do Senado Federal, 1987), p. 44, lists the five agricultural exports of Goiás as sugar, rice, cotton, wheat, and coffee in 1809.

21. On the work of cooks and slave women in the province of Rio de Janeiro, see Stein, *Vassouras*, pp. 161–79.

22. As the number of slaves declined in the second half of the nineteenth century, slaveowners in Goiás tended to keep at least one woman as a cook for the household. One almost has the sense that owners retained their slave female cooks in preference to other slaves. Small slaveowners in particular used their one slave woman as a cook.

23. *Quitandeiras*, slave women who sold fruits and vegetables, appear on the slave registries (matriculas); see n. 3. Women who received licenses to sell *agoaardente* (white rum) are listed in the tax records, AHG, caixa 38, pacote 1, Fazenda, 1843. On the custom of slave women selling foodstuffs and liquor in the mining regions, see my "Suppliers, Sellers, Servants, and Slaves," in *Cities and Society in Colonial Latin America*, ed. Louisa S. Hoberman and Susan M. Socolow (Albuquerque: University of New Mexico Press, 1986), p. 271, and Higgins, "Masters and Slaves," p. 9. The copy of a Mina's will, dated 10 July 1787, is at the BFEG in the collection of Frei Simão Dorvi, Testamento de Catarina Fernandes de nação mina.

24. On the number of businesses—stores and taverns—in the City of Goiás (1819), see Saint Hilaire, *Viagem*, p. 52.

25. Karasch, "Suppliers, Sellers, Servants, and Slaves," p. 270. Freedwomen who were identified as beggars or poor when they died are listed frequently in BFEG, Livro de Obitos, Natividade, 1809–1859.

26. Karasch, *Slave Life*, pp.208–10, and Lauderdale Graham, *House and Street*, pp. 31–58.

27. Not all the tax records list occupations. Among those that had occupational data were those for Jaraguá (AMB, no. 1004, Impostos, 1870–1871), which reported the name of the slaveowner and the slave's name (hence sex), place of birth, age, color, and occupation. Almost all slave women were cooks or laundresses. The most consistent occupational data for slave women occurs in the matriculas; see n. 3.

28. Marivone Matos Chaim, *Os Aldeamentos Indígenas na Capitania de Goiás* (Goiânia: Oriente, 1974), is the best general study on the aldeias of Goiás.

29. The employees of the textile factory are listed in RJBN, I–32,13,12, Goiás (Província), Documentos relativos a fábrica de fiação e tecelagem e malha estabelecida por João Duarte Coelho na Capital da Província de Goiás, 1838. Three Indian women and one cabra woman were "*cardadores*" (carders), while at least sixteen women worked as *tecilloes* (weavers) outside the factory. Only one of the women was identified as a slave woman. On cotton plantations and production in Meiaponte, see Saint-Hilaire, *Viagem*, pp. 99–100. He reported on exports of cotton to Bahia and Rio de Janeiro and plans to use women and children in making cotton threads (*fiação*). In my collection of coverlets, I have one from Goiás in the same design as a coverlet from Delaware (c. 1750). One of the best modern studies on weaving in Goiás is Marcolina Martins Garcia, *Tecelagem Artesanal: Estudo Etnográfico em Hidrolândia—Goiás* (Goiânia: Ed. da Universidade Federal de Goiás, 1981).

30. The evidence for the use of Indian ceramic styles derives from recent archaeological excavations in the City of Goiás (personal observations). Unglazed pottery and baskets are still made in Goiás, although the quality has declined in recent years.

31. See n. 25.

32. The best general study in English on the black brotherhoods is Patricia A. Mulvey, "The Black Lay Brotherhoods of Colonial Brazil: A History," Ph.D. dissertation, City University of New York, 1976. See also my *Slave Life*, pp. 82–86.

33. Churches built by the black lay brotherhoods are illustrated in Anna Maria Borges and Luiz Palacin, *Patrimônio Histórico de Goiás*, 2d ed. (Brasília: SPHAN/próMemória/8ª Diretoria Regional, 1987). Documents regarding some of the black brotherhoods have been preserved at BFEG.

34. Ibid., pp. 53–60.

35. The diverse locations of burials within or outside the churches in the town of Natividade were carefully recorded by the priests. See BFEG, Livro de Obitos, Natividade, 1809–1859.

36. Karasch, *Slave Life*, p. 300. Of the 165 *compromissos* (charters) studied by Mulvey, eleven brotherhoods granted loans to help slaves buy their freedom. Brotherhoods in Rio, such as Nossa Senhora dos Remedios, also provided legal counsel to slaves who had sued their owners for their freedom. Another brotherhood in Rio was formed specifically to help slaves buy their freedom papers (the Brotherhood of the Rosary and Ransom). See Mulvey, "Black Lay Brotherhoods," pp. 92–96.

37. In the document listing the women elected to the board of the brotherhood of Our Lady of the Rosary in 1827, eight slave women and one freedwoman were members of the board along with nine slave men. Only six of the members of the board were free. Although the queen was free, the female judge (*juiza*) was a slave. In contrast, in 1862 the board members, the king, the queen, the judges, and the other officers were free. BFEG, Irmandade de N. S. do Rosário, Livro dos Termos de Meza, 1826–1864. The compromisso of this brotherhood with a beautiful illustration of Our Lady of the Rosary on its cover is also at BFEG. The compromisso was registered in Rio de Janeiro in 1811.

38. There was a donation by Maria Francisca da Sᵃ of a dwelling house to the brotherhood of St. Benedict, November 9, 1792. She was described as a cabra freedwoman. BFEG, Cartório do Primeiro Oficio, 1792–1799, f. 41.

39. Motivations for celebrating the feast day of Our Lady of the Rosary were expressed in the minutes as "not only to praise Our Lady as for the consolation of the brothers." BFEG, Rosário, Livro, 14 May 1843, f. 58. Also at BFEG are the account books of the Irmandade do Rosário e Sancta Efigenia (the black female saint, who was a princess of Nubia, Karasch, *Slave Life*, p. 270) *dos homens pretos* (of the black men), Natividade, 1786–1844; and the receipt records of the gold paid for masses, funerals, and feast day expenses of the Irmandade de N. S. do Rosário of Santa Luzia, 1794–1845. See also BFEG, Rosário, Livro dos Termos de Meza, 1826–1864, for the type of luxury items imported from Rio for the feast days.

40. BFEG, Rosário, Livro dos termos de Meza, 1826–1864.

41. Mulvey, "Black Lay Brotherhoods," p. 131, notes that women played an important role in organizing the brotherhoods' festivals elsewhere in Brazil, but whether they did so in Goiás is thus far uncertain. They may have had less authority in Goiás because only two women—the queen and the judge—exercised leadership roles among the officers. Elsewhere in Brazil, black women were procurators and stewardesses—positions that were filled by men in Goiás.

42. Personal observations and photographs, City of Goiás, Feast of Pentecost, 1987 and 1988.

43. City of Goiás, Arquivo Geral da Diocese de Goiás, has slave baptismal registries from the churches of Our Lady of the Rosary and others in Goiás. See, for example, baptisms at Our Lady of the Rosary, 1871–1895, Livros 10 and 14.

44. See n. 3.

45. For Latin American concepts of legitimacy and illegitimacy, see Asunción Lavrin, ed., *Sexuality and Marriage in Colonial Latin America* (Lincoln: University of Nebraska Press, 1989). Katia de Queirós Mattoso, *Família e Sociedade na Bahia do Século XIX*, trans. James Amado (São Paulo: Corrupio, 1988), has demographic data on legal and natural families by color and civil status in Bahia.

5

"LOOSE, IDLE AND DISORDERLY"
SLAVE WOMEN IN THE
EIGHTEENTH-CENTURY
CHARLESTON MARKETPLACE

Robert Ol̦well

> Black and White all mix'd together
> Inconstant, strange, unhealthful weather
> . . . .
> The markets dear and little money
> Large potatoes, sweet as honey
> Water Bad, past all drinking
> Men and Women without thinking
> Every thing at a high price
> But rum, hominy and rice
> . . . .
> Many a bargain, if you strike it,
> This is Charles-town, how do you like it?
>
> —A Description of Charleston in 1769[1]

An old Charleston adage holds that a person standing at the intersection of Broad and Meeting streets in the center of the old town can turn about and see embodied in the buildings on each corner of the crossroads the various "laws" that govern the city. On the southeast corner stands St. Michael's Church, representing God's law, on the west side are the Federal Post Office and the Courthouse, representing man's law, and on the northeast corner stands the old Bank of the United States, representing the law of money or the market.[2]

Although most of the present buildings postdate the American Revolution, the adage applied just as well to the same spot in the colonial period. In 1774, for example, an English visitor to the city and to the intersection of Broad and Meeting wrote, "At one of the four corners . . . stands the new English church [St. Michael's], and at another is the State House . . . [while] Opposite to it [on another corner] stands the Town Watch House." The anonymous tourist thought these buildings were "handsome [and] substantial" but noted that on "the fourth corner," where the Bank of the United States would later be built, there "is only a low dirty looking brick market house."[3] Despite the visitor's disparaging opinion of the market house, his account indicates that institutions representing the three "laws" of Charleston were already in place at the crossroads.

Perhaps one reason for the contemporary disregard of the marketplace in descriptions of colonial Charleston lies in the fact that activities in the market could not readily be reconciled with those that prevailed on the other three corners of the junction. In contrast to the subordinate position allotted to African slaves in the church and the law, they played a central role in the Charleston marketplace. In 1741, two years after the market house was built, the clerk appointed to regulate trade there noted that "Negroes went so much to Market."[4] With the exception of butchers and fishermen, the vast majority of the slaves who traded in the market were women. In February 1778 one observer "counted in the market and different corners of this town, sixty-four Negro wenches selling cakes, nuts, and so forth."[5]

Like eighteenth-century tourists, most historians of colonial Charleston have chosen to overlook evidence about the "low and dirty looking . . . market house" for the more "substantial" records provided by the church and state. Consequently, both "God's law," that is, religion and the church, and "man's law," statutes and courts, have received considerable scrutiny from scholars, while the other "law" that governed the colonial metropolis, the "law of the market" and its immediate institutional representative, the town marketplace, have seldom been the subject of historical analysis. Nonetheless, the town marketplace was a place of considerable significance in the day-to-day life of the city, and an examination of activities in the Charleston marketplace reveals much about the nature of colonial South Carolina's society.

To succeed as both an economic and social system, New World slavery constantly had to balance and reconcile the contradictory requirement of patriarchy and the market. A final resolution of the conflict or a simple rejection of one in favor of the other was neither possible nor desirable. Slavery could not long survive in a social order based entirely upon market relations. Similarly, a perfectly patriarchal slave society would not be economically profitable. The fault line that resulted from the slave society's need to respect the dictates of both patriarchy and the market profoundly shaped relations between slaves and masters.

In most cases, whether as individual masters on their plantations or collectively in their churches, law courts, or legislature, eighteenth-century slaveholders sought to employ the metaphors of patriarchy to implement the domination that they exercised over their own slaves and over the slave society in general. According to patriarchal metaphors, slaves were to be completely subordinate and dependent upon their masters. All relations between slaves and masters were to be based upon a reciprocal exchange of duties and rewards, obligations and gratitude. However, early modern patriarchy implied more than the rightful superiority of masters over slaves. It also demanded the subordination of women to men. The patriarch was expected to be a lordly father as well as a fatherly lord. Therefore, in regard to gender as well as race, day-to-day activities in the market defied ordinary rules.

Metaphors of patriarchy, however, were only the means low country slaveholders employed to achieve their profit-making ends. The market house is a reminder that South Carolina slaveholders were merchant capitalists as well as plantation patriarchs. From the plantation "great house," masters sought to use patriarchy to define the slaves' labor in terms of love, gratitude, and obligation; but, at the same time, in the "counting house" of trade and commerce, masters aimed to transform the product of their slaves' labor into economic capital.

In their effort to exercise a profitable domination over their slaves, slaveholder patriarchs had to recognize and concede somewhat to the "law of the market." In this realm, the dictates of property and price rather than those of deference and duty determined relations between slaves and masters. Through the utilization of market relations, slaves could escape the smothering metaphors of patriarchy, assert their own property right, and gain a degree of autonomy and self-control. Conversely, while masters could not completely deny the legitimacy of the market, they constantly strove to restrict its application and to construct master-slave relations in patriarchal terms.[6]

The Charleston marketplace was the crucible of this conflict and struggle. Encounters which took place there every day between slaveholders and slave marketeers offer a glimpse of how the social order of the colonial slave society was constructed and perpetuated. As E. P. Thompson has pointed out, "the market . . . [was] a social as well as an economic nexus" in the preindustrial world.[7] Here town met country and news and gossip were exchanged along with goods and money.

In Charleston, public markets were the creation of both statute and custom. The Charleston marketplace was largely established in 1739, but other markets had long existed, and continued to exist, in the city. In a 1741 petition to the Assembly, the commissioner of the newly established market complained that although the "[Market] Act appoints but one public Market Place . . . there were two in the . . . Town; the one established by Law, the other by Custom."[8]

The Negro Act of 1740 permitted slaves to attend the market to buy or sell on behalf of their masters provided they carried tickets "particularly enumerating" what was to be bought or sold.[9] From the beginning, however, slave marketeers sought to do more. Many worked out an arrangement with their masters by which they not only sold their master's produce but used their earnings to purchase goods in their own right and resell them for their own personal profit. After they paid their master an agreed-upon "wage," these slave marketeers could retain whatever surplus they had earned. Most of the marketeers were slave women, perhaps because other casual work as porters or day laborers was closed to them. As market traders these women took on the roles traditionally allocated to women in West African, Caribbean, and most other preindustrial societies.[10]

In the short term, such commercial arrangements suited slaveowners who could thereby collect a steady income from their slaves and from the market even when they had no work for the slaves to do, or produce of their own to sell. In the long run, however, as slaves came to play an expanding role in the marketplace and increasingly provided the city's inhabitants, white and black, with basic necessities, whites resented both the independence of the slave marketeers and their control over the city's food supply. Thus, even while individual slaveowners allowed their slaves to become "independent" marketeers, white society collectively acted to censure the practice. Attempts to prohibit, or at least limit, the subversive aspects of slave trading go back to the late seventeenth century. In 1686 the South Carolina Assembly enacted a law that prohibited any person from buying goods from servants or slaves.[11] In 1734, the Charleston grand jury complained that "Negroes are suffered to buy and sell, and be Hucksters of Corn, Pease, fowls, &c. whereby they watch night and day on the several wharves, and buy up many articles necessary for the support of the inhabitants and make them pay an exorbitant rate."[12]

The "official" marketplace was established in 1739 partly to "prevent the injurious and illegal Practice of . . . Negro-huckstering." A year later, when the assembly revised the slave code in response to the Stono rebellion, it renewed the prohibition on independent trading by slaves.[13] However, the stern words and prescribed penalties of the new law did not stop the slave marketeers. In 1744 the grand jury again objected that "many Negroes in Charlestown (in defiance of the 31st paragraph of the Negro Act) do openly buy and sell sundry sorts of wares."[14] The recurrent complaints of Charleston grand juries, to give only the most obvious example, indicate that the sight of slave women acting as independent traders in the market was a common and accepted "illegality."[15]

The discrepancy between statute and custom suggests that the constant reassertion of a patriarchal ideal of master-slave relations in the legislature may actually have allowed slaveholders to accept the intrusion of the market into their everyday relations with their slaves. The law may have served as an ideological citadel in which the masters' absolute and patriarchal authority could be secured, while in practice and on the ground the master-slave interactions were conducted on a very different and far more negotiated basis.

Two accounts, a generation apart, provide a fair picture of the nature and extent of the participation of slaves in the Charleston marketplace in the mid–eighteenth century. A 1747 petition to the assembly complained that as a result of the competition of black marketeers "white people . . . are . . . entirely ruined and rendered miserable . . . by the great liberty and indulgence which is given to Negroes and other slaves in Charles Town to buy, sell and vend . . . valuable commodities."[16] The petitioners' description of the slave marketeers is worth quoting at length:

> [Their masters] give them all imaginable liberty, not only to buy and sell those commodities, but also, . . . to forestall the markets of Charles Town by buying up the Provisions, &c. which come to town for sale, at dear and exorbitant prices, and take what other indirect methods they please, provided they pay their masters their wages, which they seldom or never enquire how they came by the same, . . . [further] those Negroes and other slaves, being possessed of large sums of money, purchase quantities of flour, butter, applies, &ca., all [of] which they retail out to the inhabitants of Charles Town, by which means leading lazy lives, and free from the government of their masters.[17]

Another equally vivid portrayal of the market scene, printed in the *Gazette* in 1772, documents the continuing presence of slaves at the market. An anonymous observer wrote that

> almost every day . . . in and near the Lower Market, . . . poultry, fruit, eggs, c. are brought thither from the country for sale. Near that market, constantly resort a great number of loose, idle and disorderly negro women, who are seated there from morn till night, and *buy* and *sell* on *their own accounts*, what they please, in order to pay their wages, and get so much more for themselves as they can; for their owners care little, how their slaves get the money, so they are paid.[18]

Similarly, runaway slaves were often described in the colony's newspapers to be "well known in Charlestown" for their activities at the market. One fugitive, Bella, was said to be "almost every day at Market selling diverse things." An advertisement also drew attention to "the widow Brown's old Negro wench, named Lizette, who attends the lower market and frequently has things to dispose of there."[19]

Slave market women "free from the government of their masters" soon outnumbered and displaced white traders and made the Charleston market their own particular domain.[20] By the mid–eighteenth century, in terms of race as well as tolerated illegalities, the public marketplace of Charleston might be justly termed a "black market." The public market was therefore the only "official" institution in the colony where slaves played not only a central but a dominant role.[21]

The slaves' predominance in the market had important social as well as economic ramifications. Much of the produce sold by the slave marketeers "on their own accounts" had been grown by other slaves in their private gardens. In this way, slave market women became an important source of cash and manufactures to their country counterparts, and the marketplace became one of the central crossroads of the slave community. In trade, town and country slaves could cooperate to their mutual advantage. Studies of present-day markets in Jamaica and Haiti have detailed the existence of "trading partnerships" between rural peasant producers and urban market traders.[22] Such economic ties and clientage may have existed among colonial South Carolina slaves. One observer reported that [slave market] women have such a connection with and influence on, the country negroes who come to market, that they generally find means to obtain whatever they may chuse, in preference to any white person; . . . I have seen the country negroes take great pains, after having been first spoke to by those women to *reserve* whatever they chose to sell to them only, either by keeping the particular article in their canows [canoes], or by sending them away and pretending they were not *for sale*; and when they could not be easily retained by themselves, then I have seen the wenches so briskly hustle them about from one to another that in two minutes they could no longer be traced.[23]

The numerical predominance of slaves at the Charleston market may have given them an opportunity to collectively defy white authority in ways that would have been impossible individually. According to Thompson, "the market was the place where the people, because they were numerous, felt for a moment that they were strong."[24] Whites in Charleston also may have recognized that in the marketplace the ordinary powers of the slave society were to some extent suspended. In 1770, the commissioners noted that the fish market, where "the business . . . is principally carried out by negroes . . . [was] apt to be riotous and disorderly."[25]

The most common sentiment expressed in the collected grand jury presentments and other white complaints against the slave marketeers was a frustration at the large degree of discretion that market women exercised during transactions in the market and the subsequent powerlessness of white inhabitants. As slaveholders, Carolina whites felt that slaves should be generally subordinate, but as property holders and capitalists they also had to recognize the legitimacy of the market in which sellers had the right to seek the highest price for their goods. In the market, slaves could turn the contradictions of slavery to their own advantage. They could use the "law of the market" to deflect and reject the patriarchal authority under which slaveholders ordinarily sought to contain their relations with their slaves. Despite their patriarchal pretensions, slaveholders were very familiar with the "law of the market" and were bound to respect it. For slaves, the distance which market relations allowed them to create between themselves as unfree laborers and the commodities they produced could be a source of liberation. Behind the mask of a commodity and governed only by the "law of the market," slave marketeers could challenge their masters and assert a de facto equality every time they refused to sell except upon their own terms.[26]

Furthermore, because slave marketeers did not trade themselves (in the form of their labor) but instead merely exchanged goods for money, the relationship between them and the white "customer" ended as soon as the bargain was transacted. Buyer and seller were momentarily equal and no other connection existed or was thereby created. As a result, no reassuring restoration of the proper social hierarchy took place after the threatening equality of the bargaining process was concluded.

For slaveholders, an easy alternative to having to negotiate as an equal with a slave was to send their own slaves to the market to make purchases on their behalf. Doubtless, this course was taken by many if not most of Charleston's white inhabitants. Nonetheless, when their slaves returned and reported having paid a slave marketeer thirty-two shillings for a quarter of a hog, masters may still have felt a sense of humiliation at having been "out-bargained" by a slave.[27]

The grand jurors and others who objected to the "black market" protested most often against this so-called profiteering. That market slaves, "free from the government of their masters," should take profits from the slaveholders' pockets rather than contribute their labor to produce wealth for their masters was a galling contradiction of the social ideal. Black marketeers were accused of selling goods "at 100 or 150 per cent advance" from what they had paid for them.[28] In 1763, Charleston's market commissioners protested that "Negroes and other slaves . . . have of late actually raised the price of almost every necessity of life beyond anything heretofore known."[29]

Through the market, slaves in Charleston appeared to have evaded the basic principles of South Carolina slave society. To many whites, this development may have pricked latent fears that the slaves might begin to assert their independence in other areas of society as well. Consequently, many whites couched complaints about the slave marketeers in terms that seemed to describe a far more direct insubordination and rebellion. One complaint accused slave market women of acting "in open violation and contempt" of the law and of "combining together in the most impudent and notorious manner." After depicting the little regard blacks paid to white supremacy in the market, an observer remarked that *"they* are *your slaves"*—as if the matter was in doubt.[30]

In extreme cases whites spoke of the market as if their world had already been turned upside down. They described their relationship to market slaves in terms that revealed both their unease at slaves' control of the market and their own feelings of dependency. The commissioners wrote of the "manifest oppression . . . of the inhabitants" by the market slaves.[31] Another account was even more explicit: "[i]t plainly appears that we are at the mercy even of the lowest and most abandoned scoundrels, who dispose not only of our fortunes but our lives . . . this is permitted in contempt of government, which ought to exert itself."[32]

Exchange is a cultural as much as an economic phenomenon. It cannot be separated from its social context or from the structures of power within which it is conducted. Even if the transaction itself takes place within a momentary "social vacuum" of de facto equality, each participant can remember what came before and, more importantly, can anticipate what will follow after the exchange is concluded. Therefore a truly "free market" can exist only when both participants in the exchange are in a relation to each other that is genuinely equal.[33]

In Charleston two factors acted to deflect or contain the challenge which the activities of slave market women posed to the authority of the slaveholders. First, the fact that the majority of the market slaves were women may have rendered their challenge to the social order less threatening. Even if black marketeers defied the principle of white supremacy, as women they could still be subordinated under the larger patriarchal social order.[34]

It is interesting in this vein to note the vocabulary that was used to describe slave marketeers. In 1768 jurymen complained of the "many idle negro wenches, selling dry goods, cakes, rice, etc. in the markets." Four years later, market women were similarly described as "loose, idle and disorderly." Some complainants characterized these women as "insolent," "abusive," "notorious," and "impudent." Female slave marketeers were also perceived to be both "free from the government" and contemptuous of it.[35] Such descriptions of women's actions by male authorities were not confined to slave societies. Natalie Davis has noted that similar language and imagery representing "disorderly women" who protested against authority was common in early modern Europe.[36] Market women in eighteenth-century England were portrayed in the same way. A description of bread riots in England in 1807 observed that "women are more disposed to be mutinous; they stand less in fear of law, partly from ignorance, partly because they presume upon the privileges of their sex, and therefore in all public tumults they are foremost in violence and ferocity."[37]

As long as the actions of slave marketeers could be read as a female challenge to male authority and not as a black or slave challenge to white authority, they could be fit into this existing tradition of "unruly women" and contained within the parameters of what constituted acceptable manifestations of social conflict. To some degree, therefore, female market slaves in Charleston may have been "hiding behind their sex" in their defiance of laws and statutes.[38] Their behavior may thus provide an example, in microcosm, of how gender differences in a patriarchal society may have shaped slave resistance. When complainants described the resistance of market women they referred mostly to verbal aggression and linguistic "impudence." Ridicule, bluster, and wit were the market women's strongest weapons. In 1741, the clerk of the market complained that the "insolent abusive Manner" of slave marketeers rendered him "afraid to say or do Anything in the Market" and left him to be made "a Game of."[39]

Female slave marketeers may have been permitted to act in "contempt of government" precisely because white authorities felt confident that their verbal insolence was unlikely to escalate into violent rebellion. A visitor to the market wrote, "I have known those black women to be so insolent as even to *wrest* things out of the hands of white people, pretending they had been bought before, for their masters or mistresses, yet expose *the same* for sale again within an hour after, for their own benefit."[40] A black man would hardly have been permitted to make such an overt challenge to the authority of the slave society. Consequently, only the continuing subordination of the slave marketeers as women may have allowed them momentarily to overcome the limitations imposed by slavery and race.

Occasional public punishment of slave offenders provided the second outlet for the anxieties and resentments that the slaves' domination of the market caused among slaveholders. The laws against slaves' trading "on their own accounts" in the market were never strictly enforced, partly because of the effort required to do so but largely because whites had no ready alternative through which the city could gain a regular supply of fresh food. In the ordinary course of events, the "black market" was permitted to continue and whites merely complained, doubtless largely in conversation but also through the presentments of grand juries, regarding the market slaves' defiant behavior and galling presumption.

Every few years, however, whether sparked by a temporary shortage in which the market slaves' monopoly power became painfully evident or merely by a general feeling among whites that the marketeers were taking their "liberty" too much for granted, the Negro Act's prohibitions against slave trading would suddenly be enforced. In May 1773, for example, the *Gazette* reported that "a large quantity of Earthen ware, &c. was seized from Negro Hawkers in Meeting, notwithstanding the many examples lately made by forfeitures for this atrocious offense."[41] Continued complaints of grand juries indicate that these sporadic efforts to enforce the law had little real effect in limiting slave marketeering.[42] Nevertheless, the momentary and public enforcement of the law asserted the authority of the slave society over the market women and may have placated white anxieties and resentments. By threatening the marketeers with the loss of what they had so painstakingly gained and punishing them with twenty lashes if they stepped too far, such tactics might also have served as a means of keeping prices down.

A similar process may have taken place far too often upon an individual and personal level. In the market, slaveholders could at any time cast their social superiority into the balance to gain an unfair advantage or to remove the humiliation of trading, or worse, of reneging upon a contract with a slave. Slaves engaged in marketplace exchange, but they were still fettered by their inferior social status. They were constantly aware of their lack of any legal right to property and knew that their white "customer" could at any time void all contracts simply by moving the relationship from one of buyer-seller to one of master-slave or white-black. Although slaveholders constantly complained of "profiteering," it seems more likely that with such a constant threat hanging over them, slave market women accepted a smaller margin of profit than genuinely free traders would have done.

Through occasional demonstrations of their power, slaveholders could draw a line around the ordinary "disorder" of the "black market" and remind the slaves and perhaps reassure themselves that the illegality of the market continued only upon their sufferance.[43] Given their very real dependence upon the slave marketeers to gather and distribute the city's food supply, this construction was based largely on wishful thinking. Through periodic punishments, however, authorities could make the point that the dependency was at least mutual. If whites were forced to rely upon the slave market women for their basic necessities, these women were just as reliant upon white forbearance for their de facto "liberty." More importantly, the occasional enforcement of otherwise dormant laws served to remind all members of the slave society where authority lay. By such actions, slaveholders contained the independence of market slaves in the realm of tolerated illegalities.

At most, several hundred slave women regularly engaged in selling "sundry sorts of wares" in the mid-eighteenth-century Charleston marketplace. Slave marketeers therefore comprised a tiny fraction of the colony's slave population. In numerical terms, the threat they posed to the slave society was of small consequence. However, the fact that market slaves posed their challenge in the colonial metropolis of Charleston gave it a significance beyond mere numbers. In Charleston, although slave marketeers were few in number, they "played" to a large audience. Along with the city population, thousands of country residents, white and black, visited the city every day and would have had contact with the "black market." The ability of slave women to dominate the proceedings at the market in the center of the slave society's metropolis and to "escape" the limitations of their condition in such a public way challenged white authority and served as an example to other slaves. The challenge was evidently more symbolic than real, striking at the ideological level against white supremacy rather than at the actual structures of power.

The transactions and encounters which took place every day in the Charleston marketplace provide a glimpse in microcosm of the complex relations which shaped the social order of the colonial slave society. The market straddled the line that divided legal code and customary practice. While the slave market women were a vital part of the domestic economy and colonial social order, the "black market" nonetheless continued to exist outside the law. Its impact on the slave community was also two-edged. By allowing slaves to hold property and accumulate wealth within slavery, the market may have acted to lessen overt slave rebelliousness in the short term. In the longer term, however, marketeers remained a focus of dissent and a challenge to notions of white supremacy and patriarchal authority in the slave society. In the market, buyer and seller negotiated over more than the price of food. They also reckoned and constructed the ongoing relations between master and slave, white and black, men and women, authority and property.

Notes

1. "A Naval Officer's View of the Metropolis, 1769," in *The Colonial South Carolina Scene: Contemporary Views, 1697–1774*, ed. and comp. H. Roy Merrens (Columbia: University of South Carolina Press, 1977), pp. 230–31. An earlier and shorter version of this chapter (under the title "The World Turned Upside Down: Slave Women in the Charleston Marketplace") was presented at the meeting of the Organization of Ameri-

can Historians in Louisville in April 1991. The author would like to thank Sylvia Frey, Colin Palmer, and, in particular, David Barry Gaspar for their helpful criticisms of that paper.

2. The adage is somewhat spoiled by the fact that the old Bank of the United States building is now the Charleston city hall.

3. "Charleston, S.C., in 1774 as Described by an English Traveler," *Historical Magazine* 9 (November 1865): 341–47, reprinted in *The Colonial South Carolina Scene*, p. 282.

4. *Journal of the Common House of Assembly* (hereafter *JCHA*), ed. J. H. Easterby et al. (Columbia Historical Commission of South Carolina, 1953), May 21, 1741, p. 16.

5. *South Carolina and American General Gazette*, February 19, 1778.

6. The research presented in this chapter and the thesis briefly sketched out here is developed at greater length in Robert Olwell, "Authority and Resistance: Social Order in a Colonial Slave Society, the South Carolina Lowcountry, 1739–1782," Ph.D. dissertation, Johns Hopkins University, 1991.

7. E. P. Thompson, "The Moral Economy of the English Crowd in the Eighteenth Century," *Past and Present* 50 (February 1971): 135.

8. *JCHA*, May 21, 1741, p. 23. The act "for establishing a Market in the Parish of St. Philips Charles Town" was passed on April 11, 1739; *JCHA*, p. 698.

9. William Simpson, *The Practical Justice of the Peace and Parish Officer of His Majesty's Province of South Carolina* (Charleston, 1761), p. 137.

10. On this point, Philip Morgan has written, "By the late eighteenth century, then, black women had assumed an important role in the town's daily economic affairs, not unlike the place traditionally held by female entrepreneurs in the trading centres of West Africa." See Morgan, "The Development of Slave Culture in Eighteenth-Century Plantation America," Ph.D. dissertation, University of London, 1977, p. 138. Likewise, Sidney Mintz notes the predominance of women in postemancipation (1838) Jamaican markets (while also noting, due to lack of evidence, that the sex of the Jamaican marketeers during slavery cannot be known). See Mintz, *Caribbean Transformations* (Baltimore: Johns Hopkins University Press, 1984), p. 216.

11. *The Statutes at Large of South Carolina*, ed. Thomas Cooper and David J. McCord (Columbia, S.C., 1836–41), vol. 2, p. 22.

12. *South Carolina Gazette*, March 30, 1734, Weber contrib., "Presentment of the Grand Jury," *South Carolina Historical and Genealogical Magazine*, 2512.22 (October 1924), pp. 193–94.

13. *JCHA*, May 21, 1741, p. 16. The Negro Act of 1740 directed that

> [n]o slave who shall dwell . . . or be usually employed in Charles Town, shall presume to buy, sell, deal, traffic, barter, exchange or use commerce for any goods, wares, provisions, grain, victuals, or commodities, of any sort or kind whatsoever . . . on pain that all such goods, wares, provisions, grain, victuals, or commodities, which by any slave shall be . . . used in commerce, shall be seized and forfeited . . . and moreover . . . every slave who shall be convicted of such offence [is] to be publicly whipped on the bare back not exceeding twenty lashes. (*The Statutes at Large of South Carolina*, pp. 407–8)

14. Journal of the Council, October 17, 1744 (microfilm), Library of Congress, Washington, D.C., pp. 527–29.

15. Michel Foucault described this process of tolerated "illegalities" in early modern France:

> each of the different social strata had its margin of tolerated illegality: the non-application of the rule, the non-observance of the innumerable edicts or ordinances were a condition of the political and economic functioning of society. . . . Sometimes it took the form of a massive general non-observance, which meant that for decades . . . ordinances would be published and constantly renewed without ever being implemented. Sometimes it was a matter of laws gradually falling into abeyance, then suddenly being reactivated; sometimes of silent consent on the part of the authorities, neglect, or quite simply the actual impossibility of imposing the law and apprehending offenders. The least-favored strata of the population did not have, in principle, any privileges: but they benefited, within the margins of what was imposed on them by law and custom, from a space of tolerance, gained by force or obstinacy. (*Discipline and Punish: The Birth of the Prison*, trans. Alan Sheridan [New York: Vintage Books, 1979], p. 82)

16. "Petition of Sundry Inhabitants of Charlestown," *JCHA*, February 5, 1747, pp. 154–55.

17. Ibid.

18. *South Carolina Gazette*, September 24, 1772.

19. *South Carolina Gazette*, December 6, 1751; November 10, 1746; May 31, 1770. Lizette was accused of "contrivance" in a robbery in which sixty-five pounds worth of exchange notes were stolen. The advertiser thought it "very probable, that she [Lizette] may endeavour to exchange some of them [the notes] for goods to sell against."

20. *JCHA*, February 5, 1747, pp. 154–55.

21. In this regard, Betty Wood has noted that "by the late eighteenth century, the Lowcountry's urban markets were dominated by black vendors"; Wood, "'White Society' and the 'Informal' Slave Economies of Lowcountry Georgia, c. 1763–1830," *Slavery and Abolition* 11 (December 1990): 317.

22. In Haiti such "trading partnerships" are known as *pratik*. Sidney Mintz provides a description of their operation: "A buying pratik who knows her selling pratik is coming will wait at the proper place and time, refusing to buy stock from others that she is sure her pratik is carrying . . . to the extent that her stock is committed in such arrangements a selling pratik will refuse to sell to others until she has met her pratik buyer." Quoted in Stuart Plattner, "Equilibrating Market Relationships," in *Markets and Marketing*, ed. Plattner (Lanham, Md.: University Press of America/Society for Economic Anthropology, 1985), p. 137.

23. *South Carolina Gazette*, September 24, 1772.

24. Thompson, "The Moral Economy of the English Crowd," p. 135.

25. *South Carolina Gazette*, November 15, 1770. The commissioners decreed that stocks be erected near the fish market and local magistrates be authorized to confine "riotous, disorderly or drunken Negroes . . . buying, selling, or being in and about the said market in the stocks, there to remain for a space not more [than] two hours."

26. On this point, Lawrence T. McDonnell writes, "Master and slave confronted each other at the moment of exchange as bearers of commodities, stripped of social dimensions. . . . In this realm each knew perfect freedom and dependence"; McDonnell, "Money Knows No Master: Market Relations and the Slave Community," in *Developing Dixie: Modernization in a Traditional Society*, ed. Winfrid B. Moore, Jr., Joseph F. Tripp,

and Lyon G. Tyler, Jr. (New York: Greenwood, 1988), p. 34. While accepting McDonnell's idea as important and illuminating, I nonetheless have some significant reservations. Most importantly, I would argue that the market can never be entirely removed from its social context and that therefore market slaves cannot achieve "perfect freedom" (if such a thing ever exists for anyone). The equality of the market is necessarily one of degree, perception, and comparison, and is full of limitations.

27. *South Carolina Gazette*, November 26, 1772.

28. *South Carolina Gazette*, September 24, 1772.

29. *South Carolina Gazette*, October 22, 1763.

30. *South Carolina Gazette*, October 22, 1763; September 24, 1772.

31. *South Carolina Gazette*, October 22, 1763.

32. *South Carolina Gazette*, November 26, 1772.

33. James C. Scott gives an example of a contemporary Malaysian agricultural worker who was given less than the expected wage for stacking rice and when asked why he didn't argue about the low rate, replied, "Poor people can't complain; when I'm sick or need work, I may have to ask him again. I am angry in my heart." Scott quotes Karl Marx as calling this dilemma "the dull compulsion of economic relations." See Scott, "Everyday Forms of Peasant Resistance," *Journal of Peasant Studies* 13 (January 1986): 14–15.

34. For more on the "patriarchal metaphor" in theory and practice, see Olwell, "Authority and Resistance," chap. 5.

35. *South Carolina Gazette*, February 1, 1768; September 24, 1772; October 22, 1763; November 26, 1772. JCHA, May 21, 1741, p. 18; February 5, 1747, pp. 154–55.

36. Natalie Davis, *Society and Culture in Early Modern France* (Stanford: Stanford University Press, 1975), pp. 124–51.

37. Thompson, "The Moral Economy of the English Crowd," pp. 115–16.

38. Davis, *Society and Culture in Early Modern France*, p. 146. Wole Soyinka vividly describes the social "power" of contemporary West African market women (who, among other things, led a successful protest against unpopular legislation) in the Nigeria of his childhood; see Soyinka, *Ake: The Years of Childhood* (New York: Random House, 1981), pp. 199–223. For the same phenomenon in present-day Peru, see Linda J. Seligmann, "To Be In Between: The *Cholas* as Market Women," *Comparative Studies in Society and History* 31 (October 1989): 694–721.

39. JCHA, May 21, 1741, p. 18.

40. *South Carolina Gazette*, September 24, 1772.

41. *South Carolina Gazette*, May 17, 1773.

42. The "many examples" of slaves' goods being seized for violation of the law in the spring of 1773 did not prevent the grand jury from complaining on May 21 "that the Huckstering and selling dry goods, cook'd rice and other victuals is still practised about the Markets and streets of Charlestown by Negroes," *Journal of the Court of General Sessions [Charleston], 1769–1776* (South Carolina Department of Archives and History, Columbia, S.C.), p. 241.

43. Owing to lack of evidence it is impossible to prove how often (or how seldom) the laws against trading by slaves in the market were enforced. Certainly the impression gained from the presentments, which were generally directed as much at white law officers as slaves (for example, a presentment published in the *South Carolina Gazette* on

June 8, 1765, complained of "the magistrates and constables of Charlestown . . . not carrying into execution the laws . . . particularly those against . . . negroes hawking and selling . . ."), would indicate that the laws were rarely enforced. This is also indicated by the "surprised" tone adopted in the account of slaves being punished for illicit trading in 1773.

6

BLACK FEMALE SLAVES AND WHITE HOUSEHOLDS IN BARBADOS

Hilary Beckles

Most eighteenth–century accounts of British Caribbean slave societies contain fairly detailed descriptions of the life experiences of groups of so-called privileged or elite slaves. Generally these accounts contrast the "superior" life-styles of these skilled and supervisory slaves with those of the slaves of the field gangs. The lives of the field slaves are portrayed as materially impoverished, intensively monitored and restricted, and socially dishonorable. More often than not, contemporaries explain that this difference among the slaves was rooted within two distinct but related developments: the occupational and technological complexity of plantation production and the ability and willingness of slaveowners to grant some slaves special material benefits and social liberties commensurate with their perceived economic and social worth.

Modern historians of the Caribbean have generally recognized the heterogeneity of the slave labor force, and even the most general studies of slave society have acknowledged the relation between slave occupation and social status.[1] Such studies, however, as well as other more specific inquiries into slave life, have rarely discussed status differentiation in an empirically rigorous and conceptually systematic way. Through a close examination of status and labor differentiation among the female slaves of Barbados and the different life experiences of female domestics, this chapter explores how gender, work, and social relations were connected.

It is no longer contentious to suggest that analyses of social stratification among slaves which ignore the roles of gender and occupation are not likely to reflect the realities of plantation life. Although colonists in the British Caribbean perceived their slaves in broadly equalitarian terms while framing legislation for their control, considerations of gender fundamentally influenced their social attitudes and managerial policies. Consequently, slaveowners' records show that both the sex and the occupations of slaves noticeably influenced their access to material resources and social betterment. A number of recent studies on Caribbean female slavery have acknowledged the connection and have called for a major reassessment of the literature about slave production and social life.[2] Marietta Morrissey, for example, has argued that while slave men, by virtue of their greater access to certain resources (skilled positions, hiring out, provision gardens), had status and authority over slave women and children, slave women had greater access to other resources, including manumission, domestic work, sexual unions with nonslave persons, and the potential for bearing free children.[3] While Morrissey and others have given us a better understanding of the social structure of the slave community, there is still need for more research into the nature of work experiences, the relations between sex, work, and status, and the extent to which specific slave groups developed and expressed distinct identities and consciousness.[4]

If occupational and status differentiation within the slave "class" should be explained within the context of the technical and social organization of work, perhaps more attention should be paid to the structure of labor processes than to the general theme of slave treatment in master-slave relations. Some observers of slave society clearly understood this. William Dickson, private secretary to Governor Hay of Barbados and later an antislavery advocate, wrote in 1789 that although "slavery, properly speaking, admits of no distinctions of rank, yet some slaves live and are treated so very differently from others that a superficial observer would take it for granted they belong to classes of men who hold distinct ranks in society, so to speak, by tenures essentially different." The groups of slaves he described as the "privileged few" were the "porters, boatmen, and fishermen" in the towns, the "black drivers, boilers, watchmen, mechanics, and other black officers on estates," and "above all, the numerous and useless domestics, both in town and country." These slaves, he stated, live in comparative "ease and plenty" and do not "feel any of the hardships of slavery, but such that arise from the caprices of their owners." Dickson noted, however, that "truth obliges one to say that the great body of the slaves, the field people on sugar plantations, are generally treated more like beasts of burden than like human creatures."[5]

Dickson's general comments about domestics were not typical of those made in the eighteenth and early nineteenth centuries, though some household slaves were frequently described as ill-disciplined and living in excessive material comfort under an easy work regime. Elite white households, in particular, were described as overstaffed as a result of the planters' propensity to emulate the European gentry. Dickson reported a case of a lady he knew who "retained about fifty of the idlers."[6] In 1780 there were just over 5,000 slaveholders in Barbados. Scattered evidence suggests that the average slaveowning household employed three domestic slaves, which gives an approximate total of just over 15,000 of these slaves. In that year, a Select Committee of the House of Assembly reported that about 25 percent of the 62,115 slaves in the colony (15,529) were employed in "menial" domestic service. More than half of these 15,529 domestics were female, and about 20 percent (3,105) were housekeepers. It would not be unreasonable, then, to suggest that 5,000 slaveholders in

1780 employed 3,105 slave housekeepers out of a total of 15,529 domestics.[7] Barry Higman found that in 1817 about half of all slaves in Bridgetown, capital of Barbados, were domestics and that 70 percent of all domestics in plantation households were female.[8]

Slave women achieved their highest status and greatest socioeconomic rewards through household occupations. Some women did achieve limited status in the production system as drivers of the "subordinate groups" comprised of children and young adults. There is no evidence they were ever made drivers of the first or "great" gang. Women were also discriminated against in skilled artisan trades, with the exception of sewing and related crafts. While they also worked in the industrial sector of the plantations, they were generally associated with mundane, unskilled tasks, such as feeding canes to the mills and assisting boilermen.

Plantation records commonly grouped female domestics together under the title "women in office" or "house women." Such lists were headed by the housekeeper and included cooks, nannies, nurses, maids, seamstresses, and laundresses. An inventory (21 May 1796) of slaves on the Lower Estate of John Newton in Christ Church parish lists elite slaves as shown in the table. In addition to women in office, a group of superannuated women were said to work at miscellaneous tasks about the house. These women were retired and infirm fieldworkers who were called upon to do light tasks about the plantation yard, where the manager's house was located.

The origins of the integration of slave women into domestic service in Barbados date back to the crisis of white indentured servitude during the early colonizing period in the mid-seventeenth century. During the 1660s suitable white female servants were hard to come by, and the planters considered those arriving from Britain expensive and undesirable. The stereotype of female servants as deported convicts, "debauched" and "disease ridden wenches," served also to discourage many householders from employing them as domestics.[9] By the 1670s, planters expressed a distinct preference for Amerindian and black women as domestics. Barbados planters perceived slave women, unlike white servants, as having no interests or rights that transcended those of the plantation. They were considered to be economic investments that also offered nonpecuniary benefits. In 1675 John Blake, who had recently arrived on the island, informed his brother in Ireland that his white indentured domestic servant was a "slut" and he would like to be rid of her. He could not do this immediately, however, as his wife was sick. But recognizing that "washing, starching, making of drinks and keeping the house in order" was no "small taske to undergoe" in the colony, he reasoned that "until a neger wench I have, be brought to knowledge, I cannot . . . be without a white maid."[10] John Oldmixon, the early English historian of the British Empire in America, noted in 1708 that Barbados planters rarely kept white servants and that the "handsomest," "cleanliest" "black maidens" were "bred to menial services" in and about the households.[11]

Of all domestic slaves, housekeepers were the only females invested with authority in household matters. They were expected to be domestic supervisors,

Principal Slaves at Newton Plantation, Barbados, 1796

Men in Office		Women in Office	
Name	*Occupation*	*Name*	*Occupation*
Saboy	Driver	Doll	Housekeeper
Great Tobby	Smith	Dolly	In the house
Little Tobby	Smith	Dolly	In the house
Mulatto Daniel	Carpenter	Betsy	In the house
Jack	Carpenter	Jenny	In the House
William Sayers	Joiner	Mary Thomas	In the house
Hercules	Mason	Mary Ann	In the house
Thomas Sayers	Cooper		
Bob	Cooper		
Toby	Boiler		
Gloster	Basket maker		
Cuffy	Smith		
Hillos	Cooper		
Cupid	Cook		
Ned	House		

Source: Newton Papers, 1796, M. 523/225–92, Senate House Library, University of London.

confidantes to the owners, and nannies to their children. Unlike domestics such as cooks, washerwomen, and maids, who were frequently advertised for sale in the island's newspapers, housekeepers rarely changed hands. When retired, housekeepers tended to maintain close relations with household authority, which formed the basis of their social status. Dickson noted that Barbados housekeepers were often fed from the family table and that their victuals were well dressed and of good quality.[12] One visitor to the colony commented on their familiarity during household events and seemed concerned that they should be "occupied listening to any good stories and laughing at them much louder than any of the company."[13]

Karl Watson has made much of the apparent intimacy that existed between housekeepers and owners in Barbados. For Watson, the housekeeper was regarded as part of the emotional core of the planter's household, being treated as a member of the family. To support his contention, he used the correspondence of the Alleyne family, prominent members of the ruling Barbados oligarchy during the eighteenth century. He cited an 1801 letter written by John Foster Alleyne while visiting England with his wife, who had gone there to give birth. Alleyne addressed the letter to Richard Smith, his estate manager, indicating that he expected his housekeeper and other "faithful domestics will rejoice in hearing that their mistress had a very favourable time in her lying in." According to Watson, Alleyne had taken Meggy, his housekeeper, to England on an earlier trip and had sufficient confidence in her to believe that she would celebrate the birth of his child.[14]

In some cases, however, the evidence which illustrates such elements of mutual trust and confidence in the relations between housekeepers and owners also reflects a different experience for other domestics. Unlike housekeepers, who were valued for their supervisory training, other domestics were not considered skilled workers. This attitude was reflected in their market value and in the nature of their work.[15] Not all commentators agreed with Dickson that domestics were idlers treated with a degree of indulgence that frequently warranted their visitation by "jumpers" (slave whippers).[16] Many suggested, to the contrary, that the work conditions of some domestics were little better than those of field slaves. Dr. George Pinckard, who visited Barbados during the late 1790s, described the labor of washerwomen and maids with as much horror as he did that of field slaves. He drew attention to the several "callous scars" that could be found on their bodies, the result of "repeated punishments."[17]

F. W. Bayley, who visited Barbados during the 1820s, supported Pinckard's observations. Bayley noted that the arduous nature of the work of some domestics, particularly the water carriers, was comparable to that of first-gang slave women. He saw the water carriers making several trips to distant streams and rivers, "bending under the weight of wooden cans of water" which they carried on their heads.[18] Such evidence suggests that the work of various categories of domestics should be carefully differentiated so that the role and status of housekeepers can be conceptualized in terms of their co-opted submanagerial status rather than general labor subordination.

Elizabeth Fenwick's experiences with her domestic slaves in Bridgetown during the early nineteenth century reflect other dimensions of the complex arrangements and conditions under which female slaves worked and expressed their consciousness. Fenwick came to Barbados from England and established herself as a schoolteacher for white children in Bridgetown. Her correspondence (1814–1821) with Mary Hays, an English friend, deals at great length with the nature of domestic slavery. She records that the principal problems she encountered in adjusting to Barbados's colonial society were related to the management of domestic slaves. Even more than Dickson before her, Fenwick was able to capture the dialectical relations between slavery and resistance, subordination and power, as they occurred in everyday life. At the outset, she found her female domestics "a sluggish, inert, self-willed race of people, apparently inaccessible to gentle and kindly impulses." Nothing "but the dread of the whip seems capable of rousing them to exertion, and not even that, as I understand, can make them honest." Fenwick's domestics exploited her vulnerability as a newcomer, causing her to lament how they "habitually and instinctively pilfered her goods" with no regard to her opinion.[19] With these experiences dominating her daily social encounter with slavery, Fenwick had sufficient reason to believe she had fallen victim to the deviousness of domestics, whose attitudes against slavery she witnessed in the appropriation of her property and in general work inefficiency. Though she expressed moral outrage at the behavior of slaves, she admitted to being no supporter of slavery. For her the slave system itself caused the vices and mischiefs of the slave population.

This judgment, however, did not mitigate her responses to the horrors she experienced as a mistress of domestic slaves, whom she accused of being responsible for her negative attitudes to the colony and of continuously threatening to drive her away. In 1815 she complained to Mary Hays that "this mental discontent will wear away as habit enures me to new customs and manners, but one thing will ever militate against my contentment—the negro slaves." Fenwick believed that "no imagination could form an idea of the unceasing turmoil and vexation their management creates." Referring to their general attitudes against slavery, she stated that to "kindness and forbearance they return insolence and contempt," and "nothing awes or governs them but the lash of the whip or the dread of being sent into the fields of labour." She concluded with some frustration that the pursuit of "a regular course of negligence, lies, and plunder, the latter of which they carry on with a cunning and ingenuity that is surprising," constituted nothing short of concerted efforts to sabotage and exploit her household.[20]

Hired-out domestic slaves were more likely to treat their employers, rather than their owners, in the contemptuous manner that Fenwick wrote about. Several contemporaries commented on this, and Fenwick herself soon learned that the best slaves were not hired out but kept for their owner's purposes. It was not that she had chosen a bad lot but rather that she had entered the wrong labor market by hiring her domestics. In spite of her professed antislavery sentiments, peace of mind was more important, hence her constant complaint that her black servants caused her endless trouble and rendered domestic comfort unattainable.[21] Fenwick confessed that "the provocations of their dirt, disobedience and dishonesty" threatened to drive her "almost mad." One servant in particular robbed her "to a considerable amount," then boasted to her owner's other slaves that she could not be flogged and that "she knew better than to work when she was made to do so."[22]

Fenwick's domestics were employed to cook, wash, and clean, and they often also purchased household items from stores. These shopping errands presented domestics with opportunities to express their general insubordination. They never returned on time, using the "better part of the day" walking the streets and visiting friends. In addition, Fenwick explained, her hired domestics used her money to purchase items from the larger stores at low prices and retail them to slave hucksters at a markup, making a small profit for themselves. In May 1817, unable to endure the trying behavior of her domestics any more, Fenwick discharged the majority of them, including the housekeeper. "This may appear no great matter to a European," she wrote to Hays, "but if you know the slavery of managing a family in the West Indies with Negro domestics you would wonder how I support the toil. From five in the morning till evening, I have literally not an unoccupied moment, and this wretched condition is my refuge."[23] Unable to do without a housekeeper to drive the other domestics, she hired one from a friend, and two assistants, at an annual cost of £130. Much to her distress, she found that this arrangement added to, rather than diminished, the amount of supervision required of her. Fenwick wrote to Hays that the management of domestics without a reliable housekeeper is "a labour so great, so constant, so oppressive in this country, where every order must be executed under the eye of the mistress."[24]

Disturbed by the high wages of hired servants and distressed by their performance, Fenwick finally decided to purchase her own slaves. She chose a male slave to manage the kitchen. He was also responsible for the supervision of the female domestics. She hoped that by placing a male domestic over the females, she would get better results and justify her investment of £140 in him. She wrote to her friend that while "it will no doubt be repugnant to your feelings to hear me talk of buying men," it seemed the only way to manage the ungovernable domestics.[25] By August 1821, there were eight slaves in Fenwick's household, three of whom were hired and five (two men, two boys, one woman) of whom were her own. By reducing the number of hired servants and placing a male instead of a female housekeeper in charge of household supervision, Fenwick seemed to have found the domestic peace which had eluded her since arriving in the colony. By December 1821, however, she had had enough of Barbados. She left for New Haven, Connecticut, in the United States, getting rid of her five slaves "for half their value."[26]

Apart from the general character of domestic slavery, Fenwick was also concerned with wider social matters. She was particularly interested in the "evil" of white males' sociosexual manipulation of female domestic slaves. She believed that white males of Barbados considered the sexual domination of slave women to be an important and indispensable cultural benefit of their enslavement. This culture, Fenwick saw, not only corrupted individual values but also subverted public morality. She was intensely concerned when her young nephew, Orlando, arrived in Barbados from England to learn the merchant trade. She hoped that he would not "acquire those vices of manhood" which white males openly displayed in promiscuous relationships with domestics.[27] Fenwick recognized, however, that owing to the subordinate and powerless condition of domestic slaves in relation to white men, many of these slaves pursued sexual relations as a major means of betterment. She therefore considered both slaves and masters to be victims of slavery and condemned it as a "disgraceful system" not consistent with the cultivation of "excellence of character."[28]

Though housewomen sometimes experienced great psychological stress because of their close proximity to white authority and many lived in fear of sexual abuse and loss of their lives at the hands of owners and managers, they still preferred their work in the house to fieldwork. While many domestics ran away, the dread of being sent to the field gangs, which they considered a most severe punishment, was frequently sufficient to force many to conform to the wide-ranging demands of owners. If, according to Dickson, "a house negro ever chose, or seem to choose, to go into the field, it is to flee from unsupportable domestic tyranny."[29]

Some of these generalizations can be tested, using evidence from the Newton estate papers. These documents contain information on such matters as the material and social achievements of slave women, the nature of their social and sexual relations, their pursuit of freedom, and the considerations which shaped their social consciousness. From the mid-eighteenth century to the closing years of slavery in the early 1830s, one slave family of five—Old Doll, her three daughters, and her niece—dominated domestic service on Newton's estate. This family of "special status" was listed separately from other slaves in the managers' reports. They succeeded in acquiring the use of slaves for their own domestic work, some amount of integration within white society, literacy, and property of their own.

During the early 1790s, Elizabeth Newton handed over her estate to two cousins, Thomas and John Lane. One condition of the transfer was that Old Doll, her long-serving housekeeper, and Old Doll's family were to continue to enjoy the standard of living to which they had been accustomed under her management. This meant, among other things, that they would continue to dominate the key role of housekeeper on the estate. They were definitely not to work in the fields nor perform any arduous manual task. The new owners made a conscientious effort, in spite of complaints from their managers, to comply with these requests. One interesting result was that Old Doll's family became the center of social and labor disputes on the estate for over a decade.

In 1796 Sampson Wood, the Newton estate manager, sent Thomas Lane, his employer in London, a "Report on the Negroes."[30] This extremely detailed document provided information about the slaves' ages, places of birth, occupations, family patterns, sex, and market values. Included in the report was a list of the members of Old Doll's family, with descriptions of their character and general behavior. Old Doll is listed as about sixty years old; she "does nothing," having been superannuated after some forty years as the estate's housekeeper. Two of her daughters (Dolly, aged twenty-eight, and Jenny, aged thirty) were described as "doing little" about the estate.

Wood outlined the problem of keeping Dolly, Jenny, and their cousin Kitty Thomas in "high office," yet not idle. He explained that when it was possible to "just catch at a little employment now and then for them, we do so, such as cutting up and making negro clothing, but this is but once a year and but for a few days." Dolly, he added, who attended him in sickness, was "a most excellent nurse," for which he had "some obligations to her."

Wood felt that while Old Doll and her mulatto sister, Mary Ann, should be excused on account of their long service on the estate, Jenny and Kitty could not be treated similarly because they were "young, strong, healthy, and have never done anything." According to Wood, these women had been "so indulged" that any hard work on the estate "would kill them at once." William Yard, his predecessor, had "put them into the field by way of degradation and punishment," but this only caused Old Doll's entire family to resent Yard's management and to try their best to undermine it. During this time, "they were absolutely a nuisance in the field and set the worst examples to the rest of the negroes." When Wood later brought them back into the household, it was a or victory for the family in its struggle to maintain its privileged status. Mrs. V istress of the estate, put Dolly to needlework and Jenny to the more r gious occupation of housekeep Kitty vas also brought into the hou but no account was given of her precise role. Wood later complained that Dolly had told him in conversation that "neither she nor Kitty Thomas ever . . . swept out a chamber or carried a pail of water to wash"; Old Doll had other slave assistants to do that sort of work. "What think you Sir, of the hardship of slavery!" the exasperated Wood declared in his report.

Old Doll's family not only had access to slave attendants, but they also "owned" slaves who waited on them.[31] This situation accentuated their elite status in the eyes of whites and blacks. Thomas Saer, the white sexual mate of Mary Ann, had willed her a female slave named Esther. By the time of Wood's report, Esther had five children living, two boys and three girls who, though legally belonging to the Newton estate, were by custom in Mary Ann's possession. Esther's children "slaved" for Old Doll's family, and this relationship meant that Jenny, Kitty, and Dolly were raised to consider themselves "more free than slave." Ultimately the plantation house was the only place where they could work on the estate that was consistent with their social standing and consciousness.

The women in Old Doll's family aspired to sociosexual relations with free men, particularly whites. Success in such ventures was symbolic of achievement and status. It was an index by which the whole society of blacks and whites would judge them, and it was also a way to minimize the possibility of their (and their children's) relegation to field labor. By systematic "whitening" of children through conscious selection of mates, these women sought to diminish the threat of servitude. Mary Ann had four children by Saer. Wood described these children to be "as white as himself." Their color also immediately disconnected them from field labor. Dolly was the mistress of William Yard when he managed the estate, and she frequently used the relationship to gain access to plantation stores from which she and a cousin supplied the family. Wood noted in his report that all the girls "either have or have had white husbands, that is, men who keep them." Mary Thomas, daughter of Mary Ann, whom Wood described as "extremely heavy, lazy, and ignorant," had a longstanding sexual relation with the white bookkeeper, with whom she had a son. Jenny also had sexual relations with white men. The records do not show that either Mary Thomas or Jenny had intimate relations with slave men, which was unlikely because of their perceptions of elitism, authority, and self-esteem.

Elite slaves, then, went about the establishment and consolidation of their distinct social identities in a self-conscious and systematic manner. They pursued and valued the measure of recognition that white society gave them. This was the most effective way, for such slaves, of distancing themselves from the harshness of slavery and increasing their chances of attaining social freedom. One important way such recognition was conferred was for whites to address them as "miss" or "mister." Another was when owners paid them money wages for certain tasks or as an incentive to perform special duties. Artisans, drivers of the first gang, and housekeepers occasionally achieved these two objectives.

Slaves considered literacy and the attainment of professional skills to be critical in their pursuit of status and betterment in general. Michael Craton has suggested that no more than 2 percent of British Caribbean slaves were literate in the early nineteenth century, and that of the 2 percent, most were likely to be housekeepers and other elite slaves.[32] Old Doll and her daughters were literate. Dolly and Jenny were therefore able to successfully petition their absentee owner for their children's manumission between 1804 and 1818. It became increasingly common for elite slaves to pay literate members of their community to act informally as teachers, though whites opposed policies that facilitated formal schooling for the children of elite slaves. At Newton's estate in 1795, Old Doll attempted to persuade the manager, Wood, to allow her two grandsons to attend school. In his report of 1796, Wood stated that "Doll wants me to put two of her grandchildren (Jenny's children) to school to learn to read and write. I told her I should put them to some trade as soon as they were set for it, but as to putting them in school to read and write, I must consult you about, which I do now." Wood added, "If you ask my opinion about it, I shall tell you that I shall be glad to add to the little of knowledge of anyone whatsoever, and it is almost a cruelty when it is in our power to indulge them, to withhold it from them." Wood, however, had some reservations, in that "inclination must give way to policy." He believed that "it is a bad one in their situation to bestow on them the power of reading and writing. It is of little good, and very frequently producer of mischief with them."[33] Wood got his way on this occasion, but the evidence about Old Doll's family shows that overall, domestics struggled with some success to improve the social and material lot of their families against restrictive plantation policies and other constraints imposed by the wider slave system. When Old Doll died, many white persons, some of prominent families, attended her funeral. Her body was taken to the burial place on a horse-drawn hearse, accompanied by solemn music, and interred by an Anglican clergyman. For a slave, Old Doll had unquestionably achieved superior social standing.

Probably the most perplexing duties of female slave domestics were breastfeeding, weaning, and caring for their owners' white children. Popularized images of black wet nurses with their own child on one breast and that of their mistress on the other, though representing, in part, a romanticized image of slave women's ultimate subservience, were not unreal. In his notes on Barbados at the end of the 1790s, Pinckard recorded his reaction on seeing a slave nanny breast-feeding a white child in the home of a prominent planter. At the time, the planter and his wife were entertaining other European guests. As the child needed to be fed, the nanny was called upon. The planter's guests were most embarrassed by the sight of a white child sucking the black breast. To make matters worse, some "respectable" creole ladies began to assist by "slapping, pressing, shaking about and playing with the long breasts of the slave, with very indelicate familiarity . . . without seeming to be at all sensible that it was, in any degree, indecent or improper."[34] Elite white women in Barbados commonly preferred black nannies to nurse their children, and nannies were also responsible for the children until they became adults.

While black nannies, whether maids or housekeepers, socialized their own children as slaves, they also assisted their owners in raising their children in support of slavery. Within this complex orbit of psychological expectations, slave nannies moved cautiously in clear appreciation of the dangers involved. But the situation also sometimes caused slaveowners much discomfort. Many lived with the fear that nannies would murder their children, and as a result, infant mortalities were commonly enveloped in suspicion of foul play. As white doctors rarely detected poisonings, slaveowners knew that their greatest security lay in the cultivation of amicable relations with domestic staff. For some slave women, however, this condition of slavery was in itself unacceptable, and whites who recognized this never felt completely safe. In 1774, a "favourite" slave nanny was convicted for poisoning her owners' infant. Her confession revealed that it was not the first time she had poisoned an infant in the family.[35]

Many whites believed that the experience of house women varied in accordance with the character, class, and race of their owners. Pinckard, writing in the 1790s, asserted that from observing a domestic's physical appearance it was possible to judge the status of her owner. Sickly looking domestics were thus generally owned by poorer planters.[36] During the 1820s, Bayley believed that the free coloreds treated their black domestics more harshly than did whites, probably because they saw in these women the origins of their own slavery background.[37] Dickson's emphasis was more on the character of slaveowners. Many women, Dickson stated, suffered at the hands of masters who were "miscreant drunkards and desperados."[38] He acknowledged, however, that it was difficult to generalize on this matter, and he offered two opposing cases as evidence. In one, a master attempted to chop off his domestic's ear with a cutlass because he believed she had overheard an intimate family matter and broadcast it, to his detriment. In the other, he described how masters he knew deliberately fostered intimate sexual relations with domestics, whom they treated exceptionally well, as one way of obtaining information about rebellious designs.[39]

Fenwick had admittedly seen no important reason to differentiate between the use of black women as prostitutes, mistresses, or domestics. For her, these roles generally overlapped. It was generally understood, though not explicitly stated in Barbados slave society, that individuals who hired female domestics, under whatever labor titles, were entitled to sexual benefits. In 1806, a British naval officer reported that he knew a respectable creole white lady who, for a living, "lets out her negro girls to anyone who will pay for their persons, under the denomination of washer woman, and becomes very angry if they don't come home in the family way."[40] John Waller, who toured Barbados in 1808, made a similar report on the relation between prostitution, domestic servitude, and the hiring-out servant system. In his travel book he related how "a very respectable matron, who had shown a kind of motherly affection for a young friend" of his who came to Barbados on business, "advised him in the most serious manner to look out for a young mulatto or Mustee girl for his housekeeper, urging that it would greatly increase his domestic comforts and diminish his expenses." The woman also "hinted very delicately" to Waller's friend that "by being confined to one object, his health and reputation would be better secured, than by the promiscuous libertinism to which she seemed to consider every young man as habitually addicted."[41] J. Thome and J. Kimball, in their 1830s account of their "emancipation tour" of Barbados, suggested that young merchants generally took this advice on "first going to the island." It was in vogue, they added, for such new arrivals to engage "coloured females to live with them as housekeepers and mistresses." Furthermore, "it was not unusual for a man to have more than one."[42] Bayley believed that this sexual culture arose "principally from slavery, which has a bias upon everything connected with it."[43]

Domestic slaves, however, considered themselves better placed than field women to survive slavery. Not only were their life experiences more varied, but their chances of manumission were considerably greater. Higman's analysis of plantation slave mortality rates by sex and occupation shows that, next to head drivers, female domestics had the greatest chance of reaching sixty years of age; also, that urban domestics had the lowest mortality rates among all slave occupational groups.[44] Field women, of course, fared worst; hard labor, regular childbearing, malnutrition, and poor medical care did not make a formula for longevity.

Within the slave community of Barbados from 1750 to emancipation, domestic slaves, particularly housekeepers, were part of a socioeconomic elite whose lives differed from those of field hands in fundamental ways. But their special status also carried elements of an extreme form of social exploitation because of close domestic association with the rulers of the plantation world. Some women were victims of their visibility, while others used their situation to improve significantly their social and material welfare—as well as that of their families. Not all of them developed a mentality of fearful submission to the slaveowners' commands. Some expressed an aggressive consciousness in pursuit of their self-interest, in spite of disapproval from their owners. Whatever the nature of their condition, few if any would have preferred life as a field hand. Of all the slaves in Barbados, female housekeepers were the most likely to obtain legal freedom during the later years of slavery.[45]

Notes

1. See, for example, E. Goveia, *Slave Society in the British Leeward Islands at the End of the Eighteenth Century* (New Haven: Yale University Press, 1965), pp. 229–33; E. Brathwaite, *The Development of Creole Society in Jamaica, 1770–1820* (Oxford: Oxford University Press, 1971), pp. 154–62; M. Craton, *In Search of the Invisible Man: Slaves and Plantation Life in Jamaica* (Cambridge: Harvard University Press, 1978), pp. 191–223; B. W. Higman, *Slave Population and Economy in Jamaica* (Cambridge: Cambridge University Press, 1976), pp. 187–211; O. Patterson, *The Sociology of Slavery: An Analysis of the Origins, Development and Structure of Negro Slave Society in Jamaica* (London: McGibbon and Kee, 1967), pp. 216–30; K. Watson, *The Civilised Island: Barbados, A Social History, 1750–1816* (Bridgetown, 1979), pp. 69–76.

2. See B. Bush, *Slave Women in Caribbean Society, 1650–1838* (Bloomington: Indiana University Press, 1990); H. Beckles, *Natural Rebels: A Social History of Enslaved Black Women in Barbados* (New Brunswick: Rutgers University Press, 1990); M. Morrissey, *Slave Women in the New World: Gender Stratification in the Caribbean* (Lawrence: University Press of Kansas, 1989), and "Women's Work, Family Formation and Reproduction among Caribbean Slaves," *Review Journal of the Braudel Centre* 9 (1986): 339–67; R. Reddock, "Women and Slavery in the Caribbean: A Feminist Perspective," *Latin American Perspectives* 12 (1985): 63–80. For comprehensive United States analysis, see D. G. White, *Ar'n't I a Woman? Female Slaves in the Plantation South* (New York: Norton, 1985).

3. Morrissey, *Slave Women in the New World*, pp. 64–69.

4. Edited collections have appeared recently with important cross-cultural and comparative treatments of black women's historical experiences in plantation America. See *Women in Africa and the African Diaspora*, ed. R. Terborg-Penn, S. Harley, and A. Rushing (Washington, D.C.: Howard University Press, 1989); *The Black Woman Cross-Culturally*, ed. F. C. Steady (Cambridge, Mass.: Schenkman, 1981); *In Resistance: Studies in African Caribbean and Afro-Caribbean History*, ed. G. Y. Okihiro (Amherst: University of Massachusetts Press, 1986); *The Afro-American Woman: Struggles and Images*, ed. S. Harley and R. Terborg-Penn (Port Washington, N.Y.: Kennikat, 1978).

5. W. Dickson, *Letters of Slavery* (London: J. Phillips, 1789), p. 6.

6. Dickson, *Letters*, p. 6. Mrs. Carmichael, whose observations of English West Indian slave society in the early nineteenth century historians regard highly, noted that the Englishman who could easily suffice with four servants at home in the management of his household demanded fifteen in the Caribbean; see A. C. Carmichael, *Five Years in Trinidad and St. Vincent* (London: Whittaker), vol. 1, p. 120.

7. A Report of the Committee of the Council of Barbados, appointed to Inquire into the Actual Conditions of the Slaves in this Island (Bridgetown, 1822), p. 8; W. Dickson, *The Migration of Slavery* (London: J. Phillips, 1814), p. 453; Watson, *Civilised Island*, p. 75.

8. B. W. Higman, *Slave Populations of the British Caribbean, 1807–1834* (Baltimore: Johns Hopkins University Press, 1984), pp. 191–384. See also Morrissey, *Slave Women in the New World*, pp. 64–65.

9. See H. Beckles, *White Servitude and Black Slavery in Barbados* (Knoxville: University of Tennessee Press, 1989), pp. 138–39; A. Smith, *Colonists in Bondage: White Servitude and Convict Labor in America, 1607–1776* (Chapel Hill: University of North

Carolina Press, 1947), pp. 1–15; D. Souden, "Rogues, Whores and Vagabonds: Indentured Servant Emigrants to North America and the Case of Mid-Seventeenth-Century Bristol," *Social History* 3 (1978): 23–41; R. Dunn, *Sugar and Slaves: The Rise of the Planter Class in the English West Indies* (Chapel Hill: University of North Carolina Press, 1972), p. 77

10. John Blake to brother, November 1, 1675, in Caribbeana: Miscellaneous Papers Relating to the History of the British West Indies, ed. V. Oliver, 2 vols., British Library, vol. 1, pp. 55–56.

11. J. Oldmixon, *The British Empire in America*, (reprint, New York: Kelly, 1969), vol. 2, p. 129.

12. Dickson, *Letters*, p. 14.

13. "Observation upon the Oligarchy or Committee of Distant Saints in a Letter to the Rt. Hon. Viscount Sidmouth, by an Hereditary Planter," London, 1816, p. 47, British Library.

14. Watson, *Civilised Island*, p. 76.

15. Sampson Wood stated in 1796 that the field slaves, the majority of whom were women, were "the most valuable." At Seawell estate in Christ Church parish, an 1803 inventory shows that the average value of the thirty-four field women in the great gang was £100, while for the six housewomen it was £85.80. At Newton estate in the same year, the average value of women in the great gang was £114 and the average value of the eight housewomen £76. While the highest value for a Newton housewoman was £150, the highest value for a field woman was £175. At Seawell, where seventy women worked in the fields, the highest value for a field woman was £160, while the highest value for a housewoman was £120. "A Report on the Negroes at Newton Plantation, 1796." Newton Papers, M523/288, Senate House Library, University of London.

16. Dickson, *Letters*, pp. 6, 39; Watson, *Civilised Island*, p. 75.

17. G. Pinckard, *Notes on the West Indies* (London: Longman, Hurst, Rees, 1806), vol. 1, p. 258.

18. F. W. Bayley, *Four Years' Residence in the West Indies* (London: William Kidd, 1833), p. 68.

19. Elizabeth Fenwick to Mary Hayes, December 11, 1814, in *The Fate of the Fenwicks: Letters to Mary Hayes, 1788–1828*, ed. A. F. Fenwick (London: Methuen, 1927), pp. 163–64.

20. Ibid., pp. 164–68.

21. Ibid., p. 175.

22. Ibid.

23. Ibid., p. 189.

24. Ibid.

25. Ibid., p. 207.

26. Ibid., p. 213.

27. Ibid., p. 170.

28. Ibid., p. 169.

29. Dickson, *Letters*, p. 7, footnote.

30. Newton Papers, M 523/288, ff 1–20; K. Watson, "Escaping Bondage: The Odyssey of a Barbados Slave Family," paper presented at the Conference of Caribbean Historians, Barbados, 1984.

31. Newton Papers, M 523/381.

32. M. Craton, "Slave Culture, Resistance, and the Achievement of Emancipation in the British West Indies, 1738–1828," in *Slavery and British Abolition, 1776–1848* ed. J. Walvin (London: Macmillan, 1982), p. 104. See also H. Beckles, "The Literate Few: An Historical Sketch of the Slavery Origins of Black Elites in the English West Indies," *Caribbean Journal of Education* 11 (1984): 19–35.

33. Newton Papers, M 523/288, f. 13.

34. Pinckard, *Notes on the West Indies*, vol. 1, p. 260.

35. Dickson, *Letters*, p. 20.

36. Pinckard, *Notes on the West Indies*, vol. 2, pp. 112–13.

37. Bayley, *Four Years' Residence in the West Indies*, pp. 417–18.

38. Dickson, *Letters*, p. 136.

39. Ibid., p. 93.

40. Major Wyvill, Memoirs of an Old Officer (1815), f. 386, MS. Division, Library of Congress, Washington, D.C.

41. J. Waller, *A Voyage to the West Indies* (London, 1820), p. 20.

42. J. Thome and J. Kimball, *Emancipation in the West Indies* (New York: American Anti-Slavery Society, 1838), p. 79.

43. Bayley, *Four Years' Residence in the West Indies*, p. 195.

44. Higman, *Slave Populations*, pp. 334–35.

45. J. Handler, *The Unappropriated People: Freedmen in the Slave Society of Barbados* (Baltimore: Johns Hopkins University Press, 1974), p. 53; Higman, *Slave Populations*, p. 383; Morrissey, *Slave Women in the New World*, p. 67.

7

BLACK HOMES, WHITE HOMILIES
Perceptions of the Slave
Family and of Slave Women in
Nineteenth-Century Brazil

Robert W. Slenes

On August 24, 1899, Simão Alves appeared at one of the main parish churches of Campinas, in Brazil's São Paulo state, "to make a new registration of the act of marriage celebrated between Policarpo Salvador and Afra." The witnesses to this new document—Egydio Franco and José Antônio Aranha—declared that Policarpo and Afra were "husband and wife—by virtue of the fact that they were married—the religious act having been celebrated in the church which was the parish seat of this county during the time when the said couple were slaves of Mr. Thomaz Luiz Alves Cruz—more or less in the year 1858–59." Egydio and José Antônio "added that they had been companions [of Policarpo and Afra] in slavery and that for thirty and twenty-four years [respectively] they have known them always as a married couple." The testimony of these men is reliable. Although it is not possible to check their story against the original marriage certificate (perhaps because the register of slave marriages for most of 1858 and 1859 disappeared from the church archives in Campinas—a fact which may provide us with the motive for the "new registration" of 1899), another document confirms its accuracy. On October 19, 1862, a child named Benedicta, aged thirteen days, was baptized in the county; she was identified as "a daughter of Policarpo and Afra, slaves of Thomas Luis Alvares [*sic*]."[1]

Long and stable marriages like that of Policarpo and Afra were relatively uncommon among Brazilian slaves, if one accepts the arguments of the standard works which address the question. Indeed, for several important authors the conditions of bondage (the excess of men over women, the separation of families in the internal slave trade, the capriciousness and violence of masters) made slave sexual unions so unstable that affective life became virtually normless and family institutions practically nonexistent. Gilberto Freyre referred to the "animality in

Negros [who were slaves], their failure to restrain their instincts, and the prostitution that went on within the home"; Emilia Viotti da Costa pointed to "the
sexual promiscuity in which the slaves lived" and the "licentiousness of the slave
quarters"; Oracy Nogueira noted that "given the occasional and promiscuous
character of sexual relations," the slave "barely came to know his or her own
mother and siblings"; and Roger Bastide, arguing that "a [slave] woman would
sleep, now with one man now with another as the fancy took her," characterized
the sexual life of slaves as "a vast primitive promiscuity."[2] Bastides's assertion,
calling attention to the capriciousness of slave women, reveals an assumption
that seems to be shared by all of these authors: that a breakdown in sexual norms
means, above all, a disruption of controls on female sexuality. From this van-
tage point, what was distinctive about slave sexual behavior was less the inconstancy of men than the wantonness of women. In the context of these studies,
Policarpo and Afra together are certainly exceptions, and Afra seems especially
unusual.

Recent studies in slave demography, mostly unavailable in English, suggest
however that in many respects the experience of this couple, particularly of Afra,
was not uncommon. This chapter briefly reviews the results of this new research, then examines the sources which informed the earlier evaluations of the
Brazilian slave's sexual behavior and family life. It argues that the image of slave
promiscuity was drawn from an uncritical reading of nineteenth-century accounts left by European travelers and well-to-do Brazilians. The authors of
these accounts viewed blacks through an ethnocentric and elitist prism which
caused them to overlook or misinterpret the evidence regarding the intimate life
and domestic arrangements of slaves. Their distortion of the experience of slave
women was particularly severe. An examination of the biases which permeated
their writings reinforces the conclusions of recent studies in slave demography.
It also opens the way for posing new questions to these same sources, which are
replete with information that may be read in a radically different way.

In Brazil, as in the United States, the question of the slave family—or, more
precisely, of the stability or instability of the nuclear slave family—has been
linked to fundamental issues regarding black acculturation and socialization.
The four authors cited above, like virtually all students of the subject since the
1930s, have emphatically rejected racist explanations for slave sexual behavior;[3]
nonetheless, if they have lifted the burden of race from the shoulders of blacks,
they have replaced it with a sociological burden that is almost as heavy. The
affirmation that slaves in general lived in "incentiousness," in "promiscuity," or
in "prostitution" leads easily to the argument that they were profoundly marked
by that experience. Bastide and Florestan Fernandes are particularly emphatic in
positing that these conditions had an impact on the slaves' religious culture,
their sexual and family norms, and even the innermost recesses of their psyches.
Bastide asserted that given the impossibility of maintaining the existence of
the family—that is, the lineage—over time, the "cult of the ancestors" of slaves
of Bantu origin was destined to disappear rapidly or to survive only through

"indirect" ways.[4] Fernandes argues that the conditions of slavery, above all the determination of the masters to prevent "all the forms of union or of solidarity of the slaves," not only marked the sexual behavior of slaves but also undermined the norms of their family life. The result was that blacks emerged from slavery in a state of "anomie" or of "social pathology," without the psychological resources and the ties of solidarity among kin that was so necessary for engaging in competition with immigrants and achieving social mobility.[5] Finally, Bastide argued that "racial parental dualism is the most singular phenomenon of slavery," noting that if "the patriarch's son had a white father and a black mother" (the *ama de leite*, equivalent to the figure of the "mammy"), "the slave's son, on the other hand, may have known his mother but often had no idea who his real father was. In the final analysis his real father, if not his biological one, was the white patriarch, the plantation owner." In this "parental dualism" Bastide found the key to explaining the "psychic mechanisms of [the] acculturation" of blacks; "interiorizing" the white father, the black man (and, presumably, the black woman) would have "interiorized his culture, his view of the world and of life, his frames of references and his norms."[6]

We recognize here the voice of authority; the opinions are emphatic, expressed with the assurance of those who have a firm grasp on theory and an intimate acquaintance with the historical sources. Thus it is curious—or perhaps not so curious, in view of the dramatic changes in the historiography on the slave family in the United States since the late 1960s[7]—that recent studies of the slave family in Brazil indicate that the marriage of Afra and Policarpo was not entirely atypical.[8] Indeed, it would appear that sexual unions of "long duration"—not, of course, those which lasted forty years, which would be relatively rare in any society with high mortality rates, but say, those of ten years or more—were rather common among Brazilian slaves. Also common were children who not only knew their father but also passed their formative years in his company. Illustrative data exist for Campinas, a major plantation county (producing mainly sugar in the first part of the nineteenth century, then coffee after midcentury) in the state of São Paulo. According to the manuscripts of the slave *matricula* (registry) of 1872–73 for Campinas, in holdings with ten or more bondmen and women (including perhaps as many as four in every five slaves in the county), 67 percent of women above the age of fifteen were married or widowed, 87 percent of the mothers (with children under fifteen present in the same matricula list) were married or widowed, and 82 percent of children under ten lived in the same holding with both their parents or with a widowed mother or father.[9] Studies of other counties and periods, using different demographic sources, present compatible or similar results.[10]

To be sure, most of the new research focuses on localities in São Paulo, where slave marriages celebrated by the Catholic Church were considerably more common than in other provinces.[11] Nonetheless, other information strongly suggests that the data from São Paulo do not portray family structures radically different from those of slaves in the rest of Brazil, but simply indicate a greater degree of access to religious marriage.[12] In sum, in São Paulo the consensual unions among slaves were sacramented by the church and thus were documented more frequently than in other provinces. One could object that the data, above all the information from censuses, such as the matricula, may have been invented by slaveowners to deceive the authorities, or that they may simply reflect an attempt by masters to instill white standards of "morality" among their workers. In Campinas, however, the nominative linkage of the baptism and marriage registers for slaves with the matricula lists—similar to that effected between the baptism certificate of Benedicta in 1862 and reaffirmation of the marriage of her parents, Policarpo and Afra, in 1899—confirms without a doubt the authenticity of the data from 1872–73.[13] In so doing, this linkage of sources also shows that a substantial proportion of marriages recorded in the matricula had been formed ten, fifteen, even twenty years earlier.[14] Thus another possible criticism of the census data—that they may simply document the existence, at one point in time, of a large number of unions which were fundamentally unstable—is also rebutted.

The new studies about the Brazilian slave family do not aim at making life under bondage seem less harsh; nor do they mean to show that black people adopted the family norms of whites. The indices of marriage among slaves, the proportion of married mothers, and the percentage of children who lived with both parents or with one widowed parent were much lower in small holdings (those with less than ten people) which, because of their size and instability, severely limited a slave's chances of finding a marriage partner or of maintaining her or his nuclear family intact.[15] In major plantation areas like Campinas, these small holdings were relatively unimportant in demographic terms, but there is no doubt that in all of São Paulo—as in Brazil considered as a whole—they accounted for at least a very large minority of slaves.[16] Furthermore, even on the larger holdings there is no doubt that the separation of families did occur, and that the possibility of such separation was ever present. Recent studies also do not deny the impact of the great disparity between the numbers of men and women (resulting from the African trade and later, in the coffee areas of Rio, São Paulo, and Minas Gerais, from the internal commerce in slaves) on the slaves' chances of forming stable families. They simply show that the negative impact on marriage rates was felt by the men, not the women; in Campinas in 1872–73, in holdings with ten or more slaves, only 30 percent of the male population above fifteen years of age was composed of married men or widowers, a figure that was much below the proportion of married women or widows of that age.[17] Finally, the new research does not indicate that the slaves internalized the sexual family norms of their owners, or that their norms permitted only monogamous marriage. The data—which, one may presume, in the majority of studies portray marriages sanctioned by the church—practically by definition exclude the registration of cases of polygyny, or the union between a man and more than one woman, a practice which was accepted by many African societies. And even if this were not the case, a high frequency of monogamous marriages would not necessarily mean that slaves preferred this type of union. It is important to remember that in Africa polygyny tends to be a sign of relative wealth; in general, only those men who have sufficient means to sustain a larger domestic economy marry more than one woman. In sum, the practice of polygyny could only have been relatively uncommon (regardless of slave norms on the question) among slaves in Brazil, where we may presume that most men confronted an economy of scarcity, not to mention a great lack of women.[18]

What recent studies do indicate is that the weight of slavery, the disequilibrium between the sexes, and the possible (or probable) "survival" of norms favorable to polygyny did not destroy the Brazilian black family as an institution. In addition, and more important, these studies strongly suggest that a stable marital union was a cultural norm among slaves. When conditions of bondage permitted the formation of social relations with a certain continuity over time (as tended to be the case in holdings with ten or more slaves in places like Campinas), slaves opted for this type of union. In sum, there is no apparent reason to characterize the sexual and family practices of Brazilian slave women and men as unregulated, or their system of norms as destructured or in disarray. Thus the conclusions of Bastide and Fernandes, summarized above—with respect to the necessarily rapid disappearance of the cult of the ancestors among slaves of Bantu origin and descent, the prevalence of "anomie" among slaves and free blacks, and the influence of the white master/"father" or the psyche of the slave—simply have no basis.

And yet, doubts may well persist. How is it possible that researchers of the stature of those cited could have arrived at conclusions at once so emphatic and so wrong? One answer may be that they interpreted their data in the terms of a paradigm that has since been seriously questioned. Brazilian social science from the 1930s to the 1960s was strongly influenced by the sociology of Emile Durkheim, as extended and modified by American functionalism; studies about the slave family, in particular, reflected Robert K. Merton's redefinition of anomie as a concept for studying individual deviance, and also the attempt by Talcott Parsons and others to integrate Freudian thought into functionalist theories of social action, especially theories of social deviance.[19] Furthermore, authors writing on Brazil (especially Bastide and Fernandes) were acquainted with the American literature on the black family produced within the same paradigm.[20] It is not surprising, therefore, that Bastide's discussion of slave psychology, which was based on the supposed absence of the black father, paralleled that of Abram Kardiner and Lionel Ovesey in the United States, even though Bastide may have been unaware of the specific work of these authors on the subject. Nor is it strange that Fernandes independently described the Brazilian black family in terms of "social pathology" in the same year (1965) that Daniel P. Moynihan placed the family, supposedly weakened by slavery, at the center of the "tangle of pathology" in the American black community.[21]

However, if this analysis helps to explain how these students of Brazilian slavery interpreted their data, it does not go very far toward providing a critique of their sources. Is it not conceivable that the information they used—drawn mainly from the accounts of white observers, above all foreign travelers, during the time of slavery—may be more reliable than the demographic data on which recent studies are based? It is certainly true that the opinions expressed in those firsthand accounts form a coherent whole. They coincide in recording a pathological state among slaves, and it is understandable that their unanimity in this sense could have seduced many historians. Nonetheless, a closer examination of these sources reveals that the problem was not, as Bastide would have it, in the ego and superego of the slave but in the eye of the nineteenth-century beholder.[22]

Nineteenth-century accounts of Brazil employed common metaphors to describe black people. Indeed, the images are not only recurrent but also so lurid at times that one begins to suspect they were based more on white prejudices than on black realities. The novel *A Carne* (The flesh), by Júlio Ribeiro, published in 1888 and set on a plantation in western São Paulo during the time of slavery, offers a particularly good example. In one scene the white protagonist, Lenita, observes a bull and a cow mating. Immediately thereafter she witnesses a tryst between two young slave lovers. For Lenita, their encounter "was the reproduction of what had occurred, moments ago, but on a more elevated scale; the instinctive, brutish, wild, instantaneous copulation of the ruminants was followed by the premeditated, lascivious, gentle and deliberate human coitus." The scene foreshadows Lenita's fate. Later in the novel she becomes the lover of Barbosa, the son of her planter host. Lenita was interested in science; in the novel, she and Barbosa first have a platonic relationship as researchers in a laboratory he set up on the plantation where they both reside. Through science, Lenita "had hoped to fly with a bound, to ascend to the clouds"; but "the FLESH [*sic*] had held her to the earth, and she fell, she submitted herself, she fell like the feral black woman [*negra boçal*] in the copse, like the tame cow in the field."[23]

To associate cattle and slaves—not just as chattel, a category codified in law, but as beings with an unregulated sexual life—appears to have been common at the time. Other authors, who did not call themselves writers of fiction, expressed themselves in the same or in similar terms as Ribeiro. On visiting the region of Cantagalo in the province of Rio de Janeiro at the beginning of the 1860s, the Swiss traveler and diplomat Johann Jacob Von Tschudi commented upon the "frivolity and well-known inconstancy of the black in everything which has to do with sexual relations." Among slaves, according to Tschudi, "it is relatively rare to find marriages blessed by the church; but the *fazendeiro* [planter] permits couples to live together, in accordance as slaves find and choose mates among themselves, and his pronouncement that they be considered man and wife is sufficient for a union that only exceptionally will last a lifetime; normally, black women have children by two or three or even more men. On the majority of estates, even this formality [the pronouncement of the planter] is not observed, and the blacks live in sexual relationships rather like the cattle on the pampas."[24]

A few years later, in 1867, the jurist (and slaveowner) Agostinho Marques Perdigão Malheiro observed that "slave women, in general, used to live and continue to live in concubinage, or (what is worse) in lechery; only in exceptional cases does marriage guarantee to them the regular propagation of offspring."[25] In 1881, Louis Couty, a Frenchman who resided for several years in Brazil and wrote profusely on the coffee economy and slavery, affirmed that many masters, confronted by the difficulty of imposing a moral order on their bondmen and women, had decided they would no longer interfere in their slaves' sexual lives. Consequently, "in the agglomerations [of slaves] on the plantations, the two sexes are allowed to mix during two or three hours every evening; and in the towns, in the case of isolated slaves, no attempt is made to exercise any vigilance whatsoever. As a result, most slave children know only one of their parents, the mother, and she would often be embarrassed if she had to fill in an exact civil register." In addition, according to Couty, "one finds many black women who do not know how many children they have, just as one encounters those who have never bothered themselves to find out what has become of their children." Then too, when slaves did marry, the exploitation of the wife by the husband, who transformed his spouse into "his servant and his property," generally led the woman "to return . . . with usury this lack of affection." The cases of male slaves who died, poisoned by their wives, "came to be so frequent that, on almost all the plantations, it was necessary to prohibit the widows from remarrying, and to prevent them from continuing to have sexual relations."[26]

Similar declarations can be cited from accounts of the first half of the nineteenth century. Johann Moritz Rugendas, a Bavarian artist who accompanied the Langsdorff scientific expedition to Brazil and remained there from 1822 to 1825, affirmed that "generally the planters encourage marriages among the slaves"; nonetheless, "it cannot be denied that there are many exceptions to this rule, that the slaveowners very often seduce the slaves with their own example of immorality, and that the disproportion between [the numbers of] female and male slaves does not make possible a greater severity on this point and a very strict observance of conjugal fidelity."[27] In the same period, Jean Baptiste Debret, a French artist and likewise an acute observer of life in Brazil, noted that "since a slaveowner cannot, without going against nature, prevent his black men from frequenting black women, it is practically the custom, on the large properties, to bestow one black woman on every four men; it is then up to them to reach an agreement as to how to share peacefully the fruit of this concession, which is made as much to avoid any pretext for flight, as with a view toward encouraging procreation so as to counter, some day, the effects of mortality."[28]

Debret's assertion is somewhat ambiguous—it could be a simple demographic observation or a suggestion of promiscuity—as is also another sentence in his book, in which the black woman is described as "endowed to an extraordinary degree with the ardour of the senses, although [she is] faithful and chaste in marriage."[29] The other authors, however, leave little room for doubt. They created the image of sexual license and unstable families which most later historians accepted as a faithful portrayal of the lives of Brazilian slaves.

It is an image which is suspect, to say the least. Actually, contemporary observations of slavery in Brazil regarding the intimate life of bondwomen and men are short and scarce; worse, on the whole they simply do not stand up to critical examination. Accounts of European travelers, from which most of the citations are drawn, are extremely useful when they describe aspects of material culture which are easily visible and relatively unambiguous (for example, the structure, arrangement, and internal divisions of the slave quarters of the plantation which were seen firsthand). These accounts are much less reliable, however, when they convey opinions about the intimate lives of an entire social group, especially such an "exotic" group as African slaves and their descendants. George Gardner, an Englishman who traveled through the interior of Brazil in 1836, did not restrain his criticism of "voyagers, *en passant*, who have derived their knowledge from others, and not from personal observation. The most ridiculous stories are told by the European residents to strangers on their arrival, as I well know from personal experience."[30] Even careful travelers, like the majority of those cited, would have had difficulty in freeing their observations about the Brazilian slave family from the influence of preconceived ideas, either of their own or of their white informants. Brazilian writers would not have been in a much better position. Although they were not in Brazil *en passant* and thus could recognize and discard "the most ridiculous stories" regarding their country, they were, nonetheless, almost as distant from the slaves in their culture, perceptions, and way of life as European travelers.

What would have been some of the prior images, stamped on the retina, which blurred the vision of white, mostly middle- or upper-class Europeans and Brazilians when confronted with the slave? To begin with, it would be surprising not to find a deformed image of blacks and Africans themselves, because few European travelers or well-born Brazilians could have escaped the influence of racist ideologies of the time. In this regard, it is worth referring again to the case of Louis Couty, who left what is probably the longest account by a contemporary (less than two pages) about the Brazilian slave family. To be sure, even without considering Couty's ideas about race, there is reason to question his reliability as an observer. His Dutch contemporary, C. F. Van Delden Laërne, whose study of the coffee industry in Brazil is remarkable for its careful research and meticulous exposition, complained that "it would lead me to too great a length were I to confute one by one the statements in this work [Couty's *Étude de Biologie Industrielle sur le Café*, published in 1883] which appear to me to be incorrect, nay, even untrue."[31] It is best to leave this criticism aside, however, because it may be seen as the expression of professional envy, the critique of a rival researcher, and instead focus on the paragraphs in Couty's writings which concern the slave family. If the despotic husbands, heartless mothers ("black women," not "slave women"), and murderous wives in the text already cited did not raise the reader's suspicions, let us backtrack a few pages in Couty's account to find his point of departure:

> Do not . . . [the] free citizens of Africa [in Africa itself] have a distaste for manual labor, like their slave brethren; do they cultivate the ever-so-fertile lands which are in their possession; has it not been proven that, when they are employed as workers, they provide much less labor than white workers? Do they have ideas of individual liberty, these men who find it natural to be beaten, to be sold, to be killed according to the caprices of a military chief or a despot? Do they have ideas about family or property, these unhappy people who sell their children for a few scraps of gaudily colored cloth, who kill travelers to pillage their goods and consider theft as a [legitimate] means of struggle for life? And is not the study of their societies—[which are] embryonic, transitory, barely cohesive, without manufacturing plants and without production—like the study of their brain or of their cranium, sufficient to permit a suitable reply to those who make social theories with vague words or with a priori ideas?[32]

The explicit and virulent racism of this passage makes Couty's testimony regarding slaves extremely dubious. Unfortunately, it has not kept him from becoming one of the authors most cited on the question of the Brazilian slave family.[33]

Cultural prejudices also almost certainly obstructed or interfered with the vision of white observers in nineteenth-century Brazil. It is important to remember that the great majority of European travelers who wrote about Brazil, especially in the nineteenth century, came not from Spain or Portugal but from Northern and Western Europe (principally from France, Switzerland, the Germanic states, and England). In these countries from the beginning of the sixteenth to the middle of the eighteenth century, procreation practically did not occur outside sexual unions sacramented by the church; and even in the nineteenth century the illegitimacy rate generally did not rise above 10 percent—a figure much below the proportion in the Iberian countries and Latin America. Even so, the enormous increase in illegitimacy after the mid–eighteenth century, especially in the cities (where the proportion of illegitimate births was often considerably more than the national average), caused widespread alarm in Europe and was commonly interpreted as a sign of deteriorating standards of morality.[34] Thus it is not surprising that European travelers in the nineteenth century, when confronted with the very low indices of religious marriage and the very high rates of illegitimacy which prevailed among Brazilian slaves outside São Paulo, would have recorded an impression of social pathology. The distorting lens of their culture practically prohibited a different vision of reality.

In the case of Brazilian observers, one suspects that a different cultural prejudice was more important. Suggestive in this regard is "Lucinda—the *Mucama* [slave lady-in-waiting]," a short novel which forms part of Joaquim Manoel de Macedo's *As Vitimas–Algozes* (The victim-executioners). Published in 1869, this work of fiction transmits the same negative image of the slave woman that we find in Couty, but it offers a sociological, rather than racial, explanation of her character. The novel is an antislavery tract whose theme is the malefic influence of slavery in the very bosom of the white family. In describing how the young white girl, Cândida (representing purity), is corrupted by her slave lady-in-waiting, Lucinda (whose name evokes that of the devil), Macedo reveals his vision of the moral formation of the slave and his conception of how a girl from an honorable family should be brought up. Macedo writes that the slave woman, "abandoned to the scornful neglect of slavery, growing up surrounded by the practice of the most scandalous and repugnant vices, from her childhood, from her very earliest childhood, witnessing lascivious depravities and hearing the turbid eloquence of speech that knows no restraint, becomes perverted long before she is conscious of her perversion." In contrast, "the damsel [*donzela*] is a flower whose blush is a blend of circumspection and shame." In good families, "daughters are given a certain special care, which on the part of their mothers takes the form of a religious cult of love, constantly on guard, like that of the priestesses of Vesta who stood vigil over the fire of purity, and which on the part of their fathers is a sublime source of prudish sensitivity and scruples, a saintly exaggeration of the paroxysms of zealous love."

As a result of parental vigilance, "Cândida had arrived at the age of eleven with the perfect innocence of her early childhood." Unfortunately, her parents then gave her Lucinda as a present, and "[it was] the slave who wrenched her out of her happy and serene ignorance, the fruit of her innocence, and crudely . . . [taught] her sensuous theories about woman's mission." It is clear from all this that Macedo condemns the moral formation of the slave woman because he cannot accept as legitimate any set of norms for a young girl's upbringing other than that adopted by Cândida's parents. Implicit in his praise of this couple's "saintly exaggeration of the paroxysms of zealous love," one finds his condemnation of slave parents and their daughters. The modern reader will ask if it is legitimate to measure the morality of slave women and men—or any other group—by this yardstick.[35]

Macedo's concern for the fires of Vesta, however, is only an extreme manifestation of a cultural prejudice that was probably shared by most well-born Brazilians and Europeans alike. Significantly, when confronted with one of the most visible aspects of black culture in Brazil—slave dances of African origin—most white observers could not help but perceive them, in contrast to their own dances, as extremely sensual, even lewd. Charles Ribeyrolles, a Frenchman who visited the coffee and sugar regions of Rio de Janeiro in 1858, had this to say about a slave dance called the *lundú*: "it is a mad dance in which eyes, breasts and hips provoke; it is a kind of drunken convulsion." Ribeyrolles categorized this and other dances as expressing "coarse joys, indecent sensual pleasures, libertine fevers." He himself may have viewed these performances less as manifestations of African culture than as hideous creations of slavery. But others, who described them similarly, offered a different interpretation. Enrico Giglioli, who visited a coffee plantation in Rio de Janeiro in 1865, witnessed a slave dance in which "the arms and the body . . . moved in a pantomime that was far from being chaste." He went on to observe that "it is well known that the sensual character prevails in

African dances." The perception that African culture did not place "civilized" restraints on behavior made it easy for whites to believe (as Lenita and her creator, Júlio Ribeiro, certainly did) that the sexuality and the families of Africans and their descendants were utterly different from those of Europeans or of Brazilians of European extraction. And it was at this point, in an age that frequently viewed acquired traits as transmissible from generation to generation, that what I have called "cultural" and "racial" prejudice in fact merged.[36]

In addition to these stereotypes regarding black character and African culture, one would also expect to find evidence in these nineteenth-century accounts, particularly in the last decades of the period, of an ideology that postulated radical differences in the behavior of slave and free workers. According to the Frenchman Ribeyrolles,

> Pale, wan hunger does not enter the dwelling of the slave, and there one never dies of starvation as in White Chapel or the boroughs of Westminster. But families do not exist; there are only broods. Why would a father take to himself the austere and saintly joys of labor? He has no interest whatsoever in the land, in the harvest. Work, for him, is affliction and sweat; it is servitude. Why should a mother keep her hut and children clean? Her children can be taken from her at any moment, like the chicks or the kid-goats of the estate, and she herself is no more than a chattel.
>
> At times, however, distractions and joys exist in these hovels, the brutish distractions and joys of drunkenness, in which one never speaks of the past, which is pain, nor of the future, which is closed off. . . .
>
> In the huts of the blacks, I never once saw a flower: for in them, neither hopes nor remembrances exist.[37]

The reference to the "brutish distractions and joys of drunkenness" among slaves may be an allusion to slave dances, which Ribeyrolles described elsewhere in similar terms; if so, at least there is evidence in his book that he observed these dances at first hand, whatever one makes of his opinions about them. Ribeyrolles documents nothing else in this passage, however, and his reference to kid-goats—rarely found on the cotton plantations of the time, according to data presently available—is quite revealing.[38] Indeed, Ribeyrolles provides us here with a perfect example of how a "reality" can be constructed almost exclusively from preconceived ideas which make it impossible even to think about investigating slave hopes and remembrances by declaring them, a priori, nonexistent.

The ideas brought together by Ribeyrolles—the "saintly," moralizing function of free labor which, in the crux of the happy encounter between necessity and interest, makes possible the formation of the "family," conceived as a project of accumulation—are also expressed, with certain modifications and additions, in *Theses on the Colonization of Brazil*, a report by João Cardoso de Menezes e Souza presented to the Brazilian minister of agriculture, commerce, and public works in 1875. In discussing the possibility of making use of the labor of freedpersons in agriculture, Souza calls attention to the example of "a colony of blacks founded in Goyanna" (presumably French Guiana) after the emancipation of the slaves, where it had been "demonstrated that the African race can be employed usefully in agricultural work, once it has been educated in the shadow of religion and set up on the double base of family and property." Citing a French author on this case, a certain Duval, Souza extends his analysis:

> the family, to which [male] slaves paid little attention as long as marriage did not assure them either the privileges of a husband or those of a father, rapidly constitutes itself in the emancipated population. In the wake of the family comes property, in the beginning very small, its measure set by necessities and by ambition; but with children, necessities will increase, with well-being, so too will ambition. The black man . . . will work to enlarge his cabin, where he is king; his plot of land, where nobody gives him orders. Mutual aid societies, preludes to the savings banks, ardently called for, will come to the aid of this movement, revealing habits of order and providence to races which were reputed incapable of them.[39]

In this passage, Souza (via Duval) adds to Ribeyrolles's set of ideas that the family only fully constitutes itself when the man of the household is assured of the privileges of husband and father—that is, his authority before his wife and his children—which (in the supposition of these authors) does not occur under slavery. The passage also attempts to define more precisely the mutual relation between family and property, which is no more than Ribeyrolles suggested (and, incidentally, also Couty, in the paragraph in which he denies the African any "ideas about family or property"). For Souza, "in the wake of the family comes property," because the struggle to assure the welfare of the family also becomes a struggle to increase one's patrimony; but from this initial moment on, property and family march together, hand in hand, one reinforcing the other. What we have here, then, is the clear enunciation of the idea that there was a relation of mutual support between family (defined as a nuclear kin group that is monogamous and patriarchal) and private property. This model of the family will scarcely be new to students of the nineteenth century, a period at once patriarchal and bourgeois. Nonetheless, it is worth emphasizing that those who thought in its terms—as was most likely the case with the majority of travelers and well-born Brazilians in the nineteenth century—would have faced enormous difficulty in perceiving, not to mention interpreting, the family strategies and projects of slaves.

It is also worth noting that this difficulty probably would have increased with time. In the observations of foreigners and Brazilians regarding the slave family, one would expect to find the influence of a disciplinary project that, during the course of the nineteenth century, increasingly associated the stability of the nuclear family and sobriety in sexual life with constancy and diligence in work. In Europe and the United States during this period, dominant social groups and intellectuals and professionals linked to them were commonly concerned with devising strategies for putting discipline in the home, as part of an effort to instill new values among the working classes, thereby permitting a more effective control over their labor.[40] In this, there was a tacit recognition that the *embour-geoisement* of the worker would not occur through a natural process. It depended instead on the tutelage of the bourgeoisie itself and the state. For those who thought this way in Brazil, the problem of transition from slave to free labor, which raised the specter of a profound change in disciplinary practices, probably made it seem especially necessary to adopt such tutelary strategies.[41] It should be noted, in this regard, that at least three books by Samuel Smiles, the Scottish propagandist for the "moral domestic economy" and for the advantages of "subordinating the animal appetite to reason, forethought and prudence," had been translated into Portuguese and published in Rio de Janeiro by 1880,[42] Furthermore, it appears significant that from the 1870s through the decade after abolition in 1888, the "vagrancy" of freedmen and women was a constant subject of political debate, and of the press; and it is particularly intriguing that the supposed refusal of these people to work was frequently attributed to their moral degeneration, as revealed by a whole complex of negative characteristics, among them lasciviousness and the lack of stable family institutions.[43]

In summary, racism, cultural prejudices, and contemporary ideology regarding labor predisposed European travelers and well-born Brazilians in the nineteenth century to see blacks, whose intimate lives apparently did not conform to their rules, as lacking rules altogether. In the second half of the century, when not following the rules seemed to menace labor discipline increasingly, this predisposition probably became stronger. Within this context, the stories told by Ribeiro, Tschudi, Couty, and the other authors I have cited are extremely precarious as historical sources, unless one's purpose is to understand the Lenitas of the time—that is, to capture the perceptions of the elite. To enter the world of the slave, other types of information and methods of analysis are necessary.

Or at least other readings of these nineteenth-century accounts are in order. In fact, the observers of slavery were not as blind as my analysis may have suggested. Their vision was white, but it was not altogether blank. While their writings explicitly portrayed the sexual and family life of slaves as normless, they also registered details (*en passsant*, while frequently missing the meanings) which can be interpreted in an entirely different way. Indeed, between the lines of these white homilies it is possible to glimpse black homes which *are* consistent with the new demographic data.

To demonstrate this in detail, however, requires another essay.[44] Here I will only point to some of the possibilities and ultimate limits of these sources. The accounts left by white contemporaries about slavery, as it turns out, are quite useful for studying the conjugal family group. They offer particular insights into how the slaves built a domestic economy of their own and attained greater autonomy and security. For example, Tschudi, the Swiss traveler who compared slave sexual life to that of "the cattle on the pampas," also noted that there were married slaves on the plantation he visited and that these couples were permitted to live together in spaces "duly separated" from the barrackslike quarters for single slaves.[45] Other travelers also mentioned in passing the presence of married slaves on the plantations of Rio de Janeiro and São Paulo and confirmed that slave couples were commonly permitted separate living arrangements. Furthermore, it becomes apparent from these same sources that marriage, at least on large properties in this part of Brazil, brought other material advantages: the possession of one's own hearth (a fire maintained in the middle of the slave couple's hut or cubicle for heating and cooking), probably control over the preparation of and participation in at least one of the daily meals (single slaves generally took all their meals together and ate the food prepared by the plantation kitchen), possibly greater access to land for planting garden crops, and certainly greater opportunities to build a domestic economy based upon a division of labor within the household.[46]

These sources, if they are approached with some knowledge of African societies, also provide insights into how slave couples used their cultural heritage to give order and meaning to their domestic economies. For instance, an understanding of traditional patterns of architecture and building use in West-Central Africa—the prevalence there of dwellings that were very small by middle- and upper-class European standards of the nineteenth century, the general absence of windows, the positioning of an oven or hearth in the middle of the dwelling space with no chimney for ventilation—can help one appreciate how slaves in Rio de Janeiro and São Paulo (who were mostly from this part of Africa or descended from people of this region) evaluated the small spaces available to them in the slave quarters and the possibility of obtaining a separate cubicle or hut to share with a mate.[47] At the very least, one will be able to see farther than the German traveler, Ina Von Binzer. On a visit to a coffee plantation in 1881 (in an area in Rio de Janeiro where, only a generation earlier, the large majority of adult slaves had been Africans), she was repulsed by the smoke she saw emerging from a married couple's hut in which a slave woman was preparing the late-afternoon meal, and appalled that slaves would build their cooking fires in quarters that were cramped, windowless, and without chimneys. Binzer's planter host opined that the lack of ventilation in the huts had originated long before planters' attempts to control the slaves who had since grown so accustomed that even when they were freed they built their dwellings without windows.[48] Clearly, planter and traveler in this case, as in so many others, had no idea how to interpret their observations. Nevertheless, Binzer's account provides important information to those who have the skills to read it in a different way.

Ultimately, however, these sources have their limitations. They offer virtually no information on family links beyond the nuclear unit or about the skein of relations between the living and the dead. These kinship ties, so important in African societies, were virtually invisible to travelers *en passant*, like Binzer, or planters *pas pensant*, like her Brazilian host. Almost as invisible to these observers were slave women, even those who were part of a conjugal family. For instance, while the nineteenth-century accounts do suggest that when slave couples cooked for themselves it was the wife who made the meal—and this is not surprising, given African patterns—I know of no white observer who commented on the ingredients, methods of preparation, or condiments that the slave woman used. Such themes could shed light on the cultural preferences and household economies of the slaves.[49] Binzer's lack of interest in this regard—she saw a slave woman making "some sort of food"—is typical.[50] As to the broader division of labor within the household, these contemporary accounts do not permit us to go beyond the information that historian Stanley Stein presented (drawn, apparently, from interviews with ex-slaves) regarding work patterns on Sundays and holidays, when slaves had time for themselves: "where male and female slaves cohabited, men often were accompanied to the roças [garden plots] by their children, while women washed, mended, and cooked, bringing the noon meal to their mates in the field."[51] To apprehend more of the world of women slaves and to understand broader kinship ties, other sources (such as trial records, which abound in local archives) must be explored.

Still, our knowledge of the Brazilian slave family, particularly of the experience of slave women, is substantially greater than it once was. Recent demographic studies indicate that slave marriages were considerably more common and longer-lasting than was previously believed. They show that the majority of slave children, at least on the larger estates of Rio de Janeiro and São Paulo, not only knew who their fathers were but also spent their early years in the presence of both parents. Finally, these studies provide no reason to think that promiscuity was the rule, particularly among women slaves. My criticism of the biases in the accounts of nineteenth-century travelers and well-to-do Brazilians strengthens confidence in the recent demographic data; we may now reject the conclusions regarding slave anomie, deculturation, and impressment into white ways of thinking and feeling that have been so often drawn from the belief that slave sexual life and family life were normless. An alternative reading of these white homilies is clearly one way to move sensitively beyond the new quantitative data to discover meanings that slave women and men themselves conferred on their domestic arrangements and intimate lives. In the search for meanings, an effective approach to these and other sources should surely be to focus on the ways in which Brazilian slaves created an autonomous domestic economy, shaped by their cultural heritage and by their particular conditions of bondage. We must seek to discover the "hopes and remembrances" that the French traveler Charles Ribeyrolles, with his vision fixed on the bourgeois family, so adamantly denied to slaves.

Notes

An earlier version of this chapter appeared in Portuguese as "Lares Negros, Olhares Brancos: Histórias da Família Escrava no Século XIX," *Revista Brasileira de História* 8, no. 16 (March–August 1988): 189–203. All translations from foreign-language sources are mine. I would like to thank Ute Bärnert-Fürst for her assistance in translations from the German.

1. Marriage and baptism registers, Parish of Nossa Senhora de Conceição de Campinas, in Arquivo da Cúria Metropolitana de Campinas: "Casamentos, Escravos, 1841–1858," fol. 111 ("Termo de Justificação," 8/24/1899), and "Batizados, Escravos, 1861–1867."

2. Gilberto Freyre, *The Masters and the Slaves: A Study in the Development of Brazilian Civilization*, trans. Samuel Putnam, 2d English-language ed. (Berkeley: University of California Press, 1986), p. 328; Emilia Viotti da Costa, *Da Senzala à Colônia* (São Paulo: Difusão Européia do Livro, 1966), pp. 269–70; Oracy Nogueria, *Comunidade e Família: Um Estudo Sociológico de Itapetininga* (Rio de Janeiro: Centro Brasileiro de Pesquisas Educacionais, INEP, MEC, 1962), p. 262; Roger Bastide, *The African Religions of Brazil: Toward a Sociology of the Interpenetration of Cultures*, trans. Helen Sebba (Baltimore: Johns Hopkins University Press, 1978), p. 61. Stanley J. Stein also states that passing sexual unions prevailed among Brazilian slaves; but unlike the other authors cited, he argues, with Melville J. Herskovits, that these unions represented a redefinition of African traditions of polygyny, not a normless promiscuity. See Stein, *Vassouras: A Brazilian Coffee County, 1850–1900*, 2d ed. (Princeton: Princeton University Press, 1985), p. 155, and Herskovits, *The Myth of the Negro Past* (Boston: Beacon, 1958), p. 168.

3. Freyre, for instance, in the passage cited is at pains to note that the cause of slave promiscuity was slavery itself or, more specifically, the immorality of white masters; and by "prostitution . . . within the home," he means prostitution within the big house.

4. Bastide, *The African Religions*, pp. 60–61. The problem was different for Yoruba and Dahoman slaves, according to Bastide (p. 61), since their religion was "simultaneously a lineage religion and a community religion." The first aspect "was bound to disappear," as it was among the bantu; but the community religion "was able to survive by accommodating itself to the framework of 'nations' reestablished by the Portuguese and Brazilian governments for the purpose of fomenting interethnic rivalries. . . ."

5. See Florestan Fernandes, *A Integração do Negro na Sociedade de Classes*, (São Paulo: Dominus/EDUSP, 1965), vol. 1, p. 35, for the passage cited and esp. pp. 34–38, 110–18, for the general argument.

6. Bastide, *The African Religions*, p. 72.

7. See esp. Herbert G. Gutman, *The Black Family in Slavery and Freedom, 1750–1925* (New York: Pantheon 1976).

8. I define marriage, following Herskovits, as "socially sanctioned mating entered into with the assumption of permanency" (with "permanency" understood as a relative concept defined by each culture); Melville J. Herskovits, *Man and His Works* (New York, 1948), p. 296, cited in Emílio Willems, *Latin American Culture: An Anthropological Synthesis* (New York: Harper, 1975), p. 52.

9. Data from a sample of 1,975 slaves in Robert W. Slenes, "Escravidão e Família: Padrões de Casamento e Estabilidade Familiar numa Comunidade Escrava (Campinas, Século XIX)," *Estudos Econômicos* 17, no. 2 (May–August 1987): 217–27, and "Slave Family Formation in the Context of Creolization and Crop Change: Campinas, São Paulo, 1776–1872," paper presented at the Conference on Cultivation and Culture: Labor and the Shaping of Slave Life in the Americas, University of Maryland at College Park, April 1989. Data from local Campinas censuses for 1801 and 1829, reported on in the latter paper, are similar.

10. See, in chronological order, Robert W. Slenes, "The Demography and Economics of Brazilian Slavery: 1850–1888," Ph.D. dissertation, Stanford University, 1976,

chap. 9; Richard Graham, "Slave Families on a Rural Estate in Colonial Brazil, *Journal of Social History* 9, no. 3 (1976): 382–401; Iraci del Negro da Costa and Francisco Vidal Luna, "Vila Rica: Nota sobre Casamentos de Escravos (1727–1826)," *Africa* (Centro de Estudos Africanos, Universidade de São Paulo), no. 4 (1981): 105–9; Iraci del Negro da Costa and Horacio Gutiérrez, "Nota sobre Cassamentos de Escravos em São Paulo e no Paraná (1830)," *História: Questões e Debates* 5, no. 9, (December 1984): 313–21; Stuart B. Schwartz, *Sugar Plantations in the Formation of Brazilian Society: Bahia, 1550–1835* (Cambridge: Cambridge University Press, 1985), chaps. 13, 14; João Luís R. Fragoso and Manolo G. Florentino, "Marcelino, Filho de Inocência Crioula, Neto de Joana Cabinda: Um Estudo sobre Famílias Escravas em Paraíba do Sul (1835–1872)," *Estudos Econômicos* 17, no. 2 (May–August 1987): 151–73; Alida C. Metcalf, "Vida Familiar dos Escravos em São Paulo no Século Dezoito: O Caso de Santana de Parnaíba," ibid.: 229–43; Iraci del Nero da Costa, Robert W. Slenes, and Stuart B. Schwartz, "A Família Escrava em Lorena (1801)," ibid.: 245–95; Sílvia Hunold Lara, *Campos da Violência: Escravos e Senhores na Capitania do Rio de Janeiro, 1750–1808* (Rio de Janeiro: Paz e Terra, 1988), pp. 220–30; Horacio Gutiérrez, "Crioulos e Africanos no Paraná, 1798–1830," *Revista Brasileira de História* 8, no. 16 (March–August 1988): 161–88; Kátia de Queirós Mattoso, "O Filho da Escrava (em Torno da Lei do Ventre Livre)," ibid.: 37–56; José Flávio Motta, "A Família Escrava e a Penetração do Café em Bananal, 1801–1829," *Revista Brasileira de Estudos de População* 5, no. 1 (January–July, 1988): 71–101, and "Família Escrava: Uma Incursão pela Historiografia," *História: Questões e Debates* 9, no. 16 (July 1988): 104–59; Gilberto Guerzoni Filho and Luiz Roberto Netto, "Minas Gerais: Indices de Casamento da População Livre e Escrava na Comarca do Rio das Mortes," *Estudos Econômicos* 18, no. 3 (September–December 1988): 497–508; Ida Lewkowicz, "Hernança e Relações Familiares: Os Pretos Forros nas Minas Gerais do Século XVIII," *Revista Brasileira de História* 9, no. 17 (September 1988–February 1989): 101–14. See also various studies in Associação Brasileira de Estudos Populacionais [ABEP], *Anais do VI Econtro Nacional de Estudos Populacionais (Olinda, Pernambuco, 16–20 de Outubro,* 4 vols. (Belo Horizonte: ABEP, 1988), vol. 3, esp. Francisco Vidal Luna, "Observações sobre Casamento de Escravos em São Paulo (1825)," pp. 215–33. Several papers on the question were presented at the Conference on the Population History of Latin America, Ouro Preto, Brazil, July 2–6, 1989.

11. See Slenes, "The Demography," p. 420, for the percentage of married slaves by province.

12. According to provincial censuses circa 1850 and the slave matricula of 1872–73, slave marriage rates in the provinces of Rio de Janeiro and São Paulo were higher in sugar and coffee plantation areas than in non–plantation zones. Nonetheless, the percentage of married slaves was considerably greater in the plantation counties of São Paulo than in those of Rio de Janeiro (even when one compares the São Paulo and Rio sections of the Paraíba Valley), with the highest proportions being found in central-western São Paulo. Since the percentage of married free blacks (the census categories of "blacks" and "mulattoes") was also much higher in São Paulo than in Rio, it seems more likely that the data represent contrasting institutional histories—that is, differential access to church rituals on the part of lower-class persons, slave or free—rather than different family patterns. For more discussion of this question, see Slenes, "The Demography," pp. 445–58.

13. The consistency of the information in the various sources is so striking that the data, as a whole, could not be the result of an effort to deceive or to create and maintain on paper families which had no basis in reality. See Slenes, "Slave Family Formation."

14. See Slenes, "Slave Family Formation," table 2, for data on forty-eight marriages (involving slave mothers aged fifteen to forty-four) still existing in 1872–73, in a sample of 1,163 slaves from the matrícula in Campinas. For the fourteen married mothers aged thirty-five to forty-four, the median length of marriage was sixteen years and eight months.

15. For instance, in Campinas in 1872–73, in holdings with fewer than ten slaves, only 26 percent of women over fifteen and 37 percent of mothers (with children under fifteen) were ever married; furthermore, only 27 percent of children aged one to nine lived with both parents or one widowed parent. Slenes, "Escravidão e Família," 225, 227. (The data on marriage reflect, in the first instance, the small "pool" of potential mates within these holdings and the masters' virtual prohibition of church marriages between slaves of different owners; from what is known about the relative instability of small holdings, however, one suspects that slaves in these properties also had more difficulty maintaining consensual unions across ownership boundaries than bondspeople on the plantations.)

16. Stuart B. Schwartz, "Patterns of Slaveholding in the Americas: New Evidence from Brazil," *American Historical Review* 87, no. 1 (February 1982): 313–33, and Francisco Vidal Luna and Iraci del Nero da Costa, "Posse de Escravos em São Paulo no Início do Século XIX," *Estudos Econômicos* 13, no. 1 (January–April 1983): 211–21.

17. Slenes, "Escravidão e Família," 225.

18. I exclude from the category of polygynous unions serial monogamous relationships, or concomitant unions which are not entered into "with the assumption of permanency." (See Herskovits's definition of marriage in n. 8.)

19. Robert K. Merton, *Social Theory and Social Structure*, 2d. ed. (New York: Free Press, 1968), chaps. 6, 7; Talcott Parsons et al., *Family Socialization and Interaction Process* (New York, 1955); Marshall B. Clinard and Robert F. Meier, *Sociology of Deviant Behavior* (New York: Holt, Rinehart and Winston, n.d.), chap. 3 (for a review of sociological theories of deviance). Perhaps indicative of the influence of American functionalism on Brazilian sociology is the success of the textbook by F. A. de Miranda Rosa, *Pathologia Social: Uma Introdução ao Estudo da Desorganização Social*, 5th ed. (Rio de Janeiro: Zahar, 1980), first published in 1966.

20. See Roger Bastide and Florestan Fernandes, "O Preconceito Racial em São Paulo," *Publicações do Instituto de Adminstração* [of the University of São Paulo], no. 118 (April 1951), pp. 44–45 (n. 2); in this joint proposal for research, the authors cite studies on American blacks by E. Franklin Frazier *(The Negro Family in the United States)*, Gunnar Myrdal (*An American Dilemma*), and Horace Cayton and St. Clair Drake (*Black Metropolis*), among others.

21. See Abram Kardiner and Lionel Ovesey, *The Mark of Oppression: Explorations in the Personality of the American Negro*, 2d ed. (New York: World, 1962), esp. pp. 44, 46, 359–61. Bastide, who published the original French version of *The African Religions* in 1960, was aware of Kardiner's work on "basic personality" (Bastide, *The African Religions*, pp. 8, 357, 389) but does not cite this book, first published in 1951. See also Daniel Patrick Moynihan, *The Negro Family: The Case for National Action* (Washington, D.C.: Office of Policy Planning and Research, United States Department of Labor, March 1965), republished in Lee Rainwater and William L. Yancey, *The Moynihan Report and the Politics of Controversy* (Cambridge: MIT Press, 1967), pp. 39–124. It should be noted that Fernandes's concept of anomie seems closer to Durkheim's than to Merton's, in that it points to broader functional and structural factors as causes of

deviance, even in situations of apparent social equilibrium rather than simply to the inability of individuals to achieve culturally prescribed goals by culturally accepted means. See Florestan Fernandes, *Esaios de Sociologia Geral e Aplicada*, 2d ed. (São Paulo: Livraria Pioneira Editora, 1971), pp. 143–44. In part because of this, Fernandes's book *A Integração do Negro na Sociedade de Classes* has a much stronger tone of social criticism than Moynihan's work.

22. See Bastide, *The African Religions*, p. 72, for a discussion of the effects of acculturation on slave egos and superegos. My critique of the accounts of nineteenth–century white observers in Brazil is similar to Gutman's examination of sources of this type in the United States, although the specific bibliography on Brazil has led me to use somewhat different categories of analysis. See Gutman, *The Black Family*, pp. 293–303. See also Barbara Bush, *Slave Women in Caribbean Society, 1650–1838* (Bloomington: Indiana University Press, 1990), chap. 2 ("The Eye of the Beholder"), which came to my attention after this chapter, including this particular line in the text, was written.

23. Júlio Ribeiro, *A Carne* (Rio de Janeiro: Edições de Ouro, n.d.), pp. 101, 231. In the nineteenth century the word *boçal* was commonly applied to newly arrived Africans, but here it is used to refer to a Brazilian–born slave.

24. Jochann Jacob Von Tschudi, *Reisen durch Südamerika* (Leipzig: F. A. Brockhaus, 1867), vol. 3, pp. 133–34.

25. Agostinho Marques Perdigão Malheiro, *A Escravidão no Brasil: Ensaio Histórico, Juridico, Social* (Petrópolis: Editora Vozes, 1976), vol. 2, p. 129.

26. Louis Couty, *L'Esclavage au Brésil* (Paris: Librairie de Guillaumin, 1881), pp. 74–75.

27. Johann Moritz Rugendas, *Malerische Reise in Brasilien* (Paris: Engelmann, 1835), p. 11.

28. Jean Baptiste Debret, *Voyage Pittoresque et Historique au Brésil, ou Sejour d'un Artiste Français au Brésil depuis 1816 jusq' en 1831 Inclusivement* (Paris: Firmin Didot Frères, 1834–1839), vol. 2, p. 84.

29. Ibid., vol. 3, p. 149.

30. George Gardner, *Travels in the Interior of Brazil, Principally through the Northern Provinces and the Gold and Diamond Districts during the Years 1836–1841* (Boston: Milford House, 1973), p. 14.

31. C. F. Van Delden Laërne, *Brazil and Java: Report on Coffee Culture in America, Asia and Africa* (London and The Hague: W. H. Allen/M. Nijhoff, 1885), pp. 253–54.

32. Couty, *L'Esclavage*, p. 68.

33. See Stein, *Vassouras*, p. 155; Bastide, *The African Religions*, p. 61; Fernandes, *A Integração do Negro*, vol. 1, p. 36. Couty's belief that slave men mistreated their wives and that black mothers did not provide proper care for their children probably reflected prevailing European stereotypes regarding African women; see Bush, *Slave Women*, pp. 20, 103, for a discussion of these stereotypes within the Caribbean context.

34. See, for example, Edward Shorter, "Sexual Change and Illegitimacy: The European Experience," in Robert Bezucha, ed., *Modern European Social History* (Lexington, Mass., 1972), pp. 231–69; Edward Shorter, John Knodel, and Etienne Van de Walle, "The Decline of Non-Marital Fertility in Europe, 1880–1940," *Population Studies 25*, no. 3 (November 1971): 375–93; and Peter Laslett, "Introduction to the History of the Family," in Laslett, ed., *Household and Family in Past Time* (Cambridge: Cambridge University Press, 1972), pp. 16–17. On the Iberian peninsula, see Antônio Cândido, "The Brazilian Family," in T. Lynn Smith and Alexander Merchant, eds., *Brazil: Portrait of*

Half a Continent (New York, 1951), pp. 300–301, and Willems, *Latin American Culture,* pp. 52–53. According to Willems (p. 53), in Portugal and in Spain "the consensual union . . . was a deep–rooted cultural pattern rather than a deviation; it was certainly transplanted to America, where it found a receptive environment, particularly among the peasantry and the rural laborers."

35. Joaquim Manoel de Macedo, *As Vítimas-Algozes: Quadros da Escravidão* (Rio de Janeiro: Typographia Perseverança, 1869), citations respectively from vol. 2, pp. 60, 91, 115, 21, 273.

36. Charles Ribeyrolles, *Brasil Pitoresco: História-Descrições-Viagens-Instituições-Colonização* (Rio de Janeiro: Typographia National, 1859), vol. 3, pp. 47–48 (my translation is from the French text in this French-Portuguese edition); Enrico Hillyer Giglioli, *Viaggio Intorno al Globo della Pirocorvetta Italiana Magenta negli Anni 1865–66–67–68 Sotto il Comando del Capitano di Fregata V. F. Arminjon. Relazione Descrittiva e Scientifica . . .* (Milan: V. Maisner, 1875), p. 59.

37. Ribeyrolles, *Brasil Pitoresco,* vol. 3, pp. 40–41.

38. See the detailed data on animals registered in probate inventories in the county of Paraíba do Sul in João Luis Ribeiro Fragoso, "Sistemas Agrários em Paraíba do Sul (1850–1920)—um Estudo de Relações não Capitalistas de Produção," master's thesis, Universidade Federal do Rio de Janeiro, 1983, pp. 56, 58.

39. João Cardoso de Menezes e Souza, *Theses sobre Colonização do Brasil . . . Relatorio Apresentado ao Ministerio da Agricultura, Commercio e Obras Publicas em 1875* (Rio de Janeiro, 1875), pp. 166, 169–70.

40. Isaac Joseph, Philippe Fritsch, and Alain Battegay, *Disciplines à Domicile: l'Edification de la Famille,* Thematic Issue of *Recherches,* no. 28 (November 1977); Jacques Donzelot, *La Police des Familles* (Paris: Les Editions de Minuit, 1977).

41. See the suggestive study by Jurandir Freire Costa, *Ordem Médica e Norma Familiar* (Rio de Janeiro: Graal, 1979).

42. Samuel Smiles, *Economia Domestica Moral ou a Felicidade e a Independencia pelo Trabalho e pela Economia,* trans. Jacintho Cardoso da Silva (Rio de Janeiro: B. L. Garnier, 1880), p. 19 (my translation from the Portuguese). Two other books by Smiles were advertised by Garnier in this work, with no indication of date of publication: *O Caracter* and *O Poder da Vontade, ou Caracter, Comportamento e Perseverança,* 2d ed.

43. Sidney Chalhoub, *Trabalho, Lar e Botequim: O Cotidiano dos Trabalhadores no Rio de Janeiro da "Belle Époque"* (São Paulo: Brasiliense, 1986), pp. 39–40; Célia Maria Marinho de Azevedo, *Onda Negra, Medo Branco: O Negro no Imaginário das Elites—Século XIX* (Rio de Janeiro: Paz e Terra, 1987), esp. chaps. 2 and 4; Lília Moritz Schwarcz, *Retrato em Branco e Negro: Jornais, Escravos e Cidadãos em São Paulo no Final do Século XIX* (São Paulo: Companhia das Letras, 1987), pp. 163ff., 224–26, 232–40.

44. Robert W. Slenes, "Na Senzala, uma Flor: 'As Esperanças e as Recordações' na Formação da Família Escrava," article in progress.

45. Tschudi, *Reisen,* vol. 3, p. 133.

46. Evidence presented in Slenes, "Na Senzala, uma Flor."

47. On these aspects of architecture in West–Central Africa, see John Vlach, *The Afro-American Tradition in Decorative Arts* (Cleveland: Cleveland Museum of Art, 1978), pp. 124–25, 135; Julius F. Glück, "African Architecture," in *The Many Faces of Primitive Art: A Critical Anthology,* ed. Douglas Frasier (Englewood Cliffs: Prentice-Hall, 1966), p. 225; Luiz Figueira, *Africa Bantú Raças e Tribos de Angola* (Lisbon: Oficinas Fernandes, 1938), pp. 135–36. For a summary of data on the origins of Africans imported

into Brazil's center-south region (Rio de Janeiro, São Paulo, and Minas Gerais), see Mary Karasch, *Slave Life in Rio de Janeiro, 1808–1850* (Princeton: Princeton University Press, 1987), pp. 3–28.

48. Ina von Binzer, *Os Meus Romanos: Alegrias e Tristezas de uma Educadora Alemã no Brasil,* trans. Alice Rossi and Luisita da Gama Cerqueira (São Paulo: Editora Paz e Terra, 1980), pp. 50–51. The plantation visited by Binzer probably was in the Rio de Janeiro section of the Paraíba Valley, near the border with São Paulo (see the preface by Paulo Duarte in ibid., p. 15). An 1850 census showed that 50 percent of all slaves in Rio province were Africans; in the major coffee counties of the Paraíba Valley, the proportion was 70 percent or higher. Similar figures are available for the São Paulo plantation counties, Bananal (78 percent) and Campinas (70 percent), in 1829; in the latter county, where the data can be broken down by age group, Africans accounted for 80 percent of all bondpeople over age fifteen. Sources: *Archivo Estatistico da Provincia do Rio de Janeiro: Primeira Publicação* (Niterói, 1851), table C, annexed to Rio de Janeiro [Province], *Relatório [of the President of the Province],* presented May 5, 1851 (Rio de Janeiro, n.d.); Motta, "A Família Escrava," pp. 82, 97 (n. 18); Slenes, work in progress on the 1829 census manuscripts from Campinas deposited in the Arquivo Publico do Estado de São Paulo, Box 27–27.

49. See Bush, *Slave Women,* p. 98, on gender roles with respect to cooking in Africa and among slaves in the British Caribbean. Also see the suggestive comments by Charles Joyner, *Down by the Riverside: A South Carolina Slave Community* (Urbana: University of Illinois Press, 1984), pp. 91, 106, on the cultural significance for North American slaves of "the choice of particular foods and particular means of preparation."

50. Binzer, *Os Meus Romanos,* p. 50.

51. Stein, *Vassouras,* pp. 170–71, 181.

8

"SUFFER WITH THEM TILL DEATH"
SLAVE WOMEN AND THEIR CHILDREN IN NINETEENTH-CENTURY AMERICA

Wilma King

Slave parents had unusually heavy responsibilities. They had to ensure that they survived and, at the same time, that their children survived. All too often, these responsibilities fell disproportionately upon slave mothers, who provided the initial nurturing and were the basic anchors for the young children. Mothers played major roles in helping their children adjust to work, understand plantation authority, and meet the tragedies and traumas of slavery. This chapter explores the ways slave mothers filled their roles, and the enduring bonds they formed with their children under the slave system.

Motherhood among African-American slave women had two unique characteristics. First, while many women in Africa reared children with little help from the fathers in line with an accepted pattern of matrilineal or matrifocal families, many slave women in America were forced into parenting without spouses owing to imbalances in the sex ratio on numerous plantations and the slaveholders' propensity to sell men separately. In Africa, relatives were available to assist in child rearing, whereas in America, slave women were often separated from their families and friends. Second, American slaveholders viewed motherhood as an asset, and they encouraged reproduction for pecuniary reasons alone. In 1819 Thomas Jefferson was quite clear when he wrote, "I consider the labor of a breeding woman as no object, and that a child raised every 2 years is of more profit than the crop of the best laboring man." Jefferson instructed his plantation manager to impress upon the overseers that "it is not their labor, but their increase which is the first consideration with us." Little more than a year later, Jefferson again addressed his manager. "I consider a woman who brings a child every two years as more profitable than the best man on the farm," he wrote to John W. Eppes; "what she produces is an addition to capital."

The labor of male slaves, however, disappeared "in mere consumption." While slave mothers regarded their offspring as persons, slaveholders like Jefferson saw them primarily as chattel with profit-making potential. Slave women, unlike mothers in Africa, were caught in a mire of profit making in which their children were also held fast.[1]

By the early nineteenth century when direct importation of slaves from Africa ceased, natural reproduction among American slaves was on the rise. The data about reproduction raises important questions. What did the slave woman have to say about giving birth? What could her child expect from life? What could she do to shape the child's future? Natalie Shainess argues in her studies of childbirth and the psychological experience of labor that an expectant mother's attitudes about her femininity, her values, and her relationship with the unborn child's father determine how she views pregnancy. Slave women, unable to control their fertility or to make necessary decisions about their own bodies, had little to say about femininity, values, or what would eventually happen to their children.[2]

Moreover, slave women often became pregnant through forced cohabitation and molestation by white men. While proslavery critics charged abolitionists with using stories of sexual exploitation to politicize their cause, African-American slaves passed down these accounts from one generation to another as the truth. In any case, it was unrealistic for slave women to expect any consideration from the white men who impregnated them. It was possible, however, for the slave mother to enjoy attention from the slave father if both belonged to the same owner and lived together or if they belonged to different owners but were partners in "abroad" marriages.[3]

The pregnant slave woman received no prenatal care, endangering the lives of the expectant mother and her unborn child. Generally ignorant about their bodily functions and needs during gestation, slave women did not own their persons; nor did they have the resources to assure a healthy pregnancy or safe delivery. Besides, heavy work interfered with the blood supply to the placenta, which subsequently jeopardized the health of the fetus. The onus of responsibility for overworking pregnant women rested with slaveowners, who extracted physical labor from the pregnant and nonpregnant alike. Some slaveowners acknowledged the connection between heavy physical labor and low birth weight, but they were not aware of the relation to infant mortality.[4]

Although slave women were unaware of medical reasons for poor health and miscarriages, they knew that something was awry. "I an' never been safe in de family way," Josephine Bacchus, an ex-slave from South Carolina, told federal interviewers. She attributed her inability to have a "nine month child" to the lack of "good attention" during slavery. In the late 1830s slave women on the Georgia plantation owned by Pierce Mease Butler told their pitiful stories of aborted fetuses, difficult births, and infant deaths to his wife, Frances Anne Kemble, and asked her to help modify their tasks. These women were essentially correct in believing that a link existed between heavy work and the health of an unborn child, and such work, we now believe, is probably most detrimental during the earlier stages of gestation.[5]

Childbirth in antebellum America was frightening and dangerous no matter what the expectant mother's race or class, but two changes occurred in the nineteenth-century to ease the anxieties of birth. First, while midwives, female relatives, or friends ordinarily delivered slave children, if complications arose beyond the ken of those present, a doctor was called. In the larger society, midwives were slowly being replaced by male doctors. Second, men shared in the birth of their children. The presence of doctors and husbands provided safer deliveries and emotional support. White women were the primary beneficiaries, however, since slave women saw physicians only when emergencies occurred. Moreover, abroad marriages, work schedules, and other separations generally precluded the presence of slave fathers. There is an extant account of a slave father who participated in the birth of his children, but this occurred under adverse and unusual conditions. The mother, a runaway living in a cave, bore three children, and her husband "waited on her with each child." Most slave mothers delivered their children with the assistance and solace of other slave women.[6]

The legal status of slave mothers determined the condition of their children. Slave mothers were forced to relegate their children to a life of bondage, since slavery in the United States was an inherited condition. Children belonged to slaveowners for life, even if their mothers became free after giving birth.

The size of a slave family varied. Slave mothers generally gave birth about every two years and nursed each child. Although these mothers were probably unaware of it, frequent and systematic breast-feeding renders a mother infertile for a year or more. Of course, if the infant did not survive, the woman was likely to become pregnant sooner owing to the absence of lactation.[7]

Slave children, through no fault of their mothers, entered the world with meager chances of survival. The historian John Blassingame asserts that they were neglected, were fed irregularly, and suffered from a variety of ills. "Treated by densely ignorant mothers or little more enlightened planters," he writes, "they died in droves." The deaths of slave children often had little to do with how or when they were fed, or with medical treatment. What slave mothers and children ate was of greater importance. The majority of slave mothers breast-fed their children; however, poor prenatal and postnatal diets assured a milk supply devoid of the nutrients necessary to foster life and prevent diseases.[8]

Slave mothers could not control the physical conditions that fostered a high incidence of mortality and morbidity among their children. They were mere conduits through which slaveholders received a steady labor supply. Even a cursory look at the medical research on slaves shows how limited mothers were in protecting themselves and their children. Richard Steckel, for example, answers questions about the health of slaves using height records acquired from 18,562 manifests kept by captains of American ships engaged in the coastal and interregional slave trade, as well as mortality data in plantation records and growth curves from eighteenth-, nineteenth-, and twentieth-century populations. The manifests for 1820 to 1860 contained information about more than 50,000 slaves. Steckel concludes that the quality of life for slave children was exceedingly poor. American slaves in early childhood were small compared with slaves in the Caribbean and with selected American and European populations in the eighteenth and nineteenth centuries. Furthermore, even when compared with children in modern developing countries, American slave children were smaller. Low birth weights are connected to the general poor health of women before delivery, prenatal dietary deficiency, infected amniotic fluids, and heavy work.[9]

Infant mortality rates were high and communicable diseases were color blind in antebellum America. Slaveowners and slaves lived with sickness and death. Planter diaries and the records of overseers teem with notations of illness and death. Fevers, intestinal worms, measles, whooping cough, and other maladies took their toll. Slaves faced the additional life-threatening disease of sickle-cell anemia, an incurable hereditary blood disorder. At the end of 1859 David Gavin of South Carolina noted succinctly: "Celia's child died about four months[—] died saturday the 12. This is two Negroes and three horses I have lost this year." The deaths, whether animal or human, translated into financial losses for Gavin, the slaveholder, whereas Celia experienced emotional and personal loss.[10]

Whereas daily records of plantations appear callous, slaveowners' diaries often show more consideration for the dead and bereaved. In 1848 A. C. Griffin commiserated about the death of a white neighbor's child: "I hope she bears it with fortitude." He added, "It is very seldom, a family as large as hers can be raised." Mothers, white and black, came to expect that some of their children would not live to maturity. This expectation was even more real for slave mothers. Their children died at rates twice that of their white cohorts. Kenneth and Virginia Kiple found that 51 percent of the deaths among the black population in seven slaveholding states in 1849–50 occurred among children nine years of age and under. Slave children in that age group constituted 31 percent of the sample. These statistics suggest that slave mothers needed an extraordinary amount of fortitude to adjust to the large number of deaths among their children.[11]

The Kiples admit that slave children nine years of age and under fell into an "actuarially perilous category" because of deaths related to several ailments, including tetanus, teething, and lockjaw. The chance that these children would die from these ailments was four times greater than for their white contemporaries. If slave children survived their early years and entered the labor force at ten years of age or older, their health improved owing to an increase in food allowances. Until that time, slave mothers grappled with illnesses and deaths.[12]

Slaveowners were sometimes interested in the illness and death of slave children for reasons that had nothing to do with pecuniary matters. When Lucinda, a slave belonging to Tennessee planter John Houston Bills, gave birth to her third stillborn child in 1860, he remarked that "the poor woman is much distressed." It is clear that he was concerned about the grieving mother. By contrast, when the Louisiana slave Susan's "fine mulatto boy" died, their owner's wife, Tryphena Blanche Holder Fox, charged the slave mother with neglect. The baby caught a cold and "died from the effect of it" while in Fox's arms. She commiserated, "I feel badly about its death for it was a pretty baby." To be sure, her sentiments were more deep-seated: "I took a fancy to it on account of it being near the age mine would have been." Fox mourned the death of her own infant. Rather than offer consolation, she implied that Susan was neglectful and callous. The deaths of their children did not change the mistress-maid relationship, since the women inhabited different spheres, separated by race and class. Common experiences did not bring them together.[13]

Of the many causes of death among young slaves, smothering or overlaying has received an unusual amount of attention. These deaths led to speculations that slave mothers deliberately killed their children as an act of resistance. Additionally, it was commonly assumed in antebellum America that careless, "wearied" mothers were responsible for these deaths. Victims of "suffocation," generally at ages between two weeks and one year, these infants died without obvious signs of illness during the coldest months of the year. When explaining the death of her child, Tabby Abby, a former slave in Tunica, Mississippi, told federal interviewers in the 1930s that she fell asleep while breast-feeding her only child and "rolled over him and smothered him to death." Abby, like many slave mothers, held herself liable and suffered a needless ordeal. Historian Todd Savitt compared contemporary infant mortality rates with antebellum records of suffocation and found striking similarities. He has suggested that these deaths were caused by sudden infant death syndrome (SIDS) rather than suffocation. Although there is no way of knowing if any of the deaths were deliberate, Savitt's explanation is plausible, since deaths from "suffocation" continued after slavery ended, when reasons for resistance were no longer present. Moreover, a high incidence of deaths among black infants continues into our own time, even though the working conditions of many black mothers have changed. That further suggests that the deaths were not caused by tired, careless women overlaying their children.[14]

In actuality, poor prenatal care and diets rich in caloric content but inadequate in nutrients, combined with heavy physical work, were overriding factors in low birth weights and the resulting high infant mortality rates. Frances Kemble, an astute observer of conditions among slave women on her husband's plantation in 1838–39, noted, "I think the number [of children] they bear as compared with the number they rear a fair gauge of the effect of the system on their health and that of their offspring."[15]

Slave mothers adapted to the inevitable illnesses and deaths of their children. Their responses ran the full gamut. Many mothers consoled themselves through religion. They saw death as the will of God, who freed the deceased from a life of drudgery. After the death of her child, however, Tabby Abby said, "I like to went crazy for a long time atta dat." Some slave mothers were visibly shaken by the deaths. Ex-slave Fannie Moore described her mother's reaction when her younger brother died on the South Carolina plantation where they lived. Fannie cared for her sick brother during the day except when her grandmother could get away "from the white folks' kitchen." When Fannie's mother returned from the field one night, she learned that the boy had died. "Poor mammy she kneel by the bed and cry her heart out," Fannie said. Later, her mother was at work when her brother's body was carried in a pine box to the cemetery. Fannie observed from a distance as her mother "just plow and cry as she watch 'em put George in de ground."[16]

Slave mothers had a duty to preserve life, yet they received only a short reprieve for neonatal care before going back to work. Some owners allowed one month off and then assigned light work. Others were less considerate. The demand for the labor of slave mothers impeded bonding and child care. Fanny, one of nearly thirty slaves belonging to an Alabama planter, was lying in, according to the plantation records, in early August 1844; by August 29, she was back at her duties. Another slave, Charity, delivered a child on September 4, 1844, and was back at work one month later. Both women gave birth during harvest, when there was a great need for hands. The amount of cotton they picked did not match that of the other women, perhaps because they left the field regularly to feed their infants or were not physically able to resume a full work load so soon after giving birth.[17]

While slavery determined the amount of time families could spend together, slave mothers worked continually at shaping the quality of that time. No doubt the age-old spiritual "Nobody Knows the Trouble I've Seen" had meaning for both mothers and children. Slave women were often too overburdened by the duties of laborer, wife, and mother to indulge their children, yet they never stopped trying to foster positive relationships with them. Booker T. Washington's mother was too busy "to give attention to the training of her children during the day"; therefore she "snatched" a few minutes before and after work to care for him and his siblings. As a young child in Maryland, Frederick Douglass never saw his mother "by the light of day" because of the distance between where she worked and where he lived. Her visits at night were sporadic and brief because she always came after work and left early the next day. Both mothers exerted extra effort for the well-being of their children, who remembered them and their sacrifices.[18]

While mothers worked, someone else usually looked after their children. Child care sometimes rested in the hands of slaves who were either too infirm, too old, or too young to work elsewhere. A woman "with a halt in her step" cared for the children on the White Hill plantation in Prince County, Virginia, while Friday, an aged slave belonging to David Gavin of the Colleton District in South Carolina, was to "notice the yard and the little Negroes" in 1856. Slaveholders provided nurseries on large plantations such as the Weston place in East Feliciana Parish, Louisiana, where some thirty babies were cared for by Granny, a sixty-year-old slave woman, and several older girls. One Florida plantation had forty-two children to be cared for while their mothers worked; an elderly man and woman, with the assistance of youngsters, cared for the children. Needless to say, in situations where scores of children were to be cared for, help was often inadequate and attention wanting.[19] On plantations without nurseries, other arrangements had to be made for child care. In the mid-1830s, Kentucky slave Henry Bibb and his wife, Melinda, left their young daughter with Mrs. Gatewood, the slaveowner's wife, who physically abused the child while they worked. Children sometimes accompanied their parents to the fields. Those too small to keep up were strapped to their mothers' backs or left on pallets at the end of the rows, near fences, and under trees away from the sun. Mothers returned regularly to suckle their children and move them into the shade.[20]

An alternative to carrying children to work, which yielded mixed results, was to leave them in the care of older children, who occasionally ignored the crying, fretting babies. Sometimes the caregivers were engulfed in their own play and forgot their charges. Mothers periodically returned to find their small children unattended, in the sun, covered with flies, or, even worse, with ant or mosquito bites. In their naiveté young nurses sometimes placed themselves and the babies in danger. Louisa Jones, a former slave from Petersburg, Virginia, recalled caring for babies and using meat skin tied to a string around their neck as a pacifier. The string holding the meat could have easily become entangled about the child's neck with disastrous results. On the other hand, Jones, who was only ten years old when slavery ended, used the string to retrieve the meat from the child's throat to prevent choking. The number of youngsters who were subjected to unintentional injuries by other children in their parents' absence remains unknown. Despite the dangers involved, slave mothers depended upon older children for help and made it clear that by working together they could escape slavery's worst features. Even if slave mothers did not explain the intricacies of slavery, children were not totally oblivious, for they too lived within its confines. Slave children were socialized to help each other for the common good, and they became self-sufficient and responsive to the needs of others.[21]

Parents, often mothers alone, guided youngsters through the muddle of slavery. Their primary objective was to protect their children and others from harm. In a letter from a California gold field in 1853, the slave Prine Woodfin advised his wife to "rais your children up rite," because she had total responsibility for their well-being during his absence. He admonished her to "learn them to be Smart and decent and alow them to Sauce no person." The term "Smart" in this context referred not to education but to working conscientiously. Hardworking, decent, courteous children were not likely to offend anyone; nor would they bring retribution upon their mother.[22]

Slave parents expected obedience from their children, and it is not surprising that they have been portrayed as harsh disciplinarians. The complexities of slavery were confusing when children found themselves in a tug-of-war between plantation authority and parental influence. The experience of a North Carolina slave boy and an Oklahoma slave girl illustrates the point. In the first case, Harriet Jacobs witnessed her father and their mistress call William, her brother, simultaneously. Bewildered, the boy hesitated. He then responded to the mistress. Angered by the choice, the elder Jacobs scolded the boy, "You are my child and when I call you, you should come immediately, if you have to pass through fire and water." In the second case, a Cherokee freedwoman was called Sarah as a child by her mother, while their mistress called her Annie. If the girl answered to Annie, her mother punished her; if she failed to respond to Annie, the mistress punished her. Sometimes she refused to answer to either name. Recalling the struggle between her mother and mistress, Sarah said, "that made me hate both of them."[23]

William and Sarah must have wondered about their parents' attitude. The underlying motive for their "harshness" was to demand faithfulness, dependability, and family unity. Because the lives of slave women and their children converged at so many points, the actions of one affected the others. To know when to speak and what to say were key lessons for the survival of a slave family. Children might unwittingly betray family plans or secrets and incur punishment from owners. Mothers demanded allegiance and further protected their families by teaching children not to talk too much. An axiom within the slave family which governed their behavior was "children are to be seen and not heard." Slave mothers could not tolerate "enemies" within their own families.[24]

Children learned at an early age to adopt a demeanor that masked their true feelings. The mask, a protective device, became part of their countenance. During the Civil War, Mary Chesnut commented about the impervious expressions of the household servants in Charleston, South Carolina, who appeared "proudly indifferent" to the events around them. Slaves played these roles so perfectly that whites talked freely in their presence. They either believed slaves did not understand the nature of the conversations or dismissed their presence as inconsequential. "Are they stolidly stupid," Chesnut asked, "or wiser than we are, silent and strong, biding their time?" Slaves were not stupid, and Chesnut was not entirely fooled by their demeanor. Their masks were protective covering. One former slave remarked, "Got one mind for the boss to see; got another for what I know is me." Slaves passed this tactic for deception along from one generation to another.[25]

Of equal importance to the same objective among the slaves was learning how to perform tasks satisfactorily. At early ages children supplemented the adult labor force, and they eventually replaced workers as they both grew older. The occupation of a parent played a large part in determining the kind of work a child performed. Most slaves were field hands whose children learned their jobs as they worked together on the plantation. On large plantations, young children worked in groups, commonly called the "trash gang," along with pregnant women and aged slaves. On smaller agricultural holdings, patterns differed. Nevertheless, the value of the labor of women and children in the field is not to be underestimated. In 1859 North Carolina slaveholder Alonzo Mial produced "93 bales of cotton averaging 400 lbs[,] bout 3500 lbs of corn[,] 100 bushels of peas," and potatoes with fourteen hands, mostly women and children. The children were too small and young to be counted as full hands.[26]

While slaveowners made no distinctions among field hands based on gender, the same was not true with skilled jobs. Boys became smiths, masons, and wrights, but girls did not have the opportunity to learn craft techniques. The argument that craft work was too heavy was invalid, because women plowed, felled trees, and split rails. It is more likely that childbearing was chiefly responsible for barring slave women from artisan work because it interrupted work which could not be completed as easily by a substitute as picking cotton or pulling corn. Were slaveowners more concerned about reproduction or production? "The extent to which a slaveowner consciously emphasized one or the other," Deborah Gray White has noted, "ultimately depended on his need." Jacqueline Jones argued that slaveowners did not encourage women to gain craft skills because they deemed work performed during the winter (i.e., spinning, weaving) "too important to permit protracted absences from their quarters" if, as skilled workers, females were hired out the same as male artisans and mechanics. The decision not to allow women into the craft skills meant that slaveowners did not have interruptions with either their crafts (due to childbearing) or winter chores (due to crafts). Thus slave mothers and their daughters had fewer opportunities for autonomy. They were unable to travel away from the plantation, hire their own time, or earn money through skilled extra work which might be used to purchase additional goods for their own comfort or to buy their freedom.[27]

Skilled female slaves worked at domestic or housewifery chores such as cooking, washing, and sewing. Pregnant or lactating cooks, washerwomen, or seamstresses continued with their work as usual. If women needed help with housekeeping chores, cooking, laundering, or child care, it came far more readily from children than from adult males. By the antebellum period most slaves were American born and had watched their mothers juggle work loads and rear children. Regardless of the kind of work young slaves performed, mothers taught them the value of cooperating with each other. They learned to help to ward off punishments by assisting with tasks, adding cotton to a slow picker's basket, or doing whatever possible to "help de others when dey got behind." A former slave remembered hearing his mother sing as she urged spinners in Buckingham County, Virginia, along:

> Keep yo' eye on de sun,
> See how she run,
> Don't let her catch you with your work undone,
> I'm a trouble, I'm a trouble
> Trouble don' las' always.

The disappearance of the sun signaled the end of the work day when tallies were taken and punishments meted out if laborers fell short of assigned tasks. The song was equally appropriate for slaves working in cotton fields.[28]

Young slaves encountered plantation authority first hand when they entered the work force. It was here that they also received their first whipping from whites or saw their mothers punished. Paradoxically, slaveowners' lack of a clear perception of slaves as persons or property could mitigate their circumstances. Many slaveowners were reluctant to beat slaves unmercifully because it left a visible testimony of treatment and raised questions about the slaves' behavior, which could interfere with future sales. Harsh punishments could also injure slaves and lead to time lost from work and financial losses to owners. Ultimately, however, punishment or the threat of it were the prime factors that motivated slaves to work.[29] Slave mothers often shielded their children and used their influence whenever possible to protect them from punishments, but their leverage was tenuous. They were as vulnerable as their offspring, because adults generally were whipped like children and children like adults. Jacob Stroyer recognized this at an early age. When the horse trainer on their South Carolina plantation beat Jacob severely, his mother interceded on his behalf, and she too was whipped. Desperately seeking a way to stop the punishment, Stroyer ran back and forth between the horse trainer and his mother.[30]

Slave children often tried different ways of deflecting the lash when their mothers were punished. "Many's de time I edges" up to the whip, Jacob Branch said, to "take some dem licks off my mammy." Virginia-born slave Frank Bell and his brothers saved their mother from "some of dem licks" when they decided to "pitch in" and help her because she "warn't very strong." Another slave boy in Alabama, Mingo White, helped his mother escape the whip. He mastered housewifery skills after realizing that four cuts of thread (one cut equals approximately 300 yards) was too much for any one person to spin after a full day's work elsewhere. "Many de night me an' her would spin and card," he said, "so that she could get her task de next day." He knew she would receive fifty lashes if she did not complete her chore.[31]

As a child in Virginia, Allen Wilson saw his mother beaten while stripped naked to the waist and tied to a tree, but he did not interfere. Whatever the reason, Wilson decided that he was no match for the whip. "Lawd, Lawd! I prayed Gawd dat someday he'd open a way fur me to protect mother."[32]

Slave mothers called for divine intervention when they saw their children in peril. They were not remiss in looking after the religious welfare of their children, nor did they wait until something happened to teach their children to pray. Slave children were very much a part of family devotions and religious activities that made them believe in their deliverance from bondage. Numerous ex-slaves remembered their mothers' fervent pleas for an end to slavery. Religion gave them hope, as exemplified in their spirituals. Promises of a better life rang in their ears. Spirituals such as "In That Great Getting-Up Morning" and "Run to Jesus" were as much a part of their repertoire as "A Great Camp-Meeting in the Promised Land." Many slaves came to believe that their distress would end, if not in their present life, then certainly in the afterlife. The proverb "trouble don' las' always," strongly reflected their hope for a brighter future.[33]

Slave mothers did everything within their power to buffer abuses and cushion denials in order to help youngsters make adjustments and transitions until they were free of slavery. Perhaps their most difficult job was to ease the despair of family separations precipitated through sale, relocation, or hiring out. Events within the slaveowner's household often tore slave families apart when they were scattered about by estate sales, given to newly married couples, or presented as gifts to newborns. The literature about slavery in antebellum America is therefore filled with evidence about separations by both humane and brutal masters. Some slaveowners objected to breaking up families, and several of the southern states, including Louisiana and Alabama, prohibited the sale of children separately before they reached ten years of age. Nonetheless, children too small to manage on their own were sometimes sold.[34]

It was virtually impossible for slaves who had been sold or relocated to keep in touch with those they left behind because they were too far away, or because of the lack of transportation or ignorance of geography. Slaves who never saw or heard from each other again did not forget. An 1857 letter from a slave father in Georgia is testimony of the attempts that might be made to maintain family ties. "I wish to now what has Ever become of my Presus little girl," he wrote. "I left her in goldsboro [North Carolina] with Mr. Walker and I have not herd from her Since." While his letter is stirring, it does not convey the emotional strain of parting as strongly as Solomon Northup's description of the slave woman Eliza's emotional response when her children, Emily and Randall, were sold. Northup, a kidnapped slave, first met Eliza and her family in 1841 at Williams' Slave Pen in Washington, D.C., and traveled with them through Richmond and Norfolk to a New Orleans slave market. He admitted that he had "never seen such an exhibition of intense, unmeasured, and unbounded grief." Eliza constantly talked "of them," Northup wrote, and "often to them as if they were actually present." Such conversations comforted her.[35]

While facing separation, whether by sale or relocation, slave mothers groped about for ways to prepare their children. Some mothers told stories about taking long journeys and not seeing each other for a while. Others interfered with the pending separations. They ran away, hid their children in the woods, and threatened to kill them. Still other mothers arranged for buyers in order to keep their children nearby, or to purchase the entire family. Mothers ignored their personal pride and begged slaveholders to let them keep their families together. In 1859 Lucy Skipwith, a slave belonging to Virginia planter John Hartwell Cocke, persuaded him not to sell her daughter Betsey by arguing that the girl would be better off with her. Lucy was again successful in 1863 when Cocke contemplated selling or hiring out another of her daughters, Maria. Where Lucy Skipwith succeeded, the majority of slave mothers failed.[36]

It can always be argued that teenaged slaves who were sold left home at an age comparable to that of whites who were seeking jobs and trying to make a living for themselves. Under normal conditions such assertions might have some merit; however, slavery and the sale of humans, regardless of age, did not constitute normal circumstances. Besides, white youths who left home for apprenticeships were free to make such decisions either alone or with the aid of their families or someone else who had their best interests in mind. Moreover, they could return to their families when they chose. Slave children and youths had no such options. The fear of separation and never seeing their families was ever present.[37]

Aside from being subjected to punishments and separations, slaves were vulnerable to sexual harassment. Although the sexual exploitation of slave women in antebellum America has received much attention, the topic needs more research, for it focuses almost entirely upon the molestation of female slaves by white men. Homosexual and incestuous relationships and sexual liaisons between white females and male slaves have not been investigated extensively. The sexual violation of slaves by other slaves, another area in need of further study, did not ordinarily receive legal attention; consequently, there are few legal documents available for study. Furthermore, if such cases ever went to court, the judgments did not favor the plaintiffs. Consider the 1859 case against George, a slave indicted for the rape of a slave girl less than ten years of age. This was a heinous crime; however, the Mississippi court quashed the indictment and discharged George because there was no legislation "which embraces either the attempted or actual commission of a rape by a slave on a female slave." A Tennessee jury heard the case *Grandison v. State* in December 1841 and convicted the slave Grandison of assault, battery, and intent to "ravish" Mary Douglass. He received the death sentence, but the judgment was reversed because, by law, the rape of a black woman "would not be punished with death." Ironically, two years after the Grandison decision, a Tennessee grand jury indicted a slave for intent to rape a white woman. The jury returned a guilty verdict, but the judgment was reversed because there was "no entry showing that the grand jury returned . . . 'a true bill.'" Unlike white women, slave women, regardless of age, were subject to sexual abuse by men—black and white, slave and free—with impunity.[38]

Much of the abuse heaped upon slave women by white men emanated from the erroneous belief that they were naturally promiscuous. The popularization of this belief thus served as justification for the mistreatment of slave women. The more comely a slave girl, the greater the possibility that she would experience sexual abuse and sale as a "fancy girl" for illicit purposes. Eugene Genovese suggests that much of the plantation miscegenation in the antebellum South involved young single slave "girls" who were either seduced or raped by white males. He further suggests that "married slaves did not take white sexual aggression lightly." Supporting these generalizations, Genovese writes: "Planters and overseers who confronted resistant women and dangerous men usually had the good sense to content themselves with trying to seduce attractive single girls by using a combination of flattery, bribes and the ever-present threat of force." Genovese may be correct, but this says nothing about what slave mothers, fathers, grandmothers, and grandfathers thought of white sexual aggression against their offspring or what the "girls" themselves thought. Slave fathers were as likely to disapprove of sexual aggression toward their daughters as toward their wives. This, of course, was in keeping with traditional African "rights in uxorem" and "rights in genetricem," which imposed marital obligations upon a couple. In uxorem, husbands have rights over their wives as sexual and domestic partners. The woman's rights as a mother, rights in genetricem, meant that her husband was to provide food and protection for her and the children. These traditional rights were of little consequence in antebellum America.[39]

Many slave women were victims of sexual abuse that neither they nor their parents could do much about. There is little doubt, however, about what Lucy McCullough, almost eighty years old when interviewed, meant when recounting a story about her mother seeing her "cummin' crost de yahd en she say mah dress too short." Her mother ripped the hem, and "weave more cloff on hit, twel it long enuf, lak she want it." A few inches added to the dress was little protection, yet Lucy's mother believed it would shield her daughter a while longer. "My heart was heavier than it had ever been before," an ex-slave mother wrote, "when they told me my newborn babe was a girl." Based upon her own experience, she believed that her daughter would also encounter sexual abuse.[40]

Once slave girls reached adolescence, they faced the possibility of sexual exploitation. The extent of breeding or the systematic and licentious use of slaves solely to reproduce children remains virtually undocumented, although there are suggestions that it occurred. A slave child was property; its birth added value to a slaveowner's coffers regardless of the conditions under which it was conceived.

Rose, a former slave born in Bell County, Texas, told federal interviewers that her owner forced her to live with Rufus "'gainst" her "wants." Describing herself as just an "igno'mus chile," Rose related that she was unaware of her owner's intentions, believing she was only to "tend de cabin for Rufus," who insisted upon sleeping with her. The sixteen-year-old girl's protests to her mistress brought no relief. Instead she learned that she and Rufus were to bring forth "portly chillen." She asked the interviewer, "What am I's to do?"[41] Rose feared punishment or sale if she remained belligerent toward Rufus. She finally surrendered to Rufus, however, out of a misguided sense of loyalty to her owner. Threatened with separation from her mother and father, who were sold to the same man who subsequently bought her, Rose felt an indebtedness to him for keeping her family together. Years later, when talking about her former owner, Rose observed, "I can't shut from my mind" what he did. Once freed she vowed never to marry again. It is not clear if Rose and Rufus brought forth any "portly chillen" or if they were sold. The story, however, raises questions about other slaves forced into similar situations. Were they committed to making such marriages succeed? Did they learn to love each other and build mutual respect and trust? Beyond that, questions regarding attitudes toward spouses and children from unwanted pregnancies will never be answered.[42]

Slave mothers devised ingenious ways to protect themselves and their children from slavery's worst abuses. They feigned illnesses, mistreated livestock, and destroyed property. Down through the generations slaves used tactics that historians call resistance to undermine or interfere with production. Some women took more drastic steps to undermine reproduction by refusing to conceive children or by aborting them. Certainly some of their "abortions" may have been spontaneous miscarriages. Slaveowners, in such cases, unwittingly assisted in undermining reproduction by demanding heavy physical labor, distributing nutritionally poor food, and not providing adequate prenatal care for pregnant women. It was easier to accuse slave women of practicing infanticide than to gain medical knowledge explaining the connection between low birth weights and high infant mortality rates. This is not to deny the documented reports of infanticide but to raise questions about the onus of responsibility and whether slave mothers were careful to destroy only those children resulting from unwanted pregnancies or to destroy all of their children. At least one case of infanticide in antebellum Virginia leaves few questions about the slave mother's intent. Although she was guilty of killing her mulatto child, she escaped death because white citizens petitioned for her release. The woman claimed that "she would not have killed a child of her own color." It is not easy to reconcile accounts of the unwavering love slave mothers had for their children with reports of infanticide. Mothers who resorted to such drastic acts preferred to see a child die rather than survive in slavery despite conflicting emotions or the psychological costs involved.[43]

The sure way for slaves to undermine both production and reproduction was to free themselves of slavery. The majority of those who gained their freedom before the Civil War did so by running away. Some fled into the woods temporarily, while others moved away permanently. Abolitionists and vigilance committees sometimes helped fugitives gain freedom. Between May 1, 1855, and January 1, 1856, the Colored Vigilance Committee of Detroit assisted nearly 1,000 runaways, while the New York Committee of Vigilance assisted 335 runaways during its first year of operation. Figures are equally impressive for such groups in Massachusetts, Ohio, and Pennsylvania. William Still, of the Philadelphia Vigilance Committee, kept records which show that nearly 5,000 fugitives received aid from the organization between 1852 and 1857. In a study of South Carolina runaways and the slave communities, Michael Johnson concluded that "the typical runaway was a young man who absconded alone." Herbert Gutman found that as many as 88 percent of the runaways in the years before the Civil War were males between ages sixteen and thirty-five. Slave mothers, regardless of age, were less likely to run away than childless women because they were unwilling to leave their youngsters behind. The psychological impact of deserting them was too great. Additionally, there were community and family pressures to consider. "Nobody respects a mother who forsakes her children," ex-slave Molly Horniblow told her granddaughter, Harriet Jacobs, who considered running away without her two children. Jacobs believed that if she ran away her owner would grow tired of the children and sell them. "Stand by your own children," the old woman advised, "suffer with them till death." Jacobs changed her mind about leaving. She remained in hiding, however, for seven years in an unheated and unventilated loft above a storeroom adjoining her grandmother's house, unable to rear her children, who did not know that she was nearby. Although the burden of concealing her granddaughter, caring for her children under such conditions, and leading a life of deception caused Molly Horniblow much anxiety, she did it willingly. Jacobs did not abandon the dream of freeing her children. She fought a psychological battle with her owner and manipulated him into thinking she had fled to the North, until, finally, she gained her freedom and that of her children.[44]

Slave mothers who became fugitives faced extraordinary difficulties when accompanied by children. It was virtually impossible to carry enough food to sustain oneself, let alone additional food for youngsters. Moreover, traveling overland on foot meant that children walked or were physically carried. In either case, the going was slow. Besides, children crying from hunger or weariness drew attention and increased chances of detection. Despite these obstacles, a few mothers dared to flee with their offspring. In *Uncle Tom's Cabin*, Harriet Beecher Stowe modeled her character Eliza upon the actual flight of a slave woman who carried a baby across an icy river to freedom. The sons of John Parker, an abolitionist in Ripley, Ohio, who often helped runaways secure their freedom, assisted a fugitive slave woman very much like Eliza. Certainly there were other such women.[45]

Because it was much easier for slaves to escape alone, some slave mothers motivated their children to run away. Missouri-born Lucy Delaney remembered that her mother "never spared an opportunity" to tell her children to seek freedom "whenever the chance offered." By the time she was twelve, Lucy herself planned to run away, and she was "forever on the alert for a chance to escape." William Wells Brown initially refused to escape alone. He could not leave his mother, who had carried him upon her back and had been punished for nursing him instead of working. Brown insisted that they run away together. When that plan failed, his mother encouraged him to go alone.[46]

Slave mothers lived and prospered only to the extent that their children did. They shared each other's triumphs and defeats. Their lives were so firmly interlocked that they did not behave as individuals with singular purposes. For that reason it is difficult to imagine these women without children. Upon hearing that Nancy, Lucy Delaney's sister, had succeeded in running away, their mother danced, sang, clapped, and waved her hands in joy. The girl's success was also the mother's. "I was overjoyed with my personal freedom," said Mattie Jackson, a runaway slave from St. Louis, "but the joy at my mother's escape was greater than anything I had ever known." Theirs was a symbiotic relationship based upon unselfish love and trust.[47]

During the Civil War, more and more slaves liberated themselves as Union soldiers approached. In their quest for freedom, mothers and children were often seen fleeing together. Anything to the contrary would have been incongruous, considering what some mothers had suffered to keep their families together. In the early days of the Civil War, Elizabeth Hyde Botume, a northern teacher in South Carolina, observed that a "half-grown boy had his blind daddy [on his back] toting him along to freedom." More impressive, however, was the sight of a slave woman "striding along with her hominy pot, in which was a live chicken, poised on her head. One child on her back, with its arms tightly clasped around her neck, and its feet about her waist, and under each arm was a smaller child." This woman made her way to the government steamer *John Adams*, moored at a waterfront plantation, confident that freedom was at hand for her family. Another slave mother was not so fortunate. Her owner fired upon her as she fled with a child. The child died of gunshot wounds, but the mother hastened on to the Union lines, where she could bury the child free.[48]

At slavery's end in America, newly freed slaves put forth Herculean efforts to reunite families displaced by bondage and war. "In their eyes," wrote an observer, "the work of emancipation was incomplete until the families which had been dispersed by slavery were reunited." Mothers, sometimes with the help of the Freedmen's Bureau, set out to find children from whom they had been separated many years earlier. On February 6, 1866, an Arkansas freedwoman, Lucinda Jacoway, complained that William Bryant was "restraining the freedom of her child Jane Ellen." Bryant demanded that Jacoway pay him fifty dollars for the four-year-old girl. In a letter to Bryant written for Jacoway, John Vetter of the Freedmen's Bureau demanded that the child be handed over immediately. Ellen Halleck, another newly freed mother, filed a similar complaint on the same day. There is no way of knowing if these women received their children immediately, as directed, but it is clear that they were exercising their parental rights and were not at all content with someone else holding their children. In other cases mothers worked alone. Ignorant of geography but fortified with hope, many mothers set out on foot to find their kin. Kate Drumgoold, born a slave in Virginia, remembered the many difficulties her mother encountered in locating her children, who were "all over in different places," but she was not discouraged. Several times she was told they were dead; she vowed to dig for their bones. The mother finally succeeded in finding the children alive. Many other mothers failed, not because they did not try but because the challenge was beyond their resources.[49]

Throughout the period of slavery in America, mothers accepted the responsibility to provide the salve, kindle the hope, and maintain the love that would help their children survive. Kate Drumgoold remembered her mother's tenacity, which served as an inspiration to her. "My mother was one that the master could not do anything to make her feel like a slave," she recalled after slavery ended. "She would battle with them [slaveholders] to the last that she would not recognize them as her lord and master." Numerous slave narratives recorded from both men and women speak lovingly of mothers whose mettle and prayers encouraged their children to endure. William Wells Brown's mother was very special to him. His recollection of her provides the apogee in testimonies related to the interlocked lives of slave mothers and their children. "I half forgot the name of slave," he said, "when she was by my side."[50]

Notes

1. Thomas Jefferson to Joel Yancy, January 17, 1819, and Jefferson to John W. Eppes, June 30, 1820, in *Thomas Jefferson's Farm Book: With Commentary and Relevant Extracts from Other Writings*, ed. Edwin Morris Betts (Princeton: Princeton University Press, 1953), pp. 43, 46; Nancy Tanner, "Matrifocality in Indonesia and Africa and among Black Americans," in *Woman, Culture, and Society*, ed. Michelle Zimbalist Rosaldo and Louise Lamphere (Stanford: Stanford University Press, 1974), p. 153; Herbert J. Foster, "African Patterns in the Afro-American Family," *Journal of Black Studies* 14 (December 1983): 201–32; Herbert G. Gutman, *The Black Family in Slavery and Freedom, 1750–1925* (New York: Vintage, 1979), pp. 75–76.

2. *Historical Statistics of the United States: Colonial Times to 1970*, part 2 (Washington, D.C.: Government Printing Office, 1975), pp. 18–19; Allan Kulikoff, "A 'Prolifick' People: Black Population Growth in the Chesapeake Colonies, 1700–1790," *Southern Studies* 16 (Winter 1977): 391–428; Natalie Shainess, "The Structure of the Mothering Encounter," *Journal of Nervous and Mental Disorders* 136 (February 1963): 146–61, and "The Psychologic Experience of Labor," *New York State Journal of Medicine* (hereafter cited as *NYSJM*) 63 (October 15, 1963): 2923–32; Deborah Gray White, *Ar'n't I a Woman? Female Slaves in the Plantation South* (New York: Norton, 1985), pp. 67–69.

3. E. Franklin Frazier, *The Negro Family in the United States*, 2d ed. (Chicago: University of Chicago Press, 1967), pp. 50–69.

4. John Campbell, "Work, Pregnancy, and Infant Mortality among Southern Slaves," *Journal of Interdisciplinary History* (hereafter cited as *JIH*) 14 (Spring 1984): 809; Michael P. Johnson, "Smothered Slave Infants: Were Slave Mothers at Fault?" *Journal of Southern History* (hereafter cited as *JSH*) 47 (November 1981): 519; *A Documentary History of Slavery in North America*, ed. Willie Lee Rose (New York: Oxford University Press, 1976), pp. 417–18.

5. George P. Rawick, ed. *The American Slave: A Composite Autobiography* (Westport: Greenwood, 1973), vol. 2 (South Carolina), p. 20; Frances Anne Kemble, *Journal of a Residence on a Georgian Plantation in 1838–1839*, ed. John A. Scott (Athens: University of Georgia Press), pp. 229–31; Campbell, "Work, Pregnancy, and Infant Mortality," pp. 808–9.

6. *Lay My Burden Down: A Folk History of Slavery*, ed. B. A. Botkin (Chicago: University of Chicago Press, 1965), p. 179; Catherine M. Scholten, "On the Importance of the Obstetrick Art: Changing Customs of Childbirth in America, 1760 to 1825," *William and Mary Quarterly* (hereafter cited as WMQ) 34 (July 1977): 426–45; J. Jill Suitor, "Husbands' Participation in Childbirth: A Nineteenth-Century Phenomenon," *Journal of Family History* (hereafter cited as *JFH*) 6 (Fall 1981): 278–93; Judith Walzer Leavitt, *Brought to Bed: Childbearing in America 1750 to 1950* (New York: Oxford University Press, 1986), pp. 36–40, 58; Catherine Clinton, *The Plantation Mistress: Woman's World in the Old South* (New York: Pantheon, 1982), pp. 151–54; Todd L. Savitt, *Medicine and Slavery: The Diseases and Health Care of Blacks in Antebellum Virginia* (Urbana: University of Illinois Press, 1978), pp. 117–18.

7. Ulla-Britt Lithell, "Breast-feeding Habits and Their Relation to Infant Mortality and Marital Fertility," *JFH* 6 (Summer 1981): 182–94.

8. John W. Blassingame, *The Slave Community: Plantation Life in the Antebellum South*, 2d ed. (New York: Oxford University Press, 1979), p. 181; Lithell, "Breast-feeding Habits," p. 183; Kenneth F. Kiple and Virginia H. Kiple, "Slave Child Mortality:

Some Nutritional Answers to a Perennial Puzzle," *Journal of Social History* 10 (Spring 1977): 287–89.

9. Robert A. Margo and Richard H. Steckel, "The Heights of American Slaves: New Evidence on Slave Nutrition and Health," *Social Science History* (hereafter cited as *SSH*) 6 (Fall 1982): 516–38; Richard H. Steckel, "A Peculiar Population: The Nutrition, Health, and Mortality of American Slaves from Childhood to Maturity," *Journal of Economic History* 46 (September 1986): 721–41.

10. David Gavin Diary, December 1859, vol. I, p. 180, Southern Historical Collection, University of North Carolina, Chapel Hill (hereafter cited as SHC); Bayside Plantation Book, June 18, 1861, and June 29, 1861, SHC; John Nevitt Diary, March 9, 1827, SHC; Alexander Lawton Diary, 1817, SHC; Kiple and Kiple, "Slave Child Mortality," p. 285; Nancy Schrom Dye and Daniel Blake Smith, "Mother Love and Infant Death, 1750–1920," *Journal of American History* (hereafter cited as *JAH*) 73 (September 1986): 329–53; Richard H. Steckel, "A Dreadful Childhood: The Excess Mortality of American Slaves," *SSH* 10 (Winter 1986): 427–65.

11. A. C. Griffin, August 1848, SHC; Kiple and Kiple, "Slave Child Mortality," pp. 290–91.

12. Kiple and Kiple, "Slave Child Mortality," pp. 390–92; Steckel, "A Peculiar Population," 733–36.

13. John Houston Bills Diary, March 16, 1860, SHC; Tryphena Blanche Holder Fox to Anna Holder, February 1, 1860, and March 17, 1860, Tryphena Blanche Holder Fox Papers, Mississippi Department of Archives and History, Jackson; Everard Green Baker Diary, August 22, 1850, vol. I, p. 89, SHC. See Joan R. Gunderson, "The Double Bonds of Race and Sex: Black and White Women in a Colonial Virginia Parish," *JSH* 52 (August 1986): 351–72.

14. Johnson, "Smothered Slave Infants," pp. 499, 519–20; Todd L. Savitt, "Smothering and Overlaying of Virginia Slave Children: A Suggested Exploratory," *Bulletin of the History of Medicine* 49 (Fall 1975): 400–405; Savitt, *Medicine and Slavery*, pp. 120–29, 137–38.

15. Kemble, *Journal*, pp. 222–23; Johnson, "Smothered Slave Infants," pp. 493–520; Savitt, "Smothering and Overlaying," p. 400; Steckel, "A Dreadful Childhood," pp. 450–53.

16. Johnson, "Smothered Slave Infants," p. 499; Norman R. Yetman, *Life under the "Peculiar Institution": Selections from the Slave Narrative Collection* (New York: Holt, Rinehart and Winston, 1970), p. 228.

17. James H. Ruffin Plantation Records, August–September 1843, August–October 1844, vol. 3, SHC; Thomas L. Webber, *Deep Like the Rivers: Education in the Slave Quarter Community, 1831–1865* (New York: Norton, 1978), p. 10. See the instructions to overseer requiring that "breeding and suckling" women work near the house, in the William Henry Sims Papers, SHC. McDonald Furman specified that women "near being confined must be put only to light work & after delivery & able to go about must be put to light work for a time"; McDonald Furman Papers, Perkins Library, Duke University, Durham, N.C. (hereafter cited as PL).

18. Booker T. Washington, *Up from Slavery: An Autobiography by Booker T. Washington* (New York: Bantam, 1967), p. 3; Frederick Douglass, *Frederick Douglass: The Narrative and Selected Writings*, ed. Michael Merger (New York: Random House, 1984), p. 19.

19. White Hill Plantation Books, 1817–1860, SHC; David Gavin Diary, September 13, 1856, vol. I, SHC; "A Letter from a Yankee Bride in Ante-Bellum Louisiana," ed. John Q. Anderson, *Louisiana History* 1 (Summer 1960): 248; Bobby Frank Jones, "A Cultural Middle Passage: Slave Marriage and Family in the Antebellum South," Ph.D. dissertation, University of North Carolina, 1965, p. 108; Webber, *Deep Like the Rivers*, p. 11.

20. Henry Bibb, *Narrative of the Life and Adventures of Henry Bibb: An American Slave Written by Himself*, in *Puttin' on Ole Massa: The Slave Narratives of Henry Bibb, William Wells Brown, and Solomon Northup*, ed. Gilbert Osofsky (New York: Harper 1969), pp. 80–81.

21. Charles Perdue, Jr., Thomas E. Barden, and Robert K. Phillips, eds., *Weevils in the Wheat: Interviews with Virginia Ex-Slaves* (Bloomington: Indiana University Press, 1980), p.185; Yetman, *Life under the "Peculiar Institution,"* p. 66; Frazier, *The Negro Family*, p. 38.

22. Prince Woodfin to Nickles Woodfin, April 25, 1853, Nicholas Washington Woodfin Papers, SHC.

23. Harriet A. Jacobs, *Incidents in the Life of a Slave Girl, Written by Herself*, ed. Jean Fagan Yellin (Cambridge: Harvard University Press, 1987), p. 9; Yetman, *Life under the "Peculiar Institution,"* p. 327.

24. Jacobs, *Incidents*, pp. 140, 149, 154.

25. Mary Boykin Chesnut, *A Diary From Dixie*, ed. Ben Ames Williams (Boston: Houghton Mifflin, 1950), p. 38; Charshee Charlotte Lawrence-McIntyre, "The Double Meanings of the Spirituals," *Journal of Black Studies* 17 (June 1987): 390; Jacobs, *Incidents*, p. 155.

26. Alonzo Mial to Ruffin Horton, December 6, 1859, Mial Papers, North Carolina Department of Archives and History, Raleigh; Michael P. Johnson, "Work, Culture, and the Slave Community: Slave Occupations in the Cotton Belt in 1860," *Labor History* (hereafter cited as *LH*) 27 (Summer 1986): 325–55; Charles B. Dew, "David Ross and the Oxford Iron Works: A Study of Industrial Slavery in the Early Nineteenth-Century South," *WMQ* 31 (April 1974): 197–99, 210–11.

27. White, *Ar'n't I a Woman?*, p. 69; Jacqueline Jones, *Labor of Love, Labor of Sorrow: Black Women, Work and the Family from Slavery to the Present* (New York: Vintage, 1986), p. 18; Carole Shammas, "Black Women's Work and the Evolution of Plantation Society in Virginia," *LH* 26 (Winter 1985): 5–28; Leonard Stavsky, "The Origins of Negro Craftsmanship in Colonial America," *Journal of Negro History* (hereafter cited as *JNH*) 32 (October 1947): 428, and "Afro-American Art," *Black Scholar* 9 (November 1977): 35–42. Also see Michael P. Johnson and James L. Roark, *Black Masters: A Free Family of Color in the Old South* (New York: Norton, 1984), pp. 78–79, 131–34.

28. Perdue et al., *Weevils in the Wheat*, pp. 88, 309.

29. J. Thomas Wren, "A Two-Fold Character: The Slave as Person and Property in Virginia Court Cases, 1800–1860," *Southern Studies* 24 (Winter 1985): 425–31.

30. Jacob Stroyer, *My Life in the South* (Salem, 1879), p. 20.

31. Perdue et al., *Weevils in the Wheat*, p. 26; Yetman, *Life under the "Peculiar Institution,"* pp. 40, 312.

32. Perdue et al., *Weevils in the Wheat*, p. 327; Stroyer, *My Life in the South*, pp. 22–23.

33. *Jubilee and Plantation Songs: Characteristic Favorites, as Sung by the Hampton Students, Jubilee Singers, Fisk University Students, and Other Concert Companies* (Boston: Oliver Ditson, 1887), pp. 8, 24, 57, 64–65, 68; Albert J. Raboteau, *Slave Religion: The "Invisible Institution" in the Antebellum South* (New York: Oxford University Press, 1978), pp. 218–19; Rawick, *The American Slave*, vol. 19, pp. 41–45; Yetmen, *Life under the "Peculiar Institution,"* p. 227; *"Dear Master": Letters of a Slave Family*, ed. Randall M. Miller (Ithaca: Cornell University Press, 1978), pp. 196–98, 224; Mary Ellison, "Resistance to Oppression: Black Women's Response to Slavery in the United States," *Slavery and Abolition* 4 (May 1983): 59; Washington, *Up from Slavery*, p. 5.

34. James William McGettigan, Jr., "Boone County Slaves: Sales, Estate Divisions and Families, 1820–1865," parts 1 and 2, *Missouri Historical Review* 72 (January–April 1978): 176–97, 271–95; John C. Cohoon, Account Book, 1810–1860, University of Virginia, Charlottesville; John Sterrett Papers, April 30, 1829, Library of Congress, Washington, D.C.; Wren, "Two-Fold Character," p. 424; William Chone, "Thomas Jefferson and the Problem of Slavery," *JAH* 56 (December 1969): 517–18; Frederick Bancroft, *Slave-Trading in the Old South* (Baltimore: J. H. Furst, 1931), pp. 197–99; Judith Kelleher Schafer, "New Orleans Slavery in 1850 as Seen in Advertisements," *JSH* 47 (February 1981): 36. For advertisements involving the sale of children, see *The Charleston Mercury*, February 3, February 21, March 3, March 23, April 4, April 9, July 1, July 16, August 5, August 25, October 1, October 17, October 20, November 3, November 7, and November 26, 1846.

35. Lester to Miss Patsy, August 29, 1857, James Allred Papers, PL; Solomon Northrup, *Twelve Years a Slave: Narrative of Solomon Northup*, in *Puttin' On Ole Massa*, pp. 245–46, 267–68, 280.

36. Miller, *"Dear Master,"* pp. 188–89.

37. See Barbara L. Bellows, "'My Children, Gentlemen, Are My Own': Poor Women, the Urban Elite and the Bonds of Obligation in Antebellum Charleston," in *The Web of Southern Social Relations: Women, Family, and Education*, ed. Walter Fraser, Jr. (Athens: University of Georgia Press, 1885), pp. 52–71; G. Melvin Herndon, "The Unemancipated Antebellum Youth," *Southern Studies* 23 (Summer 1984): 145–54; Durwood Dunn, "Apprenticeship and Indentured Servitude in Tennessee before the Civil War," *West Tennessee Historical Society Papers* 36 (1982): 25–40.

38. Helen Tunnicliff Catterall, ed., *Judicial Cases concerning American Slavery and the Negro* (Washington, D.C.: Carnegie Institute, 1929), vol. 2, pp. 513, 520, vol. 3, p. 363; White, *Ar'n't I a Woman?*, pp. 152–53. Catterall (vol. 3, p. 363) notes that in the Session Acts of 1860, Mississippi made "the rape by a negro or mulatto on a female negro or mulatto, under twelve years of age" punishable with death or whipping. This statute appears to apply to free persons rather than slaves, since it fails to indicate the legal status of either defendants or plaintiffs.

39. Eugene D. Genovese, *Roll, Jordan, Roll: The World Slaves Made* (New York: Vintage, 1976), pp. 415, 423; White, *Ar'n't I a Woman?*, pp. 27–34; Northup, *Twelve Years a Slave*, p. 268; Eric O. Ayisi, *An Introduction to the Study of African Culture* (London: Heinemann, 1986), pp. 8–9; Richard H. Steckel, "Miscegenation and the American Slave Schedules," *JIH* 11 (Autumn 1980): 25–63. For a discussion of an ex-slave father's successful fight to save his daughters from being sold as "fancy girls," see Catherine M. Hanchett, "'What Sort of People & Families . . .'—The Edmondson Sisters," *Afro-Africans in New York Life and History* 6 (July 1982): 21–37.

40. Rawick, *The American Slave*, vol. 13 (Georgia), p. 69; Jacobs, *Incidents in the Life of a Slave Girl*, pp. 27–36, 51–57, 77, 268.

41. Rose, *A Documentary History of Slavery*, pp. 436–37; Richard Sutch, "The Breeding of Slaves for Sale and the Westward Expansion of Slavery, 1850–60," in *Race and Slavery in the Western Hemisphere: Quantitative Studies*, ed. Stanley L. Engerman and Eugene D. Genovese (Princeton: Princeton University Press, 1975), pp. 173–210.

42. Rose, *A Documentary History*, pp. 436–37.

43. Genovese, *Roll, Jordan, Roll*, p. 497; Elizabeth Fox-Genovese, "Strategies and Forms of Resistance: Focus on Slave Women in the United States," in *In Resistance: Studies in African, Caribbean, and Afro-American History*, ed. Gary Y. Okihiro (Amherst: University of Massachusetts Press, 1986), pp. 157–58; Darlene C. Hine, "Female Slave Resistance: The Economics of Sex," *Western Journal of Black Studies* 3 (Summer 1979): 123–27; White, *Ar'n't I a Woman?*, pp. 86–88; Natalie Shainess, "Abortion: Social, Psychiatric, and Psychoanalytic Perspectives," *NYSJM* 63 (December 1, 1968): 43.3070–73; Gutman, *The Black Family*, pp. 80–82; Catterall, *Judicial Cases*, vol. 2, p. 59.

44. Michael P. Johnson, "Runaway Slaves and the Slave Communities in South Carolina, 1799 to 1830," *WMQ* 38 (July 1981): 418; Gutman, *The Black Family*, pp. 265–67; Gerald W. Mullin, *Flight and Rebellion: Slave Resistance in Eighteenth-Century Virginia* (New York: Oxford University Press, 1972), p. 40; Jacobs, *Incidents in the Life of a Slave Girl*, p. 91; Schaefer, "New Orleans Slavery in 1850," p. 43; Benjamin Quarles, *Black Abolitionists* (New York: Oxford University Press, 1969), pp. 152–53; Larry Gara, *The Liberty Line: The Legend of the Underground Railroad* (Lexington: University Press of Kentucky, 1961), pp. 175–76.

45. Frank Gregg, a Cincinnati journalist, wrote about the slave woman's flight after an interview with John Parker, Jr., who, along with his brother, guided the woman from their home to another underground railroad station as she made her way to freedom. Rankin-Parker Papers, PL; Harriett Beecher Stowe, *A Key to Uncle Tom's Cabin* (Cleveland: J. P. Jewlett, 1854), p. 34; Jennie Arnold, "Lives of Teachers Who Attended Summer Institute, 1881," Early Students Folder, Hampton University Archives, Hampton, Virginia. Also see William Still, *The Underground Railroad: A Record of Facts, Authentic Narratives, Letters, &c* (Philadelphia: Porter & Coats, 1872).

46. Lucy A. Delaney, *From the Darkness Cometh the Light, or Struggles for Freedom* (St. Louis, n. p., n.d.), in *Six Women's Slave Narratives*, ed. William Andrews (New York: Oxford University Press, 1988), pp. 15–16; Brown, *Narrative of William Wells Brown*, pp. 187–88; Loren Schweninger, "A Slave Family in the Ante Bellum South," *JNH* 60 (January 1975): 34.

47. Delaney, *From the Darkness*, p. 19; Thompson, *The Story of Mattie Jackson*, pp. 31–32.

48. Elizabeth Hyde Botume, *First Days amongst the Contrabands* (New York: Arno Press, 1968), p. 15; Jones, *Labor of Love*, p. 49. The possibilities of whole families fleeing together once Union soldiers came into their areas increased. See Leon Litwack, *Been in the Storm So Long: The Aftermath of Slavery* (New York: Vintage, 1979), pp. 93–97; Gutman, *The Black Family*, pp. 267–69; Edward L. Pierce, "The Contrabands at Fortress Monroe," *Atlantic Monthly* 3 (November 1861): 627–39.

49. Eric Foner, *Reconstruction: America's Unfinished Revolution, 1863–1877* (New York: Harper, 1988), p. 82; John Vetter to William Bryant, February 6, 1866, John Vetter to Henry Kership, February 6, 1866, Record Group 105, Bureau of Refugees, Freedmen, and Abandoned Land (Freedmen's Bureau), Record Group 105, Arkansas,

National Archives, Washington, D.C.; Kate Drumgoold, *A Slave Girl's Story: Being an Autobiography of Kate Drumgoold* (Brooklyn, 1898), in *Six Women's Slave Narratives*, p. 8; Litwack, *Been in the Storm So Long*, pp. 229–37. See also Freedmen's Bureau, Record Group 1216–1219, vols. 152–53; Record Group 2128, vol. 144.

50. Drumgoold, *A Slave Girl's Story*, p. 32; Brown, *Narrative of William Wells Brown*, p. 209. See also *The Life of Okah Tubbee*, ed. Daniel L. Littlefield, Jr. (Lincoln: University of Nebraska Press, 1988). The 1848 biography, *A Sketch of the Life of OKAH TUBBEE (called) William Chubbee, Son of the Head Chief, Mosholeh Tubbee, of the Choctaw Nation of Indians*, differs greatly from the traditional slave narratives in that unwavering love of mothers is absent, while self-hatred and sibling rivalry are present. Traditional patterns aside, the purpose of the biography was to free Tubbee from slavery. He succeeded by adopting an Indian identity and publishing his autobiography, which claims that he, the son of an Indian chief, had been kidnapped and enslaved. He refers to Franky, the freed woman with whom he lived as a young child, as his "unnatural" mother.

9

GENDER CONVENTION, IDEALS, AND IDENTITY AMONG ANTEBELLUM VIRGINIA SLAVE WOMEN

Brenda E. Stevenson

The autobiographical accounts, tales, and fantasies of Virginia slave women provide a wealth of information, collective and individual, existential and relational, about the private lives of bonded black females, their families, their overseers, their masters, and their mistresses.[1] Fortunately, these accounts also entail much more. Through the vehicle of "autobiographical story," slave women were able to construct what, for them, was an operative, legitimate identity, a "counterimage" of black womanhood that flew provocatively in the face of popular contemporary images of black female degradation, promiscuity, and passivity. Slave women's image or images of themselves, more often than not, were overwhelmingly positive, even heroic. They also included notions of their principle and purpose as slave women. This essay explores some of the positive images that slave women drew of themselves and some of the practical (i.e., material, residential, occupational) conditions or variables which can be linked to the creation and perpetuation of these images.[2]

Consider, for example, the following statement from the ex-slave woman Fannie Berry:

> There wuz an ol' lady patching a quilt an' de paddyrollers wuz looking fo' a slave named John. John wuz dar funnin' an' carrying on. All at once we herd a rap on de door. John took an' runned between Mamy Lou's legs. She hid him by spreading a quilt across her lap and kept on sewing an', do you kno', dem pattyrollers never found him?[3]

Fannie Berry was born a slave in about 1841, the property of George Abbott of Appomattox County, Virginia. Her owner was a man of moderate means. In 1850, for example, Abbott and his wife, Sarah Ann, owned real estate valued at almost $2,000 and eleven slaves, seven of whom were female. But if the younger

George was anything like his uncle and namesake, George Abbott, Senior, he probably had big plans. The elder Abbott also lived in Appomattox County in 1850, but he held real estate valued at $15,000 and owned thirty-two slaves, twelve males (8 prime hands), and twenty (nine prime hands, one elderly woman, and ten children) females.[4]

Berry grew up in the work world prescribed by people like the Abbotts—in a small, rural county in which corn, tobacco, and cotton were the farmer's financial mainstay and land and slaves his most vital resources. She also grew up in a social and cultural community of slave women. They dominated her owner's work force and those of his closest relative. They, their life events, their ideas, and their morality dominated Fannie's memory of her time as a slave and her construction of slave female identity through her stories.[5]

When interviewed during the 1930s, Berry was full of information about her life as a slave female and the other women whom she had known in Virginia's southern piedmont.[6] Her account offers vibrant, stimulating images of morally driven, dynamic slave women (moral and dynamic at least in Berry's recollections and psyche). Fannie Berry's brief description of "Mamy Lou," a woman respected for both her age and occupation, pivots on the potent symbols Berry appropriates for black "womanhood"—Mamy Lou's quilt and "between her legs." In the culture of Fannie's owners these images traditionally signified the passive domestic world females occupied (the quilt) and female sexual surrender ("between her legs"). According to Berry, however, Mamy Lou used these black, "feminine" resources to a very different end—to save a vital, young slave man from the abuse of white patrollers.

Through her image of this one woman Fannie Berry is able to convey much about what many slave women expressed as their requisite concerns and responsibilities within the designs of their limited, oppressed social worlds. Read Fannie's description of Mamy Lou's actions carefully and you will find a basic premise of slave female morality and purpose—the protection and procreation of black life. Read even more carefully and you can detect the prerogative of slave female principle, the protection and procreation of black life in the face of white opposition. Clearly in her characterization of Mamy Lou, Fannie Berry is constructing a black female identity that is complex and oppositional.

Berry's "Mamy Lou," therefore, represents some of the attributes slave women believed were their most vital contributions to their families and communities. Mamy Lou is the embodiment of slave women's ability to give and nurture life. She also symbolizes their domestic productivity (her quilt) and their feminine sexuality ("between her legs"). Berry informs her audience, through the powerful image of Mamy Lou, that despite everything, slave women did not lose their female principle or moral purpose under slavery. Rather, they defined and redefined both in order to sustain domestic slave life and domesticity, often quite successfully.

Among the various ways black women chose to describe their lives and those of the other females with whom they came in contact, they especially were forthright in their appreciation of self-reliant, self-determined survivalists who had the wherewithal to protect themselves and theirs, confrontationally if need be. Of course, most women were not able to act on these traits openly for fear of severe retaliation. But it is clear that slave women held great pride and esteem for those who did. They overwhelmingly were the women whom slave females spoke most often about in "heroic" terms, attributing to them what seem like (and may have been) fantastical deeds and attitudes. While other southern residents might have believed that a woman's exhibition of such conduct was a profound suggestion of "defeminization," slave women often utilized this kind of behavior in order to survive. Some even offered embellished accounts in order to inspire others to act or at least think similarly, and of course to bolster self-esteem among them. According to them, to be such a woman helped them to maintain their most fundamental claims to womanhood; that is, their female sexuality and physicality, and their roles as mothers, nurturers, and wives.

True stories, for example, abound about slave female rape and physical abuse despite the belief commonly held by southern whites that black women could not be raped, since they were naturally promiscuous. Most slave women found no way to fight back (and win), except perhaps in the telling of their painful stories, which exonerated the images of their sexual morality. Those slave women who found a more direct manner to resist emerged in the lore and mythology of slave women both as models for black female conduct and symbols of resistance that were unique to the black female experience. Slave mothers, in fact, often told stories of these women to their daughters as part of their socialization and to engender a sense of group pride.

Virginia Hayes Shepherd, for example, spoke in glowing terms of three slave women whom she had known or her mother had told her about, who diligently protected their female selves from the ill-treatment of white, male authority figures: one successfully avoided the sexual pursuit of her owner, while the other two refused to be treated in the fields like men, that is to be worked beyond their physical endurance as women.[7] Seventy years after her emancipation, Minnie Folkes still felt the pain associated with witnessing her mother being whipped mercilessly by her overseer. Yet her explanation of her mother's suffering (that she had refused "to be wife to dis man") and her description of how her mother had taught her to protect herself from sexual abuse ("muma had sed 'Don't let nobody bother yo principle; 'cause dat wuz all yo' had'") are tinged with pride and respect. The elder Folkes was determined to have control of the physical attributes of her womanhood even if it meant routinely withstanding brutal beatings. Her resistance was a powerful lesson to Minnie.[8] (Decades after her freedom, she lamented the lack of resolve of young women of the early 1900s to resist their sexual exploitation, drawing on her own mother's stories to suggest the kind of resistance that these women should have mounted.)

Fannie Berry too had been the target of white male sexual abuse. But she had managed to escape without harm.[9] Fannie boasted of her successful act of resistance or, to use her own word, her "rebellion." But she could barely manage to conceal her delight when she told the tale of another slave woman, Sukie Abbott, "a big strappin' nigger gal," who resisted both her owner's sexual abuse and the slave trader's physical violation, linking the two as equally dehumanizing and, therefore, necessary for her to oppose.[10]

Sukie was the Abbott's cook, and Berry tells her audience that Mr. Abbott was always trying to "make his gal." One day while Sukie was in the kitchen making soap, Mr. Abbott tried to rape her. He pulled her dress down and tried to push her onto the floor. Then, according to Berry, "dat black gal got mad."

> She took an' punch ole Marsa an' made him break loose an' den she gave him a shove an' push his hindparts down in de hot pot o' soap. Soap was near to bilin', an' it burnt him near to death. He got up holdin' his hindparts an' ran from de kitchen, nor darin' to yell, 'cause he didn't want Miss Sarah Ann [his wife and Sukie's mistress] to know 'bout it.[11]

A few days later, Mr. Abbott took Sukie down to the slave market. She again faced sexual abuse and physical invasion as potential buyers stared, poked, and pinched her and checked the soundness of her teeth. According to Fannie, Sukie got mad again. Standing on the block, "she pult her dress up an' tole those ole nigger traders to look an' see if dey could fin' any teef down dere. . . . Marsa never did bother slave gals no mo," Berry added with relish.[12]

Many witnesses at the slave market in Petersburg that day no doubt thought Sukie vulgar and promiscuous. Not surprisingly, Fannie Berry, a woman who could attest to the kind of rage which emerged from the attempts to dehumanize slave women that Sukie had withstood, concluded something altogether different. According to Fannie, Sukie had exacted a high price from her master and the slave trader. True, she lost her slave community when Mr. Abbott sold her in retaliation for her resistance, but she still managed to deny her owner his supposed right to claim her "female principle." She also demanded that her new buyer see her for what she was, a woman (i.e., her physical reference to her sexual organs), not just a new work animal whose value could be assessed by looking at its teeth. And perhaps more important for the slave girls and women who came to know her story, Sukie lived on in lore as an example of slave female heroism and humanity, as the "nigger gal" whose acts of courageous defiance quelled Abbott's sexual abuse of his slave women and girls. (The fear of being "found out" by his wife, friends, and relations through a slave woman like Sukie whom he could not control seemed to have been too much for him.)[13]

Certainly it is less difficult to discern slave female notions of acceptable, or even heroic, behavior than to comprehend the roots of these ideals which, at the very least, are patently riddled with complexity. It is clear, for example, that many variables had impact. Literate African-Americans who had access to periodicals and other literature could have been as little or as greatly affected by published lectures, sermons, and stories on this subject as were literate whites. Certainly at least a significant minority had to have had some introduction to Christian beliefs about female behavior through local ministers and biblical interpretations of slave preachers and exhorters.[14]

Virginia's early female slaves also probably came into contact with several cultural models that included various prescriptions for gender-specific behavior. Most, for example, may have been familiar with broadly defined, Western European and West and Central African bodies of tradition which they could, at least theoretically, have drawn on while trying to design their own belief systems, practices, and ordered domestic world.[15] Obviously, the cultural attributes which defined the proper behavior for slave women changed over time as slaves moved from membership in African cultural groups to the creation of an African-American culture and society intricately intertwined with those of southern whites. What resulted was influenced not only by the amount and kind of exposure that Virginia's blacks had to these cultural models and their advocates but also by their perceptions of the viability of certain aspects of each standard in relation to their individual and group needs, along with their own personal affinities.

Time and location, for example, were operable variables which helped to prescribe the cultural affinities of southern slaveholders and their slaves. So too did "class" and "ethnic" differences among slaveholders. Among the "master" class in Virginia, for example, there were many differences of class as well as ethnicity which not only may account for numerous differences in the idealized gender-specific behavior of southern European-Americans but also may have affected the kinds of idealized behavior that their slaves may have internalized from contact with them. "Class" and "ethnic" differences among the slaves themselves undoubtedly were even more influential.

Among Virginia slave women, "class" and even "ethnicity" often were associated with the kind of work that they performed because the spatial relationship, differential skill, and material reward levels of women with different occupations sometimes formed something of a social, cultural, and sometimes even moral barrier between them. To an important extent, for example, field "hands" and house "servants" constructed different identities. These boundaries often were reinforced when color (which also was a potent standard of slave female beauty and something of a prerequisite for some occupations) also fell along these occupational lines. Obviously much of this kind of class stratification can be attributed to the value impositions and needs of slaveholders who demanded that their "servant" women adopt their ideals of personal conduct, morality, marriage, and family.

At stake, as far as domestics were concerned, was their place in the plantation's occupational spectrum and the kind of rewards and privileges that place afforded juxtaposed against the morality, self-definitions, and culture of the majority of slaves who lived differently from them. The eventual range of response was great: while some still resisted, others acquiesced, and some even enjoyed their cultural assimilation and the behavioral standards it imposed. "'We never went to a party in our lives,'" explained the supposedly "handsome and lady-like Custis house servant." "Mother would not let any of her children go to parties. We were as genteely [sic] brought up as white people.'"[16] Clearly, this light-skinned, domestic female slave drew great distinction between her socialization and "identity" and those of field or less "genteely" bred slave women. She not only applauded her ability and desire to imitate the social graces, restraint, and morality of her mistress' class and culture but also believed that her doing so made her quite different from and superior to those slave women who acted otherwise.

Female field laborers, on the other hand, usually did not face the same kind of pressures from their masters and mistresses to conform. This is not to say that there were no agricultural workers who shared or purposefully adopted some of the gendered social ideals of southern whites. Yet, more often than not, their standards were influenced by the needs, priorities, and opinion of the majority of slaves who, like themselves, lived and worked outside much of the influence of the "big house."

The field slave woman's "resistance" to this kind of control of her intimate and public life, along with the other pressures of slave life and the existence of a non-European cultural heritage within her community, created codes of morality and activity and a basis for identity that sometimes were remarkably close to those of slaveholders, but also could differ profoundly. Slave women of various statuses, for example, appreciated within each other demonstrations of kindness, generosity, warmth, piety, service, and selflessness—characteristics which southern society often applauded in the personalities of antebellum white women of all classes but especially expected of the elite. Yet most slave women, except those who felt particularly intimately or emotionally tied to their owners, also applauded indications of self-determination and resistance to white male authority in their behavior that most whites believed improper female conduct.[17]

Service to one's family and community were significant commitments that slave females learned early in the quarters. Behavior indicative of selflessness, generosity, kindness, and warmth were part of the assistance or service that slave women gave their families and slave friends. These activities not only allowed slave women an opportunity to demonstrate their humanity and femininity but also were suggestive to other slaves that they recognized and respected the humanity and frailties of fellow slaves. Often the aid these women rendered was gender specific. Young slave females, for example, learned to share the domestic duties or "women's work" in their families, often caring for younger siblings, washing and making clothes for their kin, and helping to prepare meals. This sphere of labor, taught and supervised by women and performed almost exclusively by females, reinforced within these slave girls a sense of their "femaleness" and helped to maintain gender bonds and boundaries that the labor they performed outside of their homes threatened to blur.

Yet their mothers and socializing kin also taught their daughters other important sociopolitical behavioral skills that were not gender specific. Young male and female slaves learned a whole collection of dos and don'ts derived from communal concerns, such as not to abuse other slaves through lying and stealing, to keep the secrets of the quarters from whites, to protect and aid runaways, to help sick and disabled slaves by sharing their work loads, and to give covert aid to one another whenever possible.[18] Obedience and reverence of slave elders was another important lesson, as was a general and genuine attitude of respect for other slaves.[19]

The emphasis on gender-specific behavior within slave families became more important as children grew older. As slave girls reached adolescence, their mothers and other female kin prepared them to take on the most important commitments of their adult lives—marriage and motherhood. Indeed, whatever class or ethnic distinctions various occupations may have imposed on slave females, their roles as wives and mothers were universally important. "Master married me to one of the best colored men in the world," Marriah Hines told her interviewer. "I had five chillun by him."[20] It was bad luck for a girl to walk around with one shoe off, another ex-slave said. "She'll stay single as many years as the number of steps she taken."[21]

Hines's statement rightfully suggests that the significance of marriage and motherhood was intimately bound up in slave women's constructions of their identity. Yet motherhood in itself was singularly important to adult female identity and morality. Elizabeth Keckley's autobiography, for example, details the scabrous circumstances under which she, as a Virginia slave woman, gained a sense of her need to protect herself and have some control of her daily life as well as her future.[22] Mrs. Keckley confirmed that she first learned a sense of self-reliance while acting as the surrogate mother to her mistress' child, noting that when she was only four years old she was given the burdensome task of caring for the newborn baby.[23] Yet it was her own motherhood which compelled her to the realization that she had to be resilient, resourceful, and rebellious enough to protect, if not her own life, then certainly that of her son.[24] The all-important roles of bearing and rearing one's own children caused many other Virginia slave women to conclude, and act, similarly.

Slave mothers viewed their youngsters both as extensions of their identities—a continuation of their kinship lines and proof of their existence—and as providers of future care and consolation. The importance of slave children as future bearers of their mothers' family heritage especially is suggested in the naming patterns evident among slave families. Often slave women, for example, named their daughters for themselves as well as other female relations.[25] These same slave mothers also often spoke of their young as persons on whom they could depend for love, comfort, and service when they became older. "Tho I know From my heart that you and Mistress would never See me Suffer as long as my Body Lives and you Live," the slave woman Phillis wrote to Mr. and Mrs. St. George Tucker during the 1820s, "I am going down very fast to my grave and . . . I would [like to] go and Live those other few dais with master Beverly and my Children."[26] "My last child died two weeks ago," lamented a slave mother at Craney Island, Virginia. "She was amazing helpful. She could sew and knit. She could spin and weave and mind the chickens and tend the children."[27] In spite of the oppressive and inevitably painful experiences of black women trying to rear their children as slaves, most respected and embraced their motherhood.

Even though child rearing was a task that slave mothers shared with other slave females in their families and quarters, they closely supervised the upbringing of their young. Many risked altercations with slaveholding men and women by merely asserting that they should have command over their children's lives.[28] The bond that slave women felt with their youngsters caused many to make innumerable sacrifices—heroic sacrifices that they were proud to recount in their interviews and autobiographies. Some, like Mary Ann Wyatt of King and Queen County and Caroline Taylor of Norfolk, for example, worked incessantly in order to gain the right to "hire out" their "time" and that of their children.[29] Others managed to escape to freedom with some of their young.[30] Countless more refused opportunities to run away because they did not want to leave their youngsters behind.[31]

The majority of slave mothers realistically were not able to secure their children from the most devastating consequences of slavery, such as brutal whippings and permanent separation from family and loved ones. Few slaves even expected that these women would risk further harm to themselves or their families by publicly criticizing slaveholding men and women who were responsible for such acts.[32] After all, a mother's fundamental priority was to keep her family intact. More often than not, open defiance of her master or mistresses did more to threaten this hope than to promote it. Yet slave women did celebrate and "create" females who occasionally risked themselves (not their children or someone else) in order to make their feelings, as mothers, known.

Nancy Williams of Yanceville, Virginia, for example, recalled the story of "Ant Cissy," a slave woman who called their owner a "mean dirty nigger-trader" when he sold her daughter Lucy. When her son Hendley died some time later, Cissy refused to publicly acknowledge any grief for her son's death, preferring instead to again take the opportunity to voice her bitter feelings about Lucy's sale. "Ant Cissy ain't sorrored much" at the death of her child, Williams concluded. "She went straight up to ole Marsa' an' shouted in his face, 'Praise Gawd, praise Gawd! My little chile is gone to Jesus. That's one chile of mine you never gonna sell.'" In Williams's tale, Ant Cissy took tremendous risk when she criticized her master, not once but two times, for the power he exercised over her daughter's life. Through this image, however, Williams celebrates a woman who spoke for countless other slave women who suffered her pain and loss, sometimes repeatedly. If Nancy's story is completely accurate, Cissy's master probably wrote her off as a crazy old woman whose outburst posed little threat to his authority. Still the risk she took, and the cause she took on, made her a heroic image in the minds of young slave women like Nancy Williams.[33]

And slave women did not just verbally criticize their owners for mistreatment of their children. Relying on their sense of responsibility as mothers, they rebelled against the poor material support that slaveholding men and women provided their families. Slave motherhood meant not hesitating to steal, lie, and cheat in order to guarantee the physical survival of their children and themselves.[34] Their numerous stories of defiance in this regard again emphasized their determination to create self-images in which they had some control of their lives and used it to protect their children.[35]

Perhaps two of the most significant variables which affected the lifestyles of slave women and their interpretation of it, given the importance of marriage and motherhood to slave female identity, were their domestic relations and the conditions of domesticity owners imposed upon them. The size and makeup of slave holdings, as well as the domestic structures these demographic characteristics in part inspired, undoubtedly exerted influence. Let us first consider the residential patterns of slave couples and families, and then some of the possible impact these patterns may have had on the behavioral standards, identity, and morality of the women involved.

Virginia's slaves were part of a variety of marriage, family, and household types—nuclear and extended family structures; monogamous, polygamous, and serial marriages; single and multiple generational households of various combinations of kin, friends, and sometimes strangers. This was so even when conditions theoretically seemed optimal for them to be part of nuclear households, such as a large slaveholding boasting equal numbers of men and women. Moreover, even that significant minority of slaves who lived in nuclear households did not experience the kind of family or domestic life that was synonymous with those who were free and middle class.[36] Consider some characteristics of slave residential patterns in Virginia.

At least from the mid–eighteenth century through the antebellum era, slave women dominated small slaveholdings, living on farms and in households where there were few adult slave men. Matrifocality was the most common characteristic of their household and family styles. Their small slave communities and households, in fact, were those comprising largely single mothers, abroad wives, and their children. Those who were married usually had monogamous, but not coresidential, and oftentimes short-term, or serial, relationships. The situation could, however, shift drastically for women who were part of larger holdings. Marriageable-aged men, for example, often dominated the population of moderate and large holdings (of ten or more). These findings are significant because they indicate that even when the general sex ratio was virtually even within the adult age cohorts within the larger populations, most slaveholdings, whether large or small, did not have nearly equal numbers of men and women in childbearing, marriageable-age cohorts.[37]

Moreover, while there tended to be greater numerical equality between men and women of marriageable age on holdings of twenty or more slaves, the men and women who were part of these holdings often were not married to one another. Instead of these holdings producing nuclear families and coresidential spouses, a variety of residential and family forms emerged, particularly large numbers of single men living together, and again single mothers and abroad wives living with their children and sometimes other kin, but not their children's fathers.

The frequent practice of Virginia slave owners of distributing slave laborers (men and women) across several working properties with little regard for family or marriage ties, the impact of the domestic slave trade and slave rental business, the complex rules of exogamy which slaves exercised, and the significant element of slave choice with regard to marriage partners were all factors which contributed to the lack of coresidential married couples and nuclear families among large slave holdings.

George Washington, for example, was one of Virginia's largest slaveholders at the end of the eighteenth century. According to his own compilations, in 1799 Washington controlled 316 slaves whom he distributed among the five farms which comprised his Mount Vernon estate. While it is certain that Washington was opposed to breaking up and thus destroying slave families through sale, it also is obvious that he routinely determined the residences of his slaves based on his labor and production needs at the time, rather than his concern that slave couples or families share the same residences. His priorities, in turn, helped to create an expansive slave community across his property—a slave community characterized by a diversity of marriage styles and family and household structures. Particularly prevalent were examples of abroad marriage, residential matrifocality, and significant numbers of single parents (principally mothers) and single adults (especially men). Of the 183 men and women on the estate in 1799, for example, a significant number (30 percent) were not married at all: of those who were married, 66 percent were in abroad marriages and did not live with their spouse. Only 16.5 percent lived together as husband and wife. Relatedly, the large majority (74 percent) of those slave families among Washington's 316 slaves which included children did not have fathers living with them because the children's mothers either had abroad marriages or were not married at all (30 percent were single). The patterns of family life among the Washington slaves which persisted on his farms deny that there was a preponderance of residentially nuclear families and question the functional importance of monogamy even when it did exist, since most "monogamous" couples did not live together.[38]

The slaves on George Washington's farms are but one example; there is much evidence of this kind of slave distribution and residential diversity throughout the state and over time. Slave lists from Virginia counties as geographically diverse as Sussex and Gloucester in the southeast, Nottoway and Charlotte in the southern piedmont, Essex in the central tidewater region, Frederick and Fairfax in the north, Madison in the mountainous west, and the city of Richmond for the period 1756 through 1865 provide conclusive documentation of these kinds of domestic situations for slaves throughout the state.[39]

What perhaps is even more indicative of the challenges to and change of family life among these slaves is evidence of slave community dispersal and possible destruction found throughout the state and over the generations. Slave registers retained in the family papers of Colonel C. W. Gooch of Richmond, for example, provide an opportunity to view the changes that occurred in a moderate-sized slaveholding in urban tidewater Virginia during the antebellum era. The Gooch list of 1830, when compared with the lists of 1839 and 1852, suggests a clear pattern of slave family and community destruction within a relatively short period of time: twenty-one of the thirty-five Gooch slaves (or 60 percent) listed in 1830 did not reappear on the slave registers of 1839 or 1852. Nine males and eleven females, or over half of the Gooch slave community, disappeared from 1830 to 1839. Sale and high mortality rates undoubtedly produced this extreme loss in the Gooch slave community and families over this brief interim. A note written on the 1830 list provides details of the fate of some of these slaves: "Sell Juliet and child and Milly and put two boys in their places[.] Sell William and replace him with a likely Tractable boy for the house— hire some of the young females out—and put out others for their victuals and clothes—."[40]

More often than not, therefore, Virginia slave women, even domestic and other privileged slave women, were single mothers and abroad wives who faced the challenge of rearing their children and addressing their families' needs without the daily attention or resources of their husbands or the fathers of their children. Those females who lived in small holdings, in particular, effectively were raised and later reared their own children in black female-dominated communities—there were few slave men of any relation (husband, blood relation, or friend) available to share daily care, socialization, or leadership tasks. Moreover, slave women faced the mounting threat of profound change even to these kinds of domestic arrangements, since more and more women and children left the state or their previous residence as part of the domestic slave trade and slave rental business over time. And keep in mind that most did not leave with their families intact. Recall, for example, that between 1830 and 1839, more slave women than men disappeared from the Gooch slave list. Some of these women (like Milly) were sold with their youngest children or child, but increasingly they were sold alone, as were their children. Slave women in female-dominated households and communities, therefore, not only had to act practically as mother, father, and household head but also had to prepare themselves and their children to expect that one day they would have to survive even without the limited resources that they offered each other when they had the luxury of living together.

The kind of slave marital and familial diversity and instability prevalent among Virginia slaves had both practical and ideological influence on female gender convention, morality, and self-definition. Faced with profound challenges to their effectiveness or even permanence as wives, mothers, and community members, they appreciated oppositional and self-deterministic behavior. These ideals, after all, contextualized slave women's physical and psychological resistance to authority located outside of themselves and their communities.[41]

Certainly the residential patterns and consequent marital and familial structures of slave women were not the only determinants of female slave behavior. The oppositional nature of slave culture and its origins, in general, and the nature of female identity among slave women, more than anything else, were responsible for the behavioral ideals and the ideology of heroic identities they constructed. Yet, in a society in which European-American female powerlessness and passivity, submission and secondhand citizenship emerged as by-products of a powerful patriarchy operating within the designs of coresidential nuclear family, it is not difficult to understand that without this patriarchy, their nuclear families and their male household head, white women's lives, to say nothing of their ideals, also would have been quite different. This kind of gendered dichotomy found in most white southern homes at the time was not a reality for slave men and women. It was not even a reality in the minority of slave families that comprised a resident father, mother, and children.

Slave husbands never provided the sole or most significant means of financial support for their wives and children. Husbands had no legal claim to their families and, accordingly, could not legitimately demand their economic resources or offer them protection from abuse or exploitation. The primary role of the slave mother, if compared with "mainstream" American gender convention, also was deeply compromised, for she never was able to give the needs of her husband and children greatest priority. Even though most slave children were part of matrifocal families, the slave woman's most important daily activities encompassed the labor that she performed for her owner, not for her family. This responsibility claimed so much of her time and energy that childbearing was limited, while child rearing necessarily was a task she shared with a number of females, within and outside of her blood and marriage-related family. These were the usual circumstances for slave life even when they were part of nuclear families. For that majority of men, women, and children who did not live as such, idealized notions of female passivity and helplessness were even more absurd. Most slave children grew up in households with their mothers but not their fathers present on a daily basis. It was their mothers who had to make the day-to-day decisions that fashioned their lives, their mothers and other members of their female communities who had to provide whatever protection and support they received. The male presence was so tenuous because of imposed residential isolation and frequent sale and hiring that women became the stabilizing forces in slave families and communities.

It comes as no surprise, then, that there are so many exemplary and heroic women found in the autobiographical stories of Virginia slave women. Heroism in the face of such austere social conditions became an especially important characteristic in slave women's self-identity.

The historical texts comprising the interviews that slave and ex-slave women like Fannie Berry gave, therefore, are important descriptive chronicles of southern society from the black female perspective. Crisscrossing the persons, events, and attitudes which were part of her life, Berry presents her audience not only with her own story but also with an array of narratives centered on the lives of other females whom she had come to know and sometimes to respect—the courageous and clever Mamy Lou; "Poor A'nt Nellie," who chose suicide rather than face another brutal beating; the much-loved Rachel, who managed to find her way back to her family after being illegally sold; the secretive Polly Monroe, who kept her free black husband hidden in her cabin's root cellar; the conflicted child Daphne, who finally chose to live with her master and mistress rather than her slave family; the indomitable Sukie, who fought her owner for control of her body; and, of course, Berry's consistently compromised slave mistress, Miss Sarah Ann.

Curiously, but not surprisingly given their lack of numbers at her place of residence, men rarely appear in Berry's long and detailed account of her life and the lives of the other women she spoke about. Her narrative is not unique in this regard. When men are present, they lack the complexity and moral presence of the women whose lives she so vividly recalls. The men are "stock figures," almost stereotypical in character. There are, for example, the sadistic, sexually depraved slave masters; the devious, deceptive slave traders; and the fun-loving, emasculated, black male youths like Mamy Lou's John. Fannie rarely mentions her husband, a railroad man whom she sees only occasionally. She makes no mention of a father at all. Instead, the slave women she brings to life take on "typical" masculine characteristics: they are bold, active, courageous, aggressive and self-determined.[42]

The identity that Fannie Berry and others constructed for themselves stood in stark contrast to their characterizations of white women. Calling planter women "hell cats" and "devils," slave girls and women implicated the immoral, indeed "unholy," behavior of slaveholding women who they believed abandoned their promise of "Christian" or moral female behavior when they forced black women to steal food, lie about slave activities, feign illness, and generally participate in all kinds of resistance behavior.[43] Not surprisingly, slave females especially reacted strongly to those slaveholding women whose actions or attitudes had had some effect on their roles as wives and mothers or, generally, had some impact on slave family life. The fact that Liza Brown's mistress had Liza's mother stripped naked and beaten when she was pregnant, for example, seemed to incense Liza much more than the usual abuse this mistress meted out to other slaves who were not in that condition.[44] Eliza Smith was accepting of her mistress' dishonesty and abuse until she refused to pay for the appropriate medical attention for Eliza's son.[45] Cordelia Long put up with years of abuse from her mistress until this slaveholding woman sold Cordelia's two children.[46]

On the other hand, Fannie Berry thought that her female owner was especially kind to attempt to keep slave couples and families united and to purchase the husbands of her slave women. Fannie also praised another slaveholding woman, Delia Mann, and other members of her family for the respect they demonstrated for her marriage—allowing the wedding to take place in their parlor and providing food for a reception.[47] The one act of generosity that Mildred Graves described when speaking of her slave experience was that her mistress had given her a "cast off dress" in which she was married.[48]

Slave women thus conspicuously constructed not only their own identities in their recollections but also the identities of their mistresses. Consider Fannie Berry's portrayal of her slave mistress, Sarah Ann Abbott. "Miss Sarah Ann was uh fine woman, even ef she was uh slave owner," Berry noted with a sense of finality to her description. The ex-slave obviously weighed carefully her good and bad memories of the white woman who had been such a large part of her life and that of her family and community of slave women before she rendered her concluding assessment. Miss Sarah Ann, according to Berry, was not of heroic character, but she "was very good to her slaves" and for that Berry was willing to give her credit. She took care of them when they were sick, allowed them to have a pet (a cat the slaves playfully named Tom Nippy Cat), tried to keep some slave couples united, and even dared to question a neighboring slave master's harsh treatment of his slave property.[49]

Even while extolling the virtues of Sarah Ann, however, Fannie could not erase the relative quality of her description—"Miss Sarah Ann was uh fine woman, even ef she was uh slave owner." For Berry realized that regardless of what Abbott had done for her slaves, she had been a member of the slaveholding class who benefited from the oppression of Fannie and the other blacks whom she owned. Since Berry's code of morality and certainly her sense of female heroism were intricately tied to a fundamental quest for black survival, humanity, and freedom (of spirit if not body), she hardly could afford Mrs. Abbott an unambiguous character reference.

But Fannie did not view Sarah Ann as just another slaveholder with like-minded priorities. Mrs. Abbott also was a woman, and part of Fannie Berry's judgment of Sarah Ann Abbott clearly was grounded in her convictions about female identity, the purposeful and privileged behavior of women, convictions that she derived from the experiences and ideals of slave women. Time and time again in her narration of her days as a slave, Berry juxtaposes her life and those of other slave women whom she had known with that of her mistress, provocatively suggesting the profound limitations (physical, emotional, situational, moral) that Mrs. Abbott, even as a white and a member of the elite, maintained in her interactions with her slaves. It was these limitations (or her unwillingness to make certain sacrifices in order to help her slaves), in Berry's judgment, that denied a basic heroic content in Mrs. Abbott's character that could have linked her, as a woman, to slave women.

While this mistress did not sanction the sale of slaves but rather hired them out, she seemingly could not keep her husband from selling those whom he found troublesome. Nor could Sarah Ann deter him from pursuing the sexual favors of her slave cook. She could not prevent her neighbor from whipping one of his slaves to death; nor did she feel able or compelled to report it to the local authorities after witnessing the brutal crime. The conditional quality of Berry's opinion of Sarah Ann Abbott, therefore, continuously begs the question of how a woman of such power (derived from her race and socioeconomic status) could feign such powerlessness in the aid of her slaves when women like Mamy Lou, who was poor, black, and merely the property of Abbott and her husband, found the wherewithal to do otherwise.

Indeed, it is certain that while Berry concluded that Abbott's intentions toward her slaves usually were good, she often depicted this slaveholding woman's ameliorative role in the lives of her blacks as a passive one, prodigiously hemmed in by her "place" as a woman and her economic concerns and sense of class allegiance as a slaveholder.[50] These deep-seated qualities of this white woman's personality and lifestyle did not elude the sharp eye of Fannie Berry and figured prominently in her moral assessment.[51] The choices that Berry believed that Mrs. Abbott—white, socially prominent, and with relatively substantial financial resources—made with regard to her slaves clearly were not the choices that she believed that she, as a slave woman, necessarily would have made.[52]

Indeed, the combination of ideals incumbent in the self-images slave women actively created in their verbal and written texts—the one set which embraced a survivalist, self-determined philosophy and the other which emphasized service, honesty, selflessness, and good works—sometimes seemed at odds. Yet they were not conflicting value systems. Rather they comprised one system of morality, a morality whose benefits were exclusive to those who lived and acted within the community from which it derived, a morality founded on the perpetuation of black life, humanity, and femininity through good works and service within and opposition to those without who threatened this perpetuation.

Fannie Berry's autobiographical account, like those of other Virginia slave females discussed here, are provocative for several reasons. They clearly presuppose significant intellectual processes among slave women in the creation of distinct models of behavior and in their suggestion of how these codes facilitated a means of group identity and exclusion, support and pride, among bonded females.[53]

Slave women imposed their ideas and ideals about female behavior not only on each other but also on the planter women with whom they came in contact. Their demonstrations of disregard for or disobedience of slaveholding women often were fundamental indictments of their disrespect for these elite women—disrespect grounded in slave women's beliefs about appropriate female behavior. Thus, while the southern antebellum patriarchy actively mythologized the elite white woman as the model of femininity for the world to emulate, slave women relied on their own standards. They created their own practical codes and a lofty mythology from their own reality and, in the wake, constructed viable, proud self-images that helped them evade dehumanization and defeminization.

Notes

1. Relying, as I do, principally on the autobiographical accounts of slave women that often were rendered some years after the institution of slavery had ended for them, and centering much of my discussion on "heroic" behavior, might be somewhat problematic. Yet, what is clear is that even in the fantastical musings of slave women about their lives, there is much to learn about their morality, that is, about their principles and purposes as bonded females in the American South. This is particularly so when it is apparent, as it is here, that these women continuously create the same kinds of fantasies, "long" tales, and reminiscences of their lives. Repeated reminiscences across generations and locales also is substantial evidence of the "truth" of many of these accounts that, examined across cultures, space, and time seem "fantastical" to the contemporary reader.

2. Similarly, some of the conduct examined here was not just specific to female slaves, particularly that with strong political connotations and that prescribed for children. Yet, much of what these women suggested was appropriate and valued behavior for females was derived from the unique experiences of their gender and, thus, was gender specific. This specificity, in turn, suggests both strong cultural and psychological alliances among slave women over the generations and across otherwise differentiating work and material conditions. Slave women's distinct notions of what was "good," bad, or heroic female-specific activity and conduct, connote a strong sense of group identity that, despite their common oppression as blacks and their diverse experiences as bonded people, often was gender centered.

3. Charles L. Perdue, Thomas E. Barden, and Robert K. Phillips, eds., *Weevils in the Wheat: Interviews with Virginia Ex-Slaves* (Charlottesville: University Press of Virginia, 1976), p. 34.

4. Manuscript Federal Census, Appomattox County, Virginia, Free Schedule, reel 933, pp. 168, 183; Slave Schedule reel 983, pp. 17, 95.

5. For the general importance of matrifocality, consider: 82 percent of ex-slaves in the compilation of Perdue et al., *Weevils in the Wheat*, who represented the last generation of Virginia bondwomen and men from around the state, spoke of the physical presence of their mothers during most of their childhood years, while only 42 percent recalled consistent contact with their fathers. Also, fully one-third of those who did make mention of the presence of their fathers during their childhoods noted that these men did not reside on the same farm or plantation with them, but lived elsewhere. Such "abroad" husbands and fathers visited only on weekend days or holidays. Regarding matrifocality on small and large holdings, also see Fitzhugh List (Madison Co.), 1853, Ambrose Powell Hill Papers, VHS; Ledger of William and Samuel Gatewood (Essex and Bath Cos.), 1772–1863, VHS; Robert and Charles Bruce Slave Lists (City of Richmond and Charlotte Co.), 1798–1859, Bruce Family Papers, VHS; William H. Gray List, (Loudoun Co.), 1839–1865, Gray Family Papers, VHS Joshua Skinner Slave List, 1785–1835, VHS, List of the Bryan Family Slaves (Gloucester Co.), 1845–1865, Grinnan Family Papers, VHS, Slave Lists of Col. C.W. Gooch (Richmond), 1830, 1839, 1852, Gooch Family Papers, VHS; Slave List of Sarah Fitzgerald (Nottoway Co.), 1864, Fitzgerald Family Papers, VHS; Digges Slave List, 1770–1860 (Frederick Co.), Digges Family Papers, VHS.

6. Much of the information provided in this study is drawn from the Federal Writers Project interviews of Virginia ex-slaves compiled in the excellent collection *Weevils in the Wheat*. Given the long debate about the appropriateness of relying on the FWP interviews of ex-slaves, it might be useful to the reader to know something about the interviews and about the interviewers whose work is contained in this collection. Scholars who have assessed the potential merit of this type of primary source information contend that one important problem has been the inability of ex-slaves to speak openly about their bonded lives because of the racial politics of the era of the interview and their vulnerability to white hostility. Historians have concluded, therefore, that some of the most forthcoming and reliable interviews were those that black interviewers were able to give. Unlike many FWP collections descriptive of slave life in other states, however, the majority of interviewers of the ex-slaves residing in Virginia were African-American. The editors of *Weevils in the Wheat* have identified thirteen of the twenty FWP workers who interviewed Virginia ex-slaves, or 65 percent, as "negro." John Blassingame further stipulates that of those interviewers who were European-American, ex-slaves clearly felt

more comfortable and, presumably, were more open in their discussions of slave life with white women than men. Of the seven European-American interviewers who participated in the Virginia study, at least six (or 86 percent) were female. The age of the interviewee is another salient factor. The average age of the ex-slaves in the *Weevils in the Wheat* collection was 15.44 years at the time of general emancipation in 1865. While this is a young average age, the reader should note that more than 45 percent of the Virginia slave population between 1820 and 1860 was fourteen years old or younger and that a female slave had been a full-time worker for at least two years by the time she reached age fifteen. Moreover, the life expectancy of antebellum slaves was quite short. Kenneth Stampp, for example, reports that the federal census of 1850 "reported average ages of 21.4" years. Fogel and Engerman conclude that "fully 40 percent" of slaves died before age nineteen years, although they assess a much longer life expectancy. One must also consider that the knowledge of the female slave experience that these ex-slave women in the Perdue compilation offer is drawn not only from their own experiences but also from those of older generations of slave female kin and close family members who passed them down and across generational lines to form a communal oral history. Kenneth Stampp, *The Peculiar Institution: Slavery in the Ante-bellum South* (New York: Random House, 1956), pp. 318–19; Robert Fogel and Stanley Engerman, *Time on the Cross: The Economics of American Negro Slavery* (Boston: Little, Brown, 1974), pp. 125, 154; Perdue et al., eds., *Weevils in the Wheat*, appendices 1, 4, 5 and passim; *The Negro in Virginia*, compiled by the Virginia Federal Writers' Project of the Work Projects Administration in the State of Virginia (New York: Hastings, 1940); John W. Blassingame, ed., *Slave Testimony: Two Centuries of Letters, Speeches, Interviews, and Autobiographies* (Baton Rouge: Louisiana State University Press, 1977), pp. xvii–lxv, esp. pp. xlii–lxii; Paul D. Escott, "The Art and Science of Reading WPA Slave Narratives," in *The Slave's Narrative*, ed. Charles T. Davis and Henry Louis Gates, Jr. (New York: Oxford University Press, 1985), p. 48; C. Vann Woodward, "History from Slave Sources," in *The Slave's Narrative*, pp. 48–59.

7. Perdue et al., *Weevils in the Wheat*, pp. 256–60.

8. Ironically, Folkes's account of her socialization stands in perverse contrast to those passed on by another group of antebellum southerners. One Virginia ex-slave, for example, expressed the sorrow that he felt for a raped black female teen as he recounted a legacy of misogyny and violence that her owner perpetuated: "[Ethel Mae] told me 'bout Marsa bringing his son Levey . . . down to the cabin," the former bondman noted. "They both took her—the father showing the son what it was all about." Perdue et al., *Weevils in the Wheat*, pp. 300–301. Also see Perdue et al., *Weevils in the Wheat*, pp. 36, 48–49, 93, 95–96, 257. Elizabeth Keckley, in *Behind the Scenes or, Thirty Years a Slave, and Four Years in the White House*, ed. James Olney (New York: Oxford University Press, 1988), pp. 38–39, wrote that she resisted the "base designs" and "persecutions" of a "white man" for four years.

9. Perdue et al., *Weevils in the Wheat*, p. 36.

10. Perdue et al., *Weevils in the Wheat*, pp. 257–59.

11. Perdue et al., *Weevils in the Wheat*, pp. 48–49.

12. Perdue et al., *Weevils in the Wheat*, p. 49.

13. Black women who fought off white men's sexual aggression also did so to protect their reputation with slave men. Although they knew they should be sympathetic to abused women, few men felt comfortable embracing a slave woman who appeared to prefer the sexual attention of white rather than black men. Even those women who were

forced to have sexual relations with slaveholding men (and most were forced) some-times received a mixed reception in the slave community. See Perdue et al., *Weevils in the Wheat*, pp. 117, 202, 207. Neither Fannie nor Sukie would have approved of publicly baring one's sexual organs under different circumstances. Slave women gener-ally frowned on blatant female sexual exhibition or promiscuity. Yet few were ashamed of their sexuality or the promise of sexual pleasure and human procreation that they as women embodied. Still, their sexual expression and experience, like other realms of their behavior, were guided by rules, rules that they formulated and articulated. Sex in the slave female world, for example, was part of the culture of adults, ideally married adults, not children and young teens. Many mothers, in fact, went to great lengths to shield their young daughters from knowledge of the actual sexual act. Minnie Folkes's mother married her at a young age and did not instruct Minnie of her sexual duties to her husband; she refused to have sexual intercourse with her husband until her mother told her that it was her duty as a wife to do so. Minnie said that her mother had taught her that she should provide other services to her husband—cook, clean, take care of his clothes, but nothing about "bothering" her "principle," and she refused to have sex with her husband until her mother told her that it was proper for her to do so.

14. Regarding Virginia slaves and religion, see, for example, Perdue et al., *Weevils in the Wheat*, pp. 52, 93, 113, 199, 124, 201, 221, 310. Also see Albert J. Raboteau, *Slave Religion: The "Invisible Institution" in the Antebellum South* (New York: Oxford Univer-sity Press, 1978), pp. 239–43; John Blassingame, *The Slave Community: Plantation Life in the Old South*, rev. ed. (New York: Oxford University Press, 1980), pp. 130–47; Eugene Genovese, *Roll, Jordan Roll: The World the Slaves Made* (New York: Vintage, 1974), pp. 232–55.

15. Regarding the varied traditional lifestyles of African women residing in those areas affected by the Atlantic slave trade, see Sylvia A. Boone, *Radiance from the Waters: Ideals of Feminine Beauty in Mende Art* (New Haven: Yale University Press, 1986); G. Adaba, M. Bekombo-Priso, J. Mogey, and C. Oppong, eds. *Marriage, Fertility and Parenthood in West Africa* (Canberra: Australian National University, 1978); C. Oppong, ed., "Fertility, Parenthood and Development: Yoruba Experiences," in *Sex Roles, Popu-lation and Development in West Africa* (London: International Labour Organization, 1987); Jeffrey and Karen Piage, *The Politics of Reproductive Ritual* (Berkeley: University of California Press, 1981); Carolyn Sargent, *Maternity, Medicine and Power: Reproduc-tive Decisions in Urban Benin* (Berkeley: University of California Press, 1982); Mary Smith, *Baba of Karo: A Woman of the Moslem Hausa* (New York: Praeger, 1964); John S. Mbiti, *African Religions and Philosophy*, 2d ed. (Oxford: Heinemann, 1990); Denise Paulme, *Women of Tropical Africa* (Berkeley: University of California Press, 1974); Mary Douglas, "The Lele of Kasai," in Daryll Forde, ed., *African Worlds: Studies in the Cosmo-logical Ideas and Social Values of African Peoples* (Oxford: Oxford University Press, 1954), pp. 2–7, 13–15; Kenneth Little, "The Mende in Sierra Leone," in Forde, ed., *African Worlds*, pp. 111–13, 115–35; K.A. Busia, "The Ashanti," in Forde, ed., *African Worlds*, 196–207; P. Mercier, "The Fon of Dahomey," 210–33. Regarding the gender conventions of white women popular during the eras this work considers, see, for ex-ample, "A Good Wife," *American Ladies Magazine* 8, no. 4 (April 1835): 228–30, VSL; "On Domestic Industry: An Address to Young Ladies," *Ladies Magazine and Lit-erary Gazette* 6, no. 7 (July 1833): 327, VSL; "Formation of Domestic Habits," *Ladies Magazine and Literary Gazette* 8, no. 11 (November 1835): 465, VSL; "What Women

Should Do?" *Ladies Magazine and Literary Gazette* 8, no. 5 (May 1835): 241–44, VSL; and "Woman's Piety," *Ladies Magazine and Literary Gazette* 6, no. 5 (May 1833): 245, VSL. Also see Nancy Cott, *The Bonds of Womanhood: Woman's Sphere in New England* (New Haven: Yale University Press, 1970), pp. 63–100; Christopher Lasch, *Haven in a Heartless World* (New York: Oxford University Press, 1977); Michael Gordon, "The Husband as Depicted in the Nineteenth-Century Marriage Manual," in *The American Man*, ed. Elizabeth Pleck and Joseph Pleck (Englewood Cliffs, N.J.: Prentice-Hall, 1980), pp. 147–57; and Elizabeth Pleck, "Two Worlds in One," *Journal of Social History* 10, no. 2 (Spring 1976): 178–95.

16. Henry Swint, ed., *Dear Ones at Home: Letters from Contraband Camps* (Nashville: Vanderbilt University Press, 1979), p. 36.

17. Catherine Clinton, *The Plantation Mistress: Woman's World in the Old South* (New York: Pantheon, 1982), pp. 17–29; Elizabeth Fox-Genovese, *Within the Plantation Household: Black and White Women of the Old South* (Chapel Hill: University of North Carolina Press, 1988), pp. 202–3.

18. Perdue et al., *Weevils in the Wheat*, pp. 26, 55–56, 238, 267, 317; Swint, ed., *Dear Ones at Home* pp. 36, 96.

19. Perdue et al., *Weevils in the Wheat*, p. 235.

20. Perdue et al., *Weevils in the Wheat*, p. 142.

21. Perdue et al., *Weevils in the Wheat*, p. 249.

22. Keckley, *Behind the Scenes*, pp. 19–20.

23. Keckley, *Behind the Scenes*, pp. 19–20.

24. Keckley, *Behind the Scenes*, pp. 29–62.

25. List of slaves of Ann Powell Burwell, VHS; Ledger of Cyrus and William Gatewood, Gatewood Family Papers, VHS. Also see Herbert Gutman, *The Black Family in Slavery and Freedom, 1750–1925* (New York: Pantheon, 1976), pp. 197–201; Gutman makes note of the repeated naming of slave boys for their fathers as an indication of the importance of fathers in the slave family. Yet analyses of other slave lists, such as that of Ann Burwell, indicate that just as important was the naming of female slaves for their maternal kin. Also see Cheryll Ann Cody, "There Was No 'Absalom' on the Ball Plantations: Slave-Naming Practices in the South Carolina Low Country, 1720–1865," *American Historical Review* 92 (1987): 563–96.

26. Blassingame, ed., *Slave Testimony*, p. 10.

27. Swint, ed., *Dear Ones at Home*, p. 61.

28. Swint, ed., *Dear Ones at Home*, p. 127.

29. Blassingame, ed., *Slave Testimony*, pp. 454–55; Still, ed., *Underground Railroad*, p. 328.

30. See, for example, William Still, ed., *Underground Railroad* (New York: Arno Press, 1968), pp. 129, 260, 328, 411.

31. See, for example, Deborah Gray White, *Ar'n't I a Woman? Female Slaves in the Plantation South* (New York: Norton, 1985), pp. 70–71.

32. See, for example, Perdue et al., *Weevils in the Wheat*, pp. 68, 236, 292.

33. Perdue et al., *Weevils in the Wheat*, pp. 322–23. This story also is attributed, with slight variation, to Beverly Jones, p. 183 of the same text. Both stories were found in the Virginia State Library archives, but there seems little hope of determining who was its author. Beverly Jones and Nancy Williams were enslaved in different parts of the state, although Williams moved to an area close to Jones's residence after emancipation. It is possible that she could have heard the story from other ex-slaves living in the vicinity and

incorporated it into hers. There also is the possibility that the interviewers or the library staff mistakenly duplicated the one story and placed it in both files.

34. Perdue et al., *Weevils in the Wheat*, pp. 201–2, 244–45, 266–67.

35. Perdue et al., *Weevils in the Wheat*, pp. 266–67.

36. Other views of slave family structure can be found in John Blassingame's discussion of the development of a monogamous slave family in *The Slave Community: Plantation Life in the Antebellum South*, 1st ed. (New York: Oxford University Press, 1972), pp. 77–78, 80–81, 87–88; Blassingame, *The Slave Community*, pp. 149–91, esp. pp. 157–91; Genovese, *Roll, Jordan Roll*, pp. 443–501; Herbert Gutman, *The Black Family in Slavery and Freedom, 1750–1925* (New York: Pantheon, 1976); White, *Ar'n't I a Woman?*; Deborah White, "Female Slaves: Sex Roles and Status in the Antebellum Plantation South," *Journal of Family History* 3, no. 3 (Fall 1983): 248–61. For postrevisionist views, see, for example, Ann Patton Malone, *Sweet Chariot: Slave Family and Household Structure in Nineteenth Century Louisiana* (Chapel Hill: University of North Carolina Press, 1992).

37. See, for example, the distribution of males and females among Loudoun County holdings at the end of the era. The male/female ratio for those aged fifteen to forty-five years who were part of holdings of between two and ten slaves in 1850, for example, was only 43. The slave women in these size holdings outnumbered the men by more than two to one. Of those slaves between fifteen and forty-five years in slaveholdings of more than ten slaves in 1850, however, there was a male/female ratio of 1.61. Also see the following slave lists from throughout Virginia and over longer periods of time: Fitzhugh List (Madison Co.), 1853, Ambrose Powell Hill Papers, VHS; Ledger of William and Samuel Gatewood (Essex and Bath Cos.), 1772–1863, VHS; Robert and Charles Bruce Slave Lists (City of Richmond and Charlotte Co.), 1798–1859, Bruce Family Papers, VHS; Joshua Skinner Slave List, 1785–1835, VHS, List of the Bryan Family Slaves (Gloucester Co.), 1845–1865, Grinnan Family Papers, VHS, Slave Lists of Col. C.W. Gooch (Richmond), 1830, 1839, 1852, Gooch Family Papers, VHS; Slave List of Sarah Fitzgerald (Nottoway Co.), 1864, Fitzgerald Family Papers, Va. Hist. Soc; Digges Slave List, 1770–1860 (Frederick Co.), Digges Family Papers, VHS.

38. Among George Washington's five farms, the Mount Vernon or "home" plantation had the largest slaveholdings. Its size and the nature of the work of the house, yard, and skilled slaves, which would have brought them physically and perhaps emotionally "close" to their master, might have provided a conducive atmosphere for the maintenance of residential nuclear families among the slaves. To some extent it did—27 percent of these slaves lived in nuclear households. The remaining persons lived quite differently. The adult men at the Mansion House, for example, outnumbered the women by almost two to one (forty-four men, twenty-three women), allowing few of the men to marry the women who worked and resided on this part of the Washington estate. More than one-third of the Mansion House slave men were not married, and 60 percent of the married men had abroad wives. Altogether, 61 percent of the married men (twenty-one) and women (four) at Washington's home plantation, for example, did not live with their spouses but had aboard husbands or wives. There also were two single mothers. Consequently, more slave children lived in households with only their mothers present than with both parents. Moreover, a substantial number of resident men (fifteen, or 34 percent) and women (eleven) were not married at all. These single adults usually lived with extended family members or their families of birth or in gender-segregated housing. Collectively, the other four farms which Washington owned offer even more

exaggerated conditions of residential and complete matrifocality, abroad marriages, and single adults.

39. Slave lists surveyed include Fitzhugh List (Madison Co.), 1853, Ambrose Powell Hill Papers, VHS; Ledger of William and Samuel Vance Gatewood (Essex and Bath Cos.), 1772–1863, VHS; Robert and Charles Bruce Slave Lists (City of Richmond and Charlotte Co.), 1798–1859, Bruce Family Papers, VHS; Joshua Skinner Slave List, 1785–1835, VHS, List of the Bryan Family Slaves (Gloucester Co.), 1845–1865, Grinnan Family Papers, VHS; Slave Lists of Col. C. W. Gooch (Richmond), 1830, 1839, 1852, Gooch Family Papers, VHS; Slave List of Sarah Fitzgerald (Nottoway Co.), 1864, Fitzgerald Family Papers, Va. Hist. Soc; Digges Slave List, 1770–1860 (Frederick Co.), Digges Family Papers, VHS. The vast majority of ex-slaves from across Virginia who gave detailed information about their lives are represented in Perdue et al., *Weevils in the Wheat*. They overwhelmingly identified their mothers as the primary providers of care and socialization during their childhoods. Fully 82 percent of these ex-slaves, who represent the last generation of Virginia bondwomen and men from around the state, spoke of the physical presence of their mothers during most of their childhood years. Only 42 percent, however, recalled consistent contact with their fathers. Also, at least one-third of those who did make mention of the presence of their fathers during their childhood noted that these men did not reside on the same farm or plantation with them, but lived elsewhere and could visit only on weekend days or holidays.

40. Slave List, 1830, Gooch Family Papers, VHS.

41. For a discussion of ideas of gender convention available to colonial southerners, see Julia Cherry Spruill, *Women's Life and Work in the Southern Colonies* (1938; reprint, New York: Norton, 1972), pp. 220–223. Regarding antebellum conventions, see, for example, "To A Young Bride," *American Ladies Magazine* 7, no. 11 (November 1835): 487, VSL; "A Chapter from the 'Book of Marriage,'" *American Ladies Magazine* 6, no. 6 (June 1833): 262–64; "Female Influence," *Ladies Magazine and Literary Gazette* 1, no. 6 (June 1828): 268; "Female Piety, *Ladies Magazine and Literary Gazette* 1, no.4 (April 1828): 177; "To A Young Mother," *American Ladies Magazine* 9, no. 7 (July 1837): 390; and George Fitzhugh, "Sociology for the South," in *Slavery Defended: The Voices of the Old South*, ed. Eric McKitrick (Englewood Cliffs, N.J.: Prentice-Hall, 1963), pp. 37–38, 45.

42. Perdue et al., *Weevils in the Wheat*, pp. 83–89.

43. While black women believed that their political, social, and economic oppressions as slaves and their physical and moral victimization as women were valid excuses for their behavior, many assumed that the socially and economically elite status of slaveholding women left them much less justification for such conduct. Clearly, female slaves surmised that slaveholding women often had the wherewithal to act as Christians, that is, to be kind, generous, understanding, protective, loyal, and honest, when slave women, more often than not, did not. Most slave women also associated the class status of European-American southerners with behavioral ideals and the ability to assume these standards. Nancy Williams, for example, expected to be (and was) treated harshly when she was hired out by what she called "poor white trash." Plainly, she believed that elite whites were more genteel, reasonable, and benevolent in their relations with their slaves than were poorer whites. See Perdue et al., *Weevils in the Wheat*, p. 318. With regard to Virginia slave women's assessment of slaveholding women's morality see, for example, ibid., pp. 32–49, 63, 190, 257, 273–75, and Keckley, *Behind the Scenes*, pp. 31–38.

44. Perdue et al., *Weevils in the Wheat*, p. 63.

45. Blassingame, ed., *Slave Testimony*, pp. 364–65.

46. Still, ed., *Underground Railroad*, pp. 112–14.

47. Perdue et al., *Weevils in the Wheat*, p. 36.

48. Perdue et al., *Weevils in the Wheat*, p. 122.

49. Perdue et al., *Weevils in the Wheat*, pp. 32–49.

50. Perdue et al., *Weevils in the Wheat*, p. 44. Regarding the relationship of slave-holding women and slaves, see Fox–Genovese, *Within the Plantation Household*, pp. 290–371; Clinton, *The Plantation Mistress*, pp. 184–91; Suzanne Lebsock, *The Free Women of Petersburg: Status and Culture in a Southern Town, 1784–1860* (New York: Norton, 1984), pp. 136–44; Jean E. Friedman, *The Enclosed Garden: Women and Community in the Evangelical South, 1830–1900* (Chapel Hill: University of North Carolina Press, 1985), pp. 68–91; Genovese, *Roll, Jordan, Roll*, pp. 343–65; Sudie Duncan Sides, "Southern Women and Slavery," *History Today* 20 (1970): 54–60, 124–30.

51. Fannie Berry obviously was fond of her white mistress, despite her qualification that the woman was part of a class of persons who generally were harsh and oppressive to blacks. In Berry's estimation, Abbott lived up to some of the ideals of womanhood that she believed a "lady" of her status should maintain. She could be kind, compassionate, solicitous of the needs of others, and willing to make at least minimal financial concessions in order to secure the satisfaction of the people she relied on for her own livelihood, but who also had little power (because the mistress and her class actively denied them the right) to organize their lives as they ideally would. Fannie Berry's brief description of her estimation of some of the kinds of behavioral traits she believed suitable for a woman like Sarah Ann Abbott resembles strikingly the gender conventions that Anne Finor Scott, for example, argues convincingly were operative among elite white women of the antebellum South. See Scott, *The Southern Lady: From Pedestal to Politics, 1830–1930* (Chicago: University of Chicago Press, 1970). Also see Fox-Genovese, *Within the Plantation Household*, pp. 196–97.

52. Berry refers, for example, to her ability to withstand harsh physical conditions (story of her being caught in a blinding rainstorm, without any shoes or clothing, but eventually able to find her way home and not suffering any illness as a result). She also spoke boldly of her determination not to have sexual relations with a white man who tried to "throw" her to the floor. According to Berry, she fought the man off and in the process "scratched his face to pieces." She also spoke of her decision to kill a dog that whites, either her mistress or local white males, repeatedly directed to attack her brother (as a form of entertainment to the white audience). Always a female of action, or so she would have her interviewer believe, Fannie killed the dog and hid him in the woods, thus removing the threat to her younger brother. Berry also included in her interview stories of slave women who ran away rather than be beaten and of one who killed herself in order to end a life of continued abuse.

53. Perdue et al., *Weevils in the Wheat*, pp. 31–50, 190–92; Keckley, *Behind the Scenes*.

SLAVERY, RESISTANCE, AND FREEDOM

10

HARD LABOR
WOMEN, CHILDBIRTH, AND
RESISTANCE IN BRITISH
CARIBBEAN SLAVE SOCIETIES

Barbara Bush

Over the past decade scholars have shown deepening interest in the lives of slave women, particularly of the antebellum South. Until recently, however, with the exception of Lucille Mathurin Mair's pioneering work on Jamaica, slave women of the Caribbean were given scant attention and analyses of their lives tended to reiterate the more popular misconceptions of contemporary observers.[1] The pioneering works on slave demography and medical treatment by Barry Higman and Richard Sheridan aroused new interest through their concern with a major enigma of Caribbean slave populations—their failure to reproduce naturally in comparison with the slave population of the antebellum South. The importance of fertility rates of black females in the demographic analyses led to research which increasingly focused on women's experience of childbirth and the adverse effects of sugar monoculture on the family and mating patterns of slaves.[2] These studies have yielded valuable insights into the lives of slave women, but they have only marginally addressed the issues of production and reproduction from the slaves' perspective. This chapter aims to integrate production and reproduction into studies of slave resistance.

Active struggle against slavery was an enduring and ever-present feature of slave life in the Caribbean. Resistance took many forms, from outright revolt to more subtle behavior. Women were no less prominent than men in resistance, and they may even have been in the vanguard, particularly in cultural resistance. As anthropologist Melville Herskovits noted in his study of a Trinidad village in the 1940s, a distinctive characteristic of black societies in the New World was the part played by women as the "principal exponents" and protectors of traditional African-derived culture.[3] This chapter argues that tensions inherent in slave women's "dual burden" of production and reproduction, combined with attempts by slave masters to manipulate these women's cultural practices and fertility, strongly influenced the responses of slave women to childbirth and infant rearing at both conscious and unconscious levels. The discussion focuses on slave women who lived on large sugar plantations in the British territories during the later period of slavery.[4]

Women in the Plantation Economy

Women were valuable workers. A rough equality existed between slave men and women, particularly in field work on large plantations where they shared the arduous conditions of life and labor.[5] However, women played unique reproductive roles, and their lives were affected by the complex structures of African and European patriarchy which influenced the character of slave society. Patriarchal dominance was evident in the sexual division of labor in plantation and slave domestic production and in attempts by masters to control reproduction. In this context women's control over their bodies was arguably a major area of struggle involving power relations at a most basic level. According to Michel Foucault, where there is power, there is resistance, or to be more precise, a plurality of resistances. Power over women was exercised through control of their sexuality, a form of oppression rarely experienced to the same degree by slave men. As Arlette Gautier wrote, the appropriation of slave women's sexuality "redoubled women's exploitation as workers," whereas male slaves could take refuge in "the fantasies of their sexual powers."[6]

White men of British origin were the major owners of slaves and thus the wealthiest and most powerful persons in the British Caribbean. These men were also the most distant from the slave population, particularly during the late years of slavery, when many were absentee owners resident in Britain. The power of absentee owners was mediated through other white men or black male overseers, who frequently took sexual advantage of black women. Between 1807 and 1832 transient white men, particularly on the largest British Caribbean plantations of absentee owners, fathered numerous slave children. While some black women may have regarded sexual unions with whites as advantageous, providing privileges and possible manumission, such relations also represented a natural extension of the power of white over black.[7] If women resisted sexual advances, they risked physical cruelty and punishment. Power over the black woman's body in its productive capacity as an asexual labor machine was thus combined with sexual power to control both production and reproduction on slave plantations.

In this matrix of power, where patriarchal structures intermeshed with basic economic structures of labor exploitation, the position of white women was ambiguous. Many white women owned slaves, but rarely more than twenty, and these slaves were concentrated mostly in towns. Subordinate to white male authority and facing sexual competition from colored and black women for their husbands' favors, white women were arguably more brutal in their treatment of slaves than white men.[8] Yet, in the intimate area of childbirth and sexuality, white women were also subjected to the dictums on childbirth that resulted from the expropriation of the ancient art of female midwifery by male doctors. In addition, inadequate obstetric knowledge and unhygienic conditions rendered childbirth hazardous for all women, in Europe and the West Indies alike. At the same time, socially constructed distinctions based on race and class firmly separated black, colored, and white women. In contrast to white and free colored women, black female slaves were subjected to punishment and the rigors of the plantation work regime.[9] The formal plantation division of labor conflicted with the traditional African division of labor which defined the private sphere of slave women's lives. Within this sphere, women were primarily childbearers and mothers who bore sole responsibility for child care and food preparation. The conflicting demands of the plantation and household on slave women arguably placed them under psychic pressures and contradictions not experienced to the same degree by free women or, indeed, slave men.

Until near the end of slavery, planters of the British Caribbean paid scant regard to slave family bonds, and they undervalued the reproductive roles of slave women. Black women were valued mainly for their labor. From the earliest days of the slave trade, Europeans regarded women as eminently suited to field-work because of their perceived "drudge" status in polygynous marriages. A large part of the labor on sugar estates consisted of digging holes for canes, hoeing, and weeding—tasks generally accepted in slaving circles as "women's work" in Africa.[10] Planters professed a preference for males, and more males than females were brought to the Caribbean during the eighteenth century. However, in the hierarchical division of labor on large plantations, men were valued for crafts skills and for work in the semi-industrial process of the sugar mill, so that up to 50 percent of ordinary field gangs were made up of women, a pattern which was also evident in the French Caribbean.[11] As William Beckford, a prominent Jamaican planter, noted in the 1780s, "A negro man is purchased for a trade, or the cultivation and different processes of the cane—the occupations of the women are only two, the house, with its several departments and supposed indulgences, or the field with its exaggerated labors. The first situation is the most honorable the last the most independent." Apart from the chief housekeeper, who was almost always colored by the late eighteenth century, and the midwife and chief doctoress or hospital assistant, who were more highly valued after the introduction of pronatalist policies during the 1790s, men were the plantation elite. This had important implications for the working and living conditions, as well as for the health and reproductive potential of women.[12]

The most important slaves were the most robust males and females who worked the fields and sugar mills. The importance of women in the formal plantation economy (as opposed to the "informal" economy of peasant cultivation and marketing, in which some women were also prominent) is reflected in the prices of prime female slaves. Between 1790 and the end of the slave trade in

1807, the approximate purchase price in Jamaica of a "new" male slave was £50 to £70, while a healthy female brought from £50 to £60. Prices of creole slaves were roughly 20 percent higher. There is no indication that fertility increased the value of women—women of similar ages, with or without children, cost exactly the same. Men and women were often sold together in "jobbing gangs." A Jamaican advertisement in 1827, for instance, offered a "small gang of effective and well-disposed slaves, 17 males and 17 females."[13]

By the early nineteenth century at least 75 percent of the slaves in the Caribbean colonies were attached to sugar plantations. Detailed demographic analysis by Higman confirms the dominance of women in field gangs (on sugar plantations, 10 percent were domestics, compared with 20 percent on coffee and cotton plantations).[14] Although planters maintained that the general treatment of sugar slaves was "mild and indulgent," Higman's calculations confirm that slave morbidity and mortality was highest, and the birth rate the lowest, on sugar plantations of the optimum size of 250 slaves. Next highest in mortality were coffee plantations, followed by cocoa, cotton, and pimento plantations, cattle ranches or pens, the towns, and, finally, marginal subsistence holdings. Sugar plantations were generally regarded as unhealthy locations where a number of factors contributed to high mortality. The labor regime itself ensured that women shared the same backbreaking work, miseries, and punishments as men. In crop time, between October and March, plantation slaves were turned out of their quarters at sunrise and worked till sunset, with little time to call their own. There was also extended night work during this period.[15]

Despite their economic value, fieldworkers were treated as the capital stock of the plantation, on par with the animals, and maintained at bare subsistence level. Though they performed the hardest labor and worked the longest hours, their living conditions were far inferior to those of domestics and skilled craftsmen and they suffered from greater ill health and higher mortality rates. To supplement the often inadequate diets provided by masters, they produced food in their free time on their provision grounds.[16] The rigors of fieldwork often led to low productivity, which was linked to various forms of resistance—from individual shirking and malingering to sabotage, arson, and more collective discontent in the gang. Control over productivity therefore became difficult. Women were prominent in such resistance.[17] As field slaves, women were subjected to the harshest conditions, but they retained greater cultural autonomy. According to Elsa Goveia, writing about the British Leeward Islands at the end of the eighteenth century, field slaves were allowed to retain Africanisms to underscore their inferiority.[18] In practice these characteristics formed a "cultural shield" which helped field slaves to sustain their struggle against slavery. The barrier to assimilation or acculturation was more easily eroded among house slaves, who were in closer proximity to whites.

Accounts of plantation life confirm that women gave their labor unwillingly and were a constant source of frustration to managers and overseers. Plantation journals and punishment lists (required by law after slave registration in 1815) of absentee London merchants Thomas and William King, kept from the early 1820s to the beginning of apprenticeship in 1833, chart the deep level of everyday resistance that female slaves sustained. Women were far more often accused of insolence, "excessive laziness," disobedience, quarreling, and "disorderly conduct" than were male slaves. On the Kings' plantation, Good Success, there were 93 female slaves and 211 male, but the women were more consistently troublesome. As persistent offenders, women were punished on average more frequently than men.[19]

Faced with the intransigence of women, which ran to more serious crimes as flight, attempts to poison their masters, and "exciting discontent" in the gang, beleaguered managers resorted to the whip. When legislation banning the whipping of female slaves was introduced in Trinidad in 1823, planters objected strongly. They complained that female slaves were "notoriously insolent" and were kept in some "tolerable order" only through fear of punishment, which they deserved more frequently than males.[20] Profit often could be extracted only through physical coercion, and, planters argued, without constant use of the whip it was impossible to work estates. Such punishment or correction had obvious implications for the well-being of women slaves, particularly during pregnancy.

Under the overseer's whip, "neither age nor sex found any favor."[21] For women, the degradation experienced by being whipped upon the bare buttocks while held down by other slaves was made worse because the black drivers who carried out the whippings, and who were eager to establish their privileged position, showed little lenience.[22] Allowance must be made for the propaganda of abolitionist writings, but records from the Kings' plantations suggest that even alternative punishments meted out to women were harsh. Women endured the public humiliation and discomfort of the "hand and foot stocks" or solitary confinement, sometimes with the additional debasement of wearing a collar. Punishments lasted from a few hours to three days, occasionally longer in serious cases, and Sunday, the only full free day for slaves to cultivate their own plots, was a favorite day for confinement—presumably because it did not interfere with the plantation work regime.[23] Pregnancy did not guarantee immunity to such harsh punishments. A pregnant woman risked a flogging if she complained about work conditions. Until the last years of slavery, Jamaica laws limiting the number of lashes that could be inflicted on slaves made no special concessions for women, pregnant or not. Slaves of both sexes could receive up to ten lashes, except when an overseer was present, when thirty-nine lashes could be administered.[24]

Jamaica planters were renowned for their callous indifference to the special needs of pregnant women. Dr. John Williamson related how one woman, confined to the stocks for "misconduct" and liberated only a few days before delivery, subsequently died of puerperal fever. The paternalist planter Matthew "Monk" Lewis, on the basis of several adverse reports, concluded that "white overseers and bookkeepers . . . [kicked] black women in the belly from one end of Jamaica to another," harming both the women and their unborn children.[25]

For most planters, women remained, first and foremost, valuable workers and were rarely given preferential treatment. It was in slaveowners' interests, particularly during the late period of slavery when faced with abolitionist pressure, to conceal the degree of exploitation of and cruelty toward women. Written records can only provide limited insights into the punishments experienced by female slaves or the degree of resistance such treatment generated. However, by the 1790s, with the growing concern over the failure of the slave population to increase naturally, the maltreatment of women became, in principle at least, a seminal issue in the debate over the causes of low fertility. This debate brought more sharply into the focus the effect of field labor on the reproductive potential of slave women.

Female Slave Fertility: An Enduring Enigma

During the early period of slavery, planters tried to ensure an even balance between their male and female slaves and encouraged stable relationships, but conflicting accounts of women's fertility already existed. Sir Hans Sloane, recording impressions of his travels through the West Indies in the early eighteenth century, observed of female slaves that they "are fruitful and go after the birth of their children to work in the fields with their little ones tied to their backs." The seventeenth-century Barbados planter, Richard Ligon, complained, however, that "though we breed both Negroes, Horses and Cattle . . . that increase will not supply the moderate decayes which we find in all of those. . . ."[26] As sugar monoculture intensified, conditions deteriorated; however, the extremely high mortality rates, particularly of new, or "saltwater," slaves, could be counteracted by cheap fresh imports. By the mid–eighteenth century, planters no longer encouraged fertility; indeed, the treatment of women possibly discouraged reproduction.

Pregnant women were often kept at fieldwork up to the last few weeks of pregnancy and were expected to return to work no later than three weeks after delivery. They suffered from many gynecological complaints, including early miscarriage and sterility, in addition to general ill health related to plantation life. Both Mair and Higman have found that women had a higher morbidity rate than men. This may explain alleged planter preference for male slaves.[27] In 1798 Barbados planters noted that slave women were "very prone" to contract disorders of the reproductive system "which will often last for their lives." Edward Long believed that "most black women" were "subject to obstructions of the menstrua (monthly periods)." This often resulted in "incurable" sterility among Ebo women.[28] Such factors may explain why fertility rates of creole slaves were higher than those of African women in all the colonies from the registration period to abolition.

The enigma of the failure of slaves to increase naturally began to concern planters in the British and French colonies toward the end of the eighteenth century because of growing abolitionist pressure to end the slave trade. The causes of low fertility therefore became a major point of debate. Legislation designed to improve the well-being of slave women and promote a "healthy increase" among slaves was introduced after 1790. Before such "ameliorative" legislation was adopted, the slave laws of the British colonies did not discriminate between male and female slaves, offering at the same time no protection from sexual abuse, overwork, maltreatment during pregnancy, or the breakup of slave families, including the separation of mothers and children. The rare exception made for pregnant women in Jamaica was that they were "respited . . . from execution until after their pregnancy."[29] Under English law, in contrast to the laws governing French and Spanish slaves in the Caribbean, slaves were legally defined as chattels, in recognition of the sanctity of an Englishman's private property. Masters had complete control over their slaves and, as property owners, they were given wide discretion in enforcing subordination and control. Slaves could give evidence against each other, but not for or against free persons. This made it extremely difficult for slave women to protest maltreatment in pregnancy, sexual abuse, or rape.[30]

Reflecting the new pronatalist policies, incentives were introduced after 1790 to encourage women to have more children. Under the Leeward Islands Act of 1798 female slaves "five months gone" were to be employed in light work. A "roomy negro house" of two rooms was to be built for every slave woman pregnant with her first child, and rewards and bonuses were offered to slave women and midwives. Legislation passed in the Leewards and in Jamaica (1809) also included provisions that female slaves "having six children living" should be exempt from hard labor and the owner exempted from taxation on such female slaves.[31] Laws were passed to encourage stable marriages, and gratuities were offered to slave parents to provide "the several little necessaries wanted to keep infants clean and decent." As it was generally held that sexual relations between white men and black women contributed in no small degree to the general "immorality" of slave society, laws were passed which fined whites up to £100 for "having criminal commerce" with any married female slave. A Jamaica law of 1826 introduced the death sentence for rape of female slaves or sexual abuse of slave girls under ten years old.[32]

Planters built additional plantation hospitals (hothouses) and lying-in houses for pregnant women. They also employed more European doctors to care for their slaves, and as a result there emerged a new interest in slave illnesses and the causes of low fertility and high infant mortality. One doctor, William Sells, advocated keeping detailed records of slave women's childbearing experiences. He also recommended careful medical attention, light employment after the fifth month, and use of better-educated black midwives, whom Europeans often regarded as incompetent or even dangerous. However, Sells warned against indulging slave women too much. He believed that they were fit to return to the fields a month to six weeks after delivery.[33]

New pronatalist policies nevertheless continued to reflect the racist view that African women, being nearer to the animal world than white women, gave birth painlessly and "with little or no difficulty" and could be returned to hard labor soon after childbirth. In the seventeenth century Ligon noted that if the over-seer was "discreet," women slaves were allowed to rest a little more than ordinary, but if not, they were compelled "to do as others" with "times . . . of suckling their Children in the fields and refreshing themselves." In contrast, Dr. Dancer, an influential physician practicing in Jamaica at the beginning of the nineteenth century, exhorted white women to avoid "all acts of exertion" after childbirth, even so light as bending down to open a drawer. According to Lady Nugent, wife of the governor of Jamaica, writing at the beginning of the nineteenth century, medical men in the colony believed that white and mulatto women had far more difficult pregnancies and more miscarriages than black women, although slave infant mortality was much higher.[34]

Anthropological studies of modern-day Africa challenge such wild and inaccurate generalizations rooted in racial justifications of slavery. Maria Cutrafelli argues that the apparent insensitivity of African women to pain in childbirth is a result of their socialization into stoically bearing pain, first experienced in clitoridectomy (female circumcision) at puberty. Such culturally determined behavior may have influenced African slave women, but it does not change the fact that childbirth was as hazardous for them as it was for white women.[35] It has already been shown that slave women suffered from many gynecological complaints and miscarriages associated with hard labor. Long ascribed their prevalence to the "unskillfulness and absurd management of negro midwives." William Beckford had a more honest answer. Reproaching his fellow planters for failing to provide better treatment for pregnant and nursing mothers, he accused them of not wishing their women to breed "as thereby so much work is lost in attendance on their infants."[36]

The abolition of the slave trade and the increasing intervention of the metropolitan government in internal island affairs led to further ameliorative legislation in the British Caribbean. The end of the slave trade gave new urgency to the pronatalist policies, but the majority of island laws retained their "policing" character and were in many ways in conflict with the well-being of pregnant and nursing mothers. Abolitionists argued that concessions to the improved welfare of slaves were made "grudgingly and of necessity" and were inoperative in practice, "mere rags to cover the blotches and ulcers of the system." Writing at the beginning of the nineteenth century, James Stephen observed that absentee proprietorship also contributed to the failure of new laws to improve female fertility.[37] Higman and Sheridan confirm that slave conditions in general deteriorated after 1800. The new interest in female slaves may even have rendered their lives more hazardous; in the French Caribbean, where similar measures were introduced to improve slave fertility, slave women and midwives were punished for infant deaths.[38]

Some paternalist planters were genuinely concerned about the treatment of female slaves, and this gave abolitionists a degree of optimism. John Jeremie argued that after punishment of slave women was reduced in St. Lucia, there was an increase in the slave birthrate. However, genuine attempts to improve "breeding conditions" were more frequently unsuccessful, baffling well-intentioned liberal planters. Although Matthew Lewis stopped all punishment on his Jamaican plantation and provided all the "comforts and requisites" deemed necessary to healthy childbirth by eighteenth-century European medical science, there was little improvement in the fertility rates of his plantation slave women.[39] Recently compiled demographic data confirm the failure of pronatalist policies. Higman has shown that, with the exception of Barbados, the British sugar colonies did not show an absolute increase in the slave population before 1832. Indeed, between 1807 and 1834 the total slave population declined from 775,000 to 665,000 at a time when adverse sex ratios of men to women—which some planters blamed for the low fertility of women—were evening out and there was a greater number of creole slaves, supposedly more adapted to plantation life.[40]

Harsh conditions of field labor undoubtedly contributed significantly to this demographic anomaly. Modern historians tend to favor the abolitionist view that slave women whose work was "least and easiest" had more children. However, the correlation between hard labor and low fertility was not always so clear-cut. In its report to the Lords of Trade inquiry into the slave trade in 1789, the Barbados Committee admitted that on most plantations there were some hard-working females "who breed very fast," while many others who labored less "do not breed at all." Higman's research suggests that fertility was relatively high on large-scale sugar plantations, almost the same as on those where cocoa was grown, and exceeded the rates for coffee and cotton plantations.[41] The causes of low fertility are obviously more complex than would appear on superficial examination of the evidence. The harsh conditions of sugar plantations may have had a more direct impact on mortality patterns than fertility (death rates were much higher on large-scale plantations). Planters themselves believed that they could more successfully manipulate mortality than fertility, and there is no hard evidence for the conscious breeding of slaves.[42]

Much of the scholarly discussion of the fertility rate has focused almost exclusively on external influences on slave women as passive subjects, not as active agents with a degree of control over their own bodies, despite the constraints of the system.[43] However, it is also necessary to examine the experience of childbirth and infant rearing from the perspective of the slave woman through consideration of the close link between culture, material conditions, and resistance. According to Higman, variations in levels of slave fertility were determined not only by work regimes but also by the cultural practices of slaves and the attempts of masters and missionaries to alter them.[44]

Slave Culture, Childbirth, and Resistance

If the abolitionists blamed harsh conditions, the proplanter faction preferred to blame "immorality" and the inferior African cultural practices of slaves for the low fertility of women and the high infant mortality rate. Many planters believed that promiscuity of slave women and venereal disease were mainly responsible for the failure of Caribbean slaves to reproduce naturally. Edward Long declared that slaves would enjoy "robust good health" if not "prone to debauch." In testimony before the 1789 inquiry into the slave trade, the Jamaican Committee reported that "negroes committed . . . foul acts of sensuality and Intemperance" and contracted venereal diseases; the women caught colds at "nocturnal assemblies" and suffered from obstructed "natural periods." The "barbaric" mating patterns of slaves, which included the practice of polygyny, were at the core of this general lack of morality. Slave women were thus "rendered unprolific" through their own "bad practices," while slaves of both sexes concealed venereal disease to avoid abstinence from pleasure during treatment. The committee further alleged that the medicines slave women took for venereal diseases produced sterility and killed their unborn children.[45]

It is difficult to determine the actual extent of venereal disease because contemporary medical opinion on the subject is conflicting. Sir Hans Sloane wrote that it was very common, especially among plantation slaves, and both gonorrhea and "pox" (syphilis) were transmitted in the same way and had the same course as among Europeans. However, Dr. Thomas Dancer believed it took a different and milder form among blacks, who frequently transmitted it to their children.[46] Such pronouncements illustrate the confusion over definitions of diseases and diagnoses common in the field of tropical medicine at the time. In the context of slave reproduction, however, it is nevertheless important to challenge planters' moral diatribes against the general immorality of slaves. These opinions were based primarily on ethnocentric myths about the "natural promiscuity" of Africans and the planters' need to confirm the "social death" of the slave through negative stereotyping and denial of rights to family bonds. With respect to venereal disease, slaves probably suffered as much as the average inhabitant of eighteenth-century European cities, also allegedly rife with "immorality" yet with booming birthrates. Moreover, planters like Long contradicted themselves in blaming polygamy for low fertility while citing the "populousness" of West Africa, where the practice "universally prevailed."[47] Recent studies of slave family life suggest that wherever possible, slave men and women attempted to recreate African marriage patterns supported by strong African-derived moral codes that worked against "promiscuity."[48] They thus resisted plantocratic attempts to impose alien cultural practices upon them, and it was probably this resistance, not "bad practices," which affected population growth.

Planters were particularly keen to change one aspect of slave childbearing—the late weaning of slave infants. This practice derived from Africa and was commonly blamed for low fertility. Research by Herbert S. Klein and Stanley L. Engerman and by Jerome S. Handler and Robert S. Corruccini suggests that breast-feeding practices may explain fertility differentials between female slaves in the Caribbean and those in the southern United States, where late weaning was rare. Late weaning was related to the two-year postnatal taboo on intercourse common to many African societies and may have provided limited contraception. In the Caribbean this custom was not confined to African-born women. It was also practiced by creoles. Thus, as Kenneth F. Kiple argues, it did not contribute to perceived differences in fertility between the two groups.[49] Late weaning, which provides strong evidence of the durability of African culture and resistance to imposed pronatalist policies, persisted in the Caribbean well into the twentieth century. Planters viewed it as another form of shamming and idling. (Women were frequently accused of citing a multitude of "female complaints" to avoid work.) When weaning houses were introduced in Jamaica to cut down on extended suckling, women strongly resisted early separation from their infants. Lewis blamed this "obstinacy" on women's desire to "retain the leisure and other indulgencies . . . of nursing mothers." Another planter, John Baillie, reached a similar conclusion after failing to get a single mother, from 1808 to 1832, to accept the premium of two dollars which he offered women to wean their children in twelve months.[50]

Women's reluctance to return to plantation work and their resistance to forcible separation from their infants were arguably rational responses to the problems associated with childbirth, including high infant mortality. Late weaning results in wide birth spacing and, in the absence of adverse influences, can improve infant and maternal well-being, but it cannot fully explain low fertility. In modern West African societies fertility rates remain very high despite long periods of breast-feeding, restrictions on intercourse, high fetal and infant mortality, and early sterility of women. Other explanations need to be explored. For Kiple, these are located in the high infant mortality and diet and disease patterns of Caribbean slavery. Richard Dunn argues, however, that "eccentric" birth intervals are better explained by sexual abstinence, miscarriages, and abortions, suggesting a more active role for slaves in determining fertility.[51]

Certainly slave nutrition and work practices influenced childbirth patterns, particularly on large plantations. As Higman notes, few free populations of the New or Old World in the early nineteenth century were subjected to "such a persistent combination of conditions unfavorable to population growth." Dietary deficiencies could have affected slave women's ability to bear and raise healthy children. Kiple argues that women may have suffered calcium deficiencies leading to rickets (although Dr. Thomas Dancer said that this was "rarely seen" in Jamaica) and were therefore frequently anemic. Kiple also notes that high frequency of stillbirths and toxemia in pregnancy may be linked to malnutrition. Delayed menarche and early menopause are also related to poor nutrition. Caribbean slaves experienced periodic famine, and there is a well-documented medical link between starvation and amenorrhea (cessation of menstruation leading to temporary sterility). In addition, endemic diseases, such as yaws, and epidemic diseases, such as measles and smallpox, may have increased the incidence of stillbirths and miscarriages. According to Michael Craton, such factors reduced the ability and willingness of women to bear children. The symbiotic relationship between nutrition, infection and fertility remains a controversial subject. Indeed, E. Van den Boogaart and P. Emmer's study of a model plantation

in Surinam shows that the birthrate remained low even though the food provided was nutritionally excellent.[52] Thus other factors related more directly to the
responses of slave women must be examined if high sterility and miscarriage rates
are to be understood.

Planters cited sterility as a major reason for low fertility, particularly among
African-born women. Creole slaves had a higher fertility rate. Kiple suggests
that West African women who could not bear children may have fallen victim to
the slave trade there. This is not an unreasonable proposition, given the high
premium placed on female fertility in traditional African culture, but more supportive evidence is needed. Another factor which may have affected the fertility
of African slave women was that they were more likely than creoles to be living
alone. Women who lived in co-residential unions were significantly more fertile
than those who lived alone. However, the presence of large numbers of African women in the slave population is, in itself, an insufficient explanation of
low fertility.[53] Most African-born women were in the fertile age range when
they arrived in the Caribbean, but the incidence of sterility among them was
abnormally high. In African cultures sterility in mature women is regarded as a
terrible stigma and social identity for women comes solely through motherhood.
Newborn children are greeted with joy and celebration; prolific childbearing
is honored. A childless couple will explore every possible means to overcome
sterility.

A real desire for motherhood does not, however, mean that African women
shunned birth control. They may have brought knowledge of abortion and
contraception with them to the Caribbean. Apart from wide birth spacing
through long lactation, ritual abstinence, abortion, and other elaborate forms of
contraception are more widespread in traditional African societies than is generally recognized. Abortion is used when taboos are broken through adultery or
in polygynous relationships where there is jealousy between co-wives. An almost
universal reason for abortion in traditional African societies is unsanctioned
pregnancy during the lactation period; it is also common to abort girls regarded
as too young for pregnancy. Abortion allows women the only real choice in societies where female reproduction is subject to strict patriarchal control.[54] A
stronger influence of African retentions among African-born women may thus
explain fertility differentials. This operated perhaps on two levels: the psychological, where the impact of slavery weakened the desire to have children; and
the practical, where the transmission of cultural knowledge about contraception
and abortion came into play.

Plantation life provided little incentive for slave women to have children.
Even after ameliorative legislation was introduced there remained insuperable
difficulties attached to pregnancy and childbirth. Women who bore children
continued to face the threat of separation from their infants or from their husbands and kin who provided emotional support. As early as 1789, planters in
Barbados recognized that the specter of sale away from friends and relatives discouraged women from having children. In the Caribbean, it is possible that

slave women would avoid unwanted pregnancies when, in the words of an eminent slave doctor, David Collins, the slave woman's life was "upheld by no consolation, animated by no hope," her troubled pregnancy ending in the birth of a child "doomed like herself to the rigors of eternal servitude."[55]

Under extreme conditions the desire and ability of women to have children is reduced. The classic example is the concentration camp. Deportees and prisoners in World War II suffered terrible psychological conditions, anguish, and shock. Under such conditions, according to the French historian Le Roy Ladurie, amenorrhea could become a "defense mechanism" reflecting the suppression of the "luxury function" of reproduction in order to survive. The effects of physical starvation and hardship combined with psychological factors to reduce fertility. Such factors may help explain the high incidence of amenorrhea among slave women. Gynecologists now distinguish between "emotional" amenorrhea, which can occur as a result of psychological disturbance, and "secondary" amenorrhea, caused by illness or a change in environment. Slave women experienced conditions which increased their chances of developing both forms of this disorder.[56]

Caribbean planters frequently accused slave women of procuring abortions and frustrating their attempts to increase the slave population. Long linked abortion to promiscuity, arguing that slave women were no better than "common prostitutes" who frequently took "specifics" to abort so that they could resume their immoral activities "without loss or hindrance to business." Drs. John Quier and David Collins, who both practiced in Jamaica during the later period of slavery, gave their professional support to this view. They added that women induced miscarriage through "violence" or the use of "simples of the country . . . possessed of forcible powers." In 1826 Reverend Beame alleged that obeah practitioners in Jamaica administered herbs and powders known only to blacks to induce abortions—an indication of the durability of transmitted African knowledge at a time when creole slaves were in the majority.[57]

In determining the extent of such practices, however, it is necessary to distinguish between procured abortions and spontaneous miscarriages because no such distinction was made in contemporary accounts. Slave women almost certainly retained knowledge of such practices from Africa, and as primitive abortion techniques, mechanical or drug-based, can be dangerous, their use by slave women may have contributed to the high incidence of sterility and the slaves' gynecological complaints reported by whites.[58] In traditional African societies various techniques are commonly used to induce abortions in culturally prescribed circumstances. Major abortifacients used include infusions from herbs, leaves of special shrubs, plant roots, and the bark of some trees. Common plants used include manioc, yam, papaya, mango, lime, and frangipani. Mechanical means are less popular and rely mainly on the insertion of sharp sticks or stalks into the vaginal canal.[59]

Similarities between African and Caribbean practices included the use of some drugs and the important role played by "medicine men and old women" (obeah practitioners). Some older women were skilled in techniques of mid-wifery and herbalism. They had carried their skills with them to the New World and were valued as doctoresses and midwives. They also provided postnatal care for mothers and infants. Some European doctors derided the folk medicine these women practiced (possibly out of professional jealousy), but black healers and nurses were generally regarded as indispensable to the running of planta-tion hospitals, and more perceptive Europeans acknowledged the efficacy of many folk remedies derived from Africa.[60] In this context the practice of abor-tion by female slaves is a viable proposition.

On the slave plantation the formulae for herbal concoctions which induced abortions could have been passed on from mother to daughter, as in Africa. Some evidence exists that slave midwives administered abortifacients such as wild cassava and other substances. Dancer recorded the names of a number of plants indigenous to the West Indies used for "promoting terms" in women. Besides cassava, they included cerasee (an emetic also mentioned by Dr. Barham), Barba-dos pride, wild passion flower, water germander, and wild tansey (a widely recognized abortifacient also used by slaves in the Old South). Sometimes strong emetics, such as the seed of the sandbox tree, were used to bring on menstrua-tion. John Stedman referred to herbal remedies used in Surinam to induce abortion, including "green pineapple," and he observed (as in traditional African cultures) young girls who reputedly aborted "to preserve themselves as long as they were able." Jealousy in polygamous marriages was another motive for abor-tion. Writing in the 1770s, Janet Schaw alleged that black women who mated with whites possessed knowledge of "certain herbs and medicines," and in making use of them to abort, they damaged their health.[61]

This sparse contemporary evidence is strengthened by anthropological data. Among the Djukas of Surinam (culturally close to the societies which existed in eighteenth-century West Africa), abortion and contraception techniques similar to those reputedly used by slave women were still found in the 1930s. These in-cluded herbs and "crude instruments" akin to the pointed sticks used in some African societies. Methods used by slave women have arguably been transmitted down the generations. Melville Herskovits noted that in Trinidad in the 1940s salt, green mangoes, and lime juice were used to successfully abort. Women in the modern Caribbean still buy herbal concoctions from old women to induce abortion.[62] In societies where contraceptive knowledge is poor, abortion is the only means available to women to control their reproduction.

High infant mortality was also cited as a major reason for the low rate of natural increase of Caribbean slave populations, and again, African cultural prac-tices adopted by slave women were blamed for this. Most whites believed that the promiscuity of slave women led to "a neglect and want of maternal affection towards children of former connexions," and even paternalistic planters like Lewis felt that slave women put pleasure before duty where care of children was concerned.[63] Such comments reflect Eurocentric, bourgeois attitudes toward slave motherhood. Slave women could not be good mothers in the modern sense of the word, but contemporary accounts also testify to the ways in which their strictness was tempered with affection and tenderness. Evidence of strong bonds between mothers and children exists in the ways women resisted separation from their children and attempts of planters to modify African-derived childrearing practices. Women were less frequently runaways because of the stronger ties they had to the plantation through children.[64]

Strong disincentives on Caribbean plantations toward raising children, including high infant mortality, may, however, have led to the supposed indifference of slave mothers. Jamaican planters reported that slave infants had a "very precarious tenure" on life and that "one-fourth perish within fourteen days of birth." In the first nine days of life, slave infants were particularly vulnerable, and, according to Higman, contemporary estimates placed the mortality rate within this period at 25 and 50 percent of all live births. The biggest killers, according to contemporary sources, were peripneumonic fevers caused by damp air and infant tetanus, or *Trismus nascentium*, the "jawfall," regarded by many Europeans as a major barrier to population growth. Predictably, slave doctors such as John Quier blamed such deaths on "inadequate maternal attention" and "want of cleanliness."[65]

During the late period of slavery attempts were made to prevent infant deaths from tetanus. Dr. Dancer recommended applying laudanum and turpentine to the umbilicus at birth to prevent tetanus caused by the "negro usage" of tying up the cut naval string with a burnt rag and leaving it for nine days without examination (a practice derived from Africa and still practiced in part of Haiti and Surinam). Dr. Sells advocated lying-in houses and "properly instructed midwives," while the planter, Lewis, recommended plunging infants into cold baths at birth. Lewis was forced to abandon this practice, however, due to the "obstinacy" of slave mothers who "took a prejudice against it." But "care and kindness" and European medicine failed to check infant mortality from tetanus. Dancer admitted that "no adequate solution" had been found and concluded that the cause of the disease depended on "a certain state and condition peculiar to infants within [the nine-day] period." John Quier argued that the "lock-jaw" which affected infants was not tetanus.[66] One explanation of the apparent high death rate from infant tetanus was that it was mistaken for tetany, which causes convulsions and has been traced to a deficiency of calcium and other vital minerals during pregnancy. However, there were perhaps other crucial variables which affected infant mortality, namely maternal attitudes. These may well have been influenced by the symbolic nature of the first nine days of a child's life in both West Africa (where neonatal tetanus was either rare or nonexistent) and Afro-Caribbean slave society.[67]

In West Africa a newborn infant is not regarded as part of this world until eight or nine days have passed, during which period it may be ritually neglected. The infant is regarded as no more than a "wandering ghost," a capricious visitor from the underworld. Among the Akan of Ghana, a child remains within the spirit world until this period is over and it becomes a human being, recognized by its father. If a child dies before this time, it is considered never to have existed. Similar traditions are found among the Ga people.[68] The durability of West African practices relating to childbirth has already been observed. It could be argued that the nine-day period (when slave midwives reputedly held "no hope" for infants) may have reflected African beliefs rather than, as Patterson suggests, deliberate neglect and fatalism because of the high risk of tetanus. Slave women were strongly attached to their "old customs" where childbearing and rearing were concerned.[69]

Within the framework of cultural persistence, it cannot be discounted that slave babies may have been deliberately "encouraged" to die. Dr. Robert Jackson, who practiced in Jamaica, argued that slave mothers were not naturally deficient in maternal affection, but "hard usage" rendered them "indifferent" or made them wish "that their offspring may fail" rather than be subjected to the plantation regime.[70] It is very difficult to establish whether premeditated infanticide occurred, although this has existed in many diverse societies from time immemorial—particularly among non-Christian "pagan" cultures where deformity, sickliness, or sheer strain on resources provided valid reasons. In traditional African culture, deformed infants and twins were commonly killed at birth. Infanticide is the natural corollary of abortion, but historians, sociologists, and demographers rarely consider this subject because of strong taboos in Western culture. For ethical reasons, infanticide is generally far less common than abortion, but where a "strong desire" to limit infant numbers exists, it may be used in conjunction with abortion or contraception, or as a final resort if these measures fail.[71]

Eugene Genovese argued that slave women in the southern United States could successfully "arrange" for infants to die soon after birth because infant deaths from natural causes were so common. Such unexplained deaths may have resulted from sudden infant death syndrome, which may be linked to mothers' labor in the fields rather than conscious attempts to deprive the system of slave infants. However, given the slaves' cultural beliefs and inherited knowledge of herbs, infanticide, like abortion, was arguably a valid response to enslavement.[72] If infanticide existed in the Old South where better material conditions prevailed, even stronger arguments apply for its practice in the Caribbean. In "letting" their children die, women slaves would release them from a dismal future. West African religious beliefs provided the ethical rationale; an infant child, dead or alive, does not have any power for good or evil and its death is regarded as spiritually "harmless."[73] The infant mortality rate from natural causes was undoubtedly high in the Caribbean, but the unusually high death rate within the first week, not satisfactorily explained as caused by tetanus, may signify that women used preparations which effected apparently natural death. These could have been acquired from obeah men and women or herbalists, known for their dangerous knowledge of poisons of which whites were largely ignorant. In Europe in the early nineteenth century, "artificial tetanus" resulting from strychnine poisoning was not unknown.[74]

Infanticide is a highly emotive word, and in the absence of evidence the arguments presented here can only remain speculative. However, as Eric Hobsbawn pointed out, there is a place for informed speculation and creative approaches in history. Indeed, in the study of oppressed social groups, this may be essential. If, as Sheridan claimed, there was a decline in infant deaths from tetanus by 1830, this certainly cannot be explained solely by better conditions, as planters and doctors tended to be disappointed by their efforts to cut infant mortality rates.[75] The decline in infant mortality may be explained more satisfactorily perhaps by the creolization of the population and greater impact of Christian beliefs which diluted the mystical justification of the nine-day period.

Women slaves had a number of powerful reasons for procuring abortion and releasing newly born infants from misery through "letting" them die. Too many children can be an excessive burden when mothers have a hard and bitter existence. One contemporary observer argued that slaves "refused to marry" in order "to avoid generating a race of human beings to be enslaved to [brutal] masters." Indeed, a paramount reason for the lack of will to have children, and hence the practice of abortion and infanticide, was the institution of slavery itself. Contemporary observers from both anti- and proslavery factions recognized this. James Stephen agreed with Bryan Edwards, who declared that slavery "in its mildest form" was "unfriendly to population," as the offspring of slaves were "born but to perish."[76]

After the abolition of slavery in 1838, Caribbean populations began to reproduce naturally, although conditions had barely improved and in some ways may have further deteriorated. This lends support for the proposition that the failure of Caribbean slave populations to reproduce cannot be explained solely by harsh conditions. The nature of slavery and the responses of slave women to their bondage must also be considered. There is no doubt that slave women loved and cared for their children, but they had no incentive to have large families. It has been argued here that there was a strong link between slave women's productive and reproductive roles and that the enigma of low fertility needs to be explored in the context of a wider slave resistance to the system. Among slave women, deliberate management of their fertility may have been a form of hidden, individual protest against slavery. Masters had less control over these forms of resistance than they had over the more overt forms of collective resistance. As Elizabeth Fox-Genovese has suggested, it is important to look not only at the specific experience of women as women but also at their struggle for an "individual soul or consciousness" against objectification, alienation, and dehumanization.[77]

Slave women's labor on Caribbean plantations conflicted with their private domestic lives. This had important implications for the reproduction of the slave population. No "normal" pattern of marriage or parenting was fully possible until slavery ended. Women had an enforced, alien division of labor imposed upon them which negated and undermined the traditional division of labor which was part of their African cultural inheritance. According to

Jacqueline Jones, the "schizoid" character of black women's lives under slavery was a product of white aspirations for blacks and blacks' aspirations for themselves. Nowhere was this more pertinent than in the intimate area of childbirth and infant rearing. After general emancipation, black women retreated, wherever possible, from plantation labor. They reclaimed their traditional role within the family and recreated a pattern of domesticity which had not been attainable under slavery. At this time the birthrate began to rise.[78]

In refusing to "breed" when forced to perform hard labor on the plantations, slave women were protesting their slave status and the erosion of their African cultural heritage. Where sexuality and reproduction were concerned, slave women were quadruply burdened, by both black and white patriarchy and by both gender and racial oppression. Their material conditions of existence, hardly conducive to childbearing and rearing, arguably led them to seek to exercise a degree of conscious control over their own reproductive capacities which frustrated planters' attempts to naturally increase the slave population. Slave women's responses to childbirth may be viewed as part of a wider pattern of resistance informed by African cultural practices and the personal and institutional relations which developed in slave societies.

Notes

1. Lucille Mathurin Mair, "A Historical Study of Women in Jamaica from 1655 to 1844," Ph.D. dissertation, University of the West Indies, 1974. For more recent works, see Deborah Gray White, *Ar'n't I a Woman: Female Slaves in the Plantation South* (New York: Norton, 1985); Jacqueline Jones, *Labor of Love, Labor of Sorrow: Black Women, Work and the Family from Slavery to the Present* (New York: Basic, 1985); Barbara Bush, *Slave Women in Caribbean Society, 1650–1838* (Bloomington: Indiana University Press, 1990).

2. Interest in slave demography developed in the 1970s. The main debates are summarized in Barry W. Higman, *Slave Populations of the British Caribbean, 1807–1834* (Baltimore: Johns Hopkins University Press, 1984), and Richard B. Sheridan, *Doctors and Slaves: A Medical and Demographic History of Slavery in the British West Indies, 1680–1834* (Cambridge: Cambridge University Press, 1985).

3. Melville J. Herskovits and Frances S. Herskovits, *Trinidad Village* (New York: Knopf, 1947), pp. 8–9. For a comprehensive study of slave resistance in the British Caribbean, see Michael Craton, *Testing the Chains: Resistance to Slavery in the British West Indies* (Ithaca: Cornell University Press, 1982).

4. Higman, *Slave Populations*, pp. 50–67. Such large-scale units, with the exception of Jamaica (53 percent), occupied 71–80 percent of all economically active slaves by 1830, and thus had a dominant role in determining the character of Caribbean slavery.

5. For detailed analyses of the living and working conditions of women field laborers, see Sheridan, *Doctors and Slaves*, pp. 178–90; Higman, *Slave Populations*, chap. 6.

6. Arlette Gautier, "Les Esclaves femmes aux Antilles françaises, 1635–1848," *Reflexions Historiques* 10 (Fall 1983): 409–35; Michael Foucault, *The History of Sexuality*, vol. 1, *An Introduction* (London: Allen Lane, 1978), trans. Robert Hurtley, pp. 96,

103–7. According to Foucault, sexuality should be described not merely as an instinctual drive but also as a "dense transfer point" for relations of power between men and women.

7. Higman, *Slave Populations*, p. 150. For an insight into the sexual power of masters over slaves, see Orlando Patterson, *Slavery and Social Death: A Comparative Study* (Cambridge: Harvard University Press, 1982), p. 173. Patterson's general discussion of power in section 1, "The Internal Relations of Slavery," is also relevant here. Patterson argues that women were more frequently manumitted than men because they were given freedom; most men purchased their freedom. This perhaps made it easier for white men to retain power over manumitted women (pp. 263–64).

8. Gad J. Heuman, *Between Black and White: Race, Politics and the Free Coloreds in Jamaica, 1792–1865* (Westport: Greenwood, 1981), p. 14. See also Patterson, *Slavery and Social Death*, p. 175. For contemporary comments, see J. G. Stedman, *Narrative of a Five Years' Expedition against the Revolted Negroes of Surinam, 1772–1777* (London: J. Johnson and J. Edwards, 1796), vol. 1, p. 112; John Stewart, *A View of the Past and Present State of the Island of Jamaica* (Edinburgh: Oliver & Boyd, 1823), p. 170. The psychological basis of European women's racism and power in colonial societies is analyzed in a classic study by Octave Mannoni, *Prospero and Caliban: The Psychology of Colonization* (New York, 1964). Data relating to slave ownership are provided by Higman, *Slave Populations*, pp. 111–12.

9. Hilary Beckles, "'Black Men in White Skins': The Formation of a White Proletariat in West Indian Slave Society," *Journal of Imperial and Commonwealth History* 15 (October 1986): 13. Even poor white women were not allowed to work as field hands.

10. Bryan Edwards, *The History, Civil and Commercial, of the British Colonies of the West Indies* (London, 1805), vol. 1, pp. 540–41; Edward Long, *The History of Jamaica* (1774; reprint, London: Frank Cass, 1970) vol. 1, pp. 304–404; John Adams, *Sketches Taken during Ten Voyages to Africa between the Years 1786 and 1800* (London, 1822), p. 8. Anthropological studies of the sexual division of labor in traditional African societies confirm that women grow most of the food crops for consumption (as opposed to export), but men also have clearly defined tasks, which include much of the heaviest labor. See, for instance, Maria Rosa Cutrafelli, *Women of Africa: Roots of Oppression*, trans. from Italian (London: Zed, 1983), chap. 2.

11. For data on sex ratios, see Sheridan, *Doctors and Slaves*, pp. 107–8; Higman, *Slave Populations*, pp. 117–18. David W. Galenson, in an econometric analysis, suggests that the higher prices of women in the internal African slave markets (in comparison to males) may have had an impact on the availability of female slaves for transport to the West Indies. See Galenson, *Traders, Planters and Slaves: Market Behavior in Early English America* (Cambridge: Cambridge University Press, 1986), pp. 105–7. The sexual division of labor on the sugar plantation is analyzed in some detail in Higman, *Slave Populations*, pp. 189–99. For comparative data on the French Caribbean, see Gautier, "Les Esclaves femmes," 410–11.

12. William Beckford, *Remarks upon the Situation of the Negroes in Jamaica* (London: Egerton, 1788), p. 13.

13. *The Royal Gazette*, Kingston, Jamaica, August 18, 1827. Contemporary estimates of slave prices are given in Edwards, *History*, vol. 2, p. 132, and "Report of the Lords of Trade into the Slave Trade," *Parliamentary Papers*, Commons, 26 (1789), 646a, pt. 3, Jamaica, Ans. no. 29. Women were on average 81 percent as valuable as adult men in Barbados, 1673–1723 (Galenson, *Traders, Planters, and Slaves*, pp. 62–65).

14. Higman, *Slave Populations*, pp. 189–98, 224, 314–17. The dominance of women in fieldwork up to emancipation is confirmed by studies of individual plantations. See Michael Craton and James Walvin, *A Jamaican Plantation: The History of Worthy Park, 1670–1970* (London: W. H. Allen, 1970), p. 138, which gives the field gang composition for 1787–95; Richard S. Dunn, "A Tale of Two Plantations: Slave Life at Mesopotamia in Jamaica and Mount Airy in Virginia, 1799–1828," *William and Mary Quarterly* 3d Series, 34 (January 1977): 32–65.

15. Higman, *Slave Populations*, pp. 183–84, 314–17. For a comparative description of the field slave's daily toil, see Beckford, *Negroes in Jamaica*, p. 44.

16. Elsa Goveia, *Slave Society in the British Leeward Islands at the End of the Eighteenth Century* (New Haven: Yale University Press, 1965), p. 234; Craton and Walvin, *A Jamaican Plantation*, pp. 103–4, 125; Higman, *Slave Populations*, p. 188.

17. The various forms of resistance employed by women, including verbal abuse, are discussed in Barbara Bush, "Defiance or Submission? The Role of the Slave Woman in Slave Resistance in the British Caribbean," *Immigrants and Minorities* 1 (March 1982): 16–39.

18. Goveia, *Slave Society*, pp. 244–45.

19. Baillies Bacolet Plantation Returns, 1820–1833; Punishment Record Books for Friendship Sarah and Good Success Plantations, 1823–1833 (British Guiana), Atkin's Slavery Collection, Wiberforce House, Hull. The intransigent nature of female field hands was also noted in the commentaries of individual planters. See Matthew Gregory Lewis, *Journal of a Residence among the Negroes of the West Indies* (London, 1845), pp. 93, 103.

20. Public Records Office, Kew, Colonial Office Series (C.O.) 295/60, 295/66, Commandant of Chaguanas to Governor Woodford, August 20, 1823; cited in Bridget Brereton, "Brute Beast or Man Angel: Attitudes to the Blacks in Trinidad, 1802–1888," unpublished paper, Department of History, University of the West Indies, Trinidad, 1974. See also Long, *History of Jamaica*, p. 103.

21. Thomas Cooper, *Facts Illustrative of the Condition of the Negro Slaves in Jamaica* (London: Hatchard, 1824), pp. 17–18.

22. Higman, *Slave Populations*, p. 224. For comments on the power of black drivers, see, for instance, Stedman, *Narrative*, vol. 1, p. 117.

23. Baillies Bacolet Plantation Returns.

24. Cooper, *Facts Illustrative*, p. 20; "Abstract from the Slave Laws of Jamaican Slave Law, 1826," no. 37 in Bernard Martin Senior, *Jamaica as It Was, as It Is, and as It May Be* (London: Hurst, 1835), p. 145; William Sells, *Remarks on the Condition of Slaves in the Island of Jamaica* (London: Richardson, Cornhill & Ridgways, 1823), p. 17.

25. John Williamson, *Medical and Miscellaneous Observations, Relative to the West Indian Islands* (Edinburgh, 1817), vol. 1, p. 191; Lewis, *Journal*, pp. 174–75.

26. Sir Hans Sloane, *A Voyage to the Islands Madera, Barbadoes, Nieves, S. Christophers and Jamaica* (London, 1707) vol. 1, p. lii; Richard Ligon, *A True and Exact History of the Island of Barbadoes* (London, 1657; reprint, London, 1970), p. 113.

27. Higman, *Slave Populations*, pp. 290–300; Mair, "A Historical Study of Women in Jamaica," pp. 313–16.

28. "Report . . . into the Slave Trade" (1789), pt. 3, Barbados, Ans. no. 16; Long, *History of Jamaica*, vol. 2, p. 341.

29. Long, *History of Jamaica*, vol. 2, p. 490. For an analysis of the slave laws from the abolitionist perspective, see John Jeremie, *Four Essays on Colonial Slavery* (London: J. Hatchard and Son, 1831).

30. Elsa Goveia, *The West Indian Slave Laws of the Eighteenth Century* (Barbados: Caribbean Universities Press, 1970), pp. 7, 25, 48; Michael Craton, *Sinews of Empire; A Short History of British Slavery* (London: Temple Smith, 1974), p. 175.

31. "Abstract from the Leeward Islands Act 1798," Act no. 36, Clauses 37 & 38, Edwards, *History*, vol. 5, pp. 181–82, 185; "Abstract of the Laws of Jamaica," Long, *History of Jamaica*, vol. 2, p. 161; Goveia, *Slave Society*, p. 196; Stewart, *View of Jamaica*, p. 262.

32. "Abstract from the Leeward Islands Act 1798," Act no. 36, Clauses 22–25, Edwards, *History*, vol. 5, pp. 183–85; "Abstract from the Slave Laws of Jamaica, 1826," nos. 32 and 33; Senior, *Jamaica*, p. 144; Long, *History of Jamaica*, vol. 2, p. 440.

33. Sells, *Remarks*, pp. 15–18.

34. Ligon, *A True and Exact History*, p. 49; Thomas Dancer, *The Medical Assistant of Jamaica Practice of Physic, Designed Chiefly for the Use of Families and Plantations* (Kingston, 1809), pp. 263–64; Philip Wright, *Lady Nugent's Journal* (Kingston: Institute of Jamaica, 1966), p. 69. For racist attitudes, see Long, *History of Jamaica*, vol. 2, p. 385; Stedman, *Narrative*, vol. 2, p. 359. Long acknowledged that childbirth in the Caribbean was "not so easy" as in Africa. In the early days slave women were reputedly "left alone to God" in one room of their cabin and after two weeks they were back at work; see Ligon, *A True and Exact History*, p. 49; Sloane, *Voyage*, vol. 1, p. cxlvii.

35. Cutrafelli, *Women of Africa*, pp. 136–37.

36. Long, *History of Jamaica*, vol. 2, p. 436; Beckford, *Negroes in Jamaica*, pp. 24–25.

37. *Edinburgh Review* 55 (1832), Article 7, p. 148, and 38 (1823), Article 8, p. 177; James Stephen, *The Crisis in the Sugar Colonies* (London, 1802), p. 32.

38. Sheridan, *Doctors and Slaves*, pp. 246–48; Higman, *Slave Populations*, pp. 67–68; Gautier, "Les Esclaves femmes," p. 417.

39. Lewis noted, "The children do not come . . . despite encouragement"; *Journal*, pp. 45, 52. See also Jeremie, *Four Essays*, p. 97. Paternalistic planters may actually have been more far-sighted than other planters and were not necessarily "uneconomic" in their policies to conserve slave life and encourage reproduction. See Daniel C. Littlefield, "Plantations, Paternalism and Profitability: Factors Affecting African Demography in the Old British Empire," *Journal of Southern History* 47 (May 1981): 171. However, such initiatives were arguably frustrated by the absentee system and increasingly uncertain economic conditions. The absence of white women to take a personal interest in pregnant and lying-in slave women may also have resulted in the neglect of these women.

40. Higman, *Slave Populations*, pp. 3, 73, 116–17. According to Higman's data, there were more women than men between 1817 and 1832 (p. 116), yet adverse sex ratios were often exaggerated by planters, particularly as abolitionist pressure built up at the end of the eighteenth century. Edwards maintained that the ratio on some Jamaican plantations was as high as five men to one woman; see Edwards, *History*, vol. 2, pp. 118, 132. See also Long, *History of Jamaica*, p. 385; Stewart, *View of Jamaica*, pp. 308–310. The sex ratio did vary from plantation to plantation, from island to island, and between rural and urban slaves but in itself is an adequate explanation of low fertility.

41. Sheridan, *Doctors and Slaves*, pp. 246–48; "Report . . . on the Slave Trade," pt. 3, Barbados, Ans. no. 16; Higman, *Slave Populations*, pp. 361–62.

42. Higman, *Slave Populations*, pp. 259–61.

43. See, for example, Michael Craton, *Searching for the Invisible Man: Slaves and Plantation Life in Jamaica* (Cambridge: Harvard University Press, 1978), pp. 102–12; Kenneth F. Kiple, *The Caribbean Slave: A Biological History* (Cambridge: Cambridge University Press, 1984), chap. 7.

44. Higman, *Slave Populations*, pp. 347–48, 362; Herbert S. Klein and Stanley L. Engerman also stress the need to account for the active agency of slaves in examining childrearing practices; see their "Fertility Differentials between Slaves in the United States and the British West Indies: A Note on Lactation Practices and Their Possible Implications," *William and Mary Quarterly* 3d series, 35 (April 1978): 374.

45. Long, *History of Jamaica*, vol. 2, pp. 412, 436–47; "Report . . . into the Slave Trade," pt. 3, Jamaica, Ans. no. 11, no. 4. For a discussion of European attitudes to Afro-Caribbean medicine, see Sheridan, *Doctors and Slaves*, pp. 320, 330–37.

46. Sloane, *Voyage*, vol. 1, p. cxxvii; Dancer, *Medical Assistant*, pp. 212–13. Kiple notes that there was confusion over the diagnosis of syphilis and yaws in the Spanish islands, and modern research has confirmed a cross-immunity between the two diseases. It was widely believed that syphilis was a white man's disease and yaws a black disease. "Pure" blacks were allegedly never stricken by syphilis, and Kiple argues that this disease became a problem for Caribbean blacks only when yaws disappeared in the twentieth century. He also maintains that tuberculosis of the urinary tract was frequently diagnosed as gonorrhea. See Kiple, *Caribbean Slave*, pp. 243–44, n. 29. Data on mortality indicate that the death rate from venereal disease was much lower than the rates for yaws and tuberculosis. See Sheridan, *Doctors and Slaves*, pp. 194–200; Higman, *Slave Populations*, pp. 339–47.

47. Long, *History of Jamaica*, vol. 2, p. 385. Comparative conditions in eighteenth-century Europe are discussed in M. C. Buer, *Health, Wealth and Population in the Early Days of the Industrial Revolution* (London: Routledge, 1926), chaps. 3, 6. The significance of negative stereotyping is discussed in Patterson, *Slavery and Social Death*, pp. 85, 100.

48. B. W. Higman, "The Slave Family and Household in the British West Indies, 1800–1834," *Journal of Interdisciplinary History* 6 (Autumn 1975): 261–87; Barbara Bush, "The Family Tree Is Not Cut: Women and Cultural Resistance in Slave Family Life in the British Caribbean," in *In Resistance: Studies in African, Caribbean and Afro-American History*, ed. Gary Y. Okihiro (Amherst: University of Massachusetts Press, 1986), pp. 117–33.

49. Klein and Engerman, "Fertility Differentials," p. 371; Jerome S. Handler and Robert S. Corruccini, "Weaning among West Indian Slaves: Historical and Bioanthropological Evidence from Barbados," *William and Mary Quarterly* 3d ser., 43 (January 1986): 111–17; Kiple, *Caribbean Slave*, p. 110. For contemporary comments, see Stedman, *Narrative*, vol. 2, p. 368; Dr. Collins, ("A Professional Planter"), *Practical Rules for the Management and Medical Treatment of Negro Slaves in the Sugar Colonies* (London: J. Barfield, 1803), p. 146. For observations on the practice in Africa, see Daryl Forde, "Kinship and Marriage among the Matrilineal Ashanti," in *African Systems of Kinship and Marriage*, ed. A. R. Radcliffe-Brown and D. Forde (London: Oxford University Press, 1950), pp. 262–63. The Ashanti prohibited intercourse for only eighty days after birth, which suggests that factors other than late weaning may have contributed to the low fertility rate where (as in the case of Jamaica) there was a high proportion of slaves of Ashanti (Akan) origin.

50. Lewis, *Journal*, pp. 145–46; Baillie, cited in Sheridan, *Doctors and Slaves*, p. 245.

51. Kiple, *Caribbean Slave*, pp. 113–15; Dunn, "A Tale of Two Plantations," p. 61. Kiple suggests that slave infant mortality was the prime reason for the low rate of natural increase in the Caribbean and argues, contrary to existing research, that slave fertility was actually high.

52. Higman, *Slave Populations*, pp. 373–76, 397; Kiple, *Caribbean Slave*, pp. 113–15; Dancer, *Medical Assistant*, pp. 232–33; Sheridan, *Doctors and Slaves*, pp. 158–59; Craton, *Searching for the Invisible Man*, p. 99; Dunn, "A Tale of Two Plantations," pp. 62–63; E. Van Den Boogaart and P. Emmer, "Plantation Slavery in Surinam in the Last Decade before Emancipation," *Annals of the New York Academy of Sciences* 292 (June 1977): 205. For the link between starvation and amenorrhea, see E. Le Roy Ladurie, *The Territory of the Historian*, trans. from French (London, 1979), pp. 265–69.

53. Kiple, *Caribbean Slave*, pp. 107–98; Higman, *Slave Populations*, pp. 372–73.

54. Cutrafelli, *Women of Africa*, pp. 133–35; Forde, "Kinship and Marriage," pp. 262–66.

55. "Report . . . into the Slave Trade," pt. 3, Barbados, Ans. no. 5; Collins, *Practical Rules*, p. 35.

56. Stanley M. Elkins, *Slavery: A Problem in American Institutional and Intellectual Life* (Chicago: University of Chicago Press, 1959). Ladurie traces the connection between low fertility and harsh conditions from the seventeenth to the twentieth century: *Territory of the Historian*, pp. 268–69. For definitions of amenorrhea, see *The British Medical Dictionary*, ed. Sir A. S. McNulty (London, 1961). Also relevant here is Terrence Des Pres's analysis of a World War II concentration camp; see Des Pres, *The Survivor: An Anatomy of Life in the Death Camps* (New York: Oxford University Press, 1976).

57. Long, *History of Jamaica*, vol. 2, p. 346; John Quier, "A Slave Doctor's Views on Childbirth, Infant Mortality and the General Health of His Charges, 1788" in Report of the Assembly on Slave Issues, Jamaica House of Assembly, enclosed in Lt. Gov. Clarke's dispatch, November 20, 1788, no. 92, C.O. 137/88, Appendix C, p. 491; Collins, *Practical Rules*, p. 51; Reverend Henry Beame, cited in *Slavery, Abolition and Emancipation: Black Slaves and the British Empire*, ed. Michael Craton, James Walvin, and David Wright (London: Longman, 1976), p. 141.

58. For the dangerous nature of slave abortions, see Sloane, *Voyage*, p. cxlii. Cutrafelli notes that in Zaire a strong pepper (pili pili) is used, large doses of which can cause internal burns to the ovaries: *Women of Africa*, p. 141. Similarly the Guinea pepper used by the Efik of Old Calabar (Nigeria) can cause "organic lesions" and "serious constitutional disturbances"; see George Devereux, *A Study of Abortion in Primitive Societies* (New York: Julian, 1955), p. 218.

59. Cutrafelli, *Women of Africa*, pp. 141–43; Devereux, *A Study of Abortion*, pp. 218, 289; R. S. Rattray, *Religion and Art in Ashanti* (Oxford: Clarendon Press, 1927), p. 55; G. W. Harley, *Native African Medicine* (Cambridge: Harvard University Press, 1941), p. 73; Melville J. Herskovits, *Dahomey: An Ancient West African Kingdom* (New York: J. J. Augustin, 1938), vol. 1, p. 268.

60. Sheridan, *Doctors and Slaves*, p. 74; Kiple, *Caribbean Slave*, pp. 152–54. For contemporary observations on slave women's knowledge of folk medicine, see Stewart, *View of Jamaica*, p. 312.

61. Dancer, *Medical Assistant*, pp. 263–64, 368, 381, 398; Stedman, *Narrative*, vol. 1, p. 334; *Journal of a Lady of Quality: Being the Narrative of a Journey from Scotland to the West Indies, North Carolina and Portugal in the Years 1774 to 1776*, ed. Evangeline Walker Andrews and Charles McLean Andrews (New Haven: Yale University Press, 1923), pp. 112–13. For transmission of folk knowledge, see Sheridan, *Doctors and Slaves*, pp. 77, 244.

62. Morton C. Kahn, *Djuka: The Bush Negroes of Dutch Guiana* (New York: Viking, 1931), pp. 127–28; Herskovits and Herskovits, *Trinidad Village*, p. 111; oral data collected by Barbara Bush.

63. Lewis, *Journal*, p. 65. For similar contemporary comments, see Edwards, *History*, vol. 2, p. 148; A. C. Carmichael, *Domestic Manners and Social Condition of the White, Coloured and Negro Population of the West Indies* (London: Whittaker, Treacher, 1833), vol. 1, p. 201.

64. *Out of the House of Bondage: Runaways, Resistance and Marronage in Africa and the New World*, ed. Gad Heuman (London: Frank Cass, 1986), p. 6. For evidence of maternal tenderness, see Ligon, *A True and Exact History*, p. 51; Long, *History of Jamaica*, vol. 2, p. 44; Sloane, *Voyage*, pp. lvi, lvii; Lewis, *Journal*, p. 90.

65. Quier, "A Slave Doctor's Views," p. 490. See also the evidence of Jamaican planters in "Report . . . into the Slave Trade," pt. 3, Jamaica, Ans. no. 16; Edwards, *History*, vol. 2, p. 140; Lewis, *Journal*, p. 97.

66. Dancer, *Medical Assistant*, pp. 257, 267, 278; Sells, *Remarks*, p. 18; Lewis, *Journal*, pp. 50, 141, 269; Quier, "A Slave Doctor's Views," p. 490. For treatment of the umbilicus in modern Afro-Caribbean societies, see Kiple, *Caribbean Slave*, p. 121; Kahn, *Djuka*, p. 227. Statistics relating to infant mortality are given in B. W. Higman, *Slave Population and Economy in Jamaica, 1807–1834* (Cambridge: Cambridge University Press, 1976), pp. 112–13. Higman suggests that infant deaths were, if anything, underrecorded in the first few days.

67. Kiple, *Caribbean Slave*, pp. 120–25.

68. Forde, "Kinship and Marriage," p. 67; Rattray, *Religion and Art*, pp. 57–58, 67; M. J. Field, *Religion and Medicine of the Ga People* (London: Oxford University Press, 1937), p. 214; G. Parrinder, *West African Religion* (London: Epworth, 1949), p. 214; Herskovits, *Dahomey*, vol. 1, pp. 266–67; Cutrafelli, *Women of Africa*, p. 133.

69. Orlando Patterson, *The Sociology of Slavery* (London: McGibbon and Kee, 1967), p. 155; Edward Brathwaite, *The Development of Creole Society in Jamaica, 1770–1820* (Oxford: Clarendon Press, 1971). For details of twentieth-century Afro-Caribbean practices, see Martha Beckwith, *Black Roadways: A Study of Jamaican Folk Life* (Chapel Hill: University of North Carolina Press, 1929), pp. 57–58; Herskovits and Herskovits, *Trinidad Village*, pp. 113–14. For slave women's "obstinacy," see Quier, "A Slave Doctor's Views," p. 491.

70. Evidence of Dr. Jackson (Jamaica), House of Commons Report, 1791, cited in Sheridan, *Doctors and Slaves*, p. 228.

71. Herbert Apteker, *Anjea: Infanticide, Abortion and Contraception in Savage Society* (New York: W. Godwin, 1931), p. 151.

72. Eugene D. Genovese, *Roll, Jordan, Roll: The World the Slaves Made* (New York: Pantheon, 1974), p. 41; Michael P. Johnson, "Smothered Slave Infants: Were Slave Mothers at Fault?" *Journal of Southern History* 47 (November 1981): 510–15.

73. Rattray, *Religion and Art*, pp. 59–61.

74. Thomas B. Curling, *A Treatise on Tetanus* (London, 1836), p. 27. For slave knowledge of poisons, see Sloane, *Voyage*, vol. 2, pp. ix, xii; R. R. Madden, *A Twelvemonth's Residence in the West Indies* (London: James Cochran, 1835), vol. 1, p. 187.

75. Sheridan, *Doctors and Slaves*, pp. 235–36; Eric Hobsbawm, quoted by Richard Gott in "The History Man," *Guardian*, February 26, 1988.

76. Monsieur Bossue, cited in Long, *History of Jamaica*, vol. 2, p. 440; Edwards, *History*, vol. 2, p. 148; James Stephen, *The Slavery of the British West India Colonies Delineated* (London, 1824–30), vol. 1, p. 79. It may be argued that slavery in the West Indies existed in its most brutal and distorted form; see Patterson, *Slavery and Social Death*, pp. 97–101.

77. Elizabeth Fox-Genovese, "Strategies and Forms of Resistance: Focus on Slave Women in the United States," in *In Resistance*, pp. 143–65. See also Sheridan, *Doctors and Slaves*, pp. 245, 339; Higman, *Slave Populations*, p. 366.

78. Jones, *Labor of Love*, p. 340. See also Sheridan, *Doctors and Slaves*, p. 340, for reversion to a traditional division of labor after emancipation. Gautier suggests that a similar reversion occurred in Saint Domingue (Haiti) after the revolution; see "Les Esclaves femmes," p. 432.

11

FROM "THE SENSE OF THEIR SLAVERY"
Slave Women and Resistance
in Antigua, 1632–1763

David Barry Gaspar

Throughout the Americas slaves carved out more livable spaces for themselves by working to transform privileges allowed by the master class into customary rights. By the early decades of the eighteenth century, Caribbean slaves had earned the right to hold markets on Sundays, and these markets became a significant feature of slave life.[1] When the legislature of the sugar island of Antigua abolished Sunday markets in March 1831 without allowing substitute time for marketing by law, the slaves vented their frustration in a number of ways that frightened most whites into believing that a general insurrection was in the making. At the very start of this outburst of collective protest, slave women were involved conspicuously.

In a joint letter to the Methodist Missionary Society in London, four Methodist missionaries on the island filed a report about what happened when "many hundreds [of slaves] assembled in the Great Market of Saint John's [the main town] and in other places."

> It is said, more than two thirds of these people brought nothing for Sale, but were generally armed with strong bludgeons secured by twine to the wrists. The Sellers were almost to an individual females, the rest men. They asserted that Sunday was their own day, and declared their determination not to resign the right of selling on that day. Their language was frequently violent and menacing, and accompanied by furious gesticulations and brandished cudgels. Matters appeared to assume a very threatening aspect. The appearance of a detachment of the 86th Regiment which was marched to the entrance of the Great Market, and then wheeled off up the New-Street, seemed for a few Minutes to have struck the fatal spark. The Multitude was instantly in Commotion, and very alarming indications of rage and resistance were witnessed throughout. Happily, however, this ebullition did not continue long: two or three parties being persuaded to depart, others slowly followed their example, and

about half past six the last company (7 or 8) of obstinate Women retired to the Country.[2]

From this early show of defiance, the slaves later moved on to burn several sugar plantations and to organize marches to Government House in Saint John's, where they insisted on laying their complaints before the governor.[3]

The prominent involvement of slave women in the dramatic confrontation at the Saint John's Market deserves special notice because it immediately draws attention to the resistance of slave women to slavery in the years before 1831. Was their activism on the eve of general emancipation (1834) atypical and unexpected, or was it a suggestive clue to a past in which resistance among slave women was the norm rather than the exception? The primary purpose of this chapter is to probe the evidence for an answer through an examination of resistance among slave women from the late 1600s to the mid-1700s. At the same time, the inquiry is meant to put slave women back into the larger picture of the continuous struggle of Antigua slaves to cope with slavery and not be overwhelmed by it. The tasks undertaken here are encumbered, however, by the dearth of evidence that focuses on the lives of slave women; to the male authorities and others who prepared the documentary evidence that survives, slave men were the more visible figures or political actors and therefore they received the most attention. Nevertheless, a careful and sensitive sifting of the evidence can illuminate some areas of the "nature, extent, and meaning"[4] of the resistance of slave women in Antigua.

In 1729 Reverend Robert Robertson of Nevis, one of the British Leeward Islands near Antigua, made several observations about the Caribbean slaves' deep hatred of slavery. Basing his judgment on many years of "long and sure observation" of slave life in the islands, Robertson noted that

> the Sense of their Slavery seems to lie deep in the Minds of many of them, and improves (as some conceive) to a very great Degree their Love to Laziness, Stealing, Stubbornness, Murmuring, Treachery, Lying, Drunkenness, and the like; that the Desire of Change, far from being the Consequence of Colour, governs strongly among the Negroes; that many of them run away from their Owners upon slight and trifling Pretences and very often without pretending to have had any Cause or Provocation given to them at all, and generally when their Labour, or Attendance is most wanted; that some of them keep out in the Mountains (of the Leeward-Islands and Jamaica) for whole Years, which is easy in Countries where it is always Summer; and they Seldom let slip any safe Opportunities of deserting to their Masters Enemies in time of an Invasion; that, however they may disguise it, they hate their masters and wish them destroyed; that they have actually plotted against them in some of the Colonies, murther'd some of them in others, and were Power in their Hands would (as is still too probable) destroy them all. . . .

Robertson also noted with some wonder that it was not unusual for recent African recruits "(without any Provocation from their new Masters, or giving any Signs of Discontent, and after no small care has been taken to make Slavery sit easy on them) to make away with themselves." Equally suicidal, for Robertson, was the tendency among other Africans who were "stupid enough to think (and some have been found making the Experiment) that if they can but get into a Boat and thrust out a little from the Shore, the Boat of itself will carry them back to their Native Land." For all of these reasons that characterized the psychological and sociopolitical dynamics of slave resistance, and also, most importantly, because of "the Danger we must needs be in" from the overwhelming size of the population of those "sort of creatures," Robertson concluded, "the white Inhabitants keep a strict Eye over them, and are often oblig'd to treat some with great Severity."[5]

It is difficult to pinpoint the slave woman in Robertson's otherwise probing remarks. Blinded as he was by the patriarchal privilege of his class, he did not see women or consider gender differentiation an important enough category of analysis within resistance. In any case, Robertson's observations challenge scholars to retrieve the missing contribution of slave women to the struggle against slavery. That in important ways slave women experienced slavery differently from slave men must be acknowledged at the outset in attempting to meet that challenge. As Elizabeth Fox-Genovese reminds us, "It is impossible to discuss the specific roles of women in the general struggle of Afro-American slaves without taking account of male and female roles—gender roles—among the slaves."[6] These roles were shaped by the demands the total plantation environment made on slaves, and by the codes of behavior nurtured by the slaves themselves within their communities.

Some scholars have argued against the use of the term *resistance* to describe and explain largely undramatic, day-to-day slave behavior that incrementally hampered the plantation system. But these everyday forms of subversion added up and constituted the foundation upon which slaves built more ambitious schemes of subversion that matured into collective political resistance or insurrection. Broadly defined, *resistance* as a concept can be used to apply to slave behavior that cannot be equated with cooperation with slavery. It spans a continuum that takes into account important qualitative differences between individual acts and those that were collective or had collective potential. Indeed, resistance was an important organizing principle of slave life. In various ways slaves created a culture of resistance in which women played important roles.[7] Robertson's catalog of slave resistance, however incomplete, nevertheless provides an illuminating sampling of responses along the continuum of resistance and highlights a reality that most slaveowners remained acutely aware of—that slave resistance and masters' control of slave behavior were important interlocking dimensions of the overall workings of the slave system. Just as it is not possible to understand the master class apart from its relations with the slaves and vice versa, so too are slave resistance and slave control best studied together because of the resistance-control dynamic.[8]

The resistance of Antigua slave women and slaveowners' perceptions of the need to control them during the seventeenth century were shaped by the character of the Sugar Revolution, which welded sugar and slavery and brought into being a society dominated by the necessity to perfect this profitable combination for the benefit of slaveowners.

Nearly fifty years after its first settlement by the English in 1632, Antigua began to experience the sweeping and rapid socioeconomic metamorphosis that historians call the Sugar Revolution. During the last quarter of the seventeenth century, the earlier individualistic, predominantly white settler society that produced tobacco as its main cash crop was swiftly replaced by a racially stratified society of whites and blacks that produced mainly sugar. The entire institutional structure and value system of the new society centered on black slavery. The most striking changes wrought by the Sugar Revolution, apart, perhaps, from the appearance of the landscape, occurred in the disproportionate size of the white and slave populations. Antigua had a total population of 1,200 in 1655. By 1678 there were 4,480 inhabitants: 2,308 whites and 2,172 blacks. In the 1680s, as the pace of economic life quickened, the slave population surged forward to greatly outnumber whites, primarily through the importation of African slave cargoes as planters raced to acquire land and slaves for sugar cultivation on a large scale. In 1703 there were reportedly 11,000 slaves in the tiny island colony of only 280 square kilometers. By 1734 slaves (24,908) outnumbered whites (3,772) by nearly eight to one.[9]

During the last three decades of the seventeenth century, before the island's forests disappeared, sacrificed to the mania of plantation building, running away, or *marronage*, was the characteristic mode of resistance among slaves. They sought refuge particularly among the Shekerly Hills of Saint Mary's Parish in the southwestern corner of the island. Some of these fugitives formed maroon bands. Through raids on outlying plantations and the encouragement to desert extended to plantation slaves, maroons or fugitive slaves threatened to undermine the security of the colony.[10] Such resistance was included among "Divers Treasonable and felonious acts punishable with death" cited by a law passed as early as 1669. In 1680 the Antigua legislature passed a comprehensive act against runaways which strongly suggests that marronage and its effects had reached a critical point in the eyes of the authorities, who now, perhaps for the first time in the short history of the developing slave society, offered rewards for the capture of fugitives.[11] Despite such obstacles, a number of fugitives succeeded in establishing a maroon camp in the Shekerly Hills by 1684. These rebels waged guerrilla warfare against whites, harassed them through their "mischief," and induced other slaves to join them in their freedom. The authorities achieved little in curbing this bold challenge to the plantation order; indeed, matters grew steadily worse, for they held the maroons responsible in 1687 for perhaps the only genuine slave insurrection in the Leeward Islands in the seventeenth century. The Antigua authorities believed that the maroons intended to foment unrest among the plantation slaves and others and to seize control of the island. This insurrectionary plot was allegedly centered on the island's south side, where the Shekerly hills continued to attract fugitives.[12]

Where do women figure in this portrait of slave unrest during the Sugar Revolution? In 1684 the Antigua governor and council asked slaveholders to prepare lists of their fugitive slaves, and it is probably from these that the legislature compiled its own revealing record of fugitives who were reputedly still at large on March 24, 1687, lurking in the hills and elsewhere.[13] Recorded by name, owner, and ethnic group or place of origin were twenty-seven fugitives (see table). Although the list certainly does not speak for itself and is admittedly of limited value for analyzing marronage in the seventeenth century, our attention is drawn to the women who appear on it. To judge from the names, at least ten women were listed along with perhaps seventeen men. We do not know how long these women were at large, but some of them may have escaped before 1684.

The list raises a number of intriguing questions.

- Does the ratio of fugitive men to women reflect a greater tendency among men to run away? Does it also imply that men outnumbered women in the slave population?
- Did women flee on their own, with men, with other women, or were they sometimes carried off by men during raids on plantations?
- In the case of "Betty & her husband," she a "Collomantee" (Coromantee from the Gold Coast), he from Angola, did they run away together or separately? Why? How old were they? Did they belong to the same owner?
- What was the connection between Abraham & Molly, who ran away, together or separately, from their master, Belchamber?
- Does the proportion of women in the list imply that while frontier conditions still existed in seventeenth-century Antigua (though they were gradually disappearing), a much larger proportion of fugitives were women than later in the eighteenth century when, because of the small size of the island and the full expansion of the plantations, the environment no longer supported long-term flight?
- How long had the fugitive women been in Antigua before they fled? When did they first arrive?
- What were their occupations, ages, and other personal attributes?
- At what period of the year, or at what stage in the annual production cycle of the plantation did they run away?

These are only a few of the sort of probing questions for which historians seek answers when they analyze slave flight,[14] but the sparse information in the Antigua fugitive slave list of 1684 does not supply answers; neither are the other scanty source materials for the seventeenth century of much help. It is clear, however, that whatever the set of circumstances that provoked their decision to become fugitives, most of these Antigua women were Africans, not creoles or island-born slaves, who held out in the hills in symbolic and actual defiance of the plantation order. That most fugitive slaves were African is perhaps a clue to the general pattern of the responses of Africans to slavery (especially among

Runaways in the Antigua Hills, March 24, 1687

Name	Ethnic Group or Place of Origin*	Owner
Tony, Tom, Joane	Mallegascos	Jonas Langford
Will, Phillip	Mallegascos	———
Robin, Garret, Nany, Sarah Mare, One More	Collomantee and Lampo	Lynch
Sarah	Lampoe	Lucas
Will	Magasco	Governor
Joan	Ibbo	Lingham
Betty & her husband	Collomantee and Angola	———
Four Negro Men & One woman	Angola	———
Sham	Ibbo	Bushway
John Premeer	A free man	———
Abraham & Molly	———	Belchamber
Mary	Pappa	Bramble
Robin	Ibbo	———

* African regions: Mallegascos, Magasco: Madagascar; Collomantee: Gold Coast; Lampo: Slave Coast; Ibbo: Niger River delta and immediate hinterland; Pappa: Dahomey.
Source: Council Minutes, March 24, 1687, fol. 63, *CO 155/1.*

those newly arrived in the colony) under the frontier conditions of early slave society in Antigua. Indeed, in ruling on the control of slaves and the recurring plague of marronage, the Antigua legislature would later concede that the law should treat newly arrived Africans more leniently because they experienced difficulty adjusting to their new environment.[15] All of this suggests that in the evaluation of patterns of slave resistance, a number of important elements of the slaves' past and current worlds should be taken into account, as well as gender and ethnic factors. If the ethnic composition of the 1684 Antigua list of fugitives shows a strong African representation, then it also obviously reflects the degree of African presence among the slave population, as well as the distribution of slave trading on the African coast in the seventeenth century.[16] Moreover, from the point of view of cultural transfer and change, one is curious about how slave flight and the development of the slave community in Antigua carried an African imprint that was expressed in a number of adaptations, including those specifically related to gender differentiation.[17]

One fugitive slave woman of Antigua, captured in 1687, demonstrated her resourcefulness in outmaneuvering the authorities and declaring her stand as an unrepentant rebel. According to the legislature, this courageous woman, about whom we unfortunately have no personal details, belonged to Mr. Charles

Grosse. She was "one of the Number of Negroes that Apposed themselves by force and Arms against his Majesties Christian subjects, That were sent to subdue the said Negroes." When captured she "did promise that shee would doe some service that might deserve her life, which wee upon hopes she might . . . Adventured to send her out to Guide a partie of men wch she did." But after "her Retturn shee made her Escape and fled to the runaway Negroes, for wch offence and for that It appears that the said Negro woman hath Threatened to Kill and Murther her master, We doe adJudge her . . . Worthy of Death as soone as she shall be brought in." Around the same time, John Atkinson captured and brought in the fugitive slave woman Jacke, belonging to Mr. Burrows, and the legislature ordered that she "be kept in safe Custody till next meeting."[18] These two references to women are the only ones on record at a time when the Antigua authorities vigorously prosecuted a campaign to rout fugitives, especially in the wooded hill country.

During the 1690s runaway slaves were still a source of great concern, but at this time there was no mention of organized bands, although in 1692, during King William's War between England and France (1689–1697), there was talk about "the danger of Negroes riseing" stirred up by the presence of fugitives and the expected subversion of resident French slaves.[19] In 1696 the legislature awarded compensation of 3,000 pounds of sugar to Samuel Martin (who was later killed by his Coromantee slaves in 1701) for his "Negro Woman" who was executed for an undisclosed felony (most probably absence for more than three months, as covered by the fugitive slave act of 1680).[20] In 1697 the legislature passed the first comprehensive slave act of Antigua, marking an important stage in the development of tensions, or what historian Michael Craton has called the "tortured dialectic" between masters and slaves.[21] Although slave women were not specifically mentioned in the act, its regulations were obviously meant to include them as potential troublemakers and rebels.

The resistance of Antigua slave women during the seventeenth century represented only the beginnings of a New World phase of resistance that was part of a longer process that began as early as their capture in Africa and remained active aboard the slave ships.[22] Taking shape among the Africans before they actually arrived at Antigua, these acts of resistance help to underscore Robertson's astute assertion that the "Sense of their Slavery seems to lie deep in the Minds of many of them." The case of the slave ship *Florida* is illustrative.

In 1714 the *Florida*, with a crew of twenty, took in 360 slaves at Calabar, in the hinterland of the coast of the Bight of Biafra, and prepared to sail for Antigua. Aboard were about 200 adult African women and about 100 men (an unusual sexual configuration); the rest were boys and girls. While the ship moved downriver to the coast, only the men were shackled by the leg "to prevent them from swimming ashore." Slave traders generally did not shackle women, believing them to be less prone to attempt escape. According to one crew member, however, the women behaved unexpectedly on this occasion: "before we got out of ye River," three or four women "shew'd us how well they could swim, & gave us ye slip, tho' we took one of them again, that could not shift so well as ye rest being big with child." This woman's pregnancy obviously did not prevent her from being sold into slavery, nor did it deter her from trying to escape. Without much more information about the circumstances surrounding her desperate act, we can only guess that she was concerned not only about her own freedom but also about that of her unborn child. We also cannot tell from the account whether these women, who may have acted together, planned their move or responded spontaneously. After the *Florida* put out to sea the crew took firm precautions against an uprising by the African men as well as women, quartering the men forward and the women aft; "there were two Swivel Guns plac'd on ye Quarter deck to command ye main deck where they were mess'd'"; and when they were "betwixt decks at each Scuttle was plac'd a Sentry with a Cutlass in his hand, with orders not to Suffer above two to come up at a time, to do their necessary occasions." To minimize the risk of revolt enroute to Antigua, the crew, many of whom were sick, concealed the deaths of eight comrades, whose bodies were thrown overboard during the night.[23] Slave traders routinely kept a careful watch over the men and women whom they later sold into slavery in the Americas. There are cases on record where captured Africans rose up and took over ships, usually when they were still within sight of the African coast.[24]

The Africans who survived the Middle Passage and arrived at Antigua after about 1700 faced conditions similar to those which had nurtured slave resistance in earlier decades. Now, however, little forest cover remained. Deforestation, which accompanied the spread of sugar cultivation, essentially ended the maroon dimension of slave resistance. Running away, however, still continued to be the most common form of resistance, and fugitives were forced to find new ways to remain at large. Tensions between masters and slaves were of great concern to the legislature. In 1702 the lawmakers revised the slave act of 1697.[25] In the previous year the Coromantee slaves of Major Samuel Martin had attacked and killed him. The incident led the Board of Trade in Britain to suggest that Governor Christopher Codrington should pass a law "for restraining inhumane severity" to indentured servants and slaves.[26]

The new slave act of 1702 contained several regulations about the worrisome problem of slave flight. These were supplemented by another act in 1723 which dealt mainly with fugitives.[27] Although the slave acts contain much information about slave resistance, they do not provide a breakdown by gender nor any good indication of the incidence of resistance. In the absence of court records, both of these features of eighteenth-century resistance in Antigua are best traced through compensation claims that slaveowners brought before the legislature, usually when their slaves were put to death by law. Scattered through the minutes of the Antigua legislature, compensation claims contain information about the names of slaves, names of owners, offenses committed, and the estimated value of the slaves or the compensation awarded. Rarely is there indication of the circumstances regarding an offense or the motivation involved. Also, because the claims represent only cases that actually came before the magistrates and legislature, they underrepresent the incidence of slave resistance. In spite of their limitations as sources, however, the claims help throw light on the resistance of slave women.[28]

For the period 1722–1763, during which compensation claims were systematically recorded, slaves were executed for running away (152 executions), burglary (6), theft (12), highway robbery (4), assaulting whites (9), murdering other slaves (27), felony (56), burglary and felony (12), poisoning (8), robbery (3), rape (1), arson (5), unspecified murders (14), and undisclosed offenses (31). Forty-one runaways were hunted down and killed or died of wounds received. Altogether, 381 slaves were killed or lawfully executed for acts of resistance over a forty-year period, omitting the years 1751 and 1752, for which claims have not been found. If the pattern of resistance and punishment remained steady in these two years, we can safely assume that an average of ten slaves a year paid with their lives for rebellious behavior. Slave women were represented in the categories of runaways executed (11), runaways hunted down and killed (5), assault on a white person (1), felony (1), arson (1), and undisclosed offenses (1). This means that at least twenty-one slave women were executed or killed, or about 6 percent of the total number of 381 slaves; eleven, or nearly 53 percent, of these women were executed for running away.

Most planters took a close interest in the proper disciplining of their fugitive slaves. In 1731 absentee planter Josiah Martin wrote to his estate manager, Barry Anderson: "I desire yt Jenny be put in Chaines, well whipt . . . for I think the worst of treatment good enough for that wretch that run away for two years." How had Jenny been able to remain at large for so long in tiny, compact Antigua? She probably had help from sympathetic whites or blacks. Martin also asked Anderson whether another fugitive woman "Cubbah be come home, I hope if she be you treated her as her fault deserved." In this case Martin appears to have expected Cubbah's absence to be short, and that she would decide when to return.[29] Long-term and short-term flight was common in eighteenth-century Antigua. When the slave woman Maudlin, from one of the Tudway family plantations, died of "Convulsion fits" in 1759, the plantation manager decided that she was no loss because she was "subject to run away and staying two Months at a time."[30] Such habitual fugitives could be a source of great frustration to plantation owners. Some slaveowners sold their troublesome runaways. Dr. Joseph Buckshorne, perhaps driven to distraction, took a more drastic and vengeful step with the slave woman Judea, amputating one of her legs "for frequently absenting herself."[31] In the 1751 inventories of the Codrington family plantations, Little Sussannah of the Cotton Plantation was described as a "great Runaway," while from Betty's Hope Plantation the "able working Women" of the field gang, Nanno Madge, and Little Aubah, were at large. The accounts for Main Swete's plantation show payment of six shillings in January 1739 to "a white Man for taking up a Negro woman"; an entry for February 1739 stated, "To Cash 3s/9d for taking up a Negro Woman and A Collar for Ditto."[32]

Under what circumstances did such women become fugitives? Antigua slave women resisted slavery as slaves and as women in the special circumstances of these two facets of their lives. During the seventeenth and the greater part of the eighteenth centuries, however, Antigua slaveowners stressed the value of the productive rather than the reproductive capacities of their slave women, and hard physical labor was as much a dominant force in their lives as in the lives of slave men.[33] Much of the resistance of slave women therefore occurred within the context of labor or work, but slave women, like men, ran away for a wide range of reasons, including an unwillingness to cope with sudden changes imposed on them by masters. In 1731, for example, one woman belonging to Abraham Redwood's plantation fled when she "suspected something . . . against her." She was to be shipped off to Redwood in Rhode Island.[34]

The most physically demanding work on sugar plantations was associated with field operations, and because most nonfield, or so-called skilled, jobs were closed to women, most of them were field hands, the vital sinews of the plantations. The situation on Betty's Hope Plantation in 1751 illustrates the context of hard labor, compounded by the shortage of workers, within which many slave women ran away or resorted to other forms of resistance.

The plantation manager noted that at Betty's Hope "there appears to be Forty two that are called able men for the field & 59 women out of which there are several runaways." Even so, it was seldom possible to muster sixty able slaves "to make Cane holes unless it is at particular times when the Tradesmen have been taken in the Field to assist." Betty's Hope suffered from two main problems that gave rise to others: it was short of workers, and its soil was poor, "it never having been manured." As a result, the plantation badly needed an additional sixty or seventy workers to ease the workload of the existing gang. "Was it not for the little Negroes that are called the Small gang, consisting of about 30 who do much more work in proportion than the Great Gang, the Estate would be greatly distressed." It is hardly surprising that all of the Betty's Hope fugitives belonged to the field gangs.[35]

In the 1740s the plantations belonging to the Codringtons were so short of slaves that slave women were forced to do some of the strenuous work normally allocated to men. Most plantation chores in the islands were not gender specific, however, but related to the age and physical condition of the slaves. The manager of the Codringtons' Garden Plantation reported the need for fifty more slaves to add to "a wretched poor Gang not Negro men Enough to Shift the spells in Croptime." Without enough workers he was "frequently Oblig'd to make fire under ye Coppers, & stills with Women," an unusual procedure he much preferred to avoid. At the same time, Betty's Hope was so short of slaves that "the Women are oblig'd to do the Labour of men, such as making fire, Carring Potts of Sugar of 100 Weight wch often Occasions Violent Disorders, & Miscarriages, and tends greatly to the Detriment of the General Interest."[36] Under the rubric of the plantation's general interest the manager might certainly have cited a multitude of difficulties, including the uncooperative behavior of

the slave women, who had much to complain about in regard to both production and reproduction and other related areas of their lives. It was probably
in recognition of the critical need to keep the women content in order to maintain harmony on the Codringtons' Cotton Plantation that the manager, John
Jeffers, received instructions in 1715 not to permit "the wenches to be ill used
by any body."[37] This remark points to the hard life of labor and sexual exploitation slave women faced generally. Slaves, women as well as men, developed a fine
sense of the limits of the proprietorial demands masters could place on them.
They drew a line between what was reasonable and what was not.

Robertson's observations about life and labor on the sugar plantations of the
Caribbean can be used to sharpen the contextual focus of resistance among plantation slaves. Robertson pointed out that slaves ran away "when their Labour or
Attendance is most wanted." This assertion must be contextualized to be fully
understood. According to Robertson, although "the Sugar-Manufacture in our
Colonies admits of as little Respite from Labour as perhaps any sort of Business
whatsoever any where else . . . where a Plantation is weak-handed, the Master is
often oblig'd either to work his Slaves in Crop-Time for a great part of the night
as well as the whole Day, or to lose the season for taking off the Canes." In
"Planting-time all Hands are at Work; there is a Time when the Canes must be
weeded and supplied, or they will not answer; the Land must be dung'd in many
Places; Fences must be made and kept up, Pasture-Lands clean'd, the Sugar-
Works, Buildings, Negro-Huts &c. repair'd or rebuilt; and what with howing
and holeing of the Ground, carriage to and from the Plantation, &c. A Planter's
Life admits of very little Interruption at any time of the Year."[38] So too, he might
have added, did the lives of the slaves, who could not hope to enjoy the fruits of
their labor like their masters.

Slave resistance in response to work load or to masters' work expectations
took many forms besides flight. The Coromantee slaves who killed Major
Samuel Martin of Greencastle plantation in 1701 allegedly did so in response to
his unreasonable demand to work around Christmas, when they looked forward
instead to enjoying the customary work-free holiday season.[39] There may have
been several similar serious disturbances in subsequent years because in 1723
Antigua legislators felt it necessary to guarantee by law the right of slaves to
Christmas holidays, stating that "great Disorders have happened, and Murders
have been committed by Slaves because their Masters have not allowed them
the same Number of Days for their Recreation at Christmas, as several of their
Neighbours have done."[40] In 1748 six slave women of one Antigua plantation
were described as "hardly worth their food." In other words, the master could
not get enough work out of them: "One hath a Canker in her head or Pretends
So, three of the best have Sucking Children which looses One half of their
Labour, the rest very lazy."[41] In 1755 conditions on the shorthanded plantation
where she lived probably became so unbearable that Phinetta drowned herself.[42]
Even if this was an exceptional case, it does help to dramatize how in one way

or another Antigua slave women desperately tried to escape the excessive demands of work.

The typical style of resistance of Antigua slave women was unquestionably of the day-to-day variety that nibbled away most insidiously at the efficiency of the slave system. Among these forms might be included the inventive means women used to obstruct sexual exploitation by white males. Other forms of such resistance, more subtle certainly, are encapsulated in the term *insolence*, which whites frequently used.[43] A whole range of behavior was crowded into this category of resistance, the intensity and meaning of which might vary: displays such as gestures, attitudes, posture, facial expression, gait, or verbal play. Whites commonly dealt with such behavior in ways that kept the offenders out of the standard documentary sources historians rely on. For such acts, suspected acts, or intentions to act that whites construed as particularly disrespectful or challenging to their authority and status, slave women were frequently whipped in an attempt to crush their spirit and humiliate them. Evidence about whipping is frequently indicative of some form of resistance.

Apart from fugitives, the slave women who are prominently mentioned in the Antigua records are the minority who engaged in open violent resistance. What was special about these women and what made their atypical responses possible? Gemima, John Seaycraft's slave, was burned for assaulting Elizabeth Coxan, a white infant; Mimba tried to kill her master John Watkins; Omer willfully set fire to the house of Margaret Gillyatt; Mimba was outlawed for helping Jack to poison the infant Giles Blizard; Edward Otto Bayer's slave Catherine remained behind bars for 153 days before she was executed for a felony. Instead of channeling her violence directly against another, Phinetta, we have noted, drowned herself.[44]

However harsh, precarious, and degrading the lives of most slave women were, the compensation claims do not contain any cases where they killed other slaves or adult whites. In six cases, however, a total of seven slave women were killed by slave men under circumstances which remain unknown. Slave women were victims, therefore, and not perpetrators of this type of psychologically complex slave resistance which expressed the common response of long-oppressed groups to strike out not only at their tormentors but also at themselves, their families, and their communities.[45] According to the descriptions of offenses in the compensation claims, there were twenty-one claims where male slaves murdered other males, compared with nine claims for assaults on whites by either slave men or women; no whites were murdered by slaves.

Although there are no claims for slave women who were connected with the major islandwide plot for a slave rebellion in 1736,[46] other sources indicate that some women were indeed involved. The planned revolt was masterminded by Court, alias Tackey, aged about forty-five, the Coromantee slave of Thomas Kerby, justice of the peace and speaker of the Antigua Assembly. Court shared leadership with Tomboy, the creole or Antigua-born slave of Thomas Hanson, a merchant and planter. The plot grew out of a series of related developments that sharpened the slaves' awareness of the possibilities for seizing power from whites. Its etiology can be traced back to the desire of the slaves to destroy slavery, their long involvement in resistance short of revolt, a population imbalance greatly in their favor, lax enforcement of slave controls, and the general character of slavery. From these foundations emerged a volatile situation conducive to revolt. Economic recession in the 1730s, along with natural disasters, sickness, and, above all, the emergence of charismatic slave leadership, made revolt even more predictable.[47]

During the trials of the rebels, councillor Vallentine Morris of the second court sought to persuade his colleagues that the mounting expense of the proceedings was not a good enough reason to stop them prematurely. Too many slaves from different parts of the island appeared to be involved. He argued that "by the Evidence of the Witnesses, by the Examinations taken against 150 Conspirators . . . there was hardly a Sensible Negro in the Island of either Sex, but was Engaged in it Either as an Actor, Abettor, or Approver; that Most of the free Negroes, and free Mulattos were Actually Engaged in it."[48] Shaken by the revelation that free people of color had made common cause with rebellious slaves, the authorities took the extraordinary step of admitting slave evidence against some of them,[49] but they did not seek to prosecute any slave women, although evidence indicated that women participated in the organization of the plot in some way.

When the slave woman Philida, Tomboy's sister, was arrested for making "some virulent Expression . . . upon her brother's account," she was reported to have voluntarily enlightened the authorities—who were not sure where to turn after an early group of twelve rebels were executed—about the frequent Saturday night meetings of slaves at the house of Treblin, the creole slave of Samuel Morgan. Philida's disclosures gave authorities the lead they needed to pursue more suspects.[50] But did she simply sell out, or did her response emerge from a deeply complex process of internal conflict as she struggled with issues that the initial discovery of the conspiracy spawned? Philida was evidently not completely in the dark about the activities and plans of the main male conspirators, many of whom must have sought the support of their trusted female companions, friends, or wives in this bold and complicated endeavor which ultimately relied on the collective resources of the slave community. The leaders always believed that if the planned revolt showed initial success, slaves from all over the island who had not been formally recruited would join in. If male slaves organized and led the plot, they nonetheless drew upon the oppositional strength of many supportive females, though only a few of these may have been privy to its details. The evidence suggests that Philida and other slave women were often present at special gatherings when the rebel leaders recruited their men, in the roles of informed onlookers or guests, or assisting with arrangements and serving food and drink, which was an especially critical role in the ceremonial initiation into the inner circles of the plot.

Recruits were initiated at these gatherings or feasts through a ritual ceremony which included taking a solemn "Damnation Oath" to support the plot and not betray it. The oath was usually taken "by drinking a health in Liquor, either rum or some other with Grave Dirt, and sometimes cocks blood, infused; and sometimes the Person swearing, laid his hand on a live Cock." Sometimes the recruit chewed "Melageta Pepper."[51] The dirt used in the ritual concoctions came from the graves of deceased relatives or other slaves, and indeed, many induction ceremonies were performed at grave sites, as the rebels sought assistance and approval from the ancestral spirits. The slave woman Obbah (Aba among the Akan) therefore played a more central role in the organization of the plot than most other slave women when she held a feast and brought some "Dirt from her Sisters Grave (for whom this feast was made) in a Callabash," which the slave Watty mixed with wine.[52]

Besides Obbah, another slave woman played much more than a peripheral part in the plot in a way that suggests, like the initiation rites, the slaves' preservation of links to Africa and the possibilities of cultural resistance under slavery. This woman the slaves called simply Queen. At the trial of Quawcoo, an old Coromantee slave of John Pare, slave witness Quamina testified that "Court used to be very Often at Pares Plantation to go to an Old Womans house called Queen and send Butter, Bread, and other things to her to sell for him, and I have bought some of her and this man Quawcoo knew it very well. Court sent a Boy on a white horse to Old Queen to tell her they were going to put him to Death, and She might keep what things She had of his."[53]

What was the real connection between Court, the rebel leader, and Obbah and Old Queen? If the Gold Coast slaves of Antigua accepted Court as their Akan ruler, could it be that Queen or Obbah, like Abena the Akan "Queen of Kingston" in Jamaica during the slave conspiracy of 1760, was "cast in the role of a traditional Akan queen-mother?"[54]

In Akan/Asante society on the Gold Coast, the queen-mother, ohemaa, or female ruler, who was often really the chief's sister, was constitutionally regarded as his "mother." Among her state functions, according to Madeline Manoukian, "she is expected to advise the Chief about his conduct and may scold and reprimand him in a way not permitted to his councillors. When a Chief's Stool is vacant the Queen-Mother proposes his successor; she is regarded as the authority on kinship relations in the Royal lineage." The queen-mother occupied the only political office "in the Akan chiefdom or state held by women." Agnes Akosua Aidoo writes that the queen-mother's office "was not merely an elevated domestic position." While she "did not represent women's interests as such in the state government," her position was vital "in the public domain" and she was "an active political being. The queen mother's obligation to advise and guide the chief, including her right to criticize and rebuke him in public, was a constitutional duty." A queen-mother who failed to perform the counseling duty, Aidoo explains, "was liable to deposition or destoolment." The matrilineal social organization of Akan society determined the position of the queen-mother and

all Akan women. Descent is traced through the female line, so that while "political offices in the lineage and state are held almost exclusively by men, political
status is conferred by women." But certain cultural attitudes and "ideological
constraints" restricted the political role of women. Among the most important
was "the ritual disability . . . emanating from menstruation," which also circum-
scribed the queen-mother's public role. While all Asante women were excluded
from service in the state armies through "Ritual disqualification and the fear of
menstrual contamination (rather than physical inferiority)," famous fighting
queen-mothers, all of whom had reached menopause, emerged.[55]

In Antigua, while Queen and Obbah were both probably Akan or of Akan descent and both were influential in the Coromantee slave community, it was
probably Queen who acted as Court's principal advisor and confidant. She rather
than Obbah may have been cast in the role of queen-mother to Court, the Akan
king who was formally crowned "King of the Coromantees" in a public ceremony with nearly 2,000 slaves present, only a few days before the conspiracy to
revolt was revealed to the utter consternation of whites. This coronation (en-
stoolment) accompanied an Akan military "ikem" ceremony which prepared
participants for the intended war against the whites. This ceremony was a
common practice in Akan communities of the Gold Coast, where it accompanied
declarations of war. Court, who was uprooted from the Gold Coast as a child and
shipped to Antigua, came to appreciate the significance of such Akan rituals
during his rise to prominence within the Akan community of the island. The old
slave woman Queen most likely educated Court, who was of noble birth, in the
workings of Akan tradition, particularly in regard to building collective support
among his countrymen and other slaves for the revolt.[56]

In regard to her probable role as a kind of queen-mother, Queen's anglicized
creole name is most suggestive. Did her name carry more political and cultural
than personal significance among the Akan slaves? The association between
Queen and Court, which Quawcoo described in connection with petty trading,
could have been good cover for more vital political relations that ultimately
helped to pull the slave plot together. In this regard, it would be interesting to
know the sort of goods or possessions that Court, facing execution, asked her
to keep for him.

That slave women did not appear on the lists of slaves who were executed or
banished for their part in the plot can perhaps be explained partly by the lack
of understanding or interest among whites about how the slave community
worked or about the significance of African culture and social organization.
Slave women were not put on trial, even Queen or Obbah, though some
women were questioned. Operating from European male-oriented perspectives,
the authorities searched out slave men as the most dangerous conspirators or
political actors, blind to the political meaning of the supportive functions of
women within the slave community. They saw the plot primarily as a direct challenge issued by men; it was a challenge to the manhood, authority, and
hegemony of white males and masters. We know that the trials were ended be-

cause of heavy costs; eighty-eight male slaves were executed and forty-nine were banished. Had Vallentine Morris been able to persuade his colleagues on the court to continue with the trials regardless of cost, it is likely that many more slaves within the subsidiary ranks of the plot's membership would have been punished, including women. Indeed, had the revolt actually occurred, Antigua whites would have had ample evidence of the important political roles of slave women.

The Antigua authorities also may have been disinclined to seek out and prosecute women suspects because the plot did not represent the kind of resistance in which women were commonly involved. Thus it is possible that the commonly nonconfrontational resistance of Antigua slave women created the wide political space for many of them to support the plot without attracting attention from the authorities. When the time came for large-scale collective resistance, slave women were prepared by a life of day-to-day resistance and by African cultural antecedents to meet the challenge. Antigua slave women must have resisted enslavement in countless ways that the historical sources have not recorded, including the manner in which they raised their children to cope with slavery. In this way, as primary transmitters of culture, slave women were principal shapers of the culture of resistance.[57]

Notes

For comments on drafts of this chapter, I wish to thank Darlene Clark Hine, Jane M. Gaines, Connie Blackmore, Patsy Evans, and Y. Tate.

1. Sir Alan Burns, *History of the British West Indies* (London: George Allen and Unwin, 1954), pp. 548, 557, 589–96, 611–15; J. H. Parry and P. M. Sherlock, *A Short History of the West Indies*, 2d ed. (London: Macmillan, 1965), pp. 182–83; *Slavery, Abolition and Emancipation: Black Slaves and the British Empire*, ed. Michael Craton, James Walvin, and David Wright (London: Longman, 1976), pp. 231–35, 279–82; J. R. Ward, *British West Indian Slavery 1750–1834: The Process of Amelioration* (Oxford: Clarendon Press, 1988); David Barry Gaspar, "Slavery, Amelioration, and Sunday Markets in Antigua, 1823–1831," *Slavery and Abolition* 9 (May 1988): 1–28, "Working the System: Antigua Slaves and Their Struggle to Live," *Slavery and Abolition* 13 (December 1992): 131–55, and "Sugar Cultivation and Slave Life in Antigua before 1800," in *Cultivation and Culture: Labor and the Shaping of Slave Life in the Americas*, ed. Ira Berlin and Philip D. Morgan (Charlottesville: University Press of Virginia, 1993), pp. 101–23; Sidney W. Mintz and Douglas Hall, "The Origins of the Jamaican Internal Marketing System," in *Papers in Caribbean Anthropology* (New Haven: Yale University Publications in Anthropology, 1960); Mintz, "The Jamaican Internal Marketing Pattern: Some Notes and Hypotheses," *Social and Economic Studies* 4 (March 1955): 95–103; Richard B. Sheridan, "The Domestic Economy," in *Colonial British America: Essays in the New History of the Early Modern Era*, ed. Jack P. Greene and J. R. Pole (Baltimore: Johns Hopkins University Press, 1984), pp. 50–53; "The Slaves' Economy: Independent Production by Slaves in the Americas," ed. Ira Berlin and Philip D. Morgan, special issue of *Slavery and Abolition* 12 (May 1991).

2. W. Dowson et al. to the Methodist Missionary Society, London, April 5, 1831, box 130, no. 70, in Methodist Missionary Society Papers, Library of the School of Oriental and African Studies, London; Gaspar, "Slavery, Amelioration, and Sunday Markets."

3. Gaspar, "Slavery, Amelioration, and Sunday Markets," pp. 16–21, and "Amelioration or Oppression? Slave Protest in Antigua on the Eve of Emancipation," Goveia Lecture, University of the West Indies, Cave Hill, St. Michael, Barbados, November 1989.

4. Elizabeth Fox-Genovese, "Strategies and Forms of Resistance: Focus on Slave Women in the United States," in *In Resistance: Studies in African, Caribbean, and Afro-American History*, ed. Gary Y. Okihiro (Amherst: University of Massachusetts Press, 1986), p. 144.

5. Robert Robertson, *A Letter to the Right Reverend the Lord Bishop of London* (London, 1730), pp. 9, 12–13, 16, 33, 96.

6. Fox-Genovese, "Strategies and Forms of Resistance," p. 145. See also Joan W. Cott, "Gender: A Useful Category of Historical Analysis," *American Historical Review* 91 (December 1986): 1053–75.

7. George M. Frederickson and Christopher Lasch, "Resistance to Slavery," in *American Slavery: The Question of Resistance*, ed. John. H. Bracey, August Meier, and Elliott Rudwick (Belmont, Calif.: Wadsworth, 1971), pp. 179–92; Roy Simon Bryce-Laporte, "Slaves as Inmates, Slaves as Men: A Sociological Discussion of Elkins' Thesis," in *The Debate over Slavery: Stanley Elkins and His Critics*, ed. Ann J. Lane (Urbana: University of Illinois Press, 1971), pp. 269–92; Winthrop D. Jordan, *White over Black: American Attitudes toward the Negro, 1550–1812* (Chapel Hill: University of North Carolina Press, 1968), pp. 113–15; Eugene D. Genovese, *Roll, Jordan, Roll: The World the Slaves Made* (New York: Vintage, 1976), pp. 597–98; Peter H. Wood, *Black Majority: Negroes in Colonial South Carolina through the Stono Rebellion* (New York: Norton, 1974), pp. 285–87; Sidney W. Mintz, *Caribbean Transformations* (Chicago: Aldine, 1974), pp. 75–81, and "Review Article: Slavery and the Slaves," *Caribbean Studies* 8 (January 1969): 65–70; David Barry Gaspar, *Bondmen and Rebels: A Study of Master-Slave Relations in Antigua* (Baltimore: Johns Hopkins University Press, 1975), and "Working the System"; James C. Scott, "Resistance without Protest and without Organization: Peasant Opposition to the Islamic Zakat and the Christian Tithe," *Comparative Studies in Society and History* 29 (July 1987), and *Domination and the Arts of Resistance: Hidden Transcripts* (New Haven: Yale University Press, 1990).

8. Gaspar, *Bondmen and Rebels* and "Working the System."

9. Gaspar, *Bondmen and Rebels*, pp. 65–128; Richard S. Dunn, *Sugar and Slaves: The Rise of the Planter Class in the English West Indies, 1624–1713* (Chapel Hill: University of North Carolina Press, 1972), pp. 117–48; Richard B. Sheridan, *Sugar and Slavery: An Economic History of the British West Indies, 1623–1775* (Baltimore: Johns Hopkins University Press, 1973), pp. 148–207; Richard Pares, *A West India Fortune* (1950; reprint, New York: Archon, 1968).

10. Gaspar, *Bondmen and Rebels*, pp. 129–36, 171–84, and "Runaways in Seventeenth-Century Antigua, West Indies," *Boletín de Estudios Latinamericanos y del Caribe* 26 (June 1979): 3–13.

11. "An Act for publique recompense to the Masters of Slaves putt to death by Law," October 28, 1669, *Colonial Office* (hereafter *CO*) 154/2 Public Record Office, Kew, Surrey; "An Act for bringing in Runaway Negroes and Incouragement of such who shall bring them in," July 9, 1680, *CO 154/2*.

12. Minutes of Council in Assembly, July 14, 1684, *CO 1/50*; Council Minutes, February 14, March 9, 17, 1687, *CO 155/1*; Dunn, *Sugar and Slaves*, p. 259.

13. Minutes of Council in Assembly, July 14, 1684, *CO 1/50*; Council Minutes, March 24, 1687, *CO 155/1*.

14. There are numerous studies of slave fugitives. See, for example, Wood, *Black Majority*, pp. 239–68; Gerald W. Mullin, *Flight and Rebellion: Slave Resistance in Eighteenth-Century Virginia* (New York: Oxford University Press, 1972); Jean Fouchard, *The Haitian Maroons: Liberty or Death*, trans. A. F. Watts (1972; reprint, New York: Blyden, 1981); Gabriel Debien, "Le Marronage aux Antilles françaises au XVIIIe siècle," *Caribbean Studies* 6 (October 1966): 3–44; Debbasch Yvan, "Le Marronage: Essai sur la désertion de l'esclave antillais," *L'Année Sociologique*, 3d series (1961): 1–112, (1962): 117–95; *Out of the House of Bondage: Runaways, Resistance and Maroonage in Africa and the New World*, ed. Gad Heuman (London: Frank Cass, 1986); *Blacks Who Stole Themselves: Advertisements for Runaways in the Pennsylvania Gazette, 1728–1790*, ed. Billy G. Smith and Richard Wojtowicz (Philadelphia: University of Pennsylvania Press, 1989); Michael P. Johnson, "Runaway Slaves and the Slave Communities in South Carolina, 1799 to 1830," *William & Mary Quarterly*, 3d series, 38 (July 1981): 418–41; Lathan A. Windley, *Runaway Slave Advertisements: A Documentary History from the 1730s to 1790*, comp. Lathan A. Windley (Westport: Greenwood, 1983), 4 vols.

15. "An Act for the better Government of Slaves, and Free Negroes," June 28, 1702, act no. 130, articles 15 and 16, in *The Laws of the Island of Antigua consisting of the Acts of the Leeward Islands, 1690–1798, and the Acts of Antigua, 1668–1845* (hereafter *Laws of Antigua*) (London, 1805–46), vol. 1, pp. 158–64.

16. Philip D. Curtin, *The Atlantic Slave Trade: A Census* (Madison: University of Wisconsin Press, 1969), pp. 116–26; K. G. Davies, *The Royal African Company* (New York: Atheneum, 1970), p. 100; Virginia Bever Platt, "The East India Company and the Madagascar Slave Trade," *William & Mary Quarterly* 3d series, 26 (October 1969): 548–77.

17. Sidney W. Mintz and Richard Price, *The Birth of African-American Culture: An Anthropological Perspective* (Boston: Beacon, 1992).

18. Council Minutes, March 31, 1687, *CO 155/1*.

19. Council Minutes, November 24, 1692; February 21, 22, 1694, *CO 155/2*.

20. Minutes of Council in Assembly, June 7, 1696, *CO 155/2*.

21. "An Act for the better Government of Slaves," December 16, 1697, *CO 8/3*; Michael Craton, review of Gaspar, *Bondmen and Rebels*, in *Journal of Caribbean History* 22 (1988): 154.

22. Lorenzo J. Greene, "Mutiny on the Slave Ships," *Phylon* 5 (1944): 346–54; Darold D. Wax, "Negro Resistance to the Early American Slave Trade," *Journal of Negro History* 51 (January 1966): 1–15; Kenneth Scott, "George Scott, Slave Trader of Newport," *American Neptune* 12 (July 1952): 222–28; Jay Coughtry, *The Notorious Triangle: Rhode Island and the African Slave Trade, 1700–1807* (Philadelphia: Temple University Press, 1981), pp. 91–92, 145, 150–54, 155–58; James A. Rawley, *The Transatlantic Slave Trade: A History* (New York: Norton) pp. 299–300. See also Wiston McGowan, "African Resistance to the Atlantic Slave Trade in West Africa," *Slavery and Abolition* 11 (May 1990): 5–29; Richard Rathbone, "Some Thoughts on Resistance to Enslavement in West Africa," in *Out of the House of Bondage*, pp. 11–22.

23. "Narrative of a voyage from London to the West Indies (Antigua, Cuba, Hispaniola, and Barbados), 1714–16," British Library Additional Manuscripts 3994b, pp. 3, 8–12.

24. See n. 22.

25. Antigua Act no. 130 of 1702.

26. Gaspar, *Bondmen and Rebels*, pp. 185–89; Board of Trade to Codrington, March 24, 1702, *CO 153/7*.

27. "An Act for attaining several Slaves now run away from their Master's Service and for the better Government of Slaves," December 9, 1723, Act no. 176 in *Laws of Antigua* (hereafter Antigua Act no. 176 of 1723), vol. 1, pp. 214–31.

28. For a more extensive presentation of findings regarding slave resistance based on these compensation claims, see Gaspar, *Bondmen and Rebels*, pp. 191–204. See also Gaspar, "'To Bring Their Offending Slaves to Justice': Compensation and Slave Resistance in Antigua 1669–1763," *Caribbean Quarterly* 30 (September–December 1984): 45–59.

29. Martin to Anderson, October 25, 1731, Martin Letter Book, pt. 1, fol. 47, Martin Papers, British Library Additional Manuscripts, 41, 352.

30. Robert Holloway to Tudway, October 10, 1759, Tudway Papers, DD/TD, Box 15, Somerset Record Office, Taunton, England.

31. Inventory of Bridge Plantation, Antigua, 1754, Tyrell Papers, D/Dke, T33, Essex Record Office, Chelmsford, England.

32. Inventories of Betty's Hope Plantation, July 26, 1751, and Cotton Plantation, July 23, 1751, Codrington Papers, D1610/E5, Gloucestershire County Record Office, Gloucester, England; Plantation Accounts, September 10, 1738–August 13, 1739, Swete Papers, 388/E4, Devon Record Office, Exeter, England.

33. Gaspar, "Sugar Cultivation and Slave Life."

34. Walter Nugent to Redwood, April 11, 1731, Abraham Redwood Correspondence, *Commerce of Rhode Island 1726–1800* (Boston: Massachusetts Historical Society, 1914–15), vol. 1, p. 15.

35. "Observations on the Inventory sent Sr. William Codrington Augst. 12, 1751," filed with 1751 inventories, Codrington Papers, D1610/E5. See also Inventory of Betty's Hope Plantation, July 16, 1751, in ibid.

36. "A Representation of the Condition of ye Estates belonging To The Late Sir William Codrington Bart. Deces'd with Observations what is proper to bedone for Extending their produce and putting them in good Convenient Order," [1740s?], Codrington Papers, D1610/C5.

37. "Orders and Directions for Mr. Jr. Jeffers at the Cottin Plantation," June 27, 1715, Codrington Papers, D1610/C2.

38. Robertson, *Letter*, p. 54.

39. Gaspar, *Bondmen and Rebels*, pp. 185–89.

40. Antigua Act no. 176 of 1723, article 32.

41. Walter Tullideph to Francis Sanders (Nevis), November 7, 1748, Tullideph Letter Books, Scottish Record Office, Edinburgh, Scotland.

42. Tullideph to George Leonard, Tortola, December 11, 1755, in ibid.

43. Gaspar, *Bondmen and Rebels*, pp. 185–214, and "Working the System"; Raymond A. Bauer and Alice H. Bauer, "Day to Day Resistance to Slavery," *Journal of Negro History* 27 (October 1942): 388–419; Darlene Hine and Kate Wittenstein, "Female Slave Resistance: The Economics of Sex," in *The Black Woman Cross-Culturally*, ed. Filomina Chioma Steady (Cambridge, Mass.: Schenkman, 1981), pp. 289–300; Steven E. Brown, "Sexuality and the Slave Community," *Phylon* 42 (Spring 1981): 1–10. There is a growing body of literature about slave women in the Americas which throws light on various dimensions of their lives, including resistance. See, for example, Deborah Gray White, *Ar'n't I a Woman? Female Slaves in the Plantation South* (New York:

Norton, 1985); Jacqueline Jones, *Labor of Love, Labor of Sorrow: Black Women, Work and the Family from Slavery to the Present* (New York: Basic, 1985); Elizabeth Fox-Genovese, *Within the Plantation Household: Black and White Women of the Old South* (Chapel Hill: University of North Carolina Press, 1988); Melton A. McLaurin, *Celia: A True Study of Violence and Retribution in Antebellum Missouri* (Athens: University of Georgia Press, 1991); Lucille Mathurin Mair, *The Rebel Woman in the British West Indies during Slavery* (Kingston, Jamaica: Institute of Jamaica, 1975), "Reluctant Matriarchs," *Savacou* 13 (1977): 1–6, *Women Field Workers in Jamaica during Slavery* (Mona, Jamaica: University of the West Indies, 1987), and "Recollections of a Journey into a Rebel Past," in *Caribbean Women Writers: Essays from the First International Conference*, ed. Selwyn R. Cudjoe (Wellesley, Mass.: Calaloux, 1990), pp. 51–60; Barbara Bush, *Slave Women in Caribbean Society 1650–1838* (Bloomington: Indiana University Press, 1990), "Defiance or Submission? The Role of the Slave Woman in Slave Resistance in the British Caribbean," *Immigrants and Minorities* 1 (March 1982): 16–38, "'The Family Tree Is Not Cut': Women and Cultural Resistance in Slave Family Life in the British Caribbean," in *In Resistance*, pp. 117–32, and "White 'Ladies,' Coloured 'Favourites' and Black 'Wenches': Some Considerations on Sex, Race and Class Factors in Social Relations in White Creole Society in the British Caribbean," *Slavery and Abolition* 2 (December 1981): 245–62; Arlette Gautier, *Les Soeurs de Solitude: La Condition féminine dans L'esclavage aux Antilles du XVIIe au XIXe siècle* (Paris: Editions Caribéenes, 1985); Rhoda E. Reddock, "Women and Slavery in the Caribbean: A Feminist Perspective," *Latin American Perspectives* 12 (Winter 1985): 63–80; Stella Dadzie, "Searching for the Invisible Woman: Slavery and Resistance in Jamaica," *Race and Class* 32 (October–December 1990): 21–38; Marietta Morrissey, *Slave Women in the New World: Gender Stratification in the Caribbean* (Lawrence: University Press of Kansas, 1989); Hilary McD. Beckles, *Natural Rebels: A Social History of Enslaved Black Women in Barbados* (New Brunswick: Rutgers University Press, 1989); Cecilia Green, "Gender and Re/production in British West Indian Slave Societies, Part 1," *Against the Current* (September–October 1992): 31–38; Richard S. Dunn, "Sugar Production and Slave Women in Jamaica," in *Cultivation and Culture*, pp. 49–72.

44. Council Minutes, April 4, 1753, *CO9/17*; Assembly Minutes, January 2, 1761, *CO9/25*; May 3, 1739, *CO9/12*; Antigua Act No. 176 of 1723, article 5; Council Minutes, July 1, 1735, *CO9/8*: Deputy Provost Marshal's Accounts; Tullideph to Leonard, December 11, 1755, Tullideph Letter Books.

45. Leslie Howard Owens, *This Species of Property: Slave Life and Culture in the Old South* (New York: Oxford University Press, 1977), pp. 93–96; Peter Kolchin, "Reevaluating the Antebellum Slave Community: A Comparative Perspective," *Journal of American History* 70 (December 1983): 581–82; Lawrence T. McDonnell, "Slave against Slave: Dynamics of Violence within the American Slave Community," paper presented at the annual meeting of the American Historical Association, San Francsico, December 28, 1983; Gerhart Saenger, *The Psychology of Prejudice: Achieving Intercultural Understanding and Cooperation in a Democracy* (New York: Harper, 1953), p. 29.

46. Bush, in "Defiance or Submission?" is mistaken that "only one woman was executed." She apparently consulted the list of executed slaves which accompanied an official published report prepared by the trial judges. A slave "Joan" belonging to "Ned Otto" is listed. See *A Genuine Narrative of the Intended Conspiracy of the Negroes Antigua* (Dublin, 1737), p. 21. This "Joan" was in fact a male slave driver who belonged to Edward Otto Bayer and carried the French name "Jean." He was executed by burning on November 27, 1736. See "A List of the Names of Negroes that were Executed for the

late Conspiracy, Their Trades, To whom they Belonged, the day and Manner of their Respective Execution," in Governor William Mathew to the Board of Trade, May 26, 1737, *CO 152/23, X7*. The slave driver Jean may have had a background similar to the creole rebel leaders Secundi and Jacko, "the most Incendiaries under Tomboy," who were "of French Parentage, and initiated into Christianity according to the Romish Church." *Genuine Narrative*, p. 4. For the judges' sentence of Jean to execution, see Council Minutes, November 29, 1737, *CO 9/10*. For the petition of compensation following the execution which was made by John Martin, attorney for Edward Otto Bayer, see Minutes of Assembly, July 24, 1738, *CO 9/12*. For a manuscript copy of the trial judges' general report of December 31, 1736, about the slave plot (hereafter General Report), see William Mathew to Board of Trade, January 7, 1737, *CO 152/22, W94*.

47. Gaspar, *Bondmen and Rebels*.

48. Council Minutes, January 31, 1737, *CO 9/10*.

49. Gaspar, *Bondmen and Rebels*, pp. 43–62.

50. General Report; Bush, "Defiance or Submission?" pp. 23–24.

51. General Report.

52. General Report; "Tryal of London a Creole slave belonging to the Estate of John Goble Dece'd [November 1736]," Trial Record, Council Minutes, January 12, 1737, *CO 9/10*; "Tryal of Parham Watty [January 14, 1737]," "Evidence against Warner's Johnno a Cooper belonging to the Folly Plantation [January 21, 1737]," Trial Record Council Minutes, February 14, 1737, *CO 9/11*; Monica Schuler, "Akan Slave Rebellions in the British Caribbean," *Savacou* 1 (1970): 15–17, 23; Benjamin C. Ray, *African Religions: Symbol, Ritual and Community* (Englewood Cliffs: Prentice-Hall, 1976), pp. 165–71; E. P. Modum, "Gods as Guests: Music and Festivals in African Traditional Societies," *Présence Africaine*, 2d Quarter (1979); Madeline Manoukian, *Akan and Ga-Adangme Peoples of the Gold Coast* (London: Oxford University Press, 1950), pp. 55–59.

53. "Evidence against Vernons Cudjoe [January 26, 1737]"; "Tryal of Parham Watty [January 14, 1737]"; Trial Record, Council Minutes, February 14, 1737, *CO 9/11*; "Tryal of Quawcoo an Old Coromantee Negroe of Mr. John Pare [December 9, 1736]," Trial Record, Council Minutes, January 12, 1737, *CO 9/10*.

54. Gaspar, *Bondmen and Rebels*, pp. 227–54; Schuler, "Akan Slave Rebellions," p. 15. See also Rosalyn Terborg-Penn, "Black Women in Resistance: A Cross-Cultural Perspective," in *In Resistance*, ed. Okihiro, pp. 188–209; Sandra E. Greene, "From Whence They Came: A Note on the Influence of West African Ethnic and Gender Relations on the Organizational Character of the 1733 St. John Slave Rebellion," in *The Danish Slave Trade and Its Abolition*, ed. George Tyson and Arnold Highfield (St. Thomas: Virgin Islands Humanities Center, 1994).

55. Manoukian, *Akan and Ga-Adangme Peoples*, p. 39; R. S. Rattray, *Ashanti* (Oxford: Clarendon Press, 1923), pp. 77–85 and passim; K. A. Busia, *The Position of the Chief in the Modern Political System of Ashanti* (London: Oxford University Press, 1951), pp. 19–21; Agnes Akosua Aidoo, "Asante Queen Mothers in Government and Politics in the Nineteenth Century," in *The Black Woman Cross-Culturally*, pp. 65–77; Kwame Arhin, "The Political and Military Roles of Akan Women," in *Female and Male in West Africa*, ed. Christine Oppong (London: George Allen & Unwin, 1983), pp. 91–98.

56. Gaspar, *Bondmen and Rebels*, pp. 21–42; General Report.

57. Bush, *Slave Women in Caribbean Society*, and "Defiance or Submission?"; Morrissey, *Slave Women in the New World*; Mair, "Reluctant Matriarchs"; Gaspar, "Working the System."

12

SLAVE WOMEN AND RESISTANCE IN THE FRENCH CARIBBEAN

Bernard Moitt

Slave women of the French Caribbean resisted slavery in the same ways that men did and in ways that gender and allocation of tasks made possible. Most often, both sexes pursued similar goals insofar as they worked to destroy slavery or to live within the system on their own terms. In this respect, the struggle waged by males and females was complementary by nature. Slave women, however, suffered a dual oppression—from slavery itself and from men, black and white, slave and free. This chapter explores women's resistance to slavery in the French Caribbean from the late seventeenth century to 1848, when slavery was abolished.

In the French Caribbean, as in other parts of the Americas, although gender played a role in the allocation of tasks among slaves, it was obliterated by slavery, and European conventional views of women as fragile beings were cast aside. What mattered most was not sexual differentiation but the need for hard, intensive labor on the plantations. African women were perceived as slaves first rather than as women and given just as heavy tasks as men.

On French Caribbean plantations, proportionately more women than men worked in the fields, where the most arduous labor was required.[1] It was considered normal for young men to move out of the fields and join the ranks of other males who monopolized the specialized tasks and most artisanal crafts. Sugar boilers, blacksmiths, carpenters, and masons all fell into the category of skilled laborers. Women were largely relegated to the category of unskilled labor,[2] performing mostly fieldwork, such as preparing the soil for planting, weeding, and cane cutting. Jean Baptiste (Père) Labat, the Dominican priest who lived in the Caribbean between 1694 and 1705 and was the ecclesiastical administrator of his order's Martinique sugar plantation, considered such work "the easiest of all labor."[3] In the French Caribbean as a whole, women did most of the cane cutting. Mill feeding, a tiring and dangerous occupation which involved passing the canes through the vertical rollers of the sugar mills, was also carried out mostly by women after a day's work in the field. Sometimes they were drawn into the machinery and maimed or killed. Though the distillation of the local rum—*guildive* or *tafia* in slave parlance—was not solely women's work, on Labat's plantation it was done only by women, whom he believed consumed less alcohol than men.[4]

Cast in occupational roles alongside men in most phases of the plantation operations, slave women participated in common forms of resistance to slavery. Though they were oppressed by black men, slavery was the common enemy. Both women and men workers of the field gangs were likely to participate in the plotting and execution of all forms of resistance whatever the gender of leadership. Both groups also worked in the masters' household as domestics and engaged in poisoning as a means of resistance. However, some gender-specific aspects of plantation labor provided women with unique ways to resist slavery. Only women were nursemaids and midwives, and accusations of infanticide were directed solely at them. Gender made it possible for women to restrict fertility and control reproduction through abortions and other means, although it is improbable that such actions always constituted resistance. Ultimately, female resistance was varied, but this chapter will pay particular attention to the involvement of women in armed revolt, *marronage*, the use of poison, and attempts to limit reproduction. These forms of resistance were among the most prevalent in slave society.

The study of resistance to slavery in the Caribbean has resulted in the publication of a rich and distinguished literature which, in recent years, has begun to consider the resistance of slave women.[5] Insight into the slaves' perception of their condition can also be drawn from literary works of the French Caribbean in which the actions of the female protagonists illustrate the importance of adopting a broad perspective on resistance that takes into account the range of contexts in which female slaves responded to slavery collectively and as individuals.

To the superficial reader, Télumée Miracle appears to accept domination and brutality at the hands of her mate, Elie, in *Pluie et vent sur Télumée Miracle*, a novel which chronicles the life struggle of three generations of Guadeloupian women from slavery to modern times.[6] Though she suffers her misfortune largely in silence and experiences a nervous breakdown as a result, Télumée transcends the turmoil which surrounds her and establishes an identity of her own while Elie falters. Likewise, Délira Délivrance seems oblivious to her subjugation by her husband, Bienaimé, in *Gouverneurs de la rosée*, a novel which deals with bitter feuding among peasant families in independent Haiti over land and water during a period of extensive drought.[7] It is Délira, however, who is charged with, and is responsible for, ensuring a smooth transition from a society plagued by conflict to one in which men and women who were former adversaries strive for the common good. Lastly, timid but resolute Madame Christophe in *La Tragédie du roi Christophe* (a play about the rule of Henri Christophe, a former slave, compatriot of Toussaint Louverture and one of the early rulers of independent Haiti),[8] consistently reminds the tyrannic King

Christophe about the importance of Africa and the need to remain grounded in its traditions. Just before committing suicide, King Christophe conscientiously chooses to return to his roots and, like the slaves, in a final act of defiance asks to be buried in Africa. These examples demonstrate that, as was the case during slavery, what appears on the surface to be female docility is often a very subtle, calculated, and conscious form of resistance. Among slave women, resistance was a multidimensional phenomenon.

Armed revolt was an important dimension of women's resistance in the French Caribbean, even though few women actually participated in combat. This kind of resistance can best be explored for the 1790s, a period of great upheaval in the French colonies. The persistent restlessness of slaves notwithstanding, these colonies remained fairly stable and economically profitable slave societies from 1635, when Guadeloupe and Martinique were settled, until 1791, when slaves in Saint Domingue rose up against their masters in a bid for freedom, employing the ideas of "liberty, fraternity, and equality" which were the trademark of the French Revolution of 1789. The intensity of this bloody and protracted struggle for freedom, which lasted until the end of 1803, and the contradictions in French policy which it revealed, led the French National Convention to abolish slavery in the French colonies on February 4, 1794. In April 1794, French Commissioners Victor Hugues and Chrétien were scheduled to make the declaration in the colonies and set up a Provisional Council to govern the islands. In the interim, the English, on whom the French had declared war in February 1793, seized the opportunity to attack Martinique and Guadeloupe and thus maintain slavery. The British were successful at Martinique. Hugues was able to use his expeditionary force of 1,500 men and an enthusiastic slave population to repel the British invasion of Guadeloupe after a seven-month struggle, which ended in December 1794.[9] Thus, while slaves in Martinique remained under British occupation and in slavery, those in Guadeloupe and La Guyane lived in a state of quasi-freedom. This freedom was threatened by the politics of Napoléon Bonaparte, ruler of France, who, by 1799 was determined to restore the authority of France in all the colonies. In essence, this meant the restoration of slavery in Guadeloupe and La Guyane and a redoubling of efforts to subdue Saint Domingue. In March 1802, under the Treaty of Amiens, Britain returned to France Martinique and other French colonies it had occupied since 1794. The French decided to retain slavery in Martinique. It was only a question of time, therefore, before the other colonies were brought back into the fold. On May 6, 1802, General Richepance landed at Pointe-à-Pitre, the capital of Guadeloupe, with 3,400 men on Napoléon's orders to reestablish slavery.[10] With virtually no hope of winning in Saint Domingue, Napoléon spared no effort in this endeavor. On May 20, 1802, slavery and the slave trade were reimposed in Guadeloupe.[11]

During the revolutionary wars at Saint Domingue and Guadeloupe, women participated in the fighting. In Saint Domingue, Marie-Jeanne, wife of the black General Lamartinière, "took her share in the defense."[12] In Guadeloupe slave women, along with men and children, formed part of the forces of Louis Delgrès, a mulatto colonel born in Martinique, who led a slave army against General Richepance and the French forces. They were also part of the forces of Joseph Ignace and Palerme, Delgrès's commanders, who led factions of the army after it split to fight the French on several fronts to maximize its chances of success. Most of the fighting took place in Basse-Terre, the southern part of Guadeloupe. On May 12, 1802, one of the major battles fought under the slave commander Palerme took place at Dolé, an important post in the hands of the rebels, where white women and children whom the slaves had rounded up on plantations were held.[13] Here at Dolé, the mulatress Solitude, though pregnant, fought her way into history by participating in all the fighting.[14]

At Guadeloupe slave women also served as messengers, transported ammunition, food, and supplies, cared for the sick, acted as cover for men under fire, and chanted revolutionary slogans which kept spirits high among the insurrectionary forces of Delgrès, Palerme, and Ignace. On May 10, 1802, whites in Basse-Terre, fearing massacre, barricaded themselves in their homes. The silence which hung over the city was, according to Guadeloupian historian Auguste Lacour, broken only by "the gallop of horses ridden by officers carrying orders and the singing of the French National Anthem by female slaves who transported bullets and other ammunition to artillery units." Slave women transported ammunition in the fiercest of battles and risked their lives in shielding their men.[15] Their chants motivated the slave troops. Lacour highlighted this aspect of women's contribution when he wrote, "It was not their fault if their fathers, their sons, their mothers and their lovers were not endowed with superhuman courage. When a bullet whistled above their heads or a bomb exploded near them, they sang loudly, holding hands while making their hellish rounds interrupted by the chant: 'Vive la mort!' ('Long live death!')."[16]

The strength of character and bravery which women demonstrated in both Saint Domingue and Guadeloupe during the wars was striking. Undaunted by the practice of the French army in Saint Domingue of burning slaves alive and throwing them to the dogs as a way of crushing resistance, women displayed as much courage as men. According to C. L. R. James, "When Chevalier, a black chief, hesitated at the sight of the scaffold, his wife shamed him. 'You do not know how sweet it is to die for liberty!' And refusing to allow herself to be hanged by the executioner, she took the rope and hanged herself."[17] Antoine Métral reinforced this view of slave women by noting that during the war, "the weaker sex became the stronger. Young women, without voicing a single complaint either in the streets or at the public squares, went valiantly before the scaffold. By their moving examples, they encouraged those who were hesitant in dying for liberty. Some were seen to display a surprising character trait by smiling in the face of death in the presence of their masters, whose desire for vengeance was thereby thwarted."[18]

There are also indications that during the early stages of the war in Guadeloupe when casualties were high, some black male slaves fled and were admonished to follow the example of women who demonstrated incomparable zeal. Women's enthusiasm for the struggle never waned, even when defeat seemed inevitable.

In 1802 Louis Delgrès's major artillery unit was set up on the left bank of the Rivière-des-Pères, flanked by Fort Saint Charles, which the slaves held. The French troops positioned themselves on the right bank. Despite stiff resistance the French troops crossed the river and engaged Delgrès's army. As the fighting intensified, Delgrès and his slave army barricaded themselves in the fort, to which Richepance later laid siege. Richepance appealed to Delgrès to surrender and offered him a pardon, but Delgrès stood his ground. On May 22, however, after he realized that the battle could not be won, Delgrès abandoned the wounded in the fort, taking with him about 400 men and a number of black women,[19] all of whom remained active in the resistance. Some of these women remained with Delgrès, while others joined up with the forces of Palerme and Ignace. On the way to Pointe-à-Pitre from Basse-Terre, Ignace's forces burned and pillaged and scored initial successes against the French. Around May 24, Ignace staked out a position on the plantation Belle Plaine in the community of Abymes, three kilometers north of Pointe-à-Pitre, but abandoned it a day later for the fort at Baimbridge, on the outskirts of Pointe-à-Pitre. The fort proved easy to penetrate, and Ignace and the men and women he led became easy targets for a section of the French forces commanded by General Nicolas Gobert. It is believed that Ignace was killed along with 675 of his followers on May 25.[20] Most of those taken prisoner were shot in Pointe-à-Pitre, 150 of them on October 27 alone. The women who accompanied Palerme fared little better. Routed by the French, Palerme's people fled into the hills.[21]

Delgrès took his last stand on the extensive Danglemont plantation, where the battle of Matouba was fought on May 28, 1802. Unable to match the well-armed French, Delgrès resolved to commit suicide and take as many French troops with him as possible by setting fire to barrels of gunpowder he distributed among his troops. According to Oruno Lara, the women "were even more enthusiastic about dying" than the men.[22] After shouts of "Vivre libre ou mourir!" Delgrès and about 500 men, women, and children were killed when the gunpowder exploded. French casualties were put at 400. Some rebels escaped into the surrounding forest and became maroons, but the defeat of Delgrès brought organized resistance to an end. An *arrête* of July 16, 1802, reimposed slavery in Guadeloupe.[23]

Women who appeared before the military tribunal which tried rebels who were caught received no special considerations and were given the same sentences as men. The tribunal sentenced the mulattress Solitude to death. Because she was pregnant, "the execution had to be postponed. She was executed on November 29, after her delivery." Jacques Adélaïde-Merlande believes that the sentence could not be carried out until she had given birth. This may well have been the case, but Arlette Gautier's explanation that the French army "awaited the birth of the child so that it would have a slave in due time!" is also plausible.[24] Other women also received the death penalty, including Marthe (Rose Toto), Delgrès's mistress who had been at Fort Saint Charles with him. A native of Saint Lucia, one of the French islands occupied by the British in 1794, Marthe-Rose suffered a broken leg during the evacuation of the fort and appeared before the tribunal on a stretcher. Accused of influencing Delgrès to resist and of inciting slave soldiers to kill white prisoners held in the fort, Marthe-Rose was hanged publicly. With the rope around her neck, she is said to have remarked to onlookers: "Having killed their king and left their country, these men have come to ours to bring trouble and confusion. May God judge them!"[25]

In February 1831 women also appeared before similar tribunals after the slave uprising in Saint Pierre, then the capital of Martinique. This was a period when, according to a police report, slaves became unusually restless, insolent, and insubordinate, setting revolutionary words to, and singing in public, *La Parisienne*, a military patriotic tune composed in Paris in 1830 for the July Revolution. For "march against their canons," the slaves substituted "march against the colonists."[26] They also wrote the inscription "la liberté ou la more [*sic*]" on a French tricolor they removed from the Place Bertin—the main square—and placed it at the entrance of the Eglise du Mouillage on the evenings of February 5 and 6. From February 7, they set fires all over Saint Pierre; on February 9 alone they torched several houses in the city as well as eight plantations, bringing the total to eleven. The same evening slaves armed with cutlasses came down from the hills to join others in a general insurrection against slavery and set fire to cane fields. The planters were terrified and drew comparisons with the slave uprising several years before in Saint Domingue. Governor Dumas de Champvallier declared a state of siege and called out the militia, the police force, other troops, and the French marines. Massive force and superior arms were used to quell the rebellion on February 10. On May 2, 1831, a special session of the assizes court convened to judge the accused—"two hundred and sixty slaves of both sexes." Of these, 210 were set free for lack of evidence, but twenty-one of the fifty tried were condemned to death, while the others received diverse penalties.[27]

In Martinique slave women also participated, directly or indirectly, in an uprising which occurred in May 1848 when the impending abolition of slavery did not materialize. Slave unrest touched several communities in the west and south of the island but was most alarming in Saint Pierre on the evening of May 22, when twenty houses were burned, two white males were killed, and thirty-two black women and children were burned alive in a house to which rebellious slaves laid siege but which, according to public rumor, was the location of an arms depot. The following day, Brigadier General de Rostoland, the provisional governor of Martinique, yielded to the unanimous wish of the Provisional Municipal Council of Saint Pierre and declared the abolition of slavery, which was made official on June 4.[28] Thus by their own actions the slaves accelerated the process of emancipation. The circumstances surrounding the women's death are unclear as there were several members of the Désarbays family among the victims. Désarbays had helped to crush resistance movements in the 1830s and, like de Sanois, the owner of the house, was despised by mulattoes and slaves. As he was scheduled to testify on May 23 against Pory Papy,[29] the mulatto deputy mayor of Martinique who was sympathetic to the slaves' demand for emancipation, the siege may well have been designed to silence him. Thus the fire which resulted from the struggle between the rebels and Désarbays may not have been intentional, as the ammunition stores allegedly belonged to the slaves. If the slaves stored ammunition in the house, it is logical to assume that it was done with the knowledge of the women, who would not likely have been suspected by Désarbays of being party to such a scheme. If in this case, as in others, the women or their men exploited stereotypical views of women which resulted in females playing "background" roles, they likely did so with the knowledge that in slave society, role playing in and by itself was a form of resistance which had its rewards.

Women also successfully deployed their sexuality in resistance against slavery. Prostitution was a fact of Saint Domingue slave society, and some slave women used it to support resistance. Malenfant, a French soldier who fought with the French army in Saint Domingue in the 1790s, observed that there was "a particular type of prostitution solely associated with slave girls and women. . . . They entered soldiers' camps shamelessly and exchanged sexual favors for bullets and gunpowder."[30]

The contributions that women made to armed struggle were therefore significant and varied, and this conclusion can be supported further by their participation in flight. In the French Antilles, more males than females engaged in slave flight, or marronage. But, though the proportion of women was a little less than 50 percent, their number is significant. Explanations of this pattern of resistance remain largely male-centered and unsatisfactory. Orlando Patterson argued that male slaves "were better able to bear the vicissitudes of such an undertaking." Similarly, Michael Craton declared that runaways had to have the stomach, as well as the arms and skill, to fight on the move and the knowledge, ingenuity, and hardihood to live off the bush. Gautier, on the other hand, attributed the lesser participation of women to less mobility in Africa, their relations with whites, and the advantages derived therefrom.[31]

These issues are more complex than they appear. Women may have been less mobile in Africa, but they were, and remain, the primary producers in agriculture.[32] That being the case, they would have been valuable, even essential, to cultivation, particularly in the case of *grand marronage* (running away to form a permanent and independent community in the forest), if not in *petit marronage* (running away for short periods, which many planters considered tantamount to absenteeism). Gautier tied mobility to maternity, suggesting that the specter of women chained along with their children in the fields—"a ghastly and effective scene in restraining the desire of a mother to run away no matter the degree of opposition to slavery"—served as a powerful deterrent to would-be fugitives. If we agree with Patterson that the Caribbean was a "theatre of European imperial horrors," however, it is not farfetched to suggest that women were not strangers to, or intimidated by, punishment and suffering. Thus Nicole Vanony-Frisch may well be right in stating that neither child care nor the unforeseen dangers which characterized marronage deterred women. There are a large number of cases where women left with children, including those born aboard slave ships bound for Saint Domingue.[33]

Neither pregnancy nor the age of the child seems to have prevented some women in the French Caribbean from fleeing, but women without children generally fled more often. In La Guyane Française, Anne-Marie Bruleau, et al. wrote, "Pregnant women as well as those carrying babies in their arms took to marronage." Some women left with infants only seven or eight days old. Marie, aged thirty-eight, took three children aged seventeen, four, and two years with her into marronage in Saint Domingue. Similarly, Blandine, aged thirty-five, and her daughter, Adélaide, fled together. Of the forty-two female fugitives in Vanony-Frisch's sample (1768–1783) of the Lepreux plantation in Guadeloupe, seven left their children behind. One of these was Bénée, a thirty-one-year-old creole slave who had run away several times and who left without her two-year-old son, Séverin. Scholastique, aged twenty-eight, with her two-year-old son, Cazinir, was one of two women who brought their children along. The other was Dorothée, aged fifty-three, with her daughter Jeanneton, aged twelve.[34]

Marronage was not restricted to any particular age group of women, although adult women constituted the majority. Fugitives over the age of forty in Saint Domingue during the eighteenth century were few. In the French colonies generally, most fugitives were seventeen to thirty-five years old. On the Lepreux plantation, according to Vanony-Frisch's calculation, 75 percent of the 104 maroons who could be identified by age were between fifteen and fifty years. There were also younger fugitives and others of advanced age in the French Antilles. On January 14, 1782, seventeen slaves, including a number of young girls, fled from the Saint-Denis de Capestere estate in Saint Domingue. Among them were Constance, aged eleven, Marie-Ann, aged thirteen, and Constance, aged nine.[35]

In the eighteenth century, slave women of the French Antilles generally ran away alone or in groups with other women and not with their husbands, as was the case in the seventeenth century. This led Jean Fouchard to conclude that "female slaves organized their marronage only among women." Some fugitive women sought work in the cities; others hid out along the extremities of large plantations. Still others worked for free blacks who owned small plantations. Such was the case of Rose, who ran away for more than a year; she worked for the black planter Lafoucault on the Lilancour plantation in northern Saint Domingue for six months. On August 17, 1769, a group of slave women abandoned a Saint Domingue plantation, but not before attempting to persuade another group of women whose function was the pounding of millet and other domestic laborers to join the party. It is not yet clear why women began to run away with other women or individually by the eighteenth century, but some historians have speculated on the possible role of the breakdown of the slave family, in which males no longer played a leading role.[36] The issue is more complex, however, because there are cases in the eighteenth and nineteenth centuries where women and men fled plantations together.

In the 1790s, several bands of male and female fugitives terrorized the cities of Saint Domingue, incited unrest among the slaves, and plagued the French army. In 1793 the French fought several fierce battles with some of these groups around Le Cap, in the north of the island. In this region alone, according to Fouchard, "there were fourteen thousand maroon women willing to accept an amnesty then in the offing. This figure is astonishing, but authentic."[37] There is no evidence that these maroons were led by a woman or that they pursued a struggle separate from that of males. In La Guyane as well, male and female maroons formed many bands. During 1802–1806 one of the most infamous bands was led by Pompée, a male who two decades earlier had established a stable, agricultural maroon community called Maripa on the left bank of the Comté river above Brodel hill. Besides Pompée's sixty-year-old wife, Gertrude, Rosine, aged sixty-seven, and Adeline and Ester, both aged forty—all former slaves of the Sigogne plantation, which they subsequently set afire—were other female fugitives in the band. Using the forest and waterways as cover, Pompée and his band successfully fought troops sent from Cayenne, the capital, for years.[38]

When caught, female slaves could be whipped, placed in iron collars, or executed. Under article 36 of the Code Noir of 1685, fugitive slaves who remained at large for a month should have their ears cut off and be branded on one shoulder with the fleur de lys. If such fugitives ran away again and stayed away for a month, they were to have their hamstring cut and be branded on the other shoulder. A third attempt to escape or an absence brought execution.[39] Fugitive women, however, had to be concerned about dangers other than punishment. The prospect of being raped, for example, was real and may explain why women, unlike men, left more often in twos, with a brother, or even disguised as men.[40]

Planters normally exercised flexibility in administering punishment for *marronage* and other offenses, as it would have been difficult to maintain a robust slave force otherwise, but women were usually punished as severely as men. Women were sometimes killed, disfigured, and humiliated for acts of *marronage*. Take the case of Marie Jeanne, a female who was part of a maroon band at Malegrou in Guadeloupe. In February 1743, while bathing in the Rivière des Parès, she was seen by Dugez, an overseer of the plantation de Brinon, which belonged to de Sennecterre and his partner La Sègue. Dugez attempted to recapture Marie Jeanne, who either defended herself or called for help. Dugez stabbed her twice with a sword, disemboweling her. "To make this deed more hideous," the historian Lucien Abénon wrote, "it has been suggested that the negress was pregnant, but this is uncertain. Informed by Dugez of the murder, La Sègue commended him and ordered that the head of the negress be cut off and exposed on a pike opposite to her hut," a common method in the Caribbean of displaying the remains of rebels. Two months later, when Dugez went out alone to examine the cattle and the cooperage, he disappeared and was never heard from again. Later interrogation of the plantation slaves, which resulted in the deaths of nine males and the whipping and branding of a female slave with the fleur de lys, revealed that he had been killed by the slaves of de Brinon, although Sennecterre attributed the plot to an unnamed European, believing that slaves were incapable of masterminding such a plot. Abénon argued convincingly, however, that the de Brinon slaves were responsible for the disappearance of Dugez, which showed that "there was solidarity among them and that they were conscious of the effects of their action," or of *marronage*, on the slave system.[41]

Children of habitual maroons—"mauvais sujets" (mischievous subjects), in plantation parlance—were sometimes chained along with their mothers and thus bore the burden of punishment. A planter could also use this form of punishment to head off *marronage*. In 1832 Xavier Tanc, a magistrate in Guadeloupe, observed that masters made a captured fugitive woman or a slave woman suspected of intending to run away wear a large chain around her neck or foot with one of her children attached. Tanc "saw a little girl about six years old dragging this heavy and irksome burden with torment as if the crime . . . of the mother was justification for punishing this young child in such a barbarous manner. At that age, her fragile frame and delicate flesh were all battered."[42] The impact of such punishment on the slave woman's psyche can only be imagined. Slave women, however, continued to engage in *marronage* and other acts of resistance to slavery, demonstrating that punishment, however barbaric, was not an effective deterrent.

Besides armed revolt and *marronage*, women also engaged in poisoning as a form of resistance, Auguste Lacour's categorization of poisoning as "a political act" fits the situation for Guadeloupe in 1802, but it also applies to other French colonies in that slaves were conscious of the devastating impact poisoning had on slavery and the planter class. Records from the Cottineau plantation in Saint Domingue show that by 1765 planters were greatly concerned about cases of poisoning. Slaves targeted masters, other slaves, and animals, into whose nostrils they are said to have inserted poisonous wood. Labat relates an incident which occurred on the Saint-Aubin plantation in Martinique around 1697, when more than thirty slaves died painfully in rapid succession within hours of one another owing to "malice on the part of a slave who poisoned the others after observing that the master showed favoritism to another slave." The slave allegedly confessed to his master that the poison he placed in alcohol was derived from a plant.[43] That Labat severely punished his own slaves for their alleged involvement shows that even members of the clergy subscribed to the theory of sabotage.

As a result of increasing death rates in the eighteenth century among planters, slaves, and animals in Guadeloupe, Martinique, and Saint Domingue, French authorities issued a series of ordinances to curb poisoning. Some ordinances applied to all the colonies, others only to individual colonies. In Guadeloupe, an ordinance of May 10, 1720, prohibited male or female slaves from treating sick people except in the case of snake bite. The penalty for infraction was death.[44] Slave medical practitioners, male and female, used a wide range of herbal remedies to ward off snake bites and other illnesses. The skill was passed on from one generation to the next,[45] and was derived from African tradition. Planters viewed such healing practices among the slaves as a facade for the rampant use of poison. Slave healers therefore became prime targets for antipoison legislation. However, not all deaths were the result of poison. Epidemics and epizootic outbreaks occurred in the French Antilles, but doctors were ill-equipped to study them. European doctors in the French colonies, known as the "King's doctors," held official positions and performed medical operations.[46] They distinguished themselves from local healers and diviners, whom they considered quacks, but these people sometimes held important posts, owing, no doubt, to the lack of doctors. Yvan Debbasch observed that it was easier for European doctors "to conceal their ignorance behind the diagnosis of poison" and "give masters the answers they wanted to hear."[47]

In February 1724 a royal ordinance applicable to the French colonies, which characterized poisoning as the most detestable crime and the most dangerous for Europeans, was introduced. It proclaimed that all slaves suspected of administering, concocting, or distributing poison, lethal or nonlethal, would be put to death. Similarly, a Martinique ordinance of May 18, 1724, outlined measures to prevent poisonings, "which have become more frequent in the last several years."[48] That a declaration of February 1, 1743, called for the strict application of the various ordinances of the French Caribbean shows that poison remained a serious concern. In 1749 the governor of Martinique published an ordinance denouncing poisoners. In 1763 the governor of Guadeloupe ruled that anyone who bought poison or instructed slaves in the medical arts, surgery, pharmacy, or knowledge of plants and tropical roots was guilty of poisoning. The death penalty was also to be administered to slaves found in possession of drugs and to diviners who distributed amulets.[49]

In spite of the stringent measures adopted, the use of poison as a weapon among slaves against their enemies continued down to the end of slavery. In October 1741 Governor Champigny of Guadeloupe and his assistant Delacroix wrote about slaves who brought planters to ruin through acts of poisoning. They pointed out that "a number of slaves and animals are dying of poison. We cannot attribute this to anything else but the abuse which some slaves make of the knowledge they possess of herbs and juices of certain plants. They concoct powders and drugs from them which they distribute to other slaves as remedy. They are, to be sure, remedies which they sell publicly without disclosing the composition [and are used for] exacting their vengeance against masters, against whites who cross them in their dealings and against their comrades whom they bear ill will."[50]

In the French Caribbean, however, poison was used mostly against animals and other slaves rather than masters. According to French sources, this was because the slaves believed that whites were less susceptible to African poisons.[51] There may have been other factors involved, though. Few slaves had unlimited access to the master's household, so it was easier for them to vent their frustrations on cattle, mules, horses, and, rarely, other slaves. The loss of slaves and animals was a serious blow to any planter. Testimony by a female slave revealed that the rampant cases of poisoning around Le Cap and Fort Dauphin in Saint Domingue in 1756 were the work of slaves.[52]

Debien reproduced several letters written between 1765 and 1774 by François Lory de la Bernardière, an absentee planter from Nantes who owned the Cottineau plantation in Fort Dauphin, which show that planters were frequently concerned about poison. Lory consistently asked his mangers to find the slaves responsible and make an example of them. Jeannit, a male slave on the neighboring Loiseau de Montaugé plantation, who had a female slave companion, Boukmann, on the Cottineau plantation, became the prime suspect. Lory offered Jeannit's master compensation to have the slave executed, then turned his attention to Boukmann, aged forty-two, and her niece, Marie-Louise, aged twenty-six, whom she trained in the art of poisoning. Accused of being a professional, Boukmann was imprisoned in solitary confinement, along with her niece, much to the pleasure of Lory, who claimed that in spite of his concerns about poison, he was still inclined to believe that the deaths were due to epilepsy. Lory's uncertainty leaves the impression that disease may have been a factor. Once a suspected poisoner was identified, however arbitrarily, nothing else mattered. Boukmann was executed and burned in 1773. Marie-Louise was spared because of her age and working potential, but in a letter of 1774 to his manager, Lory expressed the fear that she might poison the plantation slaves by putting herbal concoctions in *tafia*. He advised that she be carefully watched by the boiler, the head slave driver, and the manager himself.[53]

Poison is said to have been responsible for the near extinction of some plantations in Martinique during the eighteenth century. Debbasch presented statistics taken from administrative reports and secondary sources which showed a massive loss of slaves and animals on several plantations in the French Caribbean after 1757, enough to put a dent in the fortunes of many owners and cause a cessation of business. However, because of the large number of slave deaths involved, Debbasch doubted the reliability of these statistics. Debbasch drew attention at the same time to some striking cases of poisoning. In 1746 a Martiniquan planter, Dessales, lost 102 head of cattle, thirty-seven mules, and twenty-five slaves in a three-month period.[54] As late as 1822, authorities in Martinique indicated that poisonings were still on the increase. As a result, the governor introduced an ordinance on August 12 establishing a military court which granted no appeals. The only sentence which it handed down was decapitation, and this had to be carried out within thirty-six hours.[55]

Women formed part of the domestic entourage of every plantation, giving them access to the master's kitchen and opportunities to poison food. On August 15, 1782, the overseer of the Bonrepos plantation in the Cul-de-Sac region of Saint Domingue, reported that he caught the plantation washerwoman about to dump poisonous powder into his water jars. Surprised in the act, the woman ran, throwing the powder away. The overseer became convinced that the slaves, whom he had found difficult to govern for a year, wanted to murder him and his family.[56] Labat warned that female domestics often plotted to kill their masters and advised planters to employ an outside surgeon, a nonresident who could visit the plantation in the mornings or whenever needed.[57]

The case of Magdeleine, a fifty-five-year-old female domestic slave on the Caroline plantation owned by Brémond and Favard in La Guyane, illustrates the possibilities open to slave women to poison food. Around 1831 the owners were impressed by Magdeleine's ability and intelligence and awarded her the post of head cook. In this role, she was responsible for the care and preparation of food for the master's household. In addition, she was in charge of surgery on the plantation. She thus had the confidence of her masters and occupied, in the slave hierarchy, a post of which other slaves on Caroline were envious. Magdeleine's position enabled her to keep a tight rein on other domestics and to voice her opinion on who should occupy the post of manager, which her son-in-law, the slave Mirtil, had occupied for thirty years. Bruleaux et al. reported that when Mirtil was replaced by Quenessou, a European, Magdeleine "launched a series of actions aimed at eliminating the new manager, and, on a larger scale, preventing all whites from maintaining management of Caroline." She chose the moment carefully to poison Quenessou, who experienced vomiting and colic a few days after Favard left for France. Quenessou accused Magdeleine of poisoning him and abandoned the plantation, but this was not the end of the story. "Pushed no doubt by his mother-in-law, Mirtil expressed his desire to be reinstated in the post of manager. Brémond refused, however, and named, in place of Quenessou, another white, named Rimal." Eight days after Rimal began work, he began to show the same symptoms as his predecessor and was treated in the hospital at Cayenne. Rimal recovered and returned to the plantation "only to suffer, one morning, the same colics and vomiting." In the end, Chrétien, a white foreman on the plantation, advised him to leave while he was still alive because it was obvious that the slaves "did not want a white manager on Caroline." Frightened, helpless, and barely able to walk, Rimal was taken to Cayenne vowing never to return to Caroline. For the moment, at least, Magdeleine was able to ward off "the threat which the white manager represented to her authority on the plantation."[58]

Without raising a cutlass against her masters or appearing to lash out at the system, Magedeleine had assessed the various players on the plantation, the relations between them, and her own capacity to act and test the outer limits of the system. She created a world of her own in which she and other slaves could live on their own terms, but she, like other slaves, was still vulnerable to the vagaries of the slave plantation system. French archival records indicate that Magdeleine admitted to giving Quenessou "la tissane" but denied that any poisonous ingredients were added to it. She was never brought before the courts, as there was insufficient evidence to convict her. However, the Superior Council of La Guyane, which made local laws, voted unanimously to expel her and her family from the colony for security reasons.[59]

The paranoia over poisoning in the French Caribbean during the eighteenth century led to false accusations and wrongful convictions of many male and female slaves, including cooks and nurses. After the failure of the 1802 slave revolt in Guadeloupe, all black nurses at the military hospital in Pointe-à-Pitre, where rising mortality among General Richepance's troops was attributed to poison, were rounded up and shot. According to Lacour, many had reportedly come down from the hills specifically to seek jobs at the hospital with the intention of poisoning French soldiers. The French commander, Pillet, gave the order to execute the black nurses only after he became suspicious that they were part of a larger slave plot which included free coloreds in the military, all from Sainte Anne near Pointe-à-Pitre. The rebels called for the death of the French military and began their revolt on October 6, 1802, but were crushed within a few days.[60] In Saint Domingue, slave women may also have targeted the military. The National Guard, which camped on the Galiffet plantation in the northern part of the island during the early years of the war of liberation, experienced high mortality. According to Métral, soldiers died in droves after repeatedly drinking water from a well into which the slaves had dumped copper utensils.[61] The water could have been contaminated before, but it is conceivable that if fetching water was usually women's work, women had a hand in it.

The occupation of midwife left women open to charges of infanticide, which planters in the eighteenth century believed was an important part of slave resistance. Their charges of sabotage by infanticide were fueled by low birthrates among slave women. Indeed, high mortality and low fertility rates were characteristic of the French slave plantations. According to Debien, the death rate was 50 percent among newly arrived slaves and about 5 to 6 percent among acclimatized slaves in the eighteenth century, while the birthrate was less than 3 percent.[62] Mortality was so high on the Cottineau plantation in Saint Domingue that the entire slave force was replaced between 1765 and 1778. On La Souche plantation in Sainte Anne, Guadeloupe, the death rate was 38 percent between 1783 and 1787.[63] Planters believed that women who aborted made a conscious choice not to reproduce and that when they did give birth, they, along with midwives, killed the infants in the first few days of life.

To ensure live births, planters in the eighteenth century introduced incentives, giving women extra days off and exempting them from plantation labor, especially already pregnant women and nursing mothers.[64] The more children slave women had, the greater were the incentives. On the Fleuriau plantation in Saint Domingue in 1765, a man was also given an extra day off if his wife had four children,[65] an incentive probably also designed to give males, who had nothing to lose since the burden of child care fell upon women, a stake in the system. Slave women suspected of self-induced abortions, a common practice,[66] were put in iron collars. Because abortions were difficult to monitor, planters were convinced that the key to live births rested with midwives. Before leaving Saint Domingue in 1775, Stanislas Foäche, owner of the Foäche sugar planta-tion, instructed his overseer to put pregnant women in the hands of midwives when they were approaching their terms. Both mother and midwife were to be compensated with money and fabric when the child was out of danger, and whipped if it died. The mother was also to be put in iron collars "until such time as she became pregnant again." Foäche also directed that "all female slaves who were expecting must, if they wished to avoid punishment, declare it to the midwife who must then report to the surgeon to have it registered."[67]

The prospect of delivering stillborn infants or infants who would perish within days must have placed great stress on midwives, whom planters believed induced the condition of lockjaw (tetanus) to deprive them of new slaves. During the late eighteenth century, midwives on the Fleuriau plantation who were suspected of such actions were put in rope collars. This happened to the midwife Arada, whose rope collar contained seventy knots, each knot represent-ing a child she had allegedly killed. In 1786, Desuré, the attorney for two Saint Domingue plantations owned by Madame Dumoranay, a widow, ordered that the midwife on one of the plantations where infant mortality was high should be got rid of "for the greater good,"[68] although no firm evidence was presented against the midwife. French observers like Thibault de Chanvallon (who visi-ted Martinique in 1751) believed tetanus was caused by infection of the um-bilical cord and was responsible for 80–90 percent of child mortality in the French Caribbean during the seventeenth and eighteenth centuries.[69] Marietta Morrissey's undocumented assertion that the "use of rusty or dirty instruments or muddied stones to cut the cord also contributed to the infection"[70] is plaus-ible. In the eighteenth century, however, planters in the French colonies sub-scribed to the theory of infanticide.

Pregnant women were certainly guilty of malingering and feigning illness to avoid work, as can be seen in the reports from the overseer Dujardin de Beau-metz written to Barre de Saint-Venant, owner of a plantation in Saint Domingue in the 1780s. On September 5, 1788, Dujardin wrote to complain about the slave woman Francine, "who has been in the convalescence house for centuries for an incurable ulcer and who has been ordered to conceive a female child in ten days as compensation for her absenteeism from work." Francine had obviously been using the excuse of being pregnant for some time until the overseer caught on. It must have been with some gratification that Dujardin reported on Oc-tober 7, 1789, that Francine had conceived but her child had become a victim of "her ill will not to nourish it. She has so far escaped the whipping she deserves, but not for long, I hope."[71] Francine obviously had no desire to reproduce but gave the overseer the impression that she was complying with his wishes, only to show him in the end who had the upper hand.

Slave women in the French Caribbean also used the law, albeit rarely, to resist slavery. In 1836 slave woman Virginie of Guadeloupe successfully freed herself and two children by using Article 47 of the Code Noir, which forbade masters to sell separately nuclear family members—husband, wife, and children under eighteen years—who belonged to the same master. Under the Code Noir, such sales were to be declared null and void and masters were to be deprived of the slaves. Masters violated this article frequently.[72] There being few legally married couples, Gautier contends, only women challenged it.[73] It took eight years for Virginie's case to be resolved, as a judgment first had to be passed at the level of the mayor's jurisdiction before a civil action could be launched. Even then it took a courageous judge, Meynier, to force the mayor's hand in registering an act of emancipation without which Virginie could not have been declared free.

This is an interesting case which draws attention to aspects of gender and slavery that require further investigation. Under Articles 30 and 31 of the Code Noir, slaves could not testify in civil and criminal matters. Virginie would therefore have been dependent on the integrity of the judiciary and the willingness of its members to pursue the case. Further, in the French Caribbean, judges normally ruled in favor of masters, not slaves. With abolition approaching in the 1840s, judges seemed more willing to prosecute masters, which means that timing may have worked in Virginie's favor. Why only women launched legal challenges against the breakup of their families remains an open question pending detailed studies of the slave family in the French Caribbean. It can hardly be overlooked that in Virginie's case, nothing was said about her husband.

Another way that slave women combated slavery was by banding together in women's associations. Some of the earliest known slave associations began in Martinique in 1793 as dance clubs organized along ethnic lines in urban centers. In the nineteenth century they sprang up all over Martinique and broadened their functions to become brotherhoods whose members pooled money to hold religious functions and funerals for members. By 1830, the city of Fort Royal alone had seventeen such associations.[74] They became less ethnic in character, attracted many slaves from rural areas, and named themselves after flowers. Leaders of slave associations carried such titles as king, queen, woman of honor, and master of ceremonies. The queen of one such association located in Petit-Bourg in Guadeloupe around 1845 was a slave. The group was united by oath, was dedicated to aiding slaves who wanted to escape, and was one of several such associations.[75] In La Guyane, the minutes of a Privy Council meeting of August 1837 acknowledged two female associations of which freed slaves were also members, noting that each had a distinct name and a leader. These associations organized entertainment evenings, principally dances with drumming. The women composed the traditional songs and competed with one another over the merits of the compositions. As in the rest of the French Caribbean, however, these associations were also mutual aid societies whose activities frightened authorities.[76] Planters viewed slave associations, male or female, as vehicles for promoting crimes such as theft and for inciting rebellious behavior. In the 1830s planters of Martinique feared that "behind the pleasant appearance of a society of roses and carnations operated a band of hardened criminals, thieves, and people dedicated to poisoning animals and Whites." Their fear was that these groups contained elements who were preparing to massacre whites, as had been done in Saint Domingue in 1791.[77]

Female slaves of the French Caribbean resisted slavery for the same reasons that male slaves did and in much the same way. Slave men and women waged a complementary struggle and died together for common ideals of liberty because slavery reduced both sexes to units of labor. Drawing on the experiences and circumstances of their occupations and gender, women participated in all aspects of resistance, including armed revolt, *marronage*, poisoning, withdrawal of labor, and legal challenges to the slave system which sought to dehumanize them. The study of slave resistance in the French Caribbean, as elsewhere in the Americas, would be grossly distorted without full consideration of the lives of slave women.

Notes

1. Bernard Moitt, "Behind the Sugar Fortunes: Women, Labour and the Development of Caribbean Plantations during Slavery," in *African Continuities*, ed. S. Chilungu and S. Niang (Toronto: Terebi, 1989), pp. 410–17; Bernard Moitt, "Women, Work and Resistance in the French Caribbean during Slavery, 1700–1848," in *Engendering History: Caribbean Women in Historical Perspective*, ed. Verene Shepherd, Bridget Brereton, and Barbara Bailey (New York: St. Martin's Press, 1995), pp. 155–75.

2. Victor Schoelcher, *Des Colonies Françaises: Abolition immédiate de l'esclavage* (Basse-Terre: Société d'Histoire de la Guadeloupe, 1976), p. 23.

3. Jean Baptiste Labat, *Nouveau voyage aux isles de l'Amérique* (Paris: Guillaume, 1722), vol. 3, p. 432.

4. Labat, *Nouveau voyage*, vol. 3, pp. 202–7, 410–20.

5. See, for example, Michael Craton, *Testing the Chains: Resistance to Slavery in the British West Indies* (Ithaca: Cornell University Press, 1982); Jean Fouchard, *Les Marrons de la liberté* (Paris: Editions de l'Ecole, 1972); David Barry Gaspar, *Bondmen and Rebels: A Study of Master-Slave Relations in Antigua* (Baltimore: Johns Hopkins University Press, 1985); Richard Price, *Maroon Societies: Rebel Slave Communities in the Americas* (New York: Anchor, 1973); C. L. R. James, *The Black Jacobins* (New York: Random House, 1963); Carolyn Fick, *The Making of Haiti: The Saint Domingue Revolution from Below* (Knoxville: University of Tennessee Press, 1990); Arlette Gautier, *Les Soeurs de Solitude* (Paris: Editions Caribéennes, 1985); Barbara Bush, *Slave Women in Caribbean Society, 1650–1838* (Bloomington: Indiana University Press, 1990), and "Towards Emancipation: Slave Women and Resistance to Coercive Labour Regimes in the British West Indian Colonies, 1790–1838," *Slavery and Abolition* 5 (December 1984): 222–43; Hilary McD. Beckles, *Natural Rebels: A Social History of Enslaved Black Women in Barbados* (New Brunswick: Rutgers University Press, 1989); Lucille Mathurin Mair, *The Rebel Woman in the British West Indies during Slavery* (Kingston: African-Caribbean Institute of Jamaica, 1975); Barbara Bush, "Slave Women in the British Caribbean, 1650–1834," in *Born out of Resistance: On Caribbean Cultural Creativity*, ed. Wim Hoogbergen (Utrecht: ISOR, 1995), pp. 126–36; Marietta Morrissey, *Slave Women in the New World: Gender Stratification in the Caribbean* (Lawrence: University Press of Kansas, 1989).

6. Simone Schwarz-Bart, *Pluie et vent sur Télumée Miracle* (Paris: Editions du Seuil, 1972).

7. Jacques Roumain, *Gouverneurs de la rosée* (Paris: Les Éditeurs Français Réunis, 1946).

8. Aimé Césaire, *La Tragédie du roi Christophe* (Paris: Présence Africaine, 1963).

9. Jacques Adélaïde-Merlande, *Delgrès ou la Guadeloupe en 1802* (Paris: Editions Karthala, 1986), pp. 5–10; André Negre, *La Rébellion de la Guadeloupe (1801–1802)* (Paris: Editions Caribbéennes, 1987), pp. 12–13; Anne Pérotin-Dumon, *Etre patriote sous les tropiques, 1789–1794* (Basse-Terre: Société d'histoire de la Guadeloupe, 1985) pp. 216–31.

10. Negre, *La Rébellion*, p. 114.

11. Oruno Lara, *La Guadeloupe dans l'histoire* (Paris: L'Harmattan, 1979), p. 126.

12. James, *Black Jacobins*, p. 315.

13. Auguste Lacour, *Histoire de la Guadeloupe* (Basse-Terre: Editions de Diffusion de la Culture Antillaise, 1976), vol. 3, p. 311.

14. Lara, *La Guadeloupe*, p. 138.

15. Lacour, *Histoire*, vol. 3, pp. 271, 275. Lacour's highly personalized account raises questions about authenticity, but his position as magistrate meant that he had access to official records. There are slight variations in some dates and details in other sources, but his work draws upon informants, many of whom were well placed in Guadeloupian society.

16. Lacour, *Histoire*, vol. 3, p. 275.

17. James, *Black Jacobins*, p. 361.

18. Antoine Métral, *Histoire de l'insurrection des esclaves dans le nord de Saint-Domingue* (Paris: F. Sceref, 1818), p. 43.

19. Lacour, *Histoire*, vol. 3, pp. 275, 291.

20. Alfred Martineau and Louis-Philippe May, *Trois siècles d'histoire antillaise: Martinique et Guadeloupe de 1635 à nos jours* (Paris: Société de l'Histoire des Colonies Françaises, 1935), p. 218; Roland Anduse, *Joseph Ignace: Le premier rebelle* (Condé-sur-Noreau: Editions Jasor, 1989), pp. 268–74.

21. Lacour, *Histoire*, vol. 3, p. 331.

22. Lara, *La Guadeloupe*, p. 154.

23. Adélaïde-Merlande, *Delgrès*, p. 149; Lacour, *Histoire*, vol. 3, pp. 325–54; Martineau and May, *Trois siècles*, p. 218.

24. Lacour, *Histoire*, vol. 3, p. 311; Adélaïde-Merlande, *Delgrès*, p. 152; Gautier, *Les Soeurs*, p. 251.

25. Lacour, *Histoire*, vol. 3, pp. 398–99; Lara, *La Guadeloupe*, p. 174; Negre, *La Rébellion*, pp. 150–51.

26. Maurice Nicolas, *L'Affaire de la Grand'Anse* (Fort-de-France, 1960), pp. 18–19.

27. B. David, *Les Origines de la population martiniquaise au fil des ans 1635–1902* (Mémoire de la Société d'Histoire de la Martinique, no. 3, 1973), p. 103; Nicolas, *L'Affaire*, p. 22.

28. David, *Les Origines*, p. 105.

29. Archives d'Outre-Mer, Guyane 129 P2 (11), July 14, 1831.

30. Malenfant, *Des Colonies et particulièrement de Saint-Domingue* (Paris, 1814), cited in Métral, *Histoire*, p. 40.

31. Nicole Vanony-Frisch, "Les Esclaves de la Guadeloupe à fin de l'Ancien Régime d'après les sources notariales, 1770–1789," extract from *Bulletin de la Société d'Histoire de la Guadeloupe* 63–64 (1985): 134–35; Gaspar, *Bondmen and Rebels*, p. 181; Barry Higman, *Slave Populations of the British Caribbean, 1807–1834* (Baltimore: Johns Hopkins University Press, 1984), p. 389; Orlando Patterson, *The Sociology of Slavery*

(London: Granada, 1973), p. 260; Craton, *Testing the Chains*, p. 61; Gautier, *Les Soeurs*, p. 236.

32. Claude Meillassoux, "Female Slavery," in *Women and Slavery in Africa*, ed. Claire C. Robertson and Martin A. Klein (Madison: University of Wisconsin Press, 1983), pp. 49–65; F. Sow, "Femme africaine, emploi et division internationale du travail," *Présence Africaine*, no. 141 (1987): 199–205.

33. Gautier, *Les Soeurs*, p. 237; Orlando Patterson, *Slavery and Social Death* (Cambridge: Harvard University Press, 1982), p. 113; Vanony-Frisch, "Les Esclaves," p. 135; Fouchard, *Les Marrons*, p. 285.

34. Anne-Marie Bruleaux et al., *Deux siècles d'esclavage en Guyane française, 1652–1848* (Paris: L'Harmattan, 1986), p. 91; Gautier, *Les Soeurs*, pp. 229–37.

35. Fouchard, *Les Marrons*, p. 286; Vanony-Frisch, *Les Esclaves*, p. 136.

36. Fouchard, *Les Marrons*, p. 289; Gautier, *Les Soeurs*, pp. 228–230.

37. Fouchard, *Les Marrons*, p. 550.

38. Bruleaux et al., *Deux siècles*, p. 196.

39. *Le Code Noir ou recueil des règlements rendus jusqu'à présent* (Basse-Terre: Société d'Histoire de la Guadeloupe, 1980), p. 47.

40. Fouchard, *Les Marrons*, p. 409; Gautier, *Les Soeurs*, p. 237.

41. Lucien Abénon, *La Guadeloupe de 1671 à 1759* (Paris: L'Harmattan, 1987), vol. 2, pp. 66–67.

42. Xavier Tanc, *De l'esclavage aux colonies et spécialment à la Guadeloupe* (Paris, 1831), cited in Gautier, *Les Soeurs*, p. 237.

43. Lacour, *Histoire*, vol. 3, p. 120; Gabriel Debien, *Plantations et esclaves à Saint-Domingue* (Dakar: Publications de la Section d'Histoire, 1962), pp. 56, 61; Labat, *Nouveau voyage*, vol. 4, pp. 198, 307.

44. M. Santineau, *Histoire de la Guadeloupe sous l'Ancien Régime* (Paris: Payot, 1928), p. 289.

45. Frantz Tardo-Dino, *Le Collier de servitude* (Paris: Editions Caribéennes, 1985), p. 234.

46. Abénon, *La Guadeloupe*, vol. 1, p. 256.

47. Yvan Debbasch, "Le Crime d'empoisonnement aux îls pendant la période esclavagiste," *Revue Français d'Histoire d'Outre-Mer* 50 (1963): 146–47.

48. Satineau, *Histoire*, p. 289, cited in David, *Les Origines*, p. 82.

49. Satineau, *Histoire*, pp. 289–90; Gabriel Debien, *Les Esclaves aux Antilles françaises* (Basse-Terre: Société d'Histoire de la Guadeloupe, 1974), p. 400; David, *Les Origines*, p. 82.

50. Cited in Abénon, *La Guadeloupe*, vol. 1, p. 255.

51. Debien, *Les Esclaves*, p. 401; Debbasch, "La Crime d'empoisonnement," p. 150.

52. Debien, *Les Esclaves*, pp. 400–401.

53. Debien, *Les Esclaves*, pp. 405, 408; Debien, *Plantations*, pp. 63, 67.

54. Debbasch, "Le Crime d'empoisonnement," pp. 141–52.

55. David, *Les Origines*, p. 96.

56. Debien, *Les Esclaves*, p. 408.

57. Labat, *Nouveau voyage*, vol. 3, pp. 446–47.

58. Bruleaux et al., *Deux siècles*, pp. 188–89, cited in Antoine Gisler, *L'Esclavage aux Antilles françaises* (Fribourg: Editions Universitaires Fribourg, 1965), p. 54.

59. Bernard Moitt, "Slave Resistance in Guadeloupe and Martinique, 1791–1848," in *Journal of Caribbean History* 25, nos. 1 and 2 (1991): 151–52.

60. Lacour, *Histoire*, vol. 3, pp. 399–404; Adélaïde-Merlande, *Delgrès*, p. 162; Lara, *Histoire*, pp. 170–72.

61. Métral, *Histoire*, p. 75.

62. Debien, *Les Esclaves*, pp. 343–47.

63. Debien, *Plantations*, p. 50; Vanony-Frisch, *Les Esclaves*, pp. 62–63.

64. Gautier, *Les Soeurs*, p. 107; Debien, *Les Esclaves*, pp. 363–66; Bernard Moitt, "Transcending Linguistic and Cultural Frontiers in Caribbean Historiography: C.L.R. James, French Sources and Slavery in San Domingo," in *C.L.R. James: His Intellectual Legacies*, ed. Selwyn Cudjoe and William Cain (Amherst: University of Massachusetts Press, 1995) pp. 147–57.

65. Jacques Cauna, *Au Temps des isles à sucre* (Paris: Karthala, 1987), p. 54.

66. Gautier, *Les Soeurs*, p. 134; Médéric-Louis Elie Moreau de Saint-Méry, *Description de la partie française de l'Isle Saint-Domingue* (Paris: Société d'Histoire des Colonies Françaises, 1958), vol. 3, p. 1272; Debien *Les Esclaves*, pp. 363–66.

67. Debien, *Plantations*, p. 130.

68. Cauna, *Au Temps*, pp. 102–4.

69. Tardo-Dino, *Le Collier*, p. 187.

70. Morrissey, *Slave Women*, p. 108.

71. Gabriel Debien and Françoise Thésée, *Un Colon niortais à Saint-Domingue* (Niort: Imbert-Nicolas, 1975), p. 123.

72. Louis Sala-Molins, *Le Code noir ou le calvaire de Canaan* (Paris: Presses Universitaires de France, 1987), pp. 184–85; Bernard Moitt, "Gender and Slavery: Women and the Plantation Experience in the Caribbean before 1848," in *Born out of Resistance*, pp. 121–22.

73. Gautier, *Les Soeurs*, p. 147.

74. Yvan Debbasch, "Les Associations serviles à la Martinique au XIXe siècle," in *Etudes d'histoire du droit privé*, ed. Pierre Petot (Paris: Editions Montchrestien, 1959), p. 124.

75. Gautier, *Les Soeurs*, pp. 223–24.

76. Bruleaux et al., *Deux siècles*, pp. 185–86.

77. Debbasch, "Les associations," p. 125.

13

SLAVE AND FREE COLORED WOMEN IN SAINT DOMINGUE

David P. Geggus

For much of the eighteenth century, the French colony of Saint Domingue (modern Haiti) was one of the most productive parts of the New World. After 1770 it became the world's major producer not only of sugar but also of coffee. Its economy was thus more diversified than that of the average West Indian "sugar island" and its slave society was correspondingly more varied. Although its social structure was broadly typical of the non-Hispanic Caribbean, its institutions had much in common with those of the other Catholic colonies. At the peak of its prosperity Saint Domingue was destroyed by the most remarkable of all slave rebellions.

Apart from Arlette Gautier's pioneering general study of female slaves in the French West Indies, *Les Soeurs de Solitude*,[1] black women in Saint Domingue have not been the subject of any specific historical research. This chapter, based on a wide range of contemporary manuscript and printed sources, attempts to delineate the place of females within the slave population and free colored sector, the roles they played in the labor force, their family and sexual relations, their experiences of motherhood and ill health, and their access to freedom through manumission and resistance.

Females were always a minority of the slave population of Saint Domingue. From the late seventeenth century, when buccaneering and ranching gave way to agriculture, to the abolition of slavery in the midst of the Haitian Revolution, the colonial censuses generally show six to eight male slaves for every five females.[2] In Saint Domingue as elsewhere in the West Indies, there are signs that the sexes were sometimes evenly balanced in the colony's pioneering decades,[3] when slave ships were infrequent visitors and carried a smaller excess of men over women than during the eighteenth century.[4] The spread of sugar cultivation, however, brought with it higher male-to-female ratios that, among the working adult slaves, remained around 150 to 100 during the fifty years after 1710, briefly reaching a peak in 1730 of 180 to 100. In the creole (locally born) segment of the slave population, females slightly outnumbered males because of their lower mortality rates,[5] and so once creoles became a substantial minority of the slave population, the sex ratio fell, to 130 to 100 in the 1770s and 120 to 100 in the 1780s.

The majority of Saint Domingue's slaves were nonetheless always Africans. On the eve of the French Revolution, the colonial lawyer M.-L.-E. Moreau de Saint-Méry guessed that two-thirds of the slaves were African-born, of whom two-thirds were male.[6] Although slave imports were extremely heavy in the 1780s and were dominated by males as never before,[7] both of Moreau's estimates were certainly exaggerations. The populous, long-settled North Province contained at least as many locally born as African slaves. The West and particularly the South provinces were less creolized, but the main regional contrasts in population structure were between areas of sugar and coffee cultivation—that is, between the plains and the mountains.[8] Taking the North Province in the final decade of slavery as an example, on a typical sugar estate there would be eleven creole men, twelve African men, and nine African women for every twelve creole women. On a coffee plantation there would be fourteen creole men, fifty-six African men, and thirty-nine African women for every twelve creole women.[9]

The slave population of Saint Domingue, therefore, was never distorted by the extremely high sex ratios found in Brazil and Cuba. But males, especially African males, always formed its largest component down to the end of the colonial period. Female slaves were never as numerous as in the other French colonies or most of the British colonies because of Saint Domingue's high rate of slave importation and the higher sex ratio of its imported slaves.[10]

This sexual imbalance in the slave trade was the result of a variety of forces in both Africa and the Americas, but one of the most important appears to have been the demand of sugar planters for male workers.[11] To some degree this demand may have reflected a perceived need for physical strength, because sugar was the most demanding of plantation crops. It may also have reflected the high male mortality rates experienced on sugar estates. Most probably, however, it was the sexual division of labor in sugar production that created the excess of males over females.

Apart from agricultural workers, sugar plantations needed boilermen and furnacemen to work long hours in the stifling factory building; a substantial number of artisans, such as coopers, carpenters, masons, and wheelwrights; carters, who hauled canes and hogsheads; and stockmen, who cared for the cattle that pulled the carts and the mules that turned the mills. All these posts were given to male slaves as a matter of course, and nothing in the European or African past would lead one to expect otherwise. Similarly, the few hunters and fishermen employed by plantations were invariably men; so too were the woodcutters who cleared the forests and, in the colony's early days, provided fuel for the factories.

Females were strongly represented among the domestic slaves as house servants, washerwomen, and, occasionally, seamstresses. They were sometimes presided over by a slave housekeeper, who was frequently the mistress of the plantation owner or manager. Scullions, valets, hairdressers, postillions, and coachmen were always male, however. More surprisingly, the great majority of cooks were also men, including the few who were Africans (French traditions overrode African taboos).[12] The only areas of employment monopolized by females were midwifery and nursing. Most sugar estates had a small "hospital" by the last quarter of the eighteenth century, and planters regarded the position of nurse as one that required responsibility and independence. The designation of midwife was usually accorded to women too old to work in the fields. Thus it was not really a high status position, though such women wielded a degree of power and, presumably, enjoyed prestige in the slave quarters.

Other minor posts were given to the aged or, on occasion, adolescents. Females were in charge of poultry, sheep, and goats. They prepared cassava, spun thread, minded children, and tied up bundles of canes in the fields, working behind the cane cutters. Men were watchmen and gardeners, and tended the irrigation canals. Both sexes provided hedgecutters and gatekeepers. The most prestigious and powerful post open to a slave was that of slavedriver. Large plantations of 400 slaves might possess a half-dozen, and most sugar estates had at least two. All were men, though on some large estates an aging *commandeuse* directed the activity of a children's gang charged with collecting forage.

This predominance of males among the "specialist" slaves meant that most of the agricultural work on sugar plantations was performed by females. This was true at the end of the seventeenth century in the time of Père Labat, and in the 1770s and 1780s we find that more than 60 percent of fieldworkers were women.[13] Although during the intervening years the male proportion of the slave population increased, it is unlikely that males ever formed a clear majority of field slaves on the sugar estates. For the majority of transplanted Africans, this arrangement was more familiar for the female field slaves than for the males. About half the Africans sold in Saint Domingue came from West Central Africa, where males did little agricultural work. Among most of the main ethnic groups of that region, females were traditionally prominent in field labor.[14]

How far a sexual division of labor operated among these "unskilled" slaves is not clear. Particularly uncertain is the extent to which women shared in the backbreaking and relentless work of cane cutting with the machete.[15] According to Jean Baptiste Labat, they did the same work as men in the fields, although feeding canes through the mill was regarded as women's work that was degrading for males.[16] Men monopolized use of the ax to clear terrain, and they did most of the heavy lifting, as their high incidence of hernias suggests. There was a tendency for women to do weeding and manuring, and some observers said only the strongest men could make the cane holes in which the weaker slaves (including women) then planted.[17] However, all these tasks were performed by both sexes, as was the harvesting of coffee on the mountain plantations. Planters sought in a field gang, writes Gabriel Debien, "homogeneity of strength, which meant homogeneity of age and of acclimation. The exact balancing of the sexes did not count."[18]

In Saint Domingue's northern plain in the 1770s and 1780s, men were eight times as likely as women to escape from the drudgery of fieldwork into a post offering some independence and status. Only 5 percent of the adult females, including the midwives, were "specialists," as compared with 40 percent of the men, not counting the various supernumerary posts.[19] This was perhaps an extreme case. In earlier times, when more sugar planters resided in the colony, retinues of domestic slaves may have been somewhat larger. And on estates producing only muscovado, as opposed to semirefined sugar, factory workers were fewer. Most important, on plantations growing crops other than sugar, occupational diversity and social mobility were much more limited, and by the 1780s fewer than one-third of Saint Domingue's slaves lived on sugar estates. The position of the sexes in the slave labor force was therefore less divergent than the sugar plantation evidence suggests. Coffee plantations, for example, provided specialist posts for fewer than 15 percent of their adult male slaves. Nevertheless, the percentage of female specialists varied little according to time and crop type.[20] The overwhelming majority of women slaves were always field hands.

This generalization holds true whether or not one includes the slave population of Saint Domingue's towns. Scarcely one in twenty of the colony's slaves were urban dwellers, and the little evidence that exists suggests that most of these urbanites were males.[21] They worked on the waterfront and in craft and retail trades. The female urban slaves were probably mainly domestic servants, who lived in cramped sheds that lined the backyards of townhouses or slept on their owners' floors. The inns and taverns of the seaports also needed numerous chambermaids and washerwomen to cater to the colony's huge transient population. The restricted lifestyle of most domestics contrasted with that of the street vendors, who paid their owners a monthly sum and were left to find their own lodgings in the Little Africa districts of the major towns.[22]

Although the typical slave—male or female—was always a field hand, females had much less access than their male counterparts to positions of independence, skill, and prestige. The number of specialist positions open to women was extremely small, and they offered only limited rewards. Washerwomen passed much of their working day unsupervised with fellow workers, but none had the mobility of the carters, coachmen, and muleteers, or the hunters and fishermen. Seamstresses could earn money sewing for other slaves,[23] but the drivers and artisans were routinely rewarded, as a matter of rank, with extra food and clothing, and sometimes better housing. Domestic slaves, it is true, might receive extra food and clothing adventitiously. However, slaves generally preferred life in the slave quarters, noted Père Labat, to confinement in the master's house.[24] Such attitudes may have changed somewhat with the evolution of a creole and mixed-race "elite" (which preferred minuets and gavottes to the sensuous chica and calenda), but life under the master's eye and roof inevitably brought its own varieties of suffering. Housekeepers possessed authority, nurses exercised responsibility, and itinerant vendors enjoyed personal autonomy. However, such posts were exceedingly rare and none brought with it the power of the slave-driver, the glamor of the coachman, or the skill of the master craftsman.

Creole slaves were preferred, at least in the late eighteenth century, for all specialist positions.[25] Raised in the colony, they had a familiarity with plantation work, white society, and the creole language that made them easier to train than African outsiders, whose skills were generally ignored beyond those of cultivator and herdsman. It was also a wiser investment to train slaves who were young and likely to live longest. Yet openings existed for African males, especially as boilermen, stockmen, and artisans. By contrast, African women had virtually no opportunity for social mobility. Moreover, as colored creoles were preferred as domestic servants, females with a white father had five or six times the chance of even a black creole of avoiding labor in the fields. Even so, although colored males were almost never put to work as field slaves, their sisters sometimes were.

Within the slave quarters, of course, there existed other hierarchies of occupational status not necessarily recognized by the whites. Women acted as herb doctors as often as men did. Their ministrations were much preferred by the slaves to European medicines, and whites, too, occasionally acknowledged their skills.[26] Slave women also practiced sorcery and occasionally found whites for customers.[27] And in the different cults known as voodoo, women of different backgrounds acted as priests alongside male counterparts. They included both Africans and creoles, and the woman who officiated at the famous Bois Caiman ceremony that launched the 1791 slave revolt is said to have been a green-eyed mulatress.[28] Here it might be noted that on occasion the enslaved wives of African kings managed to retain authority over fellow countrymen in the colony, who carried their burdens, did work for them, and brought them food.[29]

Saint Domingue's slaves were fed from a variety of sources, including communal provision grounds which were cultivated like the commercial crops, and weekly distributions of imported foodstuffs, notably salt fish. In large measure, however, slaves produced their own food on personal provision grounds that they cultivated on Sundays. Much about the system remains obscure, such as how the marketing of surpluses, cultivation, and cooking were organized. Debien observes that once women predominated among field slaves, the African pattern prevailed whereby men prepared the soil and women planted, weeded, harvested, and usually went to market.[30] In modern Haiti, as in Africa, women control the marketing of food crops, which suggests direct continuity. Yet in the seventeenth century we find men selling their wife's produce, and around 1800 young men rode to market followed by a retinue of concubines carrying produce.[31] The following description by Lieutenant-Colonel Desdorides, dates from about 1780:

> All slaves who work receive a very small provision ground, which somehow suffices, although on Sundays and holidays the women go to local or town markets to sell produce. . . . When a man and woman [are persuaded to] form a settled relationship [*on amacorne un nègre avec une négresse*][32] they are given a hut, a pig, a sow, a cock and hens. If the woman is industrious, the couple gain a second income from . . . selling eggs and poultry in addition to their ground provisions. They go fishing and sell their fish. The woman fattens the pigs, and hard-working couples manage to achieve a sort of prosperity.[33]

It is difficult to know how common or stable such unions were, but it is clear that only a small fraction of slave couples were married in church. Slave marriages were recognized under the Code Noir of 1685, which forbade the separation of spouses and of mothers and children under seven. However, this probably diminished the interest of planters in encouraging matrimony among their slaves. Until about 1690, many French West Indian planters and administrators took their religion seriously and slave marriages were quite common, though this was truer of the longer-settled Windward Isles than of Saint Domingue.[34] Thereafter, as sex ratios rose and piety went out of style, colonists seem to have paid little attention to their slaves' religious lives or, indeed, any aspect of their well-being, for more than half a century. In a parish of indigo plantations in the south of Saint Domingue, Gautier found that the proportion of slaves who were married fell from 9 percent in the 1720s to under 3 percent in the 1730s and was insignificant for the remaining thirty years covered in her study.[35]

Prior to 1720 plantation inventories usually listed slaves by families, but almost never in the later period when the excess of males became larger.[36] One of the rare estates to do so was the D'Aux plantation in the northern plain. Its 1786 inventory groups 60 percent of its 170 slaves in seventeen families, ranging in size from twelve to two persons.[37] Nine of the families spanned three generations, but only two contained more than one couple. This meant that most of the children lived with only one parent, usually the mother. Even among the couples, about half the women had children by men who were not their current partner. Of the thirteen couples, six were married, and the great majority were aged over forty; none was under thirty. Most consisted of male artisans and female field slaves whose children had a tendency to become specialists. The extended families were usually virilocal, the woman being classified (and presumably living) with her partner's family. Of course, many ostensibly single persons may have had partners on other plantations, in which case it was invariably the man who visited the woman. Planters complained frequently that nocturnal visiting debilitated male slaves. Resident unions on the D'Aux plantation involved nearly half of the creoles but only one-fifth of the Africans aged over thirty.

Nearby, the plantation attorney of the famous Galliffet plantations also tried to encourage slaves to marry, but he met with the same result. Only a few old couples wished to make their unions permanent.[38] Slaves "changed their wives more frequently than their shirts," remarked a visitor to the South Province.[39] Promiscuity, observed another, was one of their few pleasures and their sole liberty: "These sorts of free unions, formed out of mutual attraction, without the help of the church, the opinion of parents or the master's consent, might seem to be inevitably happy, fruitful, and of long duration, but on most plantations they do not last long, and they produce very few children. The men and women united in this manner often split up for the simple pleasure of changing. The children generally remain the mother's responsibility, but there is no law on the subject."[40]

Neither monogamy nor parenthood appears to have been especially attractive to slaves prior to middle age. If such partnerships could bring economic benefits, they also demanded more work from women than men. In the minds of both males and females, African cultural patterns probably also helped to undermine the nuclear family within slavery, particularly the prevalence of polygyny and the facility of divorce. Acceptance in some societies of premarital sexual relations may also have played a role, though this did not apply to the Bakongo women, considered especially promiscuous in Saint Domingue.[41] Many sources state that slave women, particularly creoles, profited financially by their sexual activity or that of their daughters.[42] Along with their marketing activities, this helps explain, perhaps, how female slaves were able to acquire gold and silver jewelry and the expensive muslins and Madras handkerchiefs which they wore on Sundays. In the seventeenth century Labat noted how male slaves took pride in dressing up their wives and children. Ninety years later, Desdorides observed that it was slave women, using the proceeds of their "intrigues," who took pride in dressing their lovers.[43]

There is perhaps a danger here in generalizing from evidence drawn from around the major seaports. Nevertheless, the paucity of females in both the white and the black communities in Saint Domingue[44] evidently put the sexual favors of slave women at a premium. Lacking legal personalities, female slaves were exceptionally vulnerable to rape, and sexual harassment by whites occasionally extended to the most vicious sadism.[45] Their slavery thus had a psychophysical dimension that male slaves did not experience, so far as is known.[46] On the other hand, slave women were able to use their sexuality to obtain material advantages from whites, free coloreds, and fellow slaves, and sometimes to gain their freedom. Females slaves were manumitted more than twice as frequently as males.

Sexual relations with whites ranged along a continuum, including the sordid and violent to rare cases of marriage (more frequent with free men of color). [47] A free colored pamphleteer writing in 1789 described most French plantations as harems for their owners and white employees. Female slaves submitted to their advances, he wrote, out of a mixture of fear and hope.[48] Seamen on slave ships routinely selected personal concubines from among the women captives, giving them additional rations in exchange. According to a ship's officer, such women "adjusted better" than other slaves to the voyage; they formed attachments to their captors and were prepared to betray shipboard revolts. He does not tell us, however, whether they expected to be sold at the voyage's end. While visiting plantations in Saint Domingue, the same young Frenchman found that local hospitality included parading before male guests after dinner a choice of the most attractive female slaves "to serve you in the bath and in bed."[49]

On the sugar estates of the North Province in the late colonial period, about one in twenty-five babies born to slave women were fathered by whites.[50] As the mothers were invariably creoles and close to twenty years old, it appears that interracial sex involved only a small segment of the female population. African women maintained a strong preference for black males, wrote Moreau de Saint-

Méry, although they did reluctantly have relations with whites.[51] Opportunities for prostitution were considerable in the vicinity of seaports and garrison towns. Washerwomen in particular enjoyed an erotic reputation.[52] At the end of the American Revolutionary War, the attorney of the Bréda estate at Haut-du-Cap, where soldiers had been billeted, complained that three-quarters of the slave women had contracted venereal disease. A few years earlier he had sacked a white employee who "as soon as I had my heels turned was in his room with the slave women," to whom he gave extra food.[53] Such cases abound in planta-tion records, where they are singled out for reprobation, usually because of the effect they had on slave men.

It is not easy to say whether women slaves wielded "sexual power." Gautier argues that patriarchal relations, common to Europe and Africa, continued under slavery. Despite their differences, whites and male slaves found common interest in keeping the enslaved woman in servitude to them both.[54] Although it seems that only elite slaves were able to have numerous concubines, Moreau de Saint-Méry asserted that all the Africans in Saint Domingue remained polygynous.[55] Both Moreau and Girod Chantrans commented on how jealously possessive male slaves were of their partners. They demanded deference from females, did not eat with them, and abused violently those they suspected of being unfaithful. Women usually "accepted" such mistreatment and, accustomed to polygyny in Africa, did not generally reciprocate the males' jealousy.[56]

There are two ways to reconcile these conflicting images, besides doubting their accuracy. One is to assume that Africans and creoles had substantially different lifestyles. The other is to postulate an uneasy tension in slave culture between patriarchal tendencies and sexual freedom, both of which had African roots and were reinforced by different aspects of the slave system. This we see in Moreau de Saint-Méry's description of African co-wives who, though rivals, cheerfully colluded to facilitate one another's infidelities.[57] Even in Desdorides's account of slave women whose discreet "intrigues" helped support a lover who himself responded with gifts and infidelity, one glimpses the co-existence of unions of greater and lesser stability.[58]

With a few exceptions, white commentators usually described slave women in Saint Domingue as good mothers. "Never did children, those feeble creatures, have more assiduous care," wrote Moreau de Saint-Méry. "The slave woman who finds the time every night to bathe her children and give them clean clothes is a person worthy of respect."[59] Those same commentators, who noted that women took pride in the status of mother, also reproached them for the practice of abortion, said to be "fairly common" in and around the colony's towns. Moreau de Saint-Méry attributed this "to promiscuity, and sometimes to gloomy ideas."[60] As colonists tended to perceive abortion more willingly than miscarriages, and to attribute neonatal tetanus to infanticide, it is impossible to know what part female slaves really played in restricting the reproduction of the slave population. Moreover, the failure to record the births or deaths of infants who died young obscures the relative importance of low fertility and infant mortality. What is absolutely clear, however, is that slave women had extremely few children who lived past infancy.[61]

Measured fertility levels for Saint Domingue slaves are among the lowest known in any American slave society. In plantation inventories, well under half of adult females are listed as mothers. Perhaps one in four never gave birth at all. Average fertility indexes (1,000 children 0–4 years/females 15–44 years) typically ranged between 250 and 350 on sugar estates in all parts of the colony in the last three decades of the eighteenth century. On coffee and indigo plantations the general range was about 350-500.[62] In an eighteenth-century European or twentieth-century African society, a range of 700-950 would be normal. This difference suggests that the work regimes associated with different crop types were of considerable importance in determining the incidence of either infertility or infant mortality or both. No single factor has been found to correlate well with low measured fertility. However, for sugar estates, high work load (measured as cane acreage per slave) stands out as the most significant in the colony's North Province, where slave-to-cane ratios were lower than else-where.[63] This suggests there was a critical threshold beyond which the punishing labor of sugar estates began to impinge on slave women's fertility (or the life expectancy of their infants). On the coffee plantations, by contrast, the size of the work force and the proportion of nubile females who were Africans were more important influences.

On both types of plantations creole women gave birth at much earlier ages than Africans, and there is evidence that they may have continued to give birth later. Creole mothers had, on average, more children and (evidence suggests) gave birth at slightly shorter intervals.[64] Calculations are complicated by lack of knowledge of when most Africans arrived in the colony, but it seems that few gave birth during their first decade in the colony. This may have been due to the difficulty in finding suitable partners or to an unwillingness to procreate in an alien world. Africans may have also experienced a shorter childbearing span owing to nutritional deficiencies in childhood. The fact that creoles were taller than most Africans (in the 1780s)[65] shows they had enjoyed a better level of nutrition than those who had been sold across the Atlantic. Moreau de Saint-Méry observed that creole girls achieved menarche earlier than Africans.[66] It is surprising to find both Africans and creoles giving birth at much younger ages on coffee plantations than on sugar plantations. Just why sugar plantation life limited the fertility of young females is not certain; this is an area where much remains to be learned.

From about 1770 onward, as the price of slaves rose, planters began to display a greater interest in encouraging their slaves to reproduce.[67] They tried to purchase greater numbers of female slaves, demanded less work from pregnant women, supervised midwives, and ordered small payments to mothers and midwives on the successful birth and weaning of a child. Planters also freed from work the mothers of six live children and tried to persuade slaves to marry. Some planters punished women slaves and midwives suspected of abortion or infanticide. Punishments typically included whipping and wearing of an iron collar or ball and chain. Some contemporaries claimed this only increased the incidence of abortion among women fearful of miscarrying or of seeing their babies perish from an unidentified disease.[68] The trend toward pronatalism affected women in different ways. It could result in increased oppression and interference; it could also bring small financial rewards, some recognition of the needs of pregnant women and nursing mothers, and about a one-in-a-hundred chance of freedom from fieldwork.

One advantage women slaves seem to have had over their male counterparts was better health.[69] At least as regards the permanent disabilities recorded on plantation slave lists, women were healthier than men on the majority of plantations. Gender was often a more important determinant of a slave's health than creolization, which brought with it both epidemiological and occupational advantages. Creole women everywhere were much healthier than all other slaves, but there was frequently a larger percentage of creole men incapacitated than of African women.[70] Despite their near monopoly of the privileged occupations on plantations, males still performed the heaviest and most dangerous tasks. Their vulnerability to hernia and maiming largely explains the different health records of the two sexes. Women were also less likely to suffer the large leg ulcers called *malingres*, possibly caused by hookworm, but they were somewhat more susceptible to pulmonary ailments, probably tuberculosis and pneumonia. No other clear patterns appear in the data, except that vague terms such as "sick," "weak," and "infirm" were applied more often to women than men. The male death rate seems to have been about 20 percent higher than that for females.[71]

Another area in which female slaves were relatively favored was access to official freedom. Women greatly outnumbered men among those slaves whose owners granted the informal "liberty of the savanna," which freed slaves from plantation work, though they continued to live on the estate. Women also formed the majority of those officially freed by act of manumission. More men were freed in the seventeenth century than women, but in the period 1721–70, in the southern parish of Nippes, manumitted women outnumbered men four to one, though the majority of slaves so freed were mulatto children.[72] In the five years before the French Revolution, females formed almost two-thirds of the slaves manumitted. Their numbers ranged from 737 in 1785 to a low of 256 in 1789.[73] As 1785 was said to be an exceptional year, it seems that a female slave's chances of being officially freed, though better than a male's, never exceeded three in one thousand and were usually much less.

In fact, a black slave's prospects for manumission were even more remote, as over half the slaves freed each year were of mixed racial descent. The predominance of females was roughly the same among the black and mulatto manumittees, though more marked among the former. Among the quadroons,[74] however, males were slightly more numerous. They were no doubt children freed by their fathers, whereas the mulattoes and the blacks included many concubines. Colonists of Saint Domingue thus appear to have freed their sons more frequently than their daughters.[75]

Female servants who had nursed a sick master or mistress were fairly prominent among the slaves freed in Nippes, but at least half of the total were concubines and their children.[76] The colonial government had long deplored this encouragement of undesirable behavior, as the authorities saw it, and in 1775 the manumission tax for female slaves under forty years old was raised to double that for males. In 1786, the minister of the navy ordered that the number of testamentary manumissions be restricted. Though this did not reduce the proportion of females, it cut by more than half the total number of slaves freed.

The manumission figures for 1789 reveal a considerable contrast between the North Province and the rest of Saint Domingue as regards the gender of slaves freed. In the wealthy North females formed 78 percent of black and mulatto manumittees, as opposed to 57 percent in the West and South provinces.[77] It is unclear if this regional contrast was of long duration, but it raises an interesting question concerning the political economy of manumission. The American Revolution and the 1780s saw a large influx of single white males into the colony, especially into the booming port cities. At the same time, the number of free colored females grew faster than any other element in the urban population. In elegant Cap Français, where most free colored women were said to be prostitutes or white men's mistresses, the sex ratios of the white and free colored communities remained mirror images of each other.[78] It may be that under such circumstances, masters and administrators were more willing to free females, or perhaps slave women became more able to purchase their liberty. This period may also have seen increased migration of free women from the countryside.

Great uncertainty surrounds both the size and the structure of the free colored sector of Saint Domingue's population. When publishing the last colonial census (1789), the intendant observed that although statistics regarding free coloreds were too inaccurate to be included, women were much more numerous than men. The figures actually showed a majority of males in a total of some 24,000, along with 30,000 whites and 434,000 slaves.[79] Earlier censuses sometimes showed male and sometimes female majorities in the colony's three provinces. One is left to wonder how reliable the statistics are and whether the administration was trying to cover up either the true size of the free colored community or the number of fugitive male slaves who had been absorbed successfully into it.[80]

In any event, Saint Domingue's free colored population was undoubtedly large by the standards of non-Hispanic America. It was also unusually prosperous, in the sense that it included many middling planters, usually of coffee or indigo, some of whom had been educated in France. Only about 15 percent of the *gens de couleur* lived in the towns; they made up 11 percent of the urban population.[81] About two-thirds were said to be of mixed racial descent. The free

coloreds were thus a very diverse group in terms of wealth, occupation, phenotype, and culture. Lightness of complexion generally correlated with wealth,
free birth, legitimacy, and knowledge of French (as distinct from the local
creole). The free black minority tended to form a culturally distinct group
closest to the slaves. Some had been born in Africa; many of the females were
ex-slaves, former mistresses or wet nurses of their erstwhile owners.[82]

Women fairly certainly formed a majority of the urban free coloreds.[83] The
prostitutes of the seaports and those who were white men's mistresses often inspired passages of purple prose in descriptions of the colony written during its
final decades. They were usually of mixed racial descent, the illegitimate children
of slave concubines, and they rarely had children themselves. White male
commentators depicted them as elegant and sensual; young white women
copied their mannerisms and style of dress. They enjoyed their notoriety. In the
largest towns they hosted weekend dances to entertain wealthier whites. Although they often lived in only one or two rooms, some amassed modest
fortunes that were invested in jewelry and elaborate wardrobes. Those of Cap
Français were considered the most prosperous and glamorous; those of Port-au-
Prince and provincial Saint Marc rather less so.[84] Even in the smaller settlements
of the southern peninsula, however, the free colored women were accounted
"more elegant in dress and manners" than those of Jamaica.[85] They could be
severe to their own slaves, but in general they enjoyed free and easy relations
with slave women. They were notably charitable to the poor and sick.

The towns of Saint Domingue also contained a contrasting group of free
coloreds, whom Girod de Chantrans called "a sort of urban bourgeoisie, whose
conduct is very respectable."[86] Free for several generations and legitimately married, they included numerous artisans and their families and, no doubt, the
numerous women engaged in retail trade who purchased dry goods from
import merchants for resale to the black population. Some received an income
from urban rents. A cadastral survey of 1776 shows that about one-fifth of the
private houses in Cap Français belonged to nonwhites. This meant that the
average free colored resident owned at least one house, usually the cheapest of
the dwellings that lined the alleyways of the Little Africa district. One-fifth of
the owners were females; four-fifths were black.[87]

In the countryside, the free colored presence was similarly diverse. Frequently the census listed one-third or more of the women in a parish as domestics. More common in rural than urban districts, they were presumably the
housekeepers/mistresses of white men whom contemporaries often referred to.
Children were also much more numerous in the countryside, and in the mountain parishes there could be found very large families and interlinked clan groups.
Of those free coloreds who married, the great majority chose a spouse of the
same phenotype. Women landowners varied from solitary ex-slaves living in ram-
shackle cabins on an acre of land to the proprietors of coffee plantations with
large families and forty or more slaves.[88]

To judge from those free coloreds who used the services of a notary to record property transactions, marriage contracts, and the like, a quarter of these women were able to sign their names, as could two-thirds of the men.[89] Among the quadroons, both men and women were almost all literate, but only one in four mulatresses could sign, as opposed to three-quarters of the mulatto males. Nearly half the free black men could write their names, but very few black women could do so. Given the nature of the sources, these figures doubtless overstate even the technical literacy of the free colored population as a whole.

If those slaves who gained their freedom through official channels were mainly female, those who sought to escape from slavery on their own initiative were predominantly men. Through the eighteenth century, females typically made up 12–15 percent of the slaves who became fugitives.[90] Bearing in mind the sex ratio of the young adult population from which most fugitives came, it appears that males were three to four times as likely as females to *partir marron*. However, there were considerable differences between different sectors of the slave population. Using the runaway statistics of 1788 and 1790, compiled from local newspaper advertisements,[91] we find that African males made up approximately three-quarters of fugitives but that foreign creoles, both men and women, easily were the slaves most prone to running away. Locally born black creole women were more than fifty times less likely to flee. Only slightly more likely were African women and local colored women. Among creole adults, males fled five times as often as females. Among Africans the gender difference was even more marked.

Family ties probably explain part of these contrasts. Creole women were more likely than Africans to have children to care for, especially in the fifteen- to thirty-year-old age group that supplied the great bulk of runaways. The prospects for a successful escape also had some bearing. A comparison of the numbers of slaves advertised as missing with the numbers of recaptured fugitives suggests that light-skinned females had by far the best chances of evading recapture and that African women had the least success of all slaves. Young colored females had a ready market for their sexual favors and domestic skills and could merge into the free colored population more easily than blacks. African women were unfamiliar with both the local geography and the local language, and they were the least likely of slaves to possess marketable skills. Finally, as experienced house builders and hunters, men were better equipped for life in the mountains and forests. Females appear to have fled more often to Saint Domingue's small urban area. Among female fugitives were those who dressed as men when traveling the colony's roads. One case per year shows up in the runaway advertisements of 1788–90. All three were creoles. One of them dressed as a horseman in the rural mounted police.[92]

The types of resistance most closely associated with women were infanticide and abortion. Although the evidence is difficult to interpret and not all planters even wanted their slaves to procreate, some midwives apparently confessed to systematically killing newborns.[93] Poisoning is another controversial area where the colonial mind probably perceived more than reality warranted, particularly during the twenty years of paranoia that followed the Macandal affair of 1758. Women were quite frequently implicated, usually for administering poisons rather than making them. As domestic servants they had easy access to whites. The poisoning of livestock, conversely, was always attributed to males.[94]

In the great revolution and war of independence that stretched from 1791 to 1803, there was considerable continuity in women's roles with the colonial past.[95] The provision of food for the insurgent forces became, in large degree, the work of women. Women continued to raise families, often under perilous conditions, fleeing with their children from camp to camp and enduring extreme hunger during the early years of the slave revolt. Like male slaves, women played a diversity of roles in the initial uprisings. Some helped whites to flee or fled with them. Others killed off the dying, smashing their heads with bricks and "mutilating corpses in a thousand ways, ceasing only when the body was in pieces."[96] Women predominated among the slaves who took refuge in the towns or abandoned the rebel camps to surrender. However, white prisoners in the camps found that "the women were infinitely harsher and more insolent than the men, and less inclined to return to their duties."[97] "A refiner, having been shot," an eyewitness recalled, "was left for dead, and afterward some slave women insisted on the barbaric pleasure of making him smell their private parts."[98] Black women mocked their female captives: "You're now my slave." They made them their servants, undressed them, and beat them for minor pretexts.[99] As the world turned upside down, lifetimes of suppressed rage spilled forth.

In the early battles, when African styles prevailed, rows of women and children preceded the fighters, dancing, chanting, and screaming to encourage their men and to scare their opponents. Some female slaves visited the camps of the colonists to trade sexual favors openly for powder and shot. And at least a few women fought as soldiers, as in Biassou's daring raid on Cap Français hospital, in which he carried off his female relatives.[100] How common this was is difficult to ascertain, not least because some rebel women dressed as men.[101] After the Spanish entered the war in 1793 on the side of the slave insurgents, the black leaders became generals and colonels, and their womenfolk made the transition to society ladies. They learned to speak French and to read, and attended balls in the frontier towns in finery.[102] With the defeat of the Spanish, they accompanied their menfolk into pensioned exile.[103]

Plantation life continued in many parts of Saint Domingue through the course of the Haitian Revolution. Under the remunerated forced labor regime introduced by the French Republic, women laborers were paid usually one-third less than men.[104] On the western and southern estates where slavery was maintained by British invaders, females, especially creoles, still ran away less often than males, although when large-scale desertions took place participation was more equal.[105] Those who remained behind were often regarded as spies for the insurgents. The British occupation of 1793–98 critically divided the free colored population in several ways, and when the British withdrew they were accompanied by several hundred free coloreds, mostly females.[106]

The Haitian Revolution involved more than ever the entire population in its final epic stages, during the War of Knives (between the former slaves and free coloreds) and the War of Independence (1802–3). In the countryside, women and children acted as spies, and they were known to shoot at passing French troops and to kill off the wounded left after ambushes.[107] It is also in this period that women emerged more clearly as individuals. The stories of Sanite Bélair before the firing squad and Marie-Jeanne at La Crête a Pierrot are told in most histories of the revolution. Less known is Henriette de Saint-Marc, executed by the French, who was among several free colored women who prostituted themselves to French soldiers to obtain munitions, which they passed to the insurgents. Along with the "tigresses" of the siege of Jacmel and the untold numbers of women bayoneted, drowned, or hanged by Rochambeau's troops, these women's heroism has become part of the legend of Haiti's struggle for freedom. Haiti's freedom was purchased nevertheless mainly with the lives of men. More than reversing the sexual imbalance of the colonial period, this probably helped enracinate polygyny in the countryside and enabled the new state to begin life with a strongly positive growth rate.

Notes

1. A. Gautier, *Les Soeurs de Solitude: La Condition féminine dans l'esclavage aux Antilles du XVIIe au XIX siècle* (Paris, Editions Caribéennes: 1985); also A. Gautier, "Les Esclaves femmes aux Antilles françaises," *Reflexions Historiques* 10, no. 3 (Fall 1983), an abridgement of the larger work.

2. Archives Nationales, Section d'Outre-Mer, Aix en Provence (hereafter "ANOM"), G1/509, censuses 1681–1788; University of Florida Library, Gainesville, Rare Books, MS., "Tableau de la population . . . 1789." The claim that only 5 percent of the slaves were female, made in the abolitionist tract *Le More Lack* (Paris, 1789) and bizarrely attributed to the historian Gabriel Debien in M. Morrissey, *Slave Women in the New World: Gender Stratification in the Caribbean* (Lawrence: University Press of Kansas, 1989), pp. 35, 170, is an error; so, too, is the statement that men "were more than twice as numerous as the women," in Carolyn Fick, *The Making of Haiti: The Saint Domingue Revolution from Below* (Knoxville, 1990), p. 51.

3. See the 1687 census figures in H. Pauleus Sannon, *Histoire de Toussaint-Louverture* (Port-au-Prince, 1920–33), vol. 1, viii.

4. D. Geggus, "Sex Ratio, Age and Ethnicity in the Atlantic Slave Trade," *Journal of African History* 30, no. 1 (1989), pp. 24, 26n.

5. The lower female mortality rates seem attributable chiefly to genetic factors.

6. M.-L.-E. Moreau de Saint-Méry, *Description . . . de la partie françoise de l'isle Saint-Domingue* [1797], ed. B. Maurel and E. Tailemite (Paris: Société Française d'Histoire d'Outre-Mer, 1958; hereafter "MSM"), vol. 1, pp. 44, 57.

7. The average sex ratio of imported slaves was 201 in the 1780s, 175 in the 1760s and 1770s, and 189 in the period 1715–57; D. Geggus, "The Demographic Composition of the French Caribbean Slave Trade," in *French Colonial Historical Society: Proceedings of the 13/14th Annual Conferences*, ed. P. Boucher (Lanham, Md.: University Press of America, 1990), p. 24.

8. D. Geggus, "Sugar and Coffee Cultivation in Saint Domingue and the Shaping of the Slave Labor Force," in *Cultivation and Culture: Labor and the Shaping of Slave Life in the Americas*, ed. I. Berlin and P. Morgan (Charlottesville: University Press of Virginia, 1993), pp. 73–98. This study is based on slave lists from several hundred plantations.

9. This statement is based on analysis of ethnicity data concerning nearly 8,000 slaves of known origin from eighty sugar, coffee, and indigo plantations in the period 1778–91.

10. Geggus, "Sex Ratio," pp. 23–26, and "Demographic Composition," pp. 24, 28; Gautier, *Les Soeurs*, pp. 79–80; N. Vanony-Frisch, "Les Esclaves de la Guadeloupe à la fin de l'Ancien Régime d'après les sources notariales, 1770–1789," *Bulletin de la Société d'Histoire de la Guadeloupe* 63 (1985): 50–55. However, Jamaica in 1789 seems to have had a slightly higher sex ratio; *Two Reports on the Slave Trade to Jamaica* (London, 1789), p. 9. As the sex ratio of its imported slaves was consistently lower, this suggests perhaps that Saint Domingue's slaves suffered a much higher mortality rate.

11. Geggus, "Sex Ratio," pp. 40–44, and "Demographic Composition," pp. 17, 21. Planters always paid higher prices for males. The male/female price differential apparently was considerable in the mid-seventeenth century, and some sources show a gap of at least 17 percent as late as the 1770s. However, a differential of 5 percent or so was more typical of the 1770s and 1780s, when most imported slaves went to coffee plantations: P. Pelleprat, *Relations des missions des R.P. de la Compagnie de Jesus* (Paris: 1655), p. 55; H. de Branche et al., *Plantations d'Amérique et papiers de famille* (Mâcon, 1960), vol. 2, p. 42; Archives Nationales, Paris (hereafter "AN"), 18 AP 3, letters of 3 November 1774, 8 February 1777, 24 February and 28 December 1778; AN, 107 AP 128, dossier 1, letter of 28 February 1789. Rising demand for slaves in general also seems to have pulled up the price of females, and the high sex ratios of the 1780s were due primarily to concentration on the Bantu regions.

12. Gautier, *Les Soeurs*, p. 204, lists only ten women among a sample of thirty-nine cooks in the period 1721–70. Later in the century almost all cooks were men; D. Geggus, "The Slaves of British-Occupied Saint Domingue: An Analysis of the Workforces of 197 Absentee Plantations," *Caribbean Studies* 18 (1978): 33, and "Sugar and Coffee," table 11.

13. J. B. Labat, *Nouveau Voyage aux isles de l'Amérique* (Paris, 1742), vol. 4, p. 191; D. Geggus, "Les Esclaves de la plaine du Nord à la veille de la Révolution française partie IV," *Revue de la Société Haïtienne d'Histoire* 149 (1985): 29; M. Robinson, "Population Structure on Saint Domingue Sugar Plantations during the 1770s," term paper, 1988, History Department, University of Florida.

14. Geggus, "Sex Ratio," p. 37; O. Dapper, *Description de l'Afrique* (Amsterdam, 1686), pp. 326, 367.

15. Fewer than half the field slaves actually cut cane at any one time; J. Barre de Saint-Venant, *Des Colonies modernes sous la zone torride* (Paris, 1802), pp. 368–69.

16. Labat, *Nouveau voyage*, vol. 4, p. 191.

17. Barré de Saint-Venant, *Des Colonies*, pp. 346–48; S. J. Ducoeurjoly, *Manuel des habitants de Saint-Domingue* (Paris, 1802), vol. 1, p. 180.

18. G. Debien, *Les Esclaves aux Antilles françaises* (Basse-Terre: Société d'Histoire de la Guadeloupe, 1974), pp. 135, 353 (my translation). On indigo plantations all tasks were shared by both sexes except the extremely arduous beating of fermenting pulp done only by men; G. Debien, "A Saint-Domingue avec deux jeunes économes," *Revue de la Société Haïtienne d'Histoire* 58 (1945): 30.

19. Geggus, "Les Esclaves . . . partie IV," and "Sugar and Coffee," table 10 and n. 30.

20. See Gautier, *Les Soeurs*, pp. 266–67; Geggus, "Slaves," pp. 8–9, 33. Geggus, "Sugar and Coffee," p. 84, gives 12.7 percent of men and 4.1 percent of women as specialists in a sample of 2,000 coffee plantation slaves.

21. D. Geggus, "Urban Development in Eighteenth-Century Saint Domingue," *Bulletin du Centre d'Histoire des Espaces Atlantiques* 5 (1990), 197–228.

22. The renting or purchase of accommodations by slaves was banned in 1785, but it is not known with what results.

23. Labat, *Nouveau voyage*, vol. 4, p. 203; Debien, *Les Esclaves*, p. 90.

24. Labat, *Nouveau voyage*, vol. 4, p. 196.

25. This paragraph is based on data in Geggus, "Sugar and Coffee," tables 10 and 11, and "Slavery," table 10.

26. MSM, vol. 1, 61, p. 520; Ducoeurjoly, *Manuel*, vol. 2, pp. 116–21; J. Girod de Chantrans, *Voyage d'un Suisse dans différentes colonies d'Amérique* [1785], ed. P. Pluchon (Paris: Tallandier, 1980), pp. 136, 152.

27. P. Pluchon, *Vandou, sorciers, empoisonneurs* (Paris: Karthala, 1987), pp. 223–29.

28. D. Geggus, "Haitian Voodoo in the Eighteenth Century: Language Culture, Resistance," *Jahrbuch für Geschichte von Staat, Wirtschaft und Gessellschaft Lateinamerikas* 28 (1991): 24, 32, 35, 47, 49, and "The Bois Caiman Ceremony," *Journal of Caribbean History* 25 (1991): 41–57.

29. Pelleprat, *Relation*, pp. 51–52.

30. Debien, *Les Esclaves*, pp. 156, 208.

31. Gautier, "Les Esclaves femmes," p. 414; M. E. Descourtilz, *Voyages d'un naturaliste* (Paris, 1809), vol. 3, p. 192.

32. A creole expression, from the Spanish *mancornar*, "to tie by the horns."

33. Bibliothèque Mazarine, Paris, MS. 3453, pp. 28–29 (my translation).

34. Debien, *Les Esclaves*, pp. 250–79; Labat, *Nouveau voyage*, vol. 4, p. 454.

35. Gautier, "Les Esclaves femmes," pp. 420–21.

36. Debien, *Les Esclaves*, pp. 350–51.

37. D. Geggus, "Les Esclaves de la plaine du Nord . . . partie II," *Revue de la Société Haïtienne d'Histoire* 136 (1982): 18–20.

38. A.N., Paris, 107 AP 127–130, Odeluc's letterbooks; Geggus, "Les Esclaves . . . partie III," *Revue de la Société Haïtienne d'Histoire* 144 (1984): 34.

39. F. Wimpffen, *Voyage to St. Domingo in the Years 1788, 1789 and 1790* (London, 1817), p. 234.

40. Girod de Chantrans, *Voyage*, pp. 132–35.

41. Cf. Gautier, *Les Soeurs*, pp. 38, 53; MSM, vol. 1, p. 53.

42. Bibliothèque Municipale, Auxerre, MS. 331; Bibliothèque Mazarine, MS. 3453, pp. 31–33; Girod de Chantrans, *Voyage*, p. 136; MSM, vol. 1, pp. 57, 59–61. Several other sources add that slaveowners took a share of the money their slaves made through prostitution; see Gautier, *Les Soeurs*, p. 164.

43. Labat, *Nouveau voyage*, vol. 4, p. 470; Bibliothèque Mazarine, MS. 3453, pp. 31–33.

44. Even by Caribbean standards, the sex ratio was exceptionally high among whites; MSM, vol. 1, p. 107.

45. P. Pluchon, *Nègres et Juifs au XVIIIe siècle* (Paris: Tallandier, 1984), pp. 166–72; also see Girod de Chantrans, *Voyage*, pp. 140–41, and n. 57 below.

46. Had the Inquisition operated in the French colonies, historians might well have found documentation of a much broader range of sexual abuses and activities, as Luiz Mott has uncovered for colonial Brazil; see Mott, *O sexo prohibido: Virgens, gays e escravos* (Campinas: Papinas, 1988), pp. 17–74.

47. Gautier, *Les Soeurs*, pp. 168–71.

48. *Précis des gémissements des sang-mêlés dans les colonies françoises, par J. M. C. Américain, Sang-Mêlé* (Paris, 1789), p. 12.

49. De Branche et al., *Plantations d'Amérique*, vol. 2, pp. 42–43.

50. Geggus, "Sugar and Coffee," pp. 92–93, and "Slaves," p. 34.

51. MSM, vol. 1, pp. 57–58.

52. MSM, vol. 2, p. 585.

53. A.N. Paris, 18 AP 3, Bayon de Libertat to Comte de Bréda, 18 April 1784, 8 February 1777.

54. Gautier, *Les Soeurs*, pp. 261–65.

55. See n. 57. This view is incompatible with the assertion in P. F. Venault de Charmilly, *Lettre à M. Bryan Edwards* (London, 1797), p. 14, that creole females would not have sexual relations with Africans. Probably neither is correct.

56. Girod de Chantrans, *Voyage*, pp. 138–39; Labat, *Nouveau voyage*, vol. 4, p. 470; Descourtilz, *Voyages*, vol. 3, pp. 193–95; n. 57.

57. MSM, vol. 1, p. 57.

58. Bibliothèque Mazarin, MS. 3453, pp. 31–33.

59. MSM, vol. 1, 60–61.

60. Ibid. Cf. note 38; P.J. Laborie, *The Coffee Planter of St. Domingo* (London, 1797), pp. 169–70; M. R. Hilliard d'Auberteuil, *Considérations sur l'état présent de la colonie française de Saint-Domingue* (Paris, 1776–77), vol. 2, p. 66; Gautier, *Les Soeurs*, 97–98; MSM, vol. 3, p. 1272; Girod de Chantrans, *Voyage*, pp. 129, 136; Descourtilz, *Voyages*, vol. 3, pp. 201–3.

61. On the Galliffet estates in the 1780s, 36 percent of infants whose births were recorded died before the age of two; Geggus, "Esclaves . . . partie III," p. 35.

62. Geggus, "Sugar and Coffee," table 12.

63. Spearman's correlation test yielded $p = .09$; $r = .29$; $N = 33$. This was the only correlation found to be significant at the 10 percent level. Other variations tested were workforce size and sex ratio, the proportion of females sick/disabled, the percentage of females in the fertile age-band who were creoles and who were aged 25–34 (the late twenties being the period of peak fertility).

64. MSM, vol. 1, p. 60, mentions the practice of a long breast-feeding period accompanied by a taboo on sexual intercourse but does not link it specifically to African women. Moreau de Saint-Méry added that the taboo applied only to intercourse with men other than the child's father. On the Galliffet plantations babies were weaned at two years: AN, Paris, 107 AP, pp. 127–30, Odeluc letterbooks.

65. Geggus, "Sugar and Coffee," table 9. The height data derive from runaway notices in the colonial newspaper, *Les Affiches Américaines*.

66. MSM, vol. 1, p. 60.

67. Debien, *Les Esclaves,* pp. 352–56; Gautier, *Les Soeurs,* pp. 107–24.

68. Gautier, *Les Soeurs,* pp. 113–14.

69. However, see Debien, *Les Esclaves,* p. 319.

70. Geggus, "Slaves," pp. 29–30, and "Sugar and Coffee."

71. Geggus, "Esclaves . . . partie IV," p. 39.

72. Gautier, *Les Soeurs,* p. 172.

73. Data from A.N., Paris, C9A/158, p. 37, and C9A 159, p. 183; C9B/37, letter of 16 January 1787; F. Barbé de Marbois, *Etat des finances de Saint-Domingue* (Port-au-Prince, 1789); Chevalier de Proisy, *Etat des finances de Saint-Domingue* (Paris, 1790).

74. Quadroons were persons with one white and one mulatto parent.

75. Most censuses show that boys in the free colored population outnumbered girls, although women outnumbered men; ANOM, Aix, G1/509.

76. Gautier, *Les Soeurs,* pp. 174–75.

77. De Proisy, *Etat,* table iv.

78. David P. Geggus, "The Major Port Cities of Saint Domingue," in *Atlantic Port Cities: Economy, Culture, and Society,* ed. P. Liss and F. Knight (Knoxville: University of Tennessee Press, 1991), pp. 87–116.

79. De Proisy, *Etat,* table x; University of Florida Library, Rare Books, MS., "Tableau de la population . . . 1789."

80. D. Geggus, "The Major Port Cities," attempts to reconcile some of the discrepancies in colonial statistics.

81. Geggus, "Urban Development."

82. MSM, vol. 1, p. 102; D. Geggus, *Slavery, War and Revolution: The British Occupation of Saint Domingue* (Oxford University Press, 1982), pp. 18–23, 325–27.

83. I am assuming that the free *domestiques* listed in the censuses were mainly women.

84. MSM, vol. 1, pp. 104–10; Girod de Chantrans, *Voyage,* pp. 152–55; Bibliothèque Mazarine, MS. 3453, p. 9; C. Malenfant, *De Saint-Domingue* (Paris, 1814), pp. 162–63.

85. Geggus, *Slavery,* p. 326.

86. Girod de Chantrans, *Voyage,* p. 154.

87. ANOM, G1/495.

88. ANOM, Notariat de Saint-Domingue.

89. ANOM, Notariat de Saint-Domingue, sample of 154 cases taken from the North Province, 1775–89.

90. D. Geggus, "On the Eve of the Haitian Revolution: Slave Runaways in Saint Domingue in the Year 1790," in G. Heuman, ed., *Out of the House of Bondage* (London: Frank Cass, 1985), p. 117; *Affiches Américaines,* Feuille du Cap François, 1788, no. 41, and Feuille du Port-au-Prince, 1789, no. 62, and 1790, no. 91.

91. Geggus, "On the Eve," pp. 115, 120 (2,652 cases); *Affiches Américaines,* Feuille du Cap François, 1788 (1,253 cases).

92. *Affiches Américaines,* Feuille du Cap François, 1788, no. 41, and Feuille du Port-au-Prince, 1789, no. 62, and 1790, no. 91.

93. Gautier, *Les Soeurs,* p. 98. On midwifery and infantile tetanus, see also J. Cauna, "L'Etat sanitaire des esclaves sur une grande sucrerie," *Revue de la Société Haïtienne d'Histoire* 148 (1984): 145.

94. Pluchon, *Vaudou,* chaps. 6–9.

95. This passage is based on David P. Geggus, *The Saint Domingue Slave Revolt* (forthcoming).

96. Service Historique de la Marine, Vincennes, MS. 113, p. 657 (my translation); Bibliothèque Municipal, Nantes, MS. 1809, p. 188.

97. Gros, *Isle Saint-Domingue, Province du Nord* (Paris, 1793), p. 12.

98. A.N., F3/141, p. 212.

99. Bibl. Mun., Nantes, MS. 1809, p. 193.

100. Bibl. Mun., Auxerre, MS. 331, p. 105; A.N., F3/141, p. 214. Armed slave women also joined André Rigaud's free colored slave army in the West Province in 1791: G. Debien, *Une Plantation de Saint-Domingue: La sucrerie* Galbaud du Fort (Le Caire, 1941), p. 112.

101. Archivo General de Indias, Sevilla, Aud. Santo Domingo, 1089, letter 548, enclosure no. 4. A cult priestess named Madame Paget, called "The Virgin," dressed in male clothing when she participated in the Fort Dauphin massacre of July 1794, in which she killed three of the 790 white victims; Public Record Office, London, WO 1/65, p. 809.

102. Bibl. Mun., Rouen, MS. Leber 5847, pp. 61–62. The Spanish pressed the black leaders into giving up their concubines and going through church weddings.

103. Arch. Gen. Indias, Estado, Va. Of the 780 former rebels to whom the Spanish gave asylum, 334 were women and 94 were children.

104. "Documents. Aux origines de l'abolition de l'esclavage," *Revue d'Histoire des Colonies* 36 (1949): 52, 353, 401, 422.

105. Geggus, "Slaves," pp. 36–40.

106. Geggus, *Slavery,* p. 406. Only one-third of the seventy-five free blacks but almost all of the 242 of mixed racial descent were females.

107. Drouin de Bercy, *De Saint-Domingue* (Paris, 1814), pp. 59–60.

14

ECONOMIC ROLES OF THE FREE WOMEN OF COLOR OF CAP FRANÇAIS

Susan M. Socolow

Although the role of women in twentieth-century Caribbean society has been well documented, little research has looked at women as either social or economic actors in earlier periods. Some recent studies have begun to remedy this omission, concentrating on women in slavery during the eighteenth century, but while the history of female slaves is an important topic for future research, another group of Caribbean women, the free women of color, should not be ignored.[1] In the French Caribbean, free women of color (*femmes de couleur libre*) included all black (*négresse*), mulatto (*mulâtresse*), quadroon (*cuarteronne* or *quarteronne*) and other mixed-blood (*griffe* and *mestive*) women who were either born free or manumitted.[2]

Médéric-Louis-Elie Moreau de Saint-Méry, the most famous observer of late eighteenth-century Saint Domingue (present-day Haiti), left a vivid portrait of free women of color in general and mulatto women in particular. In his view (and in the view of many of his French contemporaries), the free women of color were sensual, lascivious creatures, who made their way in life by using their sexual attraction and prowess to ensnare white lovers. Referring to these women as "priestesses of Venus" and "courtesans," he explained how "the entire being of a mulatto woman is given up to love."[3]

> Captivating all the senses, surrendering them to the most delicious ecstasies, holding them in suspense by the most seductive raptures: those are her whole study. Nature, in some way the accessory to pleasure, has given her charms, appeal, and sensibility. She also has what is definitely more dangerous: the talent for trying her hand at greater delights than ever her partner could equal. She knows pleasure of which not even the code of Paphos contains all the secrets.

Moreau de Saint-Méry also saw the mulatto women who lived for and from love as spending all their time and money in adorning their bodies.

Everything that India produces best, of the more valuable muslins, kerchiefs, and stuffs and clothes, goes for fashionable clothes to embellish the colored woman. Rich laces, jewels whose abundance even more than their kind augments their value, are used plentifully. The desire for costly attire is so insatiable that one sees plenty of mulatto women in Saint Domingue who could change their clothes completely, day by day, for a year.[4]

While the mulatto women carried their luxury to the nth degree, they disdained caring for their clothes and jewels, wastefully refusing to wear them more than a few times.[5]

This chapter is an attempt to test the validity of Moreau de Saint-Méry's charges and to describe the role of free women of color in the economy of pre-revolutionary Cap Français, the chief urban center of the colony. Were these women extravagant creatures who earned their living as mistresses or prostitutes, as Moreau de Saint-Méry suggests, or did they have varied occupational and economic roles?

To study the free women of color of Cap Français, I have examined a sample of notary records of the city. In eighteenth-century Saint Domingue, as in France, notaries were required to keep exact copies of all legally binding transactions. The notary books present a chronological record of sales, contracts, and other legal agreements; they also document the gender, race, and legal condition of the individuals involved in these transactions. These papers therefore contain a wealth of information reflecting day-to-day economic transactions of all social groups. Notary records do not contain all transactions (many sales, for example, were made informally or privately), but they do indicate what we may consider a minimal level of social and economic interaction. The wealth of information recorded in a notary's books also provides us with some of the critical outlines of the lives of individuals and groups. The sample of notary transactions which I have examined includes the agreements notarized before the notary Bordier the younger during a three-year period, 1782–1784. Bordier was the longest practicing notary in Cap Français, having worked there since 1776. His offices were located in the center of town. The period represents a sample of the late French colonial era, the apogee of the colony's prosperity.

At first glance, what is most striking about the free colored population (*gens de couleur libre*) of Cap Français is the frequency with which they appear in the notary's records. Over the three-year period under consideration, free people of color were involved in 315 recorded transactions before Bordier. Free women accounted for 178 (56.5 percent) of these. From a purely quantitative viewpoint, free people of color of the Cap were an active element in the social and economic life of the city and its surrounding region, entering into contracts, drawing up wills, buying and selling, and settling marriage contracts.

During the eighteenth century, Cap Français was the most prosperous city of the French overseas empire. One of two urban centers of colonial Saint Domingue, the Cap had been the first seat of the colonial government. As such it had monopolized all urban functions for the entire colony until the 1760s, when Saint Domingue was divided into three districts and the rival city of Port-au-Prince became the administrative center of the southern section of the colony. However, as the capital of the northern district of Saint Domingue, the Cap continued to have an important administrative and judicial role. The northern area included within the city's jurisdiction was the first zone of the colony to be transformed into an economy dependent upon the plantation production of sugar. Cap Français was, above all, a commercial city and port which provided services for the lucrative plantations of the plains. There, sugar and coffee were exported and slaves and luxury goods were imported. Moreau de Saint-Méry referred to Cap Français in 1789 as "the largest urban center in the French colony, the principal seat of its wealth and its luxury; the place of greatest commerce."[6]

According to official tabulations, the total population of Cap Français in 1771 was 6,353. By 1780 the city and surrounding regions had a population of approximately 7,000.[7] The black and mulatto slave population of the Cap far outstripped any other group, representing approximately 60 percent of the population. Next in numerical strength were whites (20.6 percent) and free people of color, who totaled 1,391 (19.5 percent). Nonetheless, free coloreds were almost as numerous as whites and, indeed, were growing at a faster rate. Women were in the majority only among free coloreds. (See table 1.) Free colored women in Cap Français, however, were outnumbered by slave women.

Occupational information about women in general is rather incomplete, but the notary records reveal that free women of color worked as housekeepers (*ménagères*), managers charged with running large domestic establishments. Because these women worked only for white men, the term *ménagère* was possibly a euphemism for mistress.[8] On the other hand, relatively few free women of color (or free colored men) seem to have been attracted to careers as less prestigious domestic servants. While the notary records contain an occasional mention of free colored servants, the aggregate population totals for Cap Français for 1780 list no one under the rubric "colored domestics."[9] Evidently, free coloreds behaved like the white population of the city, eschewing an occupation which was clearly identified with urban slaves.[10] Salaries for housekeepers seem to have been 600 livres per year. Although no proof has been found, it is possible that some free women of color owned and operated inns, as did those of eighteenth-century Barbados.[11] The notary records contain no direct mention of prostitution, but the sale of a twenty-year-old black slave named Nancy to Sieur Jean François Theize for the astronomical sum of 19,180 livres suggests that her original owner, Delphine, a free quadroon, had trained the woman in the world's oldest profession and was perhaps herself a madam.[12]

Notary records reveal that buying and selling various articles of merchandise was an important way for free black and mulatto women to earn or supplement a living. Descriptions of female occupations included shopkeeper (*marchande*), grease dealer (*marchande de graisserie*), and greengrocer (*marchande de légumes*).[13] Beyond these specific occupational designations, notary records also

TABLE 1. Sex by Racial Group, Cap Français, 1780

| | Male | | Female | | |
	N	%	N	%	Total
Free people of color	643	46.2	748	53.8	1,391
Whites	874	59.3	599	40.7	1,473
Slaves	2,299	53.6	1,988	46.4	4,287
Total	3,816	53.4	3,335	46.6	7,151

Source: Archives Nationales de France, Section Outre Mer, G1-509.

provide vivid examples of the activities of free women in the marketplace, which ran the gamut of retail trade from the management of shops to running market stalls to peddling. The role of women in the markets of West Africa is well known, and historians and social scientists have also noted the continuation of this cultural pattern in areas of the Americas to which large numbers of African slaves were brought.[14] At Cap Français, however, free women moved beyond hawking and became established small merchants, alongside white middle-class women who ran small commercial establishments and shops.[15]

Much like their white counterparts, free black and mulatto women of Cap Français appear in the notary records entering into contracts to buy and sell real property. They frequently owned both urban and rural property. Marie Archard, a free mulatto woman, appeared before Bordier in 1783 to sell a piece of rural property located in Haut du Cap to Fauchonnette Zervine, another free mulatto.[16] Archard had acquired the rhomboid-shaped property, described as sixty feet wide (along the main road) by seventy-three feet in depth, through two purchases—one in 1777 from a free black and another two years later from a white landowner. Archard had enhanced the land's value by having a two-room wooden building constructed. The land, which adjoined property belonging to a free black woman and a white widow, had a value of 2,400 livres. The free mulatto purchaser paid for the property in cash. Free women of color who owned small pieces of rural property earned their livelihood by cultivating garden plots. These lands were located primarily in Haut du Cap. Proprietors produced enough fruits and vegetables to feed themselves and to supply the markets of the city.

Free black women also owned urban property, which they either purchased themselves or, more frequently, inherited from their late husbands.[17] Jeanne Blaise, a widowed free black woman (*négresse libre*), sold a piece of the property she inherited from her free black husband, Ignace Pompée, located at the corner of Rue Royalle and Rue de la Vieille Boucherie in the city.[18] The property, which measured twenty-two by thirty feet, contained one small building with two rooms ("a room facing the street of palisade construction [poles covered with mud], tiled and covered with shingles and a smaller room of the same construction except that it was not tiled."[19] Marie, the free black widow of Alexandre

Scipion, a resident of Haut du Cap, purchased the property. When the final contract was drawn up, Marie had already paid 6,600 livres for the property.

Some of the recorded purchases of land were sales in which both buyer and seller were free people of color, but real property located in urban and rural areas was also frequently bought from or sold to white inhabitants. Sieur Jean Bauptiste Ottin, a white inhabitant of the city, sold a property measuring "7 or 8 *carreaux*" (16.4 to 18.8 acres) along the north coast to Elisabeth, a free mulatto, who also lived in Cap Français.[20] Elisabeth paid 3,550 of the 8,500 livres that the property cost in cash, promising to pay the rest within six months.[21] Likewise, Sieur Raymond Bernard Brousse, a local white merchant, sold a smaller piece of land in L'Embarcadaire de la petite Anse, directly across the river from Cap Français, to Marie Thérèse Morin, a free mulatto, who paid the full price of 3,000 livres in cash.[22] On the other hand, Marie Sanitte, a free mulatto of Cap Français, sold land in Fort Dauphin, a town forty kilometers east of Cap Français, to Sieur Charles Jean Baptiste Nicolas, a surgeon residing there.[23] Ten years earlier, Marie had purchased the property located in a section of town called Petite Guinée from Sieur Gavaret, another white inhabitant.

Widows of successful free black and mulatto artisans showed a special penchant for investing in expensive real estate. Rose Angelique, a free mulatto and the young widow of Jacques Magnon, a free mulatto, purchased a large house and the surrounding property at the corner of Rue Espagnole and Rue de Cimetière.[24] The house was bought for the handsome sum of 64,000 livres. The previous owner, a white carpenter, received 30,000 livres in cash and extended a seven-year mortgage, with a total interest payment of 1,000 livres (or 3 percent) on the outstanding balance. While some widows acted for themselves in buying and selling property, others, especially those who inherited real estate far from Cap Français, granted powers of attorney to their kinfolk to buy and sell in their name.[25]

Free women of color also participated actively in the real property market as owners, renters, subletters, and sublettees. Those with urban or semirural holdings rented to other people of color as well as to whites. Because urban property was in short supply, owners could demand more than simple rent payment. Suzanne Alestre, a free black, for example, signed a seven-year contract with Jean Baptiste Viau, a free mulatto, to rent him a house and property which she owned on the corner of the Rue Saint Louis and the Rue des Trois Visages.[26] In addition to the 12,000 livres annual rent, Viau agreed to make several improvements to the property. Both single women and widows owned rental property which, depending on its location and size, could be rented for 200 to 12,000 livres per year.[27] At least two colored widows held choice urban property that was desirable to white tenants. The widow Marie Catherine Yris, a free black, and her free mulatto sons and daughters owned a house on the Rue Penthièvre which consisted of a large room, three smaller rooms, three closets, a kitchen, a hall, a courtyard, and a well.[28] In 1784 the house was leased to Dame Geneviève Aurignac, widow of a planter from Dondon, who paid a yearly rent of 3,400 livres. An even more

elaborate building, on the corner of the Rue du Conseil and the Rue de Penthièvre, belonged to the same Marie Catherine Yris and her children and was
rented to Messieurs Faion and Desquilbe, merchants, for 8,000 livres per year.[29]

Free women of color of Cap Français sometimes acted as absentee landlords.
Suzanne Alestre resided in Limbé, a town twenty kilometers to the southwest,
when she rented a property to Jean Baptiste Viau.[30] Other prosperous free
women of color held rental property in rural areas or other towns of the colony.
Marie Marthe Cabeche, a free black widow residing in the Cap, rented several
rooms in a building she owned in the vicinity of Fort Dauphin.[31] Some widows
inherited property from deceased husbands, while others seem to have acquired
property on their own.

Not all free women of color in Cap Français owned property. Those who
owned none were usually forced to rent urban space which, because of its scarcity, was at a premium. Elisabeth Bonne Femme, a free black merchant (her
store was located on the corner of Rue Royalle and Saint François Xavier),
sublet a three-room apartment on the Rue Saint François Xavier from Sieur
Arnaud Romain, the court bailiff, who leased the entire building from Dame
Dechamflour.[32] Bonne Femme agreed to occupy the quarters for a five-year
period, paying 3,300 livres per year in rent. Nine months later, she sublet part
of her living quarters to Victoire Arelise, a free black, who, in addition to assuming half of the rent, agreed to pay half the expenses incurred in splitting the
original apartment into two.[33] We can only imagine the economic conditions
which forced Bonne Femme to subdivide her already cramped quarters so that
she could maintain a residence in the central section of the city. Bonne Femme's
limited economic circumstances are also suggested by the fact that the contract
called for Arelise to pay her half of the rent on the very same day that payment
was due Sieur Romain.

Free women of color rented property from other free people of color as well as
from whites. Claire Clairone, a free mulatto, rented a small building located on
the Rue Royalle near the Rue de la Boucherie from Guilleaume Provoyeur, a
prosperous mulatto builder.[34] According to the terms of the contract, she was to
pay an annual rent of 2,400 livres for four years. These quarters were luxurious
when compared with the small rooms rented by two free black women, Louise
Tarhigy and Maria Louise Atraitté, in a building owned by Joseph Pironneau, a
free quadroon.[35] For their one-room apartments, which they leased on a monthly
basis, each women paid between 1,385 and 1,480 livres per year. At the other
end of the rental scale, Ann Claire, a free black, was able to afford a rent of
14,500 livres per year for the house at the corner of Rue Royalle and Rue du
Hazard, which she rented from Paul le Merle, a free mulatto.[36]

In addition to their frequent appearance in the notary records in transactions involving buying or renting real property, free women of color participated in a wide variety of transactions, sometimes providing liquid capital or
availing themselves of loans to cover goods and services. Catherine, a free mulatto woman living on the Rue Saint-Joseph, lent 1,800 livres in cash to a local

mulatto butcher who mortgaged all his property and promised to repay the sum in cash or in a "black female slave which she may chose worth 1,800 livres."[37] Marie Louise, a free black widow, sold goods worth 1,000 livres on credit to the free mulatto Charles Imbert.[38] Imbert repaid her over a four-year period, both in cash and by assuming her outstanding debts or financial obligations, which included a church tax of 357 livres that had been assessed against her property over a twenty-five-year period. More usual were shorter-term loans of approximately one month, also tied to the sale of goods on credit.[39]

Free mulatto women, especially those engaged in small retail businesses, in turn looked to local white merchants for credit. Victoire Arelise, who we noted earlier had sublet an apartment, was also the owner of a small shop on Rue Royalle. In 1784 she borrowed 1,260 livres for three months from Sieur Pierre Prisot, a white merchant.[40] Likewise, Jeanne Hulla, a free black, was loaned 2,376 livres in "silver money of Spain" under the same terms.[41] The amounts involved in these transactions suggest that they were loans tied to a sale of goods on credit. Free colored small traders, generally female, purchased their stock from import wholesalers.[42] In addition to borrowing money for business, many free women of color depended on indirect credit arrangements to make improvements to their property. Marie Louise Angelique, a free black widow, employed a free black mason to complete "several masonry jobs," promising to pay him the total charge of 1,930 livres within the year.[43]

More affluent free women of color also appear in the notary registers as purchasers of luxury goods, especially fine furniture. Goods such as "a marble table with its mahogany legs," "a mirror, four and one half feet high, framed in gilded wood," "a case from China complete with twelve porcelain cups, teapot, coffeepot, and sugar bowl," and "a mahogany dressing table with mirror and diverse jars and bottle" were owned by the most prosperous free women of color. These items were among furnishings and luxury goods purchased by Helenne Leveillé, who was able to pay in cash almost 1,500 livres.[44] These articles were much like those preferred by elite white women. Free women of color, however, unlike their white counterparts, often resold personal goods and work implements when they were faced with economic hardship. Indeed, because luxury goods were so highly prized among free women of color for the social prestige that they conveyed, a secondhand market soon developed. In 1783 Marie Anne Debrée, a free black, sold her mahogany wardrobe to another free black woman.[45] Likewise, Anne Join, a free mulatto, sold her furniture to Rosalie, a free black, for 600 livres cash. Also included in this sale were "4 pairs of irons" and "a kettle to heat water for washing and a tub."[46]

While lists of purchases and sales by free women of color support Moreau de Saint-Méry's portrayal of these women as consumers of luxury goods, they also indicate that free women of color frequently bought and sold slaves. Although historians have argued that when free people of color purchased slaves they were, in fact, buying their kin out of slavery, the Cap Français notary papers suggest that free people of color bought and sold slaves for economic profit.

Table 2. Slave Sales by Race of Seller and Purchaser

| | Purchaser | | | |
Seller	White	Free Mulatto	Free Black	Total
White	N.A.	11	2	13
Free Mulatto	13	—	6	19
Free Black	6	1	12	19
Total	19	12	20	51

Indeed, such transactions were the most frequently recorded in the notary register.

Table 2 presents information on the ethnic group of the seller and that of the purchaser from a sample of fifty-one slave sales. Because the focus of this study is the free women of color, no information was collected on sales between whites. The fact that free women of color frequently sold slaves to whites (nineteen of the fifty-one, or 35 percent) points to economic motivation rather than racial solidarity. These slaves were sold to white merchants, shopkeepers, artisans, government and military officers, and landowners by mulattoes and blacks who chose not to identify with their heritage of slavery. Legal condition was far more important than ethnicity in establishing social loyalties, and the gap between a free person of color and a slave was large. The sample also suggests that whites commonly purchased slaves from free mulattoes.

Mulatto purchasers of slaves appear to have preferred to deal with whites, perhaps believing that to buy acculturated slaves who had been previously owned by whites brought them some degree of social cachet. Free blacks, on the other hand, purchased more or less equally from all groups of sellers. Indeed, in several transactions free mulattoes purchased slaves from whites and later resold some of them to free black clients. The overwhelming majority of slaves sold were black; indeed, only two slaves were described as of mixed blood.[47] Free women of color preferred to traffic in African-born slaves. This preference is understandable; massive importation of these slaves in eighteenth-century Saint Domingue made them the most numerous and the cheapest (see table 3).[48]

Not surprisingly, the ethnic origins of the slaves bought and sold by the free women of color also match closely the origins of all African-born slaves imported during the period.[49] However, it is interesting that free women of color preferred to buy and sell female rather than male slaves by approximately three to one, regardless of the origin of the slave. The preference for female slaves is perhaps surprising because the overwhelming number of slaves imported from Africa were males. Free women of color might have preferred to purchase slave women because of gender identification, because they intended to use female slaves as assistants in their occupations, or because they believed they could more easily control slave women.

Free women of color, regardless of their occupations, purchased slaves for their own personal use. To free people of color of Cap Français, as to whites, owner-

Table 3. Origin of Slaves Purchased or Sold by Free Women of Color

Origin	Sex of Slave		
	Male	Female	Total
New World			
Creole	7	11	18
English	—	1	1
Subtotal	7	12	19
Africa			
Congo	5	7	12
Io	—	4	4
Arrada	—	4	4
Sopo	1	—	1
Mandingue	2	—	2
Nago	1	3	4
Senegal	—	1	1
Mesurade	—	1	1
Paular	—	1	1
Other African	1	—	1
Subtotal	10	21	31
Unknown	—	1	1
Total	17	34	51

ship of slaves was a mark of prosperity and social distinction. Of course, slaves also had an economic function, for they were taught marketable skills and employed in money-making activities. Female slaves were commonly trained as washerwomen (*blanchisseuses*).[50] Male slaves filled a host of artisan positions ranging from mattress maker (*matelassieur*) to wig maker (*perruquier pour hommes*).[51]

Some free women of color were active enough in the slave market to suggest that they were minor slave traders or, at least, that they supplemented their income from other pursuits by trading in slaves. Zabeau Bellanton, a free mulatto living on Rue de Penthièvre, sold five slaves within a one-week period for a total of 10,692 livres.[52] Bellanton sold a black slave woman and her four-month-old son to a white merchant, and in another transaction she split up a slave mother and child. In another case, Marie Jeanne, a free black greengrocer with a shop on Rue Saint Sauveur, bought a twenty-five-year-old Congolese male slave from Mathieu Dendré, a free black mason, for 2,000 livres. Later the same day she resold the slave to Jean Pierre l'Allemand, a free black mattress maker, for 2,450 livres.[53]

To reduce costs, free women of color preferred to avoid the local middleman and acquire slaves directly from the incoming slave ship. It is likely that they purchased slaves singly, perhaps from among the "refuse" slaves who were available at bargain prices after the more coveted slaves had been sold.[54] While most slavers could depend on selling the majority of their cargo in large lots to the major slave merchants, there were always a few odd slaves who, because of their health, physical condition, or temperament, were difficult to dispose of; slavers were willing to sell these people at low prices in order to conclude an entire transaction. Mambo Agatha, a free black woman, dealt directly with the ship's captain when she purchased an African woman who had been first sold in Spanish Louisiana.[55] Other free women of color attended the public slave auctions where embargoed cargoes were put on the block. In 1784 Dauphine, a free quadroon, bought an African woman slave in the admiralty auction of the slave cargo aboard the ship *Columbus* from Ostende.[56] Purchasers who were unable to pay cash were forced to buy from the local wholesalers because only they were willing to extend terms of credit or to accept local negotiable instruments. Marie Framillon, a free mulatto, was able to pay for three new slaves "from the Nato nation" by endorsing over a credit for 4,800 livres from Chavanne, a free mulatto, to Sieurs Ceiches et fils ainé, merchants (*négociants*).[57]

Free women of color also bought and sold slaves as agents for others. Paul Lopes, a free black residing in Grande Coucan, built up a cash balance over the years with Anne Rossignol, a free mulatto.[58] When Rossignol had amassed 1,850 livres, she went to the port and purchased a black male slave from Captain Picot, the master of the ship *La Jeune Agathe* from Le Havre. A few days later the slave and a valid bill of sale were forwarded to Lopes. Although neither the purchaser nor his commission agent was literate, there is no indication that the transactions presented any problem. In addition to their roles as agents, many free women of color purchased slaves, invested some time and money in training them, then resold them for a handsome profit. This turnover is reflected in the fact that for the eight sales for which we can document the date of original purchase and resale, the average length of ownership was nearly three years. If we exclude one slave who was owned for about twelve and a half years, this average falls to a little over one year. In three sales, the slave sold by a free woman of color had been hers less than two months.

Prosperous free women of color extended credit to customers and family to facilitate the purchase of slaves. Zabeau Bellanton sold at least one slave by extending 3,300 livres credit to Monsieur Jean Pierre Prunet, a white lawyer; half was to be paid to Bellanton within six months, the rest three months later.[59] Marie Catherine Yris, the free black widow who, along with her children, inherited property on the Rue du Conseil and the Rue de Penthièvre, loaned her son 1,414 livres to purchase a slave.[60] To repay her, he agreed to forgo the rent due him on the Penthièvre property until his mother collected her money.

Like white slaveowners, free women of color branded their slaves to indicate ownership. Merchant Simone Brocard had her slave, an Arrada woman named Delorine, branded with her name ("SIMONE BROCARD") across the chest during the ten days she remained in Brocard's possession.[61] Delphine, a free quadroon, branded her Mesurade slave with the letters "DC" (Delphine cuarteronne), perhaps showing a bit more consideration than Brocard.[62] In another case, Anne Dupont, a free black, made sure that both the owner and her residence were clear in the brand placed on her Congo slave. On the right breast, the slave woman bore the information "ANNE NLN [Negresse libre] AU CAP."[63] In some transactions involving the sale of slaves, free women of color showed an even further lack of consideration. Zabeau Bellanton sold the two-year-old black son of her slave Sophie to Marie Rose, a free black. In the bill of sale, Bellanton clearly stipulated that "the purchaser cannot, under any pretext whatsoever, oblige me to sell her the mother of the said young boy."[64]

Only one sale shows that a free woman of color purchased the slave to improve the slave's condition. In 1782 Marie Claire Magdelon, a free black, purchased Emmanuel, a sixty-five-year-old male Mandingo slave suffering from ulcerated legs, from a white planter. Magdelon stated that "her only reason for buying the said Emmanuel is to help him because of the state of his illness and his advanced age."[65] Far more frequently, slaves were bought as workers or as investments for the purchaser or her children. Leonore Mathou, a free mulatto, bought two slaves from Pierre Arguiron, slaver, for her children, Françoise Minguet and Pierre Alborti, free quadroons.[66]

In Saint Domingue free blacks and mulattoes, like whites, viewed slaves as the currency of the realm. Slaves were used to settle outstanding debts. Marie Magdelaine Garette, a free mulatto and housekeeper for Sieur Vincent Oyé, a merchant, was paid 1,200 livres in back wages (two years' salary) in the form of a "newly imported little girl of the Susso nation," twelve-year-old Rosette.[67] The next year, Oyé again paid Marie Magdelaine in slaves. This time he turned over a mother and child, twenty-six-year-old Hortense "of the Mina nation" and her three-year-old daughter.[68] Because the total value of this couple was more than twice the wages due her (2,500 livres), Marie Magdelaine agreed to pay off the outstanding debt by mortgaging future wages. In essence, after six years of work as a housekeeper, Marie Magdelaine owned three female slaves. Similarly, the free black housekeeper Catin Romus converted her 600 livres per year salary working for Sieur Antoine Peyant, a planter, into one male and two female slaves worth 6,600 livres.[69] Free women of color also rented their slaves for a fixed price. Marie, a free black widow and a merchant, rented a creole black slave named Maguerite, aged about fifteen years, to Anne Claire, a free black, for three years.[70] Anne Claire signed a standard slave rental agreement, promising to treat Marguerite "as a good father of a family would, to lodge, feed, and dress her, to care for her in health as in sickness." She paid a rental charge of 600 livres per year and was absolved of responsibility for the slave girl in case she died or ran away. In another rental agreement, Marie Magdeleine Nicolle, a free *mestive*, provided eight slaves (four black men and four black women) to Messieurs Jean Pierre Correger, merchant, and Françoise Bacqueville, planter, for a three-year period.[71] The slaves, who were to work in a brick factory which Bacqueville had taken over in Rivière Sallée, were rented for 12,125 livres per year (or approximately 1,515 livres apiece).

Free women of color sometimes freed a chosen slave, but this was relatively rare; only four cases appear in the three years of our sample. These enfranchise-

ments were all granted during the life of the slaveowner and they were uncondi-
tional. Two of the slaves manumitted were a mother and young daughter;[72] the
third was an adult daughter (a *mulâtresse*) who was manumitted by her own
mother (a *négresse*).[73] The other slave was a forty-two-year-old creole man freed
by a free black woman.[74] To free a slave was an expensive process. A charge of
1,000 livres per man and 2,000 livres per woman had to be paid into the Royal
Treasury (to the *receveur général de la colonie*), and an additional charge of
twenty livres was assessed by the local authorities.[75]

Just as slaves were usually named by their first master or mistress, those joining
the ranks of the free were sometimes renamed by their former owner. After
paying the necessary manumission taxes and receiving government permission,
Pierre Balthazaré, a free black, manumitted his slave, Marie Rose, a forty-year-
old black woman of the Fond tribe. In the notarized document that gave her
freedom, Balthazaré declared that he "imposed [on her] the name of Bossy."[76]
Whether manumitted persons chose their new names themselves is not clear, but
the renaming practice was common. There was no clear preference for names;
sometimes an African name was chosen, while at other times it was a European
name. Marthe, a freed black, enfranchised a twenty-year-old creole slave woman
and her seven-month-old daughter, renaming the mother (Charlotte) Zelmire,
and the daughter (Marthe) Zaluca.[77] These names suggest a return to African origins. But when Pierre Attila, a free black, manumitted a black creole slave and her
two daughters, the mother, Marie Louise, became Bossi, while Zaboteau was re-
christened Lucinda and Rosa became Cornelie.[78] Here the evidence is ambiguous
at least, with one ex-slave receiving an African name while the other two were
given European names. In another example, Marie Louise Gothe changed the
name of her thirty-six-year-old daughter from Felicité to Hiacine when she declared her free. Although there are far too few cases to trace any meaningful
pattern, there seems to have been a slight tendency to re-Africanize names at the
time of manumission.

One of the best-documented free women of color of Cap Français was Simone
Brocard, a free-born mulatto woman, who was baptized in the Parish of Saint-
Louis, northwest of Cap Français, on March 11, 1752.[79] Exactly how she began
to amass capital is not at all clear, but by age twenty she had already become a
merchant, a woman of property, and a slaveowner. In 1782, while residing in the
central region of L'Artibonite, Simone, who was literate or at least able to sign
her name, drew up a power of attorney giving permission to a resident of Cap to
gather all the papers belonging to her which were in the hands of various notaries and lawyers.[80] She also authorized her surrogate to settle her accounts, pay
outstanding debts, collect monies due her, and reclaim "the different blacks
which belong to her . . . actually runaways."

By 1783, Simone Brocard was residing in Cap, on the Rue Saint-Pierre, three
blocks from the city's central plaza (Place d'Armes). That year she sold a twenty-
three-year-old female slave of "the Arrada nation" to Anne Claire, a free black.[81]
According to the terms of sale, the slave woman was to remain in Brocard's

hands for up to a year, at which time the final payment of the cash sum of 1,500 livres was due. The slave was turned over to Anne Claire ten months later.[82] The low price paid for this prime-age slave indicates that she was bought as "refuse" from a slaving ship.

Not all of the slaves traded by Simone Brocard, however, were purchased as "refuse" from incoming ships. Some were born in the colony. The same month that she turned over the Arrada slave to Anne Claire, Brocard sold a young creole black woman, age sixteen, to Pierre Antoine, a free black mason living in Cap Français.[83] This creole slave commanded a far higher price than the Arrada woman, but Brocard was still able to impose certain conditions on the sale, one of them being that if and when the purchaser wished to resell the young woman, she would be offered first to Brocard, who retained the option to re-purchase at the selling price. Selling slaves to a free black clientele seems to have been only one of Brocard's economic pursuits. In May 1784, for example, Marguerite Boucan, a free black woman living in Jeremie, a southern port town of Saint Domingue, declared that she owed Brocard a total of 742 livres, 10 sols—the value of two barrels of wine Brocard sent to her to be sold.[84] Transactions such as this suggest that Brocard was involved in a variety of commercial transactions, many of which depended on a clientele of free blacks, primarily women, both in Cap and in towns and cities throughout the colony.

Although little is known of Brocard's personal life, one document is tantalizingly suggestive. In June 1783, she appeared before the notary Bordier to sign a power of attorney giving François Gay, captain of the ship *La Vicomtesse de Bearu*, the right to withdraw her two daughters from a boardinghouse (*pension*) owned by the widow Couguigny in Bordeaux.[85] Although Simone was rather hazy as to their ages (the oldest was about fourteen or fifteen, the youngest between eleven and twelve), her first daughter had to have been born when Simone was only fifteen or sixteen. Furthermore, while there is no mention of their father, the girls are both described as "quadroons," daughters of the mulatto woman and a white man. Although Brocard was able to afford the luxury of sending her daughters to France to be educated, the new royal legislation forbidding free people of color to reside in the motherland forced her to rescind her plan.

Another affluent free woman of color of Cap Français was Marie Josephine, a free quadroon who drew up a power of attorney in 1783 prior to her departure for France.[86] Granting Sieur François Guilleaume Robard, a white builder, the right to collect rents and payments due her, Marie Josephine alluded to her ownership of apartments rented to or occupied by a Monsieur Demarie; Monsieur Rabié, officer of the Cap Regiment; Monsieur Langres, an artillery officer; and Monsieur Brunet.[87] In addition to listing some luxury goods, she also mentioned loans made to some of her tenants. Lastly, she owned at least two black female Senegalese slaves, both of whom worked for daily wages (*journées*) which they turned over to her.

Even for the most affluent free women of color, travel to the continent was exceptional. Some of the wealthiest of these women were also literate, or at least able to sign their names. Marie, a free black widow of Alexandre Scipion, one of the leaders of the free community, attached her signature ("Marie veu[v]e Alexandre Sipion") to documents, as did Rose Angelique, the free mulatto widow of Jacques Magnon, and the prosperous Marie Josephine.[88]

While more affluent free women of color tried to provide for the future of their daughters by giving them the luxury of a French education, those less fortunate simply provided their children with a skill that would guarantee economic survival. They prepared their sons for life by apprenticing them to local skilled craftsmen. Zabeth La Pommeraie, a free black, turned over her eleven-year-old illegitimate son Joseph (*grif*) to Sieur Français Moreau, a Cap Français tailor, to learn the trade.[89] Likewise, Marie Castagne, a free black, sent her son Guilleaume (*grif*) to Antoine Augustin, a free black carpenter.[90] Both women signed standard apprenticeship contracts, engaging their children for a five-year period, but Zabeth was so eager to have her son learn with a white tailor that she also agreed to pay Moreau 900 livres for the apprenticeship. Daughters were never apprenticed. Occupations open to women in eighteenth-century Saint Domingue did not include those of skilled artisans. Instead, mothers trained their daughters to follow their occupations.

It is difficult to know how many free women achieved their social and economic status through affective ties to men. Furthermore, the evidence is contradictory about the ethnic background of the men who left these women property. Some free black and mulatto women inherited relatively large estates from their husbands or fathers, who were also free coloreds; others inherited from free colored friends, both male and female. Pierre Guilleaume Provoyeur, a prosperous free mulatto mason and builder, left sizable legacies to at least three free women friends.[91] Some of these bequests were small, but larger ones suggest that there was a prosperous segment of free colored society in Cap Français. Still other free women of color acquired cash and property through inheritance from white men who were not legally related to them. In these cases one can assume that these men were either the illegitimate fathers or the lovers of the women who inherited from them. Sieur Antoine Foucherot, a prosperous resident of Cap Français, left a slave, furniture, and 1,200 livres in cash to Marie Dagneau, a free mulatto, and another 1,200 livres to Manon, a free black.[92] Another planter left his female ex-slave an annual pension of 300 livres and use of a room for lodging.[93] Sometimes these white men provided for legacies that suggested some social responsibility for their illegitimate children. The children of Elisabeth, a free mulatto woman, were given a gift of 3,000 livres by Sieur Noel Hot, a plantation owner who lived in Grosmorne.[94]

While clearly not as prosperous as the most important white inhabitants of Cap Français, some free women of color (those who held property and had cash to invest in buying and selling slaves) obtained a respectable level of wealth. Some of these women also achieved their economic success through inheritance or sexual liaisons, while others used the marketplace to amass capital gradually. The majority of free women of color certainly led precarious economic lives, but notary transactions suggest that many played important roles in the local economy, acting independently, unlike white women, who were rarely visible acting on their own. The role of the free women of color in the society of Cap Français was clearly far more complex than described by white elite male observers such as Moreau de Saint-Méry. While some of these women could credit their economic survival to their personal charms or their relationship to white men, many others enterprisingly built their lives through such occupations as housekeepers, small merchants, peddlers, slave traders, landlords, and agriculturalists. The free women of color of Cap Français were active therefore in various spheres of the local economy, contributing along with free men of color to the commercial dynamism of the port city.

Notes

1. For slave women, see Arlette Gautier, *Les Soeurs de Solitude: La Condition féminine dans l'esclavage aux Antilles du XVIIe au XIXe siècle* (Paris: Editions Caribéenes, 1985). One of the few studies on free women of color is Henock Trouillot, "La Condition de la femme de couleur à Saint-Domingue," *Revue de la Société Haïtienne d'Histoire* 20, no. 103 (1957): 21–80.

2. A mulatto *(mulatre* or *mulatresse* in French) was an individual who was considered to be racially half black and half white. Quadroons were those who had one black grandparent and three white ones. *Grif* and *griffe* were the offspring of black and mulatto parents (one white grandparent and three black ones). *Mestif* and *mestive* were the offspring of aboriginal and black parents. For work on free people of color in slave societies, see Harry Hoetink, *Slavery and Race Relations in the Americas: An Inquiry into Their Nature and Nexus* (New York, 1973); David W. Cohen and Jack P. Greene, eds., *Neither Slave nor Free: The Freedmen of African Descent in the Slave Societies of the New World* (Baltimore: Johns Hopkins University Press, 1972); Jerome S. Handler, *The Unappropriated People: Freedmen in the Slave Society of Barbados* (Baltimore: Johns Hopkins University Press, 1974); Jean Tarrade, "Affranchis et gens de couleur libres à la Guyane à la fin du XVIIIe siècle d'après les minutes des notaires," *Revue Française d'Histoire d'Outre-Mer* 49, no.174 (1962): 80–116; Emile Hayot, *Les Gens de couleur libres du Fort-Royal, 1679–1823* (Paris: Société Française d'Histoire d'Outre-Mer, 1971); Lucien-René Abénon, "Blancs et libre de couleur dans deux paroisses de la Guadeloupe (Capesterre et Trois-Rivières), 1699–1799," *Revue Française d'Histoire d'Outre-Mer* 60, no. 220 (1973): 297–329. For work specifically on Saint Domingue, see Laura Foner, "The Free People of Color in Louisiana and St. Domingue: A Comparative Portrait of Two Three-Caste Slave Societies," *Journal of Social History* 3 (1970): 406–30; Henock Trouillot, "Les Ouvriers de couleur à Saint-Domingue," *Revue de la Société Haïtienne d'Histoire* 18 (1955): 33–60; Gabriel Debien, "Les Colons de Antilles et leur main d'oeuvre à la fin du XVIIIe siècle," *Notes d'Histoire Coloniale* 41 (1955): 18–21.

3. M.-L.-E. Moreau de Saint-Méry, *Description topographique, physique, civile, politique et historique de la partie française de l'isle de Saint-Domingue* [1797] (Paris: Société de l'Histoire des Colonies Françaises, 1958), vol. 1, p. 104. For an abridged English version, see Ivor D. Spencer, ed., *A Civilization That Perished: The Last Years of White Colonial Rule in Haiti* (Boston: University Press of America, 1985).

4. Moreau de Saint-Méry, *Description topographique,* vol. 1, p. 105. He also believed that since 1770 mulatto women had become even more devoted to luxury.

5. Moreau de Saint-Méry, *Description topographique,* vol. 1, p. 106.

6. Moreau de Saint-Méry, *Description topographique,* vol. 1, p. 294. For a discussion of the growth of Cap Français, see Paul Butel, "Le Modèle urbain à Saint-Domingue au XVIIIe siècle: L'Investissement immobilier dans les villes de Saint-Domingue," in P. Butel and L. M. Cullen, eds., *Cities and Merchants: French and Irish Perspectives on Urban Development, 1500–1900* (Dublin, 1986), pp. 149–79.

7. Contemporary observers suggested a considerably larger urban population. Moreau de Saint-Méry claimed that the population of the Cap Français parish had grown from 6,143 in 1775 to 12,151 in 1788, while suggesting that the population of the city was actually 15,000 by the end of the 1780s. Moreau de Saint-Méry, *Description topographique,* vol. 1, p. 479.

8. Archives Nationales de France, Section Outre-Mer (hereafter ANSOM), Notariat, Saint-Domingue 182, 27 February 1783; 181, 5 May 1782. According to Moreau de Saint-Méry, "most of the [free colored] women live with white men. There, under the little-deserved title of 'housekeepers,' they have all the functions of wives . . .."; *Description topographique,* vol. 1, p. 106.

9. ANSOM, G1-509. An example of a free colored servant can be seen in ANSOM, Notariat, Saint-Domingue 181, 5 May 1782.

10. Paradoxically it was their role as household servants (housemaids, washerwomen, cooks) as well as their feminine domestic functions (wet nurses, midwives) on the plantations which had probably allowed some of the free women of color to achieve their freedom. See Gabriel Debien, "Les Affranchissements aux Antilles françaises aux XVIIe et XVIIIe siècles," *Anuario de Estudios Americanos* 24 (1967): 1183, 1185.

11. Handler, *The Unappropriated People,* pp. 133–34.

12. ANSOM, Notariat, Saint-Domingue 188, 25 October 1784. Handler finds that prostitution was the source of livelihood for freedwomen and for slaveowners who depended on slave earnings for their sustenance; see Handler, *The Unappropriated People,* p. 137.

13. For *marchandes,* see ANSOM, Notariat, Saint-Domingue 185, 12 March 1784, and ANSOM, Notariat, Saint-Domingue 188, 27 December 1784. For *marchande de graisserie,* see ANSOM, Notariat, Saint-Domingue 184, 6 August 1783. For *marchande de legumes,* see ANSOM, Notariat, Saint-Domingue 182, 3 March 1783.

14. For a discussion of market women in Saint Domingue, see Gwendolyn Midlo Hall, "Saint-Domingue," in Cohen and Greene, *Neither Slave nor Free,* p. 181. For information on the role of free men and women in the internal marketing system of Barbados, see Handler, *The Unappropriated People,* pp. 125–30.

15. In 1784, for example, at least five French women were listed as "marchande" and another gave her occupation as "marchande et couturière." Of these women, four were unmarried. ANSOM, Notariat, Saint-Domingue 184, 185, 186, 188.

16. ANSOM, Notariat, Saint-Domingue, 182, 3 March 1783.

17. Free black ownership of urban property was not at all uncommon by the last decades of the eighteenth century. According to one study, by 1776 free people of color owned 17.1 percent of the city's buildings; Butel, "Le Modèle urbain a Saint-Domingue," in Butel and Cullen, *Cities and Merchants,* p. 155.

18. ANSOM, Notariat, Saint-Domingue 184, 22 July 1783.

19. This less expensive shingle construction nonetheless had interior tiling. For a discussion of building styles and techniques, see Philippe Loupès, "Le Modèle urbain a

Saint-Domingue au xviiie siècle: La Maison et l'habitat au Cap-Français et à Port-au-Prince," in Butel and Cullen, *Cities and Merchants,* pp. 165–79.

20. ANSOM, Notariat, Saint-Domingue 188, 20 October 1784.

21. Interestingly, the cash payment was made in "silver Spanish coin."

22. ANSOM, Notariat, Saint-Domingue 184, 31 October 1783.

23. ANSOM, Notariat, Saint-Domingue 182, 22 March 1783.

24. ANSOM, Notariat, Saint-Domingue 186, 8 April 1784.

25. ANSOM, Notariat, Port-au-Prince 793, 14 March 1784.

26. ANSOM, Notariat, Saint-Domingue 185, 29 March 1784.

27. Magdeleine Francisque, a free black and widow, rented a small piece of empty land in the Petite Guinée quarter to Jean Baptiste, La Rose for 200 livres per year; ANSOM, Notariat, Saint-Domingue 187, 13 August 1784. At the other end of the spectrum is the property owned by Suzanne Alestre, already mentioned.

28. ANSOM, Notariat, Saint-Domingue 188, 19 October 1784.

29. ANSOM, Notariat, Saint-Domingue 181, 28 June 1782.

30. ANSOM, Notariat, Saint-Domingue 185, 29 March 1784.

31. ANSOM, Notariat, Saint-Domingue 180, 16 September 1782.

32. ANSOM, Notariat, Saint-Domingue 85, 3 March 1784.

33. ANSOM, Notariat, Saint-Domingue 188, 27 December 1784.

34. ANSOM, Notariat, Saint-Domingue 189, 19 July 1784.

35. ANSOM, Notariat, Saint-Domingue 187, 3 and 8 July 1784.

36. ANSOM, Notariat, Saint-Domingue 184, 4 October 1783. It is interesting to note that while black and mulatto women owned rental property, most of the men who participated in this market were white or some variant of mulatto.

37. ANSOM, Notariat, Saint-Domingue 182, 19 February 1783.

38. ANSOM, Notariat, Saint-Domingue 184, 26 October, 1783.

39. ANSOM, Notariat, Saint-Domingue 186, 20 May 1784.

40. ANSOM, Notariat, Saint-Domingue 187, 31 July 1784.

41. ANSOM, Notariat, Saint-Domingue 188, 10 December 1784.

42. For a discussion of Cap Français's trade, see David P. Geggus, "The Major Port Cities of Saint Domingue," in *Atlantic Port Cities: Economy, Culture and Society,* ed. P. Liss and F. Knight (Knoxville: University of Tennessee Press, 1991), pp. 89–100.

43. ANSOM, Notariat, Saint-Domingue 185, 5 January 1784.

44. ANSOM, Notariat, Saint-Domingue 184, 11 August 1783.

45. ANSOM, Notariat, Saint-Domingue 184, 9 August 1783.

46. The furniture consisted of "a mahogany bed, complete with lavish embroidered covering, a lacquered table, seven chairs upholstered in straw, a water jar, five bedcovers, a cruet stand, four saltcellars, and a salad bowl." ANSOM, Notariat, Saint-Domingue 184, 24 August 1783.

47. One of these slaves was a mulatto and the other a *griffe.*

48. Estimates are that between 1783 and 1792, 13,000 slaves were imported annually into Saint Domingue by French slave traders; see Robert Louis Stein, *The French Slave Trade in the Eighteenth Century: An Old Regime Business* (Madison: University of Wisconsin Press, 1979), p. 132. The total number of slaves imported during this period was probably between 26,000 and 30,000 per year; see Philip D. Curtin, *The Atlantic Slave Trade: A Census* (Madison: University of Wisconsin Press, 1969), p. 77.

49. Curtin, *The Atlantic Slave Trade,* 194–95; David Geggus, "Sex Ratio, Age and Ethnicity in the Atlantic Slave Trade: Data from French Shipping and Plantation Records," *Journal of African History* 30 (1989): 32.

50. ANSOM, Notariat, Saint-Domingue 181, 23 July 1782; Saint-Domingue 181, 24 July 1782; Saint-Domingue 187, 8 July 1784.

51. ANSOM, Notariat, Saint-Domingue 187, 28 June 1784; Saint-Domingue 187, 9 July 1784.

52. ANSOM, Notariat, Saint-Domingue 181, 23 and 31 July 1782. The three adult slaves included in these sales were all African-born women.

53. ANSOM, Notariat, Saint-Domingue 182, 3 March 1783.

54. This would be consonant with recent findings for the English Caribbean that prices tended to decrease over the course of slave sales, with the least prosperous buyers entering the market late; see David W. Galenson, *Traders, Planters, and Slaves: Market Behavior in Early English America* (New York: Cambridge University Press, 1986), pp. 71–92.

55. ANSOM, Notariat, Saint-Domingue 183, 23 May 1783.

56. ANSOM, Notariat, Saint-Domingue 188, 25 October 1784.

57. ANSOM, Notariat, Saint-Domingue 187, 10 September 1784.

58. ANSOM, Notariat, Saint-Domingue 188, 1 October 1784.

59. ANSOM, Notariat, Saint-Domingue 181, 25 July 1782.

60. ANSOM, Notariat, Saint-Domingue 186, 8 May 1784.

61. ANSOM, Notariat, Saint-Domingue 18 June 1783. According to Moreau de Saint-Méry, "the people of this French Colony brand the Africans on the chest with their name or with simple initial letters, while with the creoles it is done only in very rare cases"; *Description topographique,* vol. 1, p. 83.

62. ANSOM, Notariat, Saint-Domingue 188, 25 October 1784.

63. ANSOM, Notariat, Saint-Domingue 182, 6 March 1783.

64. ANSOM, Notariat, Saint-Domingue 181, 31 July 1782.

65. ANSOM, Notariat, Saint-Domingue 363, 19 February 1782.

66. ANSOM, Notariat, Saint-Domingue 181, 24 July 1782. For her daughter, Leonore bought a thirty-year old creole *mulâtresse* from Curaçao who was valued at 2,000 livres. (Clearly race did not prevent Leonore from purchasing a fellow *mulâtresse.*) A twenty-year-old "black Paular woman" suffering from "a dragon-shaped scar on each eye" and valued at only 792 livres was provided for Leonore's son.

67. ANSOM, Notariat, Saint-Domingue 182, 27 February 1783.

68. ANSOM, Notariat, Saint-Domingue 188, 10 November 1784.

69. ANSOM, Notariat, Saint-Domingue 181, 5 May 1782.

70. ANSOM, Notariat, Saint-Domingue 185, 12 March 1784.

71. ANSOM, Notariat, Saint-Domingue 186, 19 April 1784. Within a month Correger turned his interest in the deal over to Claude Etienne Bois Brun, another planter; ANSOM, Notariat, Saint-Domingue 186, 10 May 1784.

72. ANSOM, Notariat, Saint-Domingue 184, 16 August 1783.

73. ANSOM, Notariat, Saint-Domingue 187, 9 August 1784.

74. ANSOM, Notariat, Saint-Domingue 184, 13 September 1783.

75. Ibid.; also see Debien, "Les Affranchissements aux Antilles français," p. 1182.

76. ANSOM, Notariat, Saint-Domingue 182, 17 March 1783.

77. ANSOM, Notariat, Saint-Domingue 184, 16 August 1783. The name Zaluca is possibly a variation of Zalika, a Swahili name meaning "well-born"; see Ogonna Chuksorgi, *Names from Africa* (Chicago: Johnson, 1972), p. 29.

78. ANSOM, Notariat, Saint-Domingue 187, 1 June 1784. Bossi or Bossy is possibly related to Dossi (born after twins) or Kossi (born of a long pregnancy), two common Goun (Dahomey) names; see Ihechukwu Madabuike, *A Handbook to African Names* (Washington, D.C.: Three Continents Press, 1976), pp. 130, 132.

79. ANSOM, Notariat, Saint-Domingue 181, 20 July 1782.

80. Ibid.

81. ANSOM, Notariat, Saint-Domingue 183, 18 June 1783.

82. ANSOM, Notariat, Saint-Domingue 186, 6 April 1784.

83. ANSOM, Notariat, Saint-Domingue 187, 29 June 1784.

84. ANSOM, Notariat, Saint-Domingue 186, 20 May 1784.

85. ANSOM, Notariat, Saint-Domingue 183, 27 June 1783.

86. ANSOM, Notariat, Saint-Domingue 183, 3 April 1783. Two days later this power of attorney was revoked because all of the outstanding debts had been collected. Marie Josephine seems to have left for France in spite of the legislation forbidding free people of color to establish residency there.

87. All of the rents were quoted in "portugaises," a unit of currency worth sixty-six livres.

88. ANSOM, Notariat, Saint-Domingue 184, 22 July 1783; 188, 19 October 1784; 183, 3 April 1783.

89. ANSOM, Notariat, Saint-Domingue 181, 12 April 1782.

90. ANSOM, Notariat, Saint-Domingue 181, 24 April 1782.

91. ANSOM, Notariat, Saint-Domingue 180, 15 August 1782, and 181, 23 June 1782.

92. ANSOM, Notariat, Saint-Domingue 187, 29 August 1784.

93. ANSOM, Notariat, Saint-Domingue 186, 24 May 1784.

94. ANSOM, Notariat, Saint-Domingue 186, 24 May 1784.

15

URBAN SLAVERY–URBAN FREEDOM
The Manumission of
Jacqueline Lemelle

L. Virginia Gould

Most women's historians who have attempted to document the experiences of women of color, both slave and free, have either failed to examine such women within their own social systems or have offered a unidimensional view that limits their portrayal to one of repression and deprival. Certainly it cannot be denied that slave women and free women of color experienced severe repression, since the very nature of the slave system worked to deprive slave women of the most basic form of freedom and to limit that of free women of color. Indeed, the effects of slavery did not stop at legal condition. Slaveholders and officials also sought to deprive slave women and free women of color of their essential identities as women and of their dignity. Oppression and deprival, however, were only goals of the slaveholders and officials, and slavery had two sides. By defying the intent of slaveholders and their system, slave women and free women of color struggled to determine their own identities as well as their own dignity. In many ways, they shaped their own world as well as their own identities in it.

The task of writing the history, of capturing the experiences, of black slaves and free women of color is understandably difficult, since at its very core slavery was a depersonalizing, alienating system. Even the sources work against scholars who strive to hear the voices of women who were deprived of the most basic skills of communication. With most sources limited to scattered documents or contemporary white observations of black life, scholars must remain skeptical. They must weigh documentary evidence against the faint voices of women of color. They must resist writing of them as receptors and instead find their many roles as actors. Black women, both slave and free, helped to define the social system of slavery as it developed in Louisiana. They led rich, multidimensional existences that spanned the distance between slavery and freedom. They were slave and free, rich and poor. They formed families under the most difficult of circumstances. They bought property and sold it. They were owned as slaves, and they owned slaves. Most of all, they were women who struggled to construct their own lives, families, and households, their own identities, within the narrow confines permitted women of color.[1]

One woman whose personal history demonstrates the ways in which slavery shaped the lives of slave women and free women of color in New Orleans was Jacqueline Lemelle. Like most other slave and free women of color, Jacqueline did not leave a personal account of her life. Public documents reveal enough about her life, however, that it is possible to recover something of her identity and many of her experiences. Jacqueline appears in the property records in which she was bought and sold. She also is found in manumission records in which she was freed and in those in which she freed others. Jacqueline and three of her daughters are discussed in some detail in the inventory of the estate of Santiago Lemelle. They also appear in local census and sacramental records. Other children of Jacqueline appear in scattered documents. When taken separately, none of the records offer conclusive evidence of Jacqueline's life. Yet when taken together and placed within the broader framework of what is known about slave and free women of color, they demonstrate much about the way in which slavery and freedom were defined and redefined by one woman.[2]

To understand the way in which Jacqueline formed meaning out of her life, the way in which she shaped and reshaped her identity, it is necessary to examine her life within the social system of slavery that ordered her world. By the end of the seventeenth century, Spain, France, and Britain were actively competing for the region that bordered the Gulf of Mexico. New Orleans became the most important settlement along the gulf, but it was not the first. Spain placed an outpost settlement at Pensacola in 1698. The next year the French placed a settlement at Biloxi. After three years the French capital was moved to Mobile. The capital was finally moved to New Orleans in 1724. Yet even as Spain established dominance over Florida and France claimed Louisiana, the geopolitical struggle over the region did not end. Instead, the colonies, along with their outpost settlements, were bartered back and forth between the Spanish, the French, and the English during the eighteenth and early nineteenth centuries. Louisiana was governed by the French between 1698 and 1762. In 1762 it was secretly ceded to Spain in the Treaty of Fontainebleau. It was ceded again in the public Treaty of Paris in 1763, although Spain did not officially take control of the colony until 1769. It remained under Spanish rule between 1769 and 1803. It was ceded to the French in 1803 and then transferred to the United States a few days later.[3]

As Louisiana was transferred back and forth between the colonial powers, its inhabitants struggled to survive. Early French administrators hoped to establish a farming settlement in the colony, but the colony's settlers thought otherwise. Instead of a farming community, the disillusioned settlers demanded a slave-based plantation society. French officials finally agreed, and by 1719 the Company of the Indies had begun to bring shiploads of Africans into the region. As Gwendolyn Midlo Hall has demonstrated in *Africans in Colonial Louisiana*, between June 1719 and January 1731, sixteen slave ships arrived in Louisiana from Senegal. The company also sent five slave ships from Juda and one from Angola. Another shipload of Africans was sent to the colony in 1743, bringing the total number of Africans imported into the region to 5,951. The French stopped the wholesale importation of Africans after 1743, and the trade was not begun again until the Spanish took control of the colony.[4]

In 1724, after several hundred Africans had arrived in the colony, the French implemented an official set of laws aimed specifically at controlling the slaves and their owners. The Code Noir, or slave law, was modeled after the 1685 Code Noir that France had originally devised for its Caribbean islands. By its very intent, the Code Noir embodied the planter philosophy of Catholicism, white supremacy, and patriarchal rule. In particular, the more lenient tenents of the Code Noir proclaimed Catholicism as the state religion, provided for the baptism and marriage of slaves, and guaranteed the rights of slaves to a reasonable standard of food and clothing. Its more restrictive acts provided that slaves could not own property, could not perform official duties, and could not testify in court. Furthermore, slaves could be manumitted only with the consent of the Superior Council. Finally, freed slaves were guaranteed most of the rights of citizenship, although they were prohibited from receiving donations *inter vivos* or *mortis causae* from whites.[5]

Despite the intentions of the Code Noir, French planters relied on violence and coercion to control their slaves, and their slaves in retaliation formed an alliance with the local Native Americans. The alliance between the slaves and the Native Americans not only disrupted the labor force but also threatened the safety of the white population. Thus in order to win their slave's loyalty, planters and governing officials implemented reforms which were meant to assimilate the slaves into the colonial community and to recognize their status as men and women with rights under the law. Of course, not all slaveholders cooperated, but some did. Many slaves were introduced to Catholicism, encouraged to marry and to form stable family unions, supplied with their own plots of land, and given free time to market their own produce or other goods. Religious indoctrination, family, and self-sufficiency, officials and planters believed, would tie slaves to the community and reduce their tendency to rebel. The region's slaves, then, had successfully negotiated a certain amount of autonomy under the French.[6]

It was during the early years in French Louisiana, when the French were still importing slaves into the colony from the Senegal region of Africa, that Jacqueline was born. Neither her birth nor her baptism records have been found, so it is impossible to know exactly when or where she was born. It is doubtful, however, that she was one of the slaves brought from Africa, since she was consistently described in the records as a mulatress, which suggests that her mother was a slave and her father was white. Since later records suggest that Jacqueline was born around 1730, it is probable that her mother was one of the first Africans brought into the colony.[7]

That so little information was recorded about Jacqueline's identity was no accident. In a discussion of African slavery, Claude Meillassoux effectively argues that preclusion from ties of kinship, or social weakness, contributed to the effectiveness of the slave system and the productivity of the slave. Extant records in New Orleans suggest the same systematic weakening of the slaves ties of kinship that Meillassoux found in African slave communities. For instance, sacramental records of the St. Louis Cathedral demonstrate that at baptism infant slaves were denied the legitimate identification of a father. In virtually every case, the father of the infant was registered as unknown by the priest whose responsibility it was to record all pertinent information. But it is impossible to believe that slave women did not know the fathers of their children. Instead, local white authorities, including priests, refused to identify the father, since to do so would have interfered with the power or control of the master and therefore the effectiveness of the institution. Precluded from legitimate or operative ties with their own kin, slave women existed under the direct power of their master or mistress. Like their rural sisters, slave women in the city belonged to households that were not governed by their own male kin. Denied family ties, excluded from power over their own children, slave women suffered precarious relationships that effectively isolated them as individuals.[8]

The slave infant Jacqueline offers a case in point. As the daughter of a slave mother with no recorded lineage and an unknown father, Jacqueline had no recorded lineage. When sold away from her mother, as she ultimately was, she was isolated even further from a recognizable family. Moreover, as long as Jacqueline remained a slave, her children took on her legal status as isolated persons; Jacqueline had no legitimately recognizable lineage to pass along to them. As a slave, she was recognizable only as property. As a person, her identity and her legitimate ties to the community existed only through her master.

Such deliberate alienation of slaves from their own kin can be found in naming practices. Slaves were almost always legally denied last names or names that would have associated them with their own families. Instead they were identified by their first names only. To be accurately or legally identified, a slave had to be described as the property of a certain master. Yet there is no reason to believe that slaves did not have or want to have legitimate last names. As evidenced by colonial property records, when slaves were freed they identified themselves with last names and sometimes even with new first names. For example, the slave of Maria Francisca Robert identified herself as Maria Mariengoin at her emancipation. Maria Del Carmen, the slave of Francisco Silos, also identified herself with a last name, and the seventeen-year-old slave of Nicolas Mesa de Lizana, Sofia, identified her last name as Conesa at her emancipation.[9]

In weakening slaves' ties of kinship, urban slaveholders sought to maintain a dependent labor force. Yet the slave system in colonial Louisiana in general and the nature of slavery in New Orleans in specific mitigated against that very dependence. Scholars such as Richard Wade, Frederick Bowser, David Barry Gaspar, and Frederick Cooper, agree that the distinctive labor market in the cities of the Americas redefined the nature of slavery there. Benjamin Latrobe captured the distinctive form of slavery in New Orleans shortly after arriving there in 1797. Writing of the free mingling of the city's population without apparent reference to freedom or bondage, Latrobe described the mob he had witnessed on the levee as "white men and women, and of all hues of brown, and of all faces, from round Yankees to grizzly and lean Spaniards, black Negroes and negresses, filthy Indians, half naked, mulattoes curly and straight-haired, quadroons of all shades, long haired and frizzled, women dressed in the most flaring yellow and scarlet gowns, the men capped and hatted." Latrobe concluded that "their wares consisted of as many kinds as their faces." Slave women, so picturesquely described by Latrobe and other commentators, functioned as entrepreneurs beside free laborers in the marketplace. When away from their owners, urban slaves acted as managers of their own time and labor. It was there in the public space of the bustling city that they lost themselves in the crowd and thus created their own world. It was there too that they communicated with one another and formed friendships, sometimes even families.[10]

The public space of the city offered slaves anonymity that their private or household space denied them. Wade points out in *Slavery in the Cities* that the nature of urban slavery required unique living arrangements. Most slaves lived in the same house with their master or mistress or in a small cabin enclosed by high walls in the backyard. While differing in size and arrangement from the plantation, Wade comments, the urban facility, or compound, functioned roughly in the same way as the rural plantation: "It provided a means of social control as well as of shelter; it embodied the servile relationship between white and black; and it expressed a style of living appropriate to its setting." Yet the intimacy of the urban compound intensified the relationship between slaves and their masters and mistresses. With living quarters within a few feet of their masters' back doors, if not in the same houses, slaves spent much of their time at home under the watchful eye of their owners. Such intimacy, as many historians have previously noted, could lead to love and caring as well as to hate and cruelty. What seems especially clear is that intimacy between slave women and their masters and mistresses in New Orleans led to expressions of both.[11]

Some urban slave women who lived in the house of their owners toiled every day under their direct supervision. Others were rented out or worked independently, bringing their masters a daily, weekly, or monthly sum. Wade notes that under such arrangements slaveowners had to depend on their slaves' loyalty. Yet he also notes that it was just such arrangements that weakened their control over them. In reality, the public and impersonal environment of the city and the practical arrangements made between slaves and their owners offered slaves, who naturally resisted the restraints placed upon them, a remarkable degree of self-determination.[12]

Jacqueline is an urban slave, a domestic, when she appears in the records, so it is probable that her mother too was an urban slave. Records in the city demonstrate that urban slaves usually remained in the city, passing their skills to their children. As an urban slave, Jacqueline's mother would have taught her to take over simple chores when she was no more than three or four years old. As she became a youth, Jacqueline would have continued to work beside her mother, learning domestic and marketing skills from her. She probably would have stayed with her mother until she was approximately fourteen years of age, when she would have been sold. It was at the age of fourteen, according to the Code Noir, that slave children could be separated from their mothers. When Jacqueline was sold away from her mother, she would have taken her skills with her into the home of her new master or mistress.[13]

How many times Jacqueline was bought and sold is not clear. What is clear is that she was purchased by Santiago Lemelle from Monsieur Laquer, one of Lemelle's neighbor's, in 1762. At that time, Jacqueline would have been approximately thirty-two years old. Her new master, Santiago Lemelle, was born in Opelusus, but by 1762 he was living in New Orleans and working as a ship's captain and a merchant. Lemelle probably bought Jacqueline to perform his household chores and possibly even to market the goods that he transported into the colony. Her tasks as a domestic and marketer would have followed those of other urban slave women.[14]

Urban domestics performed a variety of skilled and unskilled labor in the city's households. They cleaned the houses of their masters and mistresses. They cooked their meals, sewed and laundered their clothes, and raised their children. When not working in the house of their master or mistress, domestic slaves could be rented out to others in the community who needed household help. Domestic slaves also worked as housekeepers, cooks, and laundresses in the city's commercial establishments. Hawkers and peddlers worked in the streets and on the levees. That urban slave women were most often assigned gender-specific tasks, however, should not be interpreted as a sign of the sensitivity of the master class. Instead, as housekeepers, cooks, laundresses, seamstresses, and marketers they were central to the household and the markets of the urban community.[15]

The tasks of urban slave women, defined by the needs of the urban community, also reflected the African heritage of the women. Accounts of life in the city clearly demonstrate that urban slaves adapted traditional African institutions of production to the circumstances of slavery that they found in the city. Those traditions can be seen most clearly in the marketing skills of the women. Women in Africa frequently dominate the petty markets, as did the women in New Orleans. Furthermore, when performing work outside the dominance of their masters or mistresses, when renting out their own time and talent, or when spending their days hawking or peddling produce in the streets or on the levee, slave women fell back on African models of self-reliance.

Since Santiago's work often took him out of the city for months at a time, it is probable that Jacqueline ran Santiago's household. It is also possible that she marketed the merchandise that he brought to New Orleans. In his journal, Latrobe discussed one aspect of the importance of women of color to the market trade of the city when he described their practice of peddling. Noting that it was the "whole of the retail trade in dry goods . . . before the United States got possession of the country" since "it was not then nor is it now, the fashion for ladies to go shopping," Latrobe remarked that the custom was one of the remarkable features of the city. During the whole day, Latrobe observed, black women "are met carrying baskets upon their heads and calling at the doors of houses." "These baskets," he continued, "contain assortments of dry goods, sometimes, to appearance, to a considerable amount."[16]

Not all slave or free women of color who were marketers hawked or peddled along the levee or in the streets. Some sold goods from the stalls along the levee or from retail shops in the city. In fact, descriptions of daily life in the city suggest that slave women and free women of color sometimes carried on their occupations in their own households or in retail establishments. Therefore it is possible that Jacqueline sold merchandise from Santiago's storefront gallery on Royal Street. The gallery was just two doors away from their residence. The inventory of Santiago's estate suggests that when he died he owned large quantities of soap, candles, fabrics, buttons, braid, and oil. It is probable that Lemelle had imported these goods into the colony. In fact, a list of his accounts suggests that he wholesaled some of his imported merchandise to retail establishments, such as that owned by the Monsanto Brothers. The account of his estate also suggests that he sold small quantities of goods directly to the public. And since it was not unusual for slaves in the city to conduct business for their owners and Santiago was frequently away from the city, it is more than likely that he entrusted Jacqueline to oversee at least some of his business in his absence.[17]

Beginning in 1762, about the time Jacqueline was purchased by Lemelle, an unexpected series of political events disrupted life in the struggling port. That year, Spain attained Louisiana with the secret Treaty of Fontainebleau. The transfer was made public with the Treaty of Paris in 1763, but it was not until 1765 that the Crown appointed Antonio de Ulloa y de la Torre Guiral to serve as the first governor of Spanish Louisiana. Even though the Spanish Crown tried to appease Louisiana's French settlers by instructing Ulloa to leave the existing French system of governance intact, in 1768 the colonists rebelled against him. The rebellion was short-lived, however, for a few months later the Crown sent Alejandro O'Reilly, a Spanish general, to restore order, to punish the French who led the rebellion, and to implement the laws of the Indies.[18]

The decision of the Crown to implement the laws of the Indies was an important one for the colony's slaves and free people of color. Unlike the Code Noir, Spanish slave law guaranteed slaves the right to own property and the right of judicial protection against cruelty. Freed slaves, and thus free people of color, had rights of citizenship, which included the right to receive *inter vivos* and *mortis causae* donations from whites. Furthermore, believing that "it is a rule of law that all judges should aid liberty, for the reason that it is a friend of nature, because not only men, but all animals love it," Spanish governing officials enacted two customs that made manumission more accessible. The first allowed slaveholders the right to manumit their slaves by a simple act recorded by a notary. This policy was significantly different from the French policy, which required slaveholders to obtain the permission of the Superior Council before manumitting their slaves.[19]

It was not unusual for slaveholders to manumit their slaves under the French system. There are countless examples of slaveholders who successfully manumitted their slaves. For instance, Jean Baptiste le Moyne, Sieur de Bienville, manumitted Jorge and Marie, who were man and wife, in 1733. Bienville noted in the manumission records that his slaves had been faithful servants for twenty-six years. Yet, not all slaveholders who wanted to free their slaves did so successfully. When Saint Pierre de Saint Julien decided to leave the colony, he personally freed his slaves Marie Charlotte and her daughter Louise. The freedom of Marie Charlotte and Louise, however, was challenged by creditors, who argued to the Superior Council that Saint Pierre de Saint Julien had freed his slaves without their permission. The outcome of the challenge to the freedom of Marie Charlotte is unclear, but it is likely that the slaves were returned to slavery, since any manumission allowed without the permission of the Superior Council was deemed to be null and void.[20]

The other more lenient custom of manumission that the Spanish brought with them into the region was the custom of *coartación*, or self-purchase. *Coartación*, as practiced throughout Spanish America, was an arrangement in which slaves were permitted to free themselves by agreeing with their masters on a purchase price or by arbitrating a sum through the courts. Such a policy not only allowed slaves the possibility of freedom—not only suggested to them that it was their natural right by its implications of liberty and humanity—but, in effect, loosened their master's control over them.[21]

Notwithstanding Spanish manumission policy, slaves did not gain their freedom easily. Usually valued at several hundred pesos, slaves had to have salable skills or access to goods over several years in order to accumulate their purchase price. Slaves with masters who were either unwilling to allow them time off for self-employment or did not allow them to retain a portion of their earnings had little opportunity to accumulate the funds necessary for their purchase price. Furthermore, within a system that expected slaves to provide much of their own food, clothing, and other necessities, the ability of slaves to save enough of their income to purchase their freedom or that of their kin would have been extremely difficult. Thus restrained by the demands of their masters and hindered by their own needs as well as the lagging colonial economy, slaves struggled against overwhelming odds for their freedom.[22]

Manumissions recorded in the notarial, court, and sacramental records demonstrate that in New Orleans between 1765 and 1803, or during the Spanish period, more than one thousand slaves were manumitted. An analysis of the manumission records demonstrates clear patterns for those who had a chance at freedom as opposed to those who did not. Most slaves who were manumitted were women and children. In 1783, Don Juan Robin manumitted his forty-eight-year-old slave Maria and three of her children: Juan Luis, eighteen; Maria Juana, twenty-seven; and Isabel, twenty. He also freed Isabel's two daughters: Juana and Francisca. Of those freed by family, it appears that approximately 40 percent were freed by a parent or grandparent. In most cases the parent or grandparent who purchased the child was free, but a few slaves purchased their children, apparently forfeiting their own freedom for that of their children. For instance, in 1779 Angelica, the negress slave of Antonio Ramis, petitioned the court to appoint an appraiser for her four-year-old grandchild, Maria Antonia, the slave of Santiago Porta, "so that she may be permitted to buy her for the price of her valuation and that an act of emancipation be issued to her." Angelica explained to the court that she had paid the price of her own freedom to her master "with the exception of a small amount" but because of "great love . . . for her grandchild" she had begged alms from various charitable people to buy the freedom of her grandchild.[23]

After children, most of those who were freed were women. In fact, a survey of the manumission records demonstrates that approximately three times as many women as men were manumitted. A few slaves, like Mariana, the mulatress slave of Santiago Maguien who was freed in 1797 for 600 pesos, were able to purchase their own freedom. Several factors increased the possibility of freedom for women. Slave women were usually ascribed a lesser monetary value than slave men. Hundreds of documents of slave sales in New Orleans demonstrate that during the Spanish occupation it was typical for slave men to be valued at approximately 100 to 200 pesos more than women of a comparable age, with the most valuable age for either being between fifteen and forty-five years. Similar evidence is contained in the manumission records, where the price of freedom for men was customarily higher than that for women. Thus slave men would have had to save longer for their freedom.[24]

In addition to being of lesser value, slave women were not so threatening to the white population as their male counterparts. The attitudes of officials toward slave and free men and women can be seen in the reaction that officials had to the refugees fleeing the rebellion in Saint Domingue. Fearing that they would bring their rebellious ideas with them, officials passed laws aimed at restricting the emigration of men into the colony. Despite their efforts, however, their worst fears were realized when a slave rebellion was barely averted at Pointe Coupée. Again, evidence of the response to the plot demonstrates that officials and planters executed or imprisoned slave and free men of color but ignored the women who were involved. Men, then, and not women, were viewed as threatening.[25]

Some slave women, living and working in close quarters with their masters and mistresses and caring for them and their children on a day-to-day basis, were awarded their freedom gratuitously by their masters or mistresses "for the great love and care that they had given." Most often, however, slave women were freed by a relative, a husband, or a cohabitant. It was not uncommon for slave women, willingly or unwillingly, to participate in concubinal relationships with their masters or with other free men in the community, and these relationships often led to manumission for themselves and their children. The manumission of the slave Jacqueline Lemelle offers one example. It appears from the records that Santiago Lemelle purchased Jacqueline for her labor, but it is just as obvious that over the years Jacqueline became more to Santiago than his slave. For after living with Santiago for ten years as his slave and bearing three of his daughters, Jacqueline and these daughters, Agata, Maria Francisca [alias Tonton], and Adelaida, were freed.[26]

Many slave women, like Jacqueline, obtained their freedom and that of their children as a direct consequence of their sexual liaisons with their masters or with other free men in the community. In fact, as Ira Berlin points out in *Slaves without Masters*, at least in New Orleans, the majority of manumissions were a direct consequence of the concubinage of slave women with white men. The Spanish census records of New Orleans demonstrate that there was a numerical preponderance of men in the white population and women in the slave and free colored population, or a race-sex imbalance that encouraged miscegenous unions. Certainly the demographic imbalance of the population was an important incentive for such relationships, but slave women also recognized that they could attain their freedom and that of their children by participating in relationships with free men.[27]

Relationships between women and their owners, as Orlando Patterson points out in *Slavery and Social Death*, could resemble de facto marriages. The debate about such relationships is whether they were parasitic—the master taking from but not giving to the slave—or symbiotic, with each achieving what they needed. It seems that at least in Spanish New Orleans, where free men often manumitted the women with whom they cohabited, the act of manumission itself, the most meaningful expression of mutuality and trust, would have been the best indicator of a symbiotic relationship.[28]

As Santiago's slave, Jacqueline may not have been able to resist his sexual demands. After all, he owned her; and even though French and Spanish law forbade him to exploit her sexually, there is no record of a slave in colonial New Orleans attempting to prosecute her master for rape or sexual exploitation. But colonial court records do clearly demonstrate that slave women were not passive victims who submitted to the advances of just any man. Indeed, evidence shows that some slave women resisted their master's advances and the advances of other free men. In one of the most obvious examples, in 1776 Maria Juana, the slave of a planter named Juan Suriray, successfully petitioned the court for freedom on the grounds that she had been the concubine of Juan for many years, but that when she had refused to consort with him after he married a prominent white woman, he had abused her, "even to deprive her of her shoes and stockings," and forced her to wear rags. Preferring to spend her time in jail rather than with Juan, Maria Juana was no longer willing to be his concubine or his slave. And Maria Juana was not alone. Innumerable court cases illuminate the ways in which slave women resisted control by white men.

Circumstances turned out differently for Jacqueline than they had for Maria Juana. It is impossible to know exactly what Jacqueline thought of her liaison with Santiago. The fact that after he gave her freedom she remained in his household suggests, though, that their relationship was mutual. That Jacqueline and her three daughters were freed and that they remained in Santiago's household, however, does not indicate that their lives would have changed dramatically, or even that they would have distanced themselves from other slaves.[29]

Free women of color shared complex relations with other slave and free women of color in the city. Slave women and free women of color, separated from white women by race, were tied together by traditions that had been brought from Africa and by others that were created in the hostile environment of Louisiana. They also forged real and fictive kinship networks that criss-crossed the city and reached into the plantation region around the city. These networks were not transcended by condition. Commitments between slave women and free women of color are especially obvious in the manumission records. For instance, Margaret, a free woman of color who was leaving the city for Havana, made arrangements with the court to sell her property on Royal Street in case she died while abroad. The proceeds of the sale, she instructed, were to purchase the freedom of her mother and her brother. In another example, the free woman of color Juana, in her will, ordered her executor to buy the slave Joseph, aged about twenty-five, and the slave Juana, aged about twenty, to liberate them from slavery because of the great love she bore from them, having raised them as her own children in her own home.[30]

Notwithstanding such bonds, however, slaves and free women of color could be distanced by legal or social status or by class. Since slavery defined the most degraded social position, distance from slavery was an essential attribute of social advancement or upward mobility within the hierarchy of social status allowable for people of color. But status in colonial Louisiana meant more than legal condition. An elaborate system of racial classification was also adhered to, especially in Spanish Louisiana, in order to designate status or distance from slavery. Gary Mills perceptively points out in *The Forgotten People: Cane River's Creoles of Color* that once freed, Louisiana's free people of color, who were overwhelmingly racially mixed, "successfully rejected identification with any established racial order and achieved recognition as a distinct ethnic group." The degree of privilege or degradation of any individual in that group, Mills argues, depended upon his or her placement within the racially based caste system. The caste system that Mills so astutely described was not a reflection of African values or traditions but rather a reflection of early modern European social tradition.[31]

Certainly not all of New Orleans' free people of color accepted the racially based caste system, but many did. Sacramental and property records note the racial classification of slaves and free people of color, and these records bear witness to the fact that racially mixed free people of color consistently formed business and personal alliances with those of their same racial classification. Census and parish records demonstrate that free women of color usually married or cohabited with those of their own racial stratum or with white men. Parish records document that godparents were usually of the same racial classification as their godchildren or lighter.[32]

Bartolome Bautista, a free grifo, personally experienced the significance of racial classification in New Orleans in 1788 after he tried to entice Catalina Labastille to elope with him. Instead of successfully enticing her away from her family, Bartolome found himself in prison. When he requested that the court release him so that he might return to his farm to gather his crop, Bartolome also asked the court to require Pedro Pablo Labastille, Catalina's father, to appear in court to explain why he objected to the marriage. Finding Bautista's request reasonable, the court released him from prison; and, at a court hearing a few days later, Labastille testified that he objected to the marriage because his daughter was a quadroon and Bautista was only a grifo. Ultimately, at the urging of his friends, Labastille allowed his daughter to marry Bautista. Where would Labastille have gotten the idea that a grifo could not marry a quadroon? The most obvious answer is that he assumed it from social tradition.[33]

Social and legal condition, then, defined and redefined relations between slaves and free people of color. Free women of color did not, on any account, ignore their kin. But neither did they reject their right to own slaves in order to benefit from their labor. Hundreds of free women of color in New Orleans owned slaves. Free women of color owned slave women who were domestics and marketers. Occasionally they owned men who were skilled craftsmen. They bought slaves and sold them. They inherited them and then willed them to their heirs. Occasionally they freed them.[34]

The complex relations between slave women and free women of color and between slavery and freedom in New Orleans can best be understood within the context of Jacqueline Lemelle's life. As Jacqueline's relationship to Santiago Lemelle was redefined from slave to cohabitant to co-parent, her relationship with her family, her legal status, and her status in the community changed. As long as Jacqueline remained in slavery, she had no legitimate say in the lives of her daughters. They could have been sold away from her, as her daughter Maria Juana was, or she from them. Furthermore, during the years that Santiago Lemelle owned Jacqueline as his slave yet cohabited with her, she would have more than likely been free to come and go much as she chose, managing the other slaves and the household, possibly even managing Lemelle's marketing business. As a cohabitant of a free man, Jacqueline would have enjoyed a certain measure of autonomy. Slavery for her would have blurred into freedom. The fabric that had been her life before she was freed would not have been torn with her manumission. With certainty, some aspects of her life would have taken on a different meaning, but on a day-to-day basis her life would have continued much as before. Patterson argues, in fact, that even when urban masters manumitted their female slaves they rarely lost much in tangible terms—either economically or politically—but that, in fact, they usually gained a great deal. Tied to their masters through concubinage, blood, or other ties, freed slave women, according to Patterson, remained accessible.[35]

Despite the continuities in her life, however, Jacqueline would not have taken her freedom or that of her children casually. As slaves, both she and her daughters were unable to inherit or to bequeath property. But freedom changed all that. After they were freed, they did not have to fear being sold by Santiago or

willed to his heirs at his death. Jacqueline and her daughters could enjoy the
benefits of their labor. Her daughters could be legally educated. Furthermore,
the women could live where they pleased, come and go as they pleased, buy and
sell as they pleased, marry or not marry as they pleased. Manumission gave
them a legitimate identity to pass on to their children, control over their own
lives, access to property, legal protection under the law, and the right to inherit.
All of these reasons, no doubt, prompted Jacqueline to negotiate her own freedom and that of their daughters with Santiago. These same reasons, in turn,
more than likely encouraged him to ensure it.

At least one other reason, however, must have compelled Jacqueline to negotiate her freedom with Santiago. Shortly after her own manumission, Jacqueline
purchased the freedom of her daughter Maria Juana and her granddaughter,
Julia, from Francisco Lemelle, Santiago Lemelle's brother.[36] Another of Jacqueline's children, Luis Dusuau, was freed by his white father, Don Joseph Dusuau
de la Crois. It was perhaps only then, after she had ensured all of her children's
freedom, that Jacqueline could enjoy her own. But her time with Santiago was
limited. A few years later, in 1784, he died, leaving Jacqueline and their daughters Agata, Tonton, and Adelaida as his heirs. Jacqueline and her daughters
inherited most of his household goods, his property on Royal Street, and his
two slaves. The slave Francisca was willed to Jacqueline, Eulalia to her daughters. Santiago also requested that Francisco Blaché be appointed their guardian
so that he might continue to "show them how to increase their property." Finally, Santiago declared that the estate could not be sold nor alienated in any
way until after Jacqueline's death.[37]

Jacqueline's transformation of slavery into freedom thus did not end with
her own manumission. Neither did it end with Santiago Lemelle's death, or
even with her own death, which occurred a few years later. Jacqueline's legacy
to her children and to their children was freedom. But it was more, since her
liaison with Santiago provided their daughters with powerful ties to the white
community, ties which could protect them from reenslavement or degradation.
Neither Jacqueline nor her children took their ties to the white community
lightly. In the waning years of the eighteenth century, before Louisiana was
ceded to the United States, Adelaida followed the example of her mother and
her African grandmother by reinforcing those ties. She entered into a liaison
with Luis Bruno Gireaudeau, a prominent white New Orleanian. Adelaida
Lemelle's arrangement with Luis lasted throughout her lifetime and produced
several children, one of whom distanced herself even further from slavery by
passing into the white community in Natchez, Mississippi.

Notes

1. For the best discussions of slave women, see Deborah Gray White, *Ar'n't I a
Woman? Female Slaves in the Antebellum South* (New York: Norton, 1985); Catherine

Clinton, *The Plantation Mistress* (New York: Pantheon, 1982); Jean Friedman, *The Enclosed Garden* (Chapel Hill: University of North Carolina Press, 1985). For free women of color, see Suzanne Lebsock, *The Free Women of Petersburg: Status and Culture in a Southern Town* (New York: Norton, 1984); Adele Logan Alexander, *Ambiguous Lives: Free Women of Color in Rural Georgia, 1789–1879* (Fayetteville: University of Arkansas Press, 1991). Also see Virginia Meacham Gould, "In Full Enjoyment of Their Liberty: The Free Women of Color of the Gulf Ports of New Orleans, Mobile, and Pensacola, 1769–1860," Ph.D. dissertation, Emory University, 1991. Kent Anderson Leslie's *Daughter of Color, Daughter of Privilege* (Athens: University of Georgia Press, 1995) examines the life of Amanda America Dixon, a slave woman who lived as if she were free. For the debate on women in the Caribbean, see Barbara Bush, *Slave Women in Caribbean Society, 1650–1838* (London: James Currey, 1990); Marietta Morrissey, *Slave Women in the New World* (Lawrence: University Press of Kansas, 1989).

2. New Orleans Sacramental Records, 1724 to the present, located in the St. Louis Archives in New Orleans. Libertad of Jacqueline, Agata, Maria Francisca [alias Tonton], and Adelaida recorded by the escribano Andres Almonaster y Roxas, January through December 1772, November 1772, located in the Civil Court Building, New Orleans. Hereafter the manumission records will be cited as acts by escribano and date. The inventory of the estate of Santiago Lemelle, Spanish Judicial Records, Louisiana State Museum.

3. For a concise history of the region, see James Thomas McGowan, "Creation of a Slave Society: Louisiana Plantations in the Eighteenth Century," Ph.D. dissertation, University of Rochester, 1976; Daniel H. Usner, Jr., *Indians, Settlers, and Slaves in a Frontier Exchange Economy: The Lower Mississippi Valley before 1783* (Chapel Hill: University of North Carolina Press, 1992); Etienne Gayarre, *A History of Louisiana*, 4 vols. (New Orleans: James A. Gresham, 1879).

4. McGowan, "Creation of a Slave Society"; Usner, *Indians, Settlers, and Slaves*; Gwendolyn Midlo Hall, *Africans in Colonial Louisiana: The Development of Afro-Creole Culture in the Eighteenth Century* (Baton Rouge: Louisiana State University Press, 1992).

5. The Code Noir was applied to Louisiana on March 23, 1724, Records of the Superior Council, Louisiana State Museum. The Code Noir can also be found at the Library of Congress microfilm, Records of the States of the United States of America: Louisiana, 1678–1810 (1949). For a discussion of the intentions of the Code Noir, see Elsa V. Goveia, "The West Indian Slave Laws of the Eighteenth Century," in *Slavery in the New World*, ed. Laura Foner and Eugene D. Genovese (Englewood Cliffs, 1969), pp. 113–38. For Louisiana, see Thomas Marc Fiehrer, "The African Presence in Colonial Louisiana: An Essay on the Continuity of Caribbean Culture," in *Louisiana's Black Heritage*, ed. Robert R. Macdonald, John R. Kemp, and Edward F. Haas (New Orleans: Louisiana State Museum, 1979), pp. 3–31; Hans W. Baade, "The Law of Slavery in Spanish Louisiana: 1769–1803," in *Louisiana's Legal Heritage*, ed. Robert R. Macdonald, John R. Kemp, and Edward R. Haas (Pensacola: Perdido Bay Press, 1983), pp. 43–86.

6. McGowan, "Creation of a Slave Society," pp. 43–174; Hall, *Africans in Colonial Louisiana*, pp. 97–155.

7. Acts of Andres Almonaster y Roxas, November 1772.

8. Claude Meillassoux, "Female Slavery," in *Women and Slavery in Africa* ed. Claire C. Robertson and Martin A. Klein (Madison: University of Wisconsin Press, 1984), pp. 49–66; Orlando Patterson, *Slavery and Social Death: A Comparative Study* (Cambridge: Harvard University Press, 1982), pp. 38–76.

9. Orlando Patterson, *Slavery and Social Death*, pp. 38–62. Acts of Pedro Pedesclaux, April 16, 1800; Pedro Pedesclaux, January 2, 1800; Acts of Pedro Pedesclaux, February 11, 1776.

10. Richard Wade, *Slavery in the Cities* (New York: Oxford University Press, 1964); Frederick P. Bowser, "Colonial Spanish America," in *Neither Slave nor Free: The Freedmen of African Descent in the Slave Societies of the New World*, ed. David W. Cohen and Jack P. Green (Baltimore: Johns Hopkins University Press, 1972); David Barry Gaspar, *Bondmen and Rebels: A Study of Master-Slave Relations in Antigua with Implications for Colonial British America* (Baltimore: Johns Hopkins University Press, 1985); Frederick Cooper, *Plantation Slavery on the East Coast of Africa* (New Haven: Yale University Press, 1977).

11. Wade, *Slavery in the Cities*, pp. 55–62. For expressions of violence and affection between masters and mistresses and their slaves, see Benjamin Henry Latrobe, *The Journal of Latrobe* (New York: D. Appleton, 1901), pp. 182–84. He comments on the slave who, after emancipation, devoted her labors to her former mistress, who was old and helpless. Also see the criminal proceedings against Pedro La Cabanne and the mulatress slave Madelon, who belonged to Nicolas Perthus, of March 28, 1778, and the criminal proceedings against Joseph Leon et al. on February 16, 1781. Census records of New Orleans consistently demonstrate the preponderance of slave women in the urban population. For instance, out of a total population in New Orleans of 1,227 in 1771, 39 percent were slaves, 55 percent of whom were women. By 1791, census records demonstrate that there were 1,604 slaves and that again 55 percent were women. Of those slaves between thirteen and forty-nine years old (the childbearing years), 59 percent were women. Court Records, Notarial Acts, and travelers' accounts of New Orleans describe the domestic roles of slave women. For instance, see Latrobe, pp. 182, 183, 204. Also see the records of Pierre Clement Laussaut, Historic New Orleans Collection.

12. Wade, *Slavery in the Cities*, pp. 29–54. See the testimony of Maria Theresa in the Spanish Judicial Records, September 4, 1782, for an example of the tradition of urban slaves who worked and lived independently but continued to turn their wages, in whole or in part, over to their masters and mistresses. In her testimony, Maria Theresa promised the court to continue to turn over her daily wages to her mistress from her occupations as a good seamstress, washer, and ironer.

13. A survey of the Notarial Acts and Court Records in New Orleans reveals occupational data for slave and free women of color and demonstrates that while some slaves were sold as young as three months, most were sold away from their mothers and their original masters around the age of fourteen years. Wade, *Slavery in the Cities*, pp. 30–33.

14. The inventory of the estate of Santiago Lemelle.

15. For a description of the occupations of slave women in colonial New Orleans, see the Records of the Superior Council for the French period and the Spanish Court Records for the Spanish period.

16. The records of Lemelle's probated estate; Latrobe, *The Journal of Latrobe*, pp. 202–3; Gaspar, *Bondmen and Rebels*, p. 109; Patterson, *Slavery and Social Death*, pp. 254–55; B. W. Higman, *Slave Populations of the British Caribbean, 1807–1834* (Baltimore: Johns Hopkins University Press, 1984), pp. 245–47.

17. The inventory of the estate of Santiago Lemelle.

18. McGowan, "Creation of a Slave Society."

19. Baade, "The Law of Slavery in Spanish Louisiana," pp. 43–67. *Inter vivos* is the transference of property from one living person to another; *mortis causae* involves transfers from the estates of deceased individuals.

20. Jean Baptiste Le Moyne, Superior Council Records, 1733, Louisiana State Museum; St. Pierre de St. Julien, Superior Council Records.

21. The practice of self-purchase in New Orleans is evident in the Notarial Archives of the Spanish period located in the Civil Court Building in New Orleans. For the debate surrounding the liberality of the Spanish practice of *coartación*, see Gwendolyn M. Hall, *Social Control in Slave Plantation Societies: A Comparison of St. Domingue and Cuba* (Baltimore: Johns Hopkins University Press, 1971) pp. 81–135; Rebecca J. Scott, *Slave Emancipation in Cuba: The Transition to Free Labor, 1860–1899* (Princeton: Princeton University Press, 1985), pp. 13–14; Franklin W. Knight, *Slave Society in Cuba during the Nineteenth Century* (Madison, 1970), pp. 130–31; Elsa Goveia, "The West Indian Slave Laws," p. 116; McGowan, "Creation of a Slave Society," pp. 175–217; Baade, "The Law of Slavery in Spanish Louisiana," pp. 67–70; Fierher, "The African Presence in Colonial Louisiana," p. 24. For the nearly complete records of manumission for the Spanish period in New Orleans, see the *cartas de libertad* included in the Notarial Acts, 1769–1803, housed in the Civil Court Building in New Orleans. A few court cases that consider the subject of self-purchase are located in the Court Records for the Spanish period which are housed in the Louisiana State Museum in New Orleans.

22. Elsa Goveia, Hans Baade, and James Thomas McGowan, among others, discuss the difficulty of self-purchase faced by slaves in New Orleans and other Spanish American colonies. The New Orleans Census of 1795 was compiled from church censuses taken by parish priests and reported to Bishop Luis Penalver y Cardenas in New Orleans and can be seen in the Records of the Diocese of Louisiana and Floridas, 1576–1803, University of Notre Dame Archives; microfilm is located at Louisiana State University, Baton Rouge.

23. An excellent discussion of manumissions in the Spanish period can be found in Kimberly S. Hanger, "Personas de Varias Clases y Colores: Free Persons of Color in the Spanish New Orleans, 1769–1803," Ph.D. dissertation, University of Florida, 1991. Angelica's petition was heard by the Spanish Court on July 29, 1779, and can be found in the Louisiana State Museum, New Orleans. Also see the Spanish Court Records for the case of Rosa and Maria Isabel, the negress slaves of Señor Raynoldo, who appealed to the court to uphold the freedom that Raynoldo had granted to them and to Rosa's daughter in his will. Denied freedom by Raynoldo's heirs, the two slaves were awarded their freedom by the court but were required to pay their appraised value to Raynoldo's heirs. For Rosa and for her daughter, the amount was 350 pesos; for Maria Isabel, 340 pesos. In their case, freedom was awarded before payment was required, but most times payment came first.

24. Almonaster y Roxas, *escribano*, January through July 1776, pp. 586 and 158; In two other examples of *coartación*, Juliana, the forty-year-old negress slave of Miguel Almonari, bought her freedom for 280 pesos in August 1776; in the same year, the forty-one-year-old negress slave Mariana paid Pedro Vieux, her master, 350 pesos for her freedom. But freedom was much more elusive for other slave women. For example, in 1773 the negress slave Maturina took the free mulatress Naneta to court on the grounds that Maturina had entrusted her with the money that she had accumulated for her purchase price but that Naneta had tricked Maturina and used the funds to free her own mother, Enriqueta. The court upheld Maturina's claim, demanding that Naneta return the sum, but the record ends with Maturina continuing to petition the court to retrieve her savings. Maturina's case was brought before the Spanish court in 1773 and can be found in the Louisiana State Museum in New Orleans. Original Notarial Acts, New Orleans, 1769–1803. In 1794, Augustin Malet, a mulatto libre, and the testamentary

executor for the estate of his mother, Juana, a mulatta libre, freed the negress Rosalia, as his mother requested, for the love and care that the slave had shown her over the years. Pedro Pedesclaux, *escribano*, Book of January through May 1794, Act of February 7, 1794, p. 117; Original Notarial Acts of New Orleans, 1769–1803.

25. Spanish Judicial Records, May 1, 1795; Jack D. L. Holmes, "The Abortive Slave Revolt at Pointe Coupée, Louisiana, 1795," *Louisiana History* 11 (1970): 341–62; Stuart O. Landry, ed. and trans., *Voyages to Louisiana by C. C. Robin, 1803–1805*, 2 vols. (New Orleans, 1966), p. 117; Alfred Hunt, *Haiti's Influence on Antebellum America: Slumbering Volcano in the Caribbean* (Baton Rouge: Louisiana State University Press, 1988), pp. 26–28.

26. The *carta de libertad* for Jacqueline, Adelaida, Maria Francisca, and Agata Lemelle was recorded by the *escribano* Almonaster y Roxas in November 1772 and is located in the book of January through December 1772. Also see the inventory and appraisement of the estate of Santiago Lemelle probated March 21, 1784.

27. Ira Berlin, *Slaves without Masters: The Free Negro in the Antebellum South* (New York: Oxford University Press, 1981), pp. 108–9; Gould, "In Full Enjoyment of Their Liberty."

28. Patterson, *Slavery and Social Death*, pp. 453–55.

29. The inventory of the estate of Santiago Lemelle; court proceedings of Maria Juana, the slave of Juan Suriray, Spanish Court Records, February 28, 1774.

30. The records of Margaret and Juana can be found in the Spanish Judicial Records. Another place to gauge relationships between slave women and free women of color is in the Archives of the St. Louis Cathedral. Sacramental records demonstrate that it was a common practice for free women of color to serve as *madrinas*, or godmothers, to the children of slave women but that nearly all who did were relatives. Furthermore, notarial and property records fail to demonstrate ties between slave and free women of color outside of kinship ties. Court records also fail to demonstrate a single case of a free woman of color leaving her estate to a slave or free woman of color who was not a relative.

31. Gary B. Mills, *The Forgotten People: Cane River's Creoles of Color* (Baton Rouge: Louisiana State University Press, 1977), pp. xiii–xiv.

32. The tradition of racial classification was formalized by the Spanish in the 1785 code, called the Codigo Negro Carolino, which institutionalized the dishonor of African descent and the honor of white descent. See Hall, *Social Control in Slave Plantation Societies*, pp. 138–39.

33. Bartolome Bautista, Spanish Judicial Records, September 6, 1788.

34. Notarial Acts and Court Records located in New Orleans demonstrate that it was not unusual for free women of color to own slaves but that when they did they overwhelmingly owned women instead of men. Also, free women of color usually freed only slaves to whom they were related. Occasionally they freed friends or fictive kin. Slaves they owned as laborers were either kept, sold, or willed to children or other heirs. For the most complete picture of the ways in which free women of color responded to slave women, see the papers of the William T. Johnson family at the Hill Memorial Library in Baton Rouge.

35. The inventory of the estate of Santiago Lemelle, Spanish Court Records, 1784; Patterson, *Slavery and Social Death*, p. 247.

36. The manumission records of Maria Juana and Julia are recorded in the acts of Juan Garic, December 1772 and October 1775.

37. The inventory of the estate of Santiago Lemelle; acts of F. Broutin, June 14, 1794.

SELECTED BIBLIOGRAPHY

Celia E. Naylor-Ojurongbe and David Barry Gaspar

Aidoo, Agnes Akosua. "Asante Queen Mothers in Government and Politics in the Nineteenth Century." In *The Black Woman Cross-Culturally.* Edited by Filomina Chioma Steady. Cambridge, Mass.: Schenkman, 1981, 65–77.

Alberro, Solange. "Juan de Morga and Gertrudis de Escobar: Rebellious Slaves." In *Struggle and Survival in Colonial America.* Edited by David G. Sweet and Gary B. Nash. Berkeley: University of California Press, 1981, 165–88.

Alonzo, Andrea Starr. "A Study of Two Women's Slave Narratives: *Incidents in the Life of a Slave Girl* and *The History of Mary Prince.*" *Women's Studies Quarterly* 17, nos. 3 and 4 (Fall–Winter 1989): 118–22.

Andrews, William, ed. *Six Women's Slave Narratives.* New York: Oxford University Press, 1988.

Arhin, Kwame. "The Political and Military Roles of Akan Women." In *Female and Male in West Africa.* Edited by Christine Oppong. London: George Allen & Unwin, 1983, 91–98.

Atkins, Leah Rawls. "High Cotton: The Antebellum Alabama Plantation Mistress and the Cotton Culture." *Agricultural History* 68 (Spring 1994): 92–104.

Axelsen, Diana E. "Women as Victims of Medical Experimentation: J. Marion Sims' Surgery on Slave Women, 1845–1850." *Sage: A Scholarly Journal on Black Women* 2, no. 2 (Fall 1985): 10–13.

Barkley Brown, Elsa. "African-American Women's Quilting: A Framework for Conceptualizing and Teaching African-American Women's History." *Signs* 14, no. 4 (1989): 921–29.

Beal, Frances M. "Slave of a Slave No More: Black Women in Struggle." *Black Scholar* 6, no. 6 (March 1975): 2–10.

Beckles, Hilary McD. *Afro-Caribbean Women and Resistance to Slavery in Barbados.* London: Karnak House, 1988.

———. *Natural Rebels: A Social History of Enslaved Black Women in Barbados.* New Brunswick: Rutgers University Press, 1989.

———. "White Women and Slavery in the Caribbean." *History Workshop: A Journal of Socialist and Feminist Historians* 36 (1993): 66–82.

Berlin, Ira. "The Revolution in Black Life." In *The American Revolution: Explorations in the History of American Radicalism.* Edited by Alfred F. Young. De Kalb: Northern Illinois University Press, 1976, 349–82.

———, Steven F. Miller, and Leslie S. Rowland. "Afro-American Families in the Transition from Slavery to Freedom." *Radical History Review* 42 (Fall 1988): 89–121.

———, and Ronald Hoffman, eds. *Slavery and Freedom in the Age of the American Revolution.* Charlottesville: University Press of Virginia, 1983.

Bernard, Jacqueline. *Journey toward Freedom: The Story of Sojourner Truth.* New York: Norton, 1967.

Bernhard, Virginia. *Southern Women: Histories and Identities.* Edited by Betty Brandon, Elizabeth Fox-Genovese, and Theda Perdue. Columbia: University of Missouri Press, 1992.

Berthoff, Rowland. "Conventional Mentality: Free Blacks, Women, and Business Corporations as Unequal Persons, 1820–1870." *Journal of American History* 76 (December 1989): 753–84.

Bilby, Kenneth, and Filomina Chioma Steady. "Black Women and Survival: A Maroon Case." In *The Black Woman Cross Culturally*. Edited by Filomina Chioma Steady. Cambridge, Mass.: Schenkman, 1981, 451–67.

Blackburn, George, and Sherman L. Ricards. "The Mother-Headed Family among Free Negroes in Charleston, South Carolina, 1850–1860." *Phylon* 42, no. 1 (March 1981): 11–25.

Bleser, Carol, ed. *In Joy and in Sorrow: Women, Family, and Marriage in the Victorian South, 1830–1900*. New York: Oxford University Press, 1991.

Bogin, Ruth. "Sarah Parker Remond: Black Abolitionist from Salem." *Essex Institute Historical Collections* 110, no. 2 (April 1974): 120–50.

Bradford, Sarah. *Harriet Tubman: The Moses of Her People*. Lecaucus, N.J.: Citadel, 1987.

Brathwaite, Edward Kamau. "Submerged Mothers." *Jamaica Journal* 9, nos. 2 and 3 (1975): 48–49.

Braxton, Joanne M. *Black Women Writing Autobiography: A Tradition within a Tradition*. Philadelphia: Temple University Press, 1989.

———. "Harriet Jacobs' *Incidents in the Life of a Slave Girl*: The Redefinition of the Slave Narrative Genre." *Massachusetts Review: A Quarterly of Literature, the Arts and Public Affairs* 27, no. 2 (Summer 1986): 379–87.

Brown, Ira V. "'Am I Not a Woman and a Sister?': The Anti-Slavery Convention of American Women, 1837–1839." *Pennsylvania History* 50 (January 1983): 1–19.

———. "Cradle of Feminism: The Philadelphia Female Anti-Slavery Society, 1833–1840." *Pennsylvania Magazine of History and Biography* 102 (April 1978): 143–66.

Brown, Steven E. "Sexuality and the Slave Community." *Phylon* 42 (March 1981): 1–10.

Burgess, Norma J. "Gender Roles Revisited: The Development of the 'Woman's Place' among African-American Women in the United States." *Journal of Black Studies* 24 (June 1994): 391–401.

Burke, Helen M. "The Rhetoric and Politics of Marginality: The Subject of Phillis Wheatley." *Tulsa Studies in Women's Literature* 10 (Spring 1991): 31–46.

Burnham, Dorothy. "The Life of the Afro-American Woman in Slavery." *International Journal of Women's Studies* 1, no. 4 (July–August 1978): 363–77.

Bush, Barbara. *Slave Women in Caribbean Society, 1650–1838*. Bloomington: Indiana University Press, 1990.

———. "Towards Emancipation: Slave Women and Resistance to Coercive Labour Regimes in the British West Indian Colonies, 1790–1838." *Slavery and Abolition* 5, no. 3 (December 1984): 222–43.

———. "White 'Ladies,' Coloured 'Favourites' and Black 'Wenches': Some Considerations on Sex, Race and Class Factors in Social Relations in White Creole Society in the British Caribbean." *Slavery and Abolition* 2, no. 3 (December 1981): 245–62.

Bush-Slimani, B. "Hard Labor: Women, Childbirth and Resistance in British Caribbean Slave Societies." *History Workshop: A Journal of Socialist and Feminist Historians* 36 (1993): 83–99.

Bynum, Victoria. "On the Lowest Rung: Count Control over Poor White and Free Black Women." *Southern Exposure* 12 (November–December 1984): 40–44.

Campbell, John. "Work, Pregnancy, and Infant Mortality among Southern Slaves." *Journal of Interdisciplinary History* 14, no. 4 (Spring 1984): 793–812.

Carby, Hazel V. "'On the Threshold of Women's Era': Lynching, Empire and Sexuality in Black Feminist Theory." *Critical Inquiry* 12, no. 1 (Autumn 1985): 262–77.

Chase-Riboud, Barbara. *Sally Hemings: A Novel*. New York: Viking, 1979.

Chauvet, Marie. *Dance on the Volcano*. Translated by Salvator Attanasio. New York: William Sloane, 1959. (Translation of *La Danse sur le volcan*, Paris: Librairie Plon, 1957).

Clinton, Catherine. "Caught in the Web of the Big House: Women and Slavery." In *The Web of Southern Social Relations: Women, Family and Education*. Edited by Walter J. Fraser, Jr., Frank Saunders, Jr., and Jon L. Wakelyn. Athens: University of Georgia Press, 1985, 19–34.

———. "Fanny Kemble's Journal: A Woman Confronts Slavery on a Georgia Plantation." *Frontiers* 9 (1987): 74–79.

———. *The Plantation Mistress: Woman's World in the Old South*. New York: Pantheon, 1982.

———. "'Southern Dishonor': Flesh, Blood, Race, and Bondage." In *In Joy and in Sorrow: Women, Family, and Marriage in the Victorian South, 1830–1900*. Edited by Carol Bleser. New York: Oxford University Press, 1991, 52–68.

———, ed. *Half Sisters of History: Southern Women and the American Past*. Durham, N.C.: Duke University Press, 1994.

Cody, Cheryll Ann. "Naming, Kinship, and Estate Dispersal: Notes on Slave Family Life on a South Carolina Plantation, 1786–1833." *William and Mary Quarterly* 3d Series, 39, no. 1 (January 1982): 192–211.

———. "A Note on Changing Patterns of Slave Fertility in the South Carolina Rice District, 1735–1865." *Southern Studies* 16, no. 4 (Winter 1977): 457–62.

———. "Slave Demography and Family Formation: A Community Study of the Ball Family Plantations, 1720–1896." Ph.D. dissertation, University of Minnesota, 1982.

Cole, Johnnetta. "Militant Black Women in Early U.S. History." *Black Scholar* 9, no. 7 (April 1978): 38–44.

Conrad, Earl. "I Bring You General Tubman." *Black Scholar* 1, no. 1 (January–February 1970): 2–7.

Cook, Charles Orson, and James M. Poteet. "'Dem Was Black Times, Sure 'Nough': The Slave Narratives of Lydia Jefferson and Stephen Williams." *Louisiana History* 20 (Summer 1979): 281–92.

Cornelius, Janet. "Slave Marriages in a Georgia Congregation." In *Class, Conflict, and Consensus: Antebellum Southern Communities*. Edited by Orville Vernon Burton and Robert C. McMath, Jr. Westport, Conn.: Greenwood, 1982, 128–45.

Craton, Michael. "Changing Patterns of Slave Families in the British West Indies." *Journal of Interdisciplinary History* 10, no. 1 (Summer 1979): 1–35.

Cunningham, Constance A. "The Sin of Omission: Black Women in Nineteenth-Century American History." *Journal of Social and Behavioral Sciences* 33, no. 1 (Winter 1987): 35–46.

Dadzie, Stella. "Searching for the Invisible Woman: Slavery and Resistance in Jamaica." *Race and Class* 32, no. 2 (October–December 1990): 21–38.

Davis, Angela Y. "Reflections on the Black Woman's Role in the Community of Slaves." *Black Scholar* 3, no. 4 (December 1971): 2–15.

———. *Women, Race and Class*. New York: Random House, 1981.

de Groot, Silvia W. "Maroon Women as Ancestors, Priests and Mediums in Surinam." *Slavery and Abolition* 7, no. 2 (September 1986): 160–74.

Diedrich, Maria. "'My Love Is Black as Yours Is Fair': Premarital Love and Sexuality in the Antebellum Slave Narrative." *Phylon* 47, no. 3 (September 1986): 238–47.

Dill, Bonnie Thornton. "The Dialectics of Black Womanhood." *Signs* 4 (Spring 1979): 543–55.

Diner, Hasia R. "Black Women in Families: From Field to Factory." *Reviews in American History* 13, no. 4 (1985): 551–56.

Dunn, Richard S. "Black Society in the Chesapeake, 1776–1810." In *Slavery and Freedom in the Age of the American Revolution*. Edited by Ira Berlin and Ronald Hoffman. Charlottesville: University Press of Virginia, 1983, 49–82.

———. "'Dreadful Idlers' in the Cane Fields: The Slave Labor Pattern on a Jamaican Sugar Estate, 1762–1831." *Journal of Interdisciplinary History* 17, no. 4. (Spring 1987): 795–822.

———. "A Tale of Two Plantations: Slave Life at Mesopotamia in Jamaica and Mount Airy in Virginia, 1799–1828." *William and Mary Quarterly* 3d Series, 34, no. 1 (January 1977): 32–65.

Eastman, Carole M. "Women, Slaves, and Foreigners: African Cultural Influences and Group Processes in the Formation of Northern Swahili Coastal Society." *International Journal of African Historical Studies* 21, no. 1 (1988): 1–20.

Ellison, Mary. "Resistance to Oppression: Black Women's Response to Slavery in the United States." *Slavery and Abolition* 4, no. 1 (May 1983): 56–63.

Emecheta, Buchi. *The Slave Girl*. New York: Braziller, 1977.

Erkkila, Betsy. "Phillis Wheatley and the Black American Revolution." In *A Mixed Race: Ethnicity in Early America*. Edited by Frank Shuffelton. New York: Oxford University Press, 1993, 225–40.

Farnham, Christie. "Sapphire? The Issue of Dominance in the Slave Family, 1830–1865." In *"To Toil the Livelong Day": America's Women at Work, 1780–1980*. Edited by Carol Groneman and Mary Beth Norton. Ithaca: Cornell University Press, 1987, 68–83.

Faust, Drew Gilpin. "Culture, Conflict, and Community: The Meaning of Power on an Ante-Bellum Plantation." *Journal of Social History* 14, no. 1 (Fall 1980): 83–98.

———. *James Henry Hammond and the Old South: A Design for Mastery*. Baton Rouge: Louisiana State University Press, 1982.

———. *Southern Stories: Slaveholders in Peace and War*. Columbia: University of Missouri Press, 1992.

———. "'Trying to Do a Man's Business': Slavery, Violence, and Gender in the American Civil War." *Gender and History* 4 (Summer 1992): 197–214.

———, ed. *Ideology of Slavery: Proslavery Thought in the Antebellum South, 1830–1860*. Baton Rouge: Louisiana State University Press, 1981.

Ferguson, Moira. *The History of Mary Prince*. London: Pandora, 1987.

———, ed. *The Hart Sisters: Early African Caribbean Writers, Evangelicals and Radicals*. Lincoln: University of Nebraska Press, 1993.

Finkelman, Paul, ed. *Women and the Family in a Slave Society*. New York: Garland, 1989.

Fogel, Robert, and Stanley Engerman. "Recent Findings in the Study of Slave Demography and Family Structure." *Sociology and Social Research* 63, no. 3 (April 1979): 566–89.

Foley, William E. "Slave Freedom Suits before Dred Scott: The Case of Marie Jean Scypion's Descendants." *Missouri Historical Review* 79 (October 1984): 1–23.

Foster, Frances Smith. "Adding Color and Contour to Early American Self-Portraitures: Autobiographical Writings of Afro-American Women." In *Conjuring: Black Women, Fiction, and Literary Tradition*. Edited by Marjorie Pryse and Hortense J. Spillers. Bloomington: Indiana University Press, 1985, 25–38.

———. *Written by Herself: Literary Production by African American Women, 1746–1892*. Bloomington: Indiana University Press, 1993.

———. "Between the Sides: Afro-American Women Writers as Mediators." *Nineteenth-Century Studies* 3 (1989): 53–64.

———. "'In Respect to Females . . .': Differences in the Portrayals of Women by Male and Female Narrators." *Black American Literature Forum* 15, no. 2 (Summer 1981): 66–70.

———. "Ultimate Victims: Black Women in Slave Narratives." *Journal of American Culture* 1, no. 4 (1978): 845–54.

Fox-Genovese, Elizabeth. "Antebellum Southern Households: A New Perspective on a Familiar Question." *Review* 7, no. 2 (Fall 1983): 215–53.

———. "Placing Women's History in History." *New Left Review* 133 (May–June 1982): 5–29.

———. "Strategies and Forms of Resistance: Focus on Slave Women in the United States." In *In Resistance: Studies in African, Caribbean and Afro-American History.* Edited by Gary Y. Okihiro. Amherst: University of Massachusetts Press, 1986, 143–65.

———. *Within the Plantation Household: Black and White Women of the Old South.* Chapel Hill: University of North Carolina Press, 1988.

Frazier, E. Franklin. "The Negro Slave Family." *Journal of Negro History* 15, no. 1 (January 1930): 198–259.

Gates, Henry Louis, Jr., general ed. *Collected Black Women's Narratives.* Schomburg Library of Nineteenth-Century Black Women Writers. New York: Oxford University Press, 1988.

Gautier, Arlette. "Les Esclaves femmes aux Antilles françaises, 1635–1848." *Reflexions Historiques* 10, no. 3 (Fall 1983): 409–35.

———. *Les Soeurs de Solitude: La Condition féminine dans l'esclavage aux Antilles du XVIIe au XIXe siècle.* Paris: Editions Caribéennes, 1985.

Genovese, Eugene D. "'Our Family, White and Black': Family and Household in the Southern Slaveholders' World View." In *In Joy and in Sorrow: Women, Family and Marriage in the Victorian South, 1830–1900.* Edited by Carol Bleser. New York: Oxford University Press, 1991, 69–87.

Getman, Karen A. "Sexual Control in the Slaveholding South: The Implementation and Maintenance of a Racial Caste System." *Harvard Women's Law Journal* 7 (Spring 1984): 115–52.

Giacomini, Sonia Maria. *Mulhere Escrava: Uma Introducao Historica ao Estudo da Mulhere Negra no Brasil.* Petrópolis: Vozes, 1988.

Giddings, Paula. "Casting of the Die: Morality, Slavery and Resistance." In *When and Where I Enter: The Impact of Black Women on Race and Sex in America.* New York: Morrow, 1984, 33–55.

Goodson, Martia Graham. "Medical-Botanical Contributions of African Slave Women to American Medicine." *Western Journal of Black Studies* 11, no. 4 (Winter 1987): 198–203.

———. "The Slave Narrative Collection: A Tool for Reconstructing Afro-American Women's History." *Western Journal of Black Studies* 3, no. 2 (Summer 1979): 116–22.

Graham, Richard. "Slave Families on a Rural Estate in Colonial Brazil." *Journal of Social History* 9, no. 3 (Spring 1976): 382–402.

Gregory, Chester W. "Black Women in Pre-Federal America." In *Clio Was a Woman: Studies in the History of American Women.* Edited by Mabel E. Deutrich and Virginia C. Purdy. Washington, D.C.: Howard University Press, 1980, 53–70.

Grimstead, David. "Anglo-American Racism and Phillis Wheatley's 'Sable Veil,' 'Length-'ned Chain,' and 'Knitted Heart.'" In *Women in the Age of the American Revolution.* Edited by Ronald Hoffman and Peter J. Albert. Charlottesville: University Press of Virginia, 1989, 338–444.

Groneman, Carol. "Nymphomania: The Historical Construction of Female Sexuality." *Signs* 19 (Winter 1994): 337–67.

Gundersen, Joan Rezner. "The Double Bonds of Race and Sex: Black and White Women in a Colonial Virginia Parish." *Journal of Southern History* 52, no. 3 (August 1986): 351–72.

Gutman, Herbert G. *The Black Family in Slavery and Freedom, 1750–1925.* New York: Pantheon, 1976.

———. "Slave Culture and Slave Family and Kin Network: The Importance of Time." *South Atlantic Urban Studies* 2 (1978): 73–88.

Gwin, Minrose C. *Black and White Women of the Old South: The Peculiar Sisterhood in American Literature.* Knoxville: University of Tennessee Press, 1985.

———. "Green-eyed Monsters of the Slavocracy: Jealous Mistresses in Two Slave Narratives." In *Conjuring: Black Women, Fiction, and Literary Tradition.* Edited by Marjorie Pryse and Hortense J. Spillers. Bloomington: Indiana University Press, 1985, 39–52.

Hanchett, Catherine M. "'What Sort of People and Families . . .': The Edmonson Sisters." *Afro-Americans in New York Life and History* 6, no. 2 (July 1982): 21–37.

Handler, Jerome S. "Joseph Rachell and Rachael Pringle-Polgreen: Petty Entrepreneurs." In *Struggle and Survival in Colonial America.* Edited by David G. Sweet and Gary B. Nash. Berkeley: University of California Press, 376–91.

———, and Robert S. Corruccini. "Weaning among West Indian Slaves: Historical and Bioanthropological Evidence from Barbados." *William and Mary Quarterly* 3d Series, 43, no. 1 (January 1986): 111–17.

Harley, Sharon, and Terborg-Penn, Rosalyn, eds. *The Afro-American Woman: Struggles and Images.* Port Washington, N.Y.: Kennikat, 1978.

Harper, C. W. "Black Aristocrats: Domestic Servants on the Antebellum Plantation." *Phylon* 46 (June 1985): 123–35.

Harris, J. William, ed. *Society and Culture in the Slave South.* London: Routledge, 1992.

Hartgrove, W. B. "The Story of Maria Louise Moore and Fannie M. Richards." *Journal of Negro History* 1, no. 1 (January 1916): 23–33.

Henke, Suzette. *"Incidents in the Life of a Slave Girl:* Autobiography as Reconstruction." *Feminist Issues* 6 (Fall 1986): 33–39.

Hewitt, Nancy. "Sisterhood in International Perspective: Thoughts on Teaching Comparative Women's History." *Women's Studies Quarterly* 16 (Spring–Summer 1988): 22–32.

Higginbotham, Elizabeth, and Sarah Watts. "The New Scholarship on Afro-American Women." *Women's Studies Quarterly* 16 (Spring–Summer 1988): 12–21.

Higginbotham, Evelyn Brooks. "African-American Women's History and the Metalanguage of Race." *Signs* 17, no. 2 (1992): 251–74.

———. "Beyond the Sound of Silence: Afro-American Women's History." *Gender and History* 1 (Spring 1989): 50–67.

Higman, Barry W. "African and Creole Slave Family Patterns in Trinidad." *Journal of Family History* 3, no. 2 (Summer 1978): 163–80.

———. "Household Structure and Fertility on Jamaican Slave Plantations: A Nineteenth-Century Example." *Population Studies* 27, no. 3 (November 1973): 527–50.

———. "The Slave Family and Household in the British West Indies, 1800–1834." *Journal of Interdisciplinary History* 6, no. 2 (Autumn 1975): 261–87.

Hine, Darlene Clark. "Female Slave Resistance: The Economics of Sex." *Western Journal of Black Studies* 3, no. 2 (Summer 1979): 123–27.

———. "Lifting the Veil, Shattering the Silence: Black Women's History in Slavery and Freedom." In *The State of Afro-American History: Past, Present and Future.* Edited by Darlene Clark Hine. Baton Rouge: Louisiana State University Press, 1986, 223–49.

———. "Rape and the Inner Lives of Black Women in the Middle West." *Signs* 14 (Summer 1989): 912–20.

———, ed. *Black Women in American History: From Colonial Times through the Nineteenth Century.* 4 volumes. Brooklyn, N.Y.: Carlson, 1990.

————, and Kate Wittenstein. "Female Slave Resistance: The Economics of Sex." In *The Black Woman Cross-Culturally*. Edited by Filomina Chioma Steady. Cambridge, Mass.: Schenkman, 1981, 289–99.

Hoffman, Nancy. "Teaching about Slavery, the Abolitionist Movement, and Women's Suffrage." *Women's Studies Quarterly* 14, nos. 1 and 2 (Spring–Summer 1986): 2–6.

Hoffman, Ronald, and Peter J. Albert, eds. *Women in the Age of the American Revolution*. Charlottesville: University Press of Virginia, 1989.

Hoffschwelle, Mary S. "Women's Sphere and the Creation of Female Community in the Antebellum South: Three Tennessee Slaveholding Women." *Tennessee Historical Quarterly* 50 (Summer 1991): 80–89.

Horton, James Oliver. "Freedom's Yoke: Gender Conventions among Antebellum Free Blacks." *Feminist Studies* 12, no. 1 (Spring 1986): 51–76.

Hull, Gloria T., Patricia Bell Scott, and Barbara Smith, eds. *All the Women Are White, All the Blacks Are Men, but Some of Us Are Brave: Black Women's Studies*. Old Westbury, N.Y.: Feminist, 1982.

Inscoe, John C. "Slave Rebellion in the First Person: The Literary 'Confessions' of Nat Turner and Dessa Rose." *Virginia Magazine of History and Biography* 97, no. 4 (October 1989): 419–36.

Jackson-Brown, Irene V. "Black Women and Music: A Survey from Africa to the New World." In *The Black Woman Cross-Culturally*. Edited by Filomina Chioma Steady. Cambridge, Mass.: Schenkman, 1981, 383–401.

Jacobs, Harriet A. *Incidents in the Life of a Slave Girl, Written by Herself*. Edited and with an introduction by Jean Fagan Yellin. Cambridge: Harvard University Press, 1987. (First published in 1861 under the pseudonym Linda Brent.)

Jennings, Thelma. "'Us Colored Women Had to Go Throug a Plenty': Sexual Exploitation of African-American Slave Women." *Journal of Women's History* 1, no. 3 (Winter 1990): 45–74.

Johnson, Michael P. "Smothered Slave Infants: Were Slave Mothers at Fault?" *Journal of Southern History* 47, no. 4 (November 1981): 493–520.

————. "Work, Culture, and the Slave Community: Slave Occupations in the Cotton Belt in 1860." *Labor History* 27, no. 3 (Summer 1986): 325–55.

————, and James L. Roark. "Strategies of Survival: Free Negro Families and the Problem of Slavery." In *In Joy and in Sorrow: Women, Family and Marriage in the Victorian South, 1830–1900*. Edited by Carol Bleser. New York: Oxford University Press, 1991, 88–102.

Johnson, Whittington B. "Free African-American Women in Savannah, 1800–1860: Affluence and Autonomy amid Diversity." *Georgia Historical Quarterly* 76 (Summer 1992): 260–83.

Johnson-Odim, Cheryl, and Margaret Strobel. "Conceptualizing the History of Women in Africa, Asia, Latin America and the Caribbean, and the Middle East." *Journal of Women's History* 1, no. 1 (Spring 1989): 31–62.

Jones, Jacqueline. *Labor of Love, Labor of Sorrow: Black Women, Work and the Family from Slavery to the Present*. New York: Basic, 1985.

————. "'My Mother Was Much of a Woman': Black Women, Work, and the Family under Slavery." *Feminist Studies* 8, no. 2 (Summer 1982): 235–69.

————. "Race, Sex, and Self-Evident Truths: The Status of Slave Women during the Era of the American Revolution." In *Half Sisters of History: Southern Women and the American Past*. Edited by Catherine Clinton. Durham, N.C.: Duke University Press, 1994.

Just, Roger. "Freedom, Slavery and the Female Psyche." *History of Political Thought* 6, nos. 1 and 2 (1985): 169–88.

Keckley, Elizabeth. *Behind the Scenes; or, Thirty Years a Slave and Four Years in the White House*. New York: Oxford University Press, 1988.

Kerber, Linda K. "Separate Spheres, Female Worlds, Woman's Place: The Rhetoric of Women's History." *Journal of American History* 75, no. 1 (June 1988): 9–39.

Kiple, Kenneth F., and Kiple, Virginia H. "Slave Child Mortality: Some Nutritional Answers to a Perennial Puzzle." *Journal of Social History* 10, no. 3 (March 1977): 284–309.

Klein, Herbert S. "African Women in the Atlantic Slave Trade." In *Women and Slavery in Africa*. Edited by Claire C. Robertson and Martin A. Klein. Madison: University of Wisconsin Press, 1983, 29–38.

———, and Engerman, Stanley L. "Fertility Differentials between Slaves in the United States and the British West Indies: A Note on Lactation Practices and Their Possible Implications." *William and Mary Quarterly* 3d Series, 35, no. 2 (April 1978): 357–74.

Kossek, Brigitte. "Racist and Patriarchal Aspects of Plantation Slavery in Grenada: 'White Ladies,' 'Black Women Slaves,' and 'Rebels.'" In *Slavery in the Americas*. Edited by Wolgang Binder. Wurzburg: Königshausen & Neumann, 1993, 277–303.

Krebs, Sylvia H. "Life without 'My Folks': Letters to Former Slaves." *Atlanta History Journal* 29 (Summer 1985): 47–50.

Kulikoff, Allan. "The Beginnings of the Afro-American Family in Maryland." In *Law, Society and Politics in Early Maryland*. Edited by Aubrey C. Land, Lois Green Carr, and Edward C. Papenfuse. Baltimore: John Hopkins University Press, 1977, 717–96.

———. "The Origins of Afro-American Society in Tidewater Maryland and Virginia, 1700 to 1790." *William and Mary Quarterly* 3d Series, 35, no. 2 (April 1978): 226–59.

———. "A 'Prolifick' People: Black Population Growth in the Chesapeake Colonies, 1700–1790." *Southern Studies* 16, no. 4 (Winter 1977): 391–428.

———. "Uprooted Peoples: Black Migrants in the Age of the American Revolution, 1790–1820." In *Slavery and Freedom in the Age of the American Revolution*. Edited by Ira Berlin and Ronald Hoffman. Charlottesville: University Press of Virginia, 1983, 143–71.

Kuznesof, Elizabeth Anne. "Household Composition and Headship as Related to Mode of Production: São Paulo 1765–1836." *Comparative Studies in Society and History* 22, no. 1 (January 1980): 78–108.

———. "The Role of the Female-Headed Household in Brazilian Modernization: 1765–1836." *Journal of Social History* 13, no. 4 (Summer 1979): 589–614.

Lamur, Humphrey E. "Fertility Differentials on Three Slave Plantations in Suriname." *Slavery and Abolition* 8, no. 3 (December 1987): 313–35.

———. "The Slave Family in Colonial Nineteenth-Century Suriname." *Journal of Black Studies* 23 (1992): 344–57.

Lantz, Herman, and Lewellyn Hendrix. "Black Fertility and the Black Family in the Nineteenth Century: A Re-Examination of the Past." *Journal of Family History* 3, no. 3 (Fall 1978): 251–61.

Lawson, Ellen N. "Sarah Woodson Early: Nineteenth-Century Black Nationalist 'Sister.'" *Umoja* 5, no. 2 (Summer 1981): 15–26.

Lebsock, Suzanne. "Free Black Women and the Question of Matriarchy: Petersburg, Virginia, 1784–1820." *Feminist Studies* 8, no. 2 (Summer 1982): 271–92.

———. *The Free Women of Petersburg: Status and Culture in a Southern Town, 1784–1860*. New York: Norton, 1984.

Lerner, Gerda. "Reconceptualizing Differences among Women." *Journal of Women's History* 1, no. 3 (Winter 1990): 106–22.

———. "Women and Slavery." *Slavery and Abolition* 4, no. 3 (December 1983): 173–98.

————, ed. *Black Women in White America: A Documentary History*. New York: Pantheon, 1972.

Levy, Andrew. "Dialect and Convention: Harriet A. Jacobs' Incidents in the Life of a Slave Girl." *Nineteenth-Century Literature* 45, no. 2 (September 1990): 206–19.

Lewis, Ronald L. "Slave Families of Early Chesapeake Ironworks." *Virginia Magazine of History and Biography* 86 (April 1978): 169–79.

Littlefield, Daniel C. "Plantations, Paternalism, and Profitability: Factors Affecting African Demography in the Old British Empire." *Journal of Southern History* 47 (May 1981): 167–82.

Loewenberg, Bert James, and Ruth Bogin, eds. *Black Women in Nineteenth-Century Life: Their Words, Their Thoughts, Their Feelings*. University Park: Pennsylvania State University Press, 1976.

Lovejoy, Paul E. "Concubinage and the Status of Women Slaves in Early Colonial Northern Nigeria." *Journal of African History* 29, no. 2 (1988): 245–66.

Mabee, Carleton, "Sojourner Truth, Bold Prophet: Why Did She Never Learn to Read?" *New York History* 69, no. 1 (January 1988): 55–77.

————. "Sojourner Truth Fights Dependence on Government: Moves Freed Slaves Off Welfare in Washington to Jobs in Upstate New York." *Afro-Americans in New York Life and History* 14 (January 1990): 7–26.

Mack, Beverly B. "Women and Slavery in Nineteenth-Century Hausaland." *Slavery and Abolition* 13, no. 1 (April 1992): 89–110.

Mair, Lucille Mathurin. "A Historical Study of Women in Jamaica from 1655 to 1844." Ph.D. dissertation. University of the West Indies, 1974.

————. *The Rebel Woman in the British West Indies during Slavery*. Kingston: Institute of Jamaica, for the African-Caribbean Institute of Jamaica, 1975.

————. "Recollections of a Journey into a Rebel Past." In *Caribbean Women Writers: Essays from the First International Conference*. Edited by Selwyn R. Cudjoe. Wellesley, Mass.: Calaloux, 1990, 51–60.

————. *Women Field Workers in Jamaica during Slavery*. Mona, Jamaica: Department of History, University of the West Indies, 1987.

Malone, Ann Patton. "Searching for the Family and Household Structure of Rural Louisiana Slaves, 1810–1864." *Louisiana History* 28, no. 4 (Fall 1987): 357–80.

Mann, Susan A. "Slavery, Sharecropping, and Sexual Inequality." *Signs* 14, no. 4 (Summer 1989): 774–98.

Marable, Manning. "Groundings with My Sisters: Patriarchy and the Exploitation of Black Women." *Journal of Ethnic Studies* 11 (Summer 1983): 1–40.

Martinez-Alier, Verena. *Marriage, Class and Colour in Nineteenth-Century Cuba: A Study of Racial Attitudes and Sexual Values in a Slave Society*. London: Cambridge University Press, 1974.

Matson, R. Lynn. "Phillis Wheatley—Soul Sister?" *Phylon* 33, no. 3 (Fall 1972): 222–30.

Matthews, Jean. "Race, Sex, and the Dimension of Liberty in Antebellum America." *Journal of the Early Republic* 6, no. 3 (Fall 1986): 275–91.

Mbilinyi, M. J. "Wife, Slave and Subject of the King: The Oppression of Women in the Shambala Kingdom." *Tanzania Notes and Records*, nos. 88–89 (1982): 1–14.

McLaurin, Melton A. *Celia, a Slave: A True Story of Violence and Retribution in Antebellum Missouri*. Athens: University of Georgia Press, 1991.

Meillassoux, Claude. "Female Slavery." In *Women and Slavery in Africa*. Edited by Claire C. Robertson and Martin A. Klein. Madison: University of Wisconsin Press, 1983, 49–66.

Miers, Suzanne, and Igor Kopytoff, eds. *Slavery in Africa: Historical and Anthropological Perspectives* Madison: University of Wisconsin Press, 1977.

Mills, Bruce. "Lydia Maria Child and the Endings to Harriet Jacobs's *Incidents in the Life of a Slave Girl.*" *American Literature* 64 (June 1992): 255–72.

Mills, Gary B. "Coincoin: An Eighteenth-Century 'Liberated' Woman." *Journal of Southern History* 42, no. 2 (May 1976): 205–22.

Mintz, Sidney W. "Economic Role and Cultural Tradition." In *The Black Woman Cross-Culturally.* Edited by Filomina Chioma Steady. Cambridge, Mass.: Schenkman, 1981, 515–34.

Mirkin, Harris. "The Passive Female: The Theory of Patriarchy." *American Studies* 25 (Fall 1984): 39–59.

Momsen, Janet, ed. *Women and Change in the Caribbean: A Pan-Caribbean Perspective.* Bloomington: Indiana University Press, 1993.

Moody, Joycelyn K. "Ripping Away the Veil of Slavery: Literacy, Communal Love, and Self-Esteem in Three Slave Women's Narratives." *Black American Literature Forum* 24, no. 4 (Winter 1990): 633–48.

Morgan, Philip D. "Black Society in the Lowcountry, 1760–1810." In *Slavery and Freedom in the Age of the American Revolution.* Edited by Ira Berlin and Ronald Hoffman. Charlottesville: University Press of Virginia, 1983, 83–141.

Morrison, Toni. *Beloved.* New York: Knopf, 1987.

Morrissey, Marietta. *Slave Women in the New World: Gender Stratification in the Caribbean.* Lawrence: University Press of Kansas, 1989.

———. "Women's Work, Family Formation and Reproduction among Caribbean Slaves." *Review Journal of the Braudel Centre* 9, no. 3 (1986): 339–67.

Mullin, Michael. "Women and the Comparative Study of American Negro Slavery." *Slavery and Abolition* 6, no. 1 (May 1985): 25–40.

Nash, Gary B. "Forging Freedom: The Emancipation Experience in the Northern Seaport Cities, 1775–1820." In *Slavery and Freedom in the Age of the American Revolution.* Edited by Ira Berlin and Ronald Hoffman. Charlottesville: University Press of Virginia, 1983, 3–48.

Newman, Debra L. "Black Women in the Era of the American Revolution in Pennsylvania." *Journal of Negro History* 61, no. 3 (July 1976): 276–89.

Noble, Jeanne L. *Beautiful, Also, Are the Souls of My Black Sisters: A History of Black Women in America.* Englewood, N.J.: Prentice-Hall, 1978.

Norton, Mary Beth. "Eighteenth-Century American Women in Peace and War: The Case of the Loyalists." *William and Mary Quarterly* 3rd Series, 33 (July 1976): 386–409.

———. *Liberty's Daughters: The Revolutionary Experience of American Women, 1750–1800.* Boston: Little, Brown, 1980.

———, Herbert G. Gutman, and Ira Berlin. "The Afro-American Family in the Age of Revolution." In *Slavery and Freedom in the Age of the American Revolution.* Edited by Ira Berlin and Ronald Hoffman. Charlottesville: University Press of Virginia, 1983, 175–91.

Obitko, Mary Ellen. "'Custodians of a House of Resistance': Black Women Respond to Slavery." In *Women and Men: The Consequences of Power.* Edited by Dana V. Heller and Robin Ann Sheets. Cincinnati: Office of Women's Studies, University of Cincinnati, 1977, 256–69.

Oden, Gloria C. "The Journal of Charlotte L. Forten: The Salem-Philadelphia Years (1854–1862) Reexamined." *Essex Institute Historical Collections* 119, no. 2 (April 1983): 119–36.

Oppong, Christine, ed. *Female and Male in West Africa.* London: George Allen & Unwin, 1983.

Painter, Nell Irvin. "Of Lily, Linda Brent, and Freud: A Non-Exceptionalist Approach to Race, Class, and Gender in the Slave South." *Georgia Historical Quarterly* 76 (Summer 1992): 241–59.

————. "Sojourner Truth in Life and Memory: Writing the Biography of an American Exotic." *Gender and History* 2 (Spring 1990): 3–16.

————. "Three Southern Women and Freud: A Non-Exceptionalist Approach to Race, Class and Gender in the Slave South." In *Feminist Revision History*. Edited by Ann-Louise Shapiro. New Brunswick, N.J.: Rutgers University Press, 1994, 195–216.

Parent, Anthony S., and Susan Brown Wallace. "Childhood and Sexual Identity under Slavery." *Journal of the History of Sexuality* 3 (1992–93): 363–401.

Parkhurst, Jessie W. "The Role of the Black Mammy in the Plantation Household." *Journal of Negro History* 23, no. 3 (July 1938): 349–69.

Patterson, Orlando. "From Endo-deme to Matri-deme: An Interpretation of the Development of Kinship and Social Organization among the Slaves of Jamaica, 1655–1830." In *Eighteenth-Century Florida and the Caribbean*. Edited by Samuel Proctor. Gainesville: University Presses of Florida, 1976, 50–59.

————. "Slavery, Alienation, and the Female Discovery of Personal Freedom." In *Home: A Place in the World*. Edited by Arien Mack. New York: New York University Press, 1993, 159–87.

Perkins, Linda. "Black Women and Racial 'Uplift' Prior to Emancipation." In *The Black Woman Cross-Culturally*. Edited by Filomina Chioma Steady. Cambridge: Schenkman, 1981, 317–34.

Porter, Dorothy B. "Sarah Parker Remond, Abolitionist and Physician." *Journal of Negro History* 20, no. 3 (July 1935): 287–93.

Prince, Mary. *The History of Mary Prince, a West Indian Slave, Related by Herself.* Edited by Moira Ferguson. London: Pandora, 1987. (First published in 1831.)

Pryse, Marjorie, and Hortense J. Spillers, eds. *Conjuring: Black Women, Fiction, and Literary Tradition*. Bloomington: Indiana University Press, 1985.

Pugh, Evelyn L. "Women and Slavery: Julia Gardiner Tyler and the Duchess of Sutherland." *Virginia Magazine of History and Biography* 88 (April 1980): 186–202.

Quarles, Benjamin. "Harriet Tubman's Unlikely Leadership." In *Black Leaders of the Nineteenth Century*. Edited by Leon Litwack and August Meier. Urbana: University of Illinois Press, 1988, 43–57.

Rapport, Sara. "The Freedman's Bureau as a Legal Agent for Black Men and Women in Georgia, 1865–1868." *Georgia Historical Quarterly* 73 (Winter 1989): 26–53.

Reddock, Rhoda E. "Women and Slavery in the Caribbean: A Feminist Perspective." *Latin American Perspectives* 12, no. 1 (Winter 1985): 63–80.

Richardson, Marilyn, ed. *Maria W. Stewart, America's First Black Woman Political Writer: Essays and Speeches*. Bloomington: Indiana University Press, 1979.

Robertson, Claire C. "Changing Perspectives in Studies of African Women, 1976–1985." *Feminist Studies* 13, no. 1 (Spring 1987): 87–136.

————, and Martin A. Klein, eds. *Women and Slavery in Africa*. Madison: University of Wisconsin Press, 1983.

Russell, Sandi. *Render Me My Song: African-American Women Writers from Slavery to the Present*. New York: St. Martin's, 1991.

Russell-Wood, A. J. R. "The Black Family in the Americas." *Societas* 8, no. 1 (Winter 1978): 1–38.

Savitt, Todd L. "The Use of Blacks for Medical Experimentation and Demonstration in the Old South." *Journal of Southern History* 48, no. 3 (August 1982): 331–48.

Schafer, Judith K. "'Open and Notorious Concubinage': The Emancipation of Slave Mistresses by Wills and the Supreme Court in Antebellum Louisiana." *Louisiana History* 28, no. 2 (Spring 1987): 165–82.

Schweninger, Loren. "Property-Owning Free African-American Women in the South, 1800–1870." *Journal of Women's History* 1, no. 3 (Winter 1990): 13–44.

————. "A Slave Family in the Antebellum South." *Journal of Negro History* 60, no. 1 (January 1975): 29–44.

Scott, Anne Firor. "Women in Plantation Culture: Or What I Wish I Knew about Southern Women." *South Atlantic Urban Studies* 2 (1978): 24–33.

————, ed. *Unheard Voices: The First Historians of Southern Women.* Charlottesville: University Press of Virginia, 1993.

Scott, Joan W. "Gender: A Useful Category of Historical Analysis." *American Historical Review* 91 (December 1986): 1053–75.

————. "History and Difference." *Daedulus* 116 (Fall 1987): 93–118.

Sealander, Judith. "Antebellum Black Press Images of Women." *Western Journal of Black Studies* 6, no. 3 (Fall 1982): 159–65.

Sears, Richard. "Working Like a Slave: Views of Slavery and the Status of Women in Antebellum Kentucky." *Register of the Kentucky Historical Society* 87 (Winter 1989): 1–19.

Shammas, Carole. "Black Women's Work and the Evolution of Plantation Society in Virginia." *Labor History* 26, no. 1 (Winter 1985): 5–28.

Shea, Deborah, ed. "Spreading Terror and Devastation Wherever They Have Been: A Norfolk Woman's Account of the Southampton Slave Insurrection." *Virginia Magazine of History and Biography* 95 (January 1987): 65–74.

Sheridan, Richard B. "The Problem of Reproduction." *Doctors and Slaves: A Medical and Demographic History of Slavery in the British West Indies, 1680–1834.* Cambridge: Cambridge University Press, 1985, 222–48.

Sherman, Sarah Way. "Moral Experience in Harriet Jacobs's *Incidents in the Life of a Slave Girl.*" *NWSA Journal* 2 (Spring 1990): 167–85.

Shockley, Ann Allen, ed. *Afro-American Women Writers, 1746–1933: An Anthology and Critical Guide.* Boston: G. K. Hall, 1988.

Sides, Sudie Duncan. "Southern Women and Slavery." *History Today* 20 (January 1970): 54–60.

Silverman, Jason H., "Mary Ann Shadd and the Search for Equality." In *Black Leaders of the Nineteenth Century.* Edited by Leon Litwack and August Meier. Urbana: University of Illinois Press, 1988, 87–100.

Simmonds, Lorna. "Slave Higglering in Jamaica, 1780–1834." *Jamaica Journal* 20, no. 1 (February–April 1987): 31–38.

Smith, Eleanor. "Black American Women and Work: A Historical Review, 1619–1920." *Women's Studies International Forum* 8, no. 4 (1985): 343–49.

Soderlund, Jean R. "Black Women in Colonial Pennsylvania." *Pennsylvania Magazine of History and Biography* 107, no. 1 (January 1983): 49–68.

Spillers, Hortense J. "Mama's Baby, Papa's Maybe: An American Grammar Book." *Diacritics: A Review of Contemporary Criticism* 17, no. 2 (Summer 1987): 65–81.

Spruill, Julia Cherry. *Women's Life and Work in the Southern Colonies.* Chapel Hill: University of North Carolina Press, 1938.

Staples, Robert. "The Myth of the Black Matriarchy." *Black Scholar* 2, no. 1 (January–February 1970): 8–16.

Steady, Filomina Chioma, ed. *The Black Woman Cross-Culturally.* Cambridge, Mass.: Schenkman, 1981.

Steckel, Richard H. "Slave Marriage and the Family." *Journal of Family History* 5, no. 4, (Winter 1980): 406–21.

Sterling, Dorothy. "To Build a Free Society: Nineteenth-Century Black Women." *Southern Exposure* 12, no. 2 (March–April 1984): 24–30.

————, ed. *We Are Your Sisters: Black Women in the Nineteenth Century.* New York: Norton, 1984.

Stetson, Erlene. "Studying Slavery: Some Literary and Pedagogical Considerations on the Black Female Slave." In *All the Women Are White, All the Blacks Are Men, but*

Some of Us Are Brave: Black Women's Studies. Edited by Gloria T. Hull, Patricia Bell Scott, and Barbara Smith. Old Westbury, N.Y.: Feminist, 1982, 61–84.

Stevenson, Brenda. "Distress and Discord in Virginia Slave Families, 1830–1860." In *In Joy and in Sorrow: Women, Family and Marriage in the Victorian South, 1830–1900.* Edited by Carol Bleser. New York: Oxford University Press, 1991, 103–34.

Streitmatter, Rodger. "Delilah Beasley: A Black Woman Who Lifted as She Climbed." *American Journalism* 11 (Winter 1994): 61–75.

Sumler-Lewis, Janice. "The Forten-Purvis Women of Philadelphia and the American Anti-Slavery Crusade." *Journal of Negro History* 66, no. 4 (Winter 1981–82): 281–88.

Sutch, Richard. "The Breeding of Slaves for Sale and the Westward Expansion of Slavery, 1850–1860." In *Race and Slavery in the Western Hemisphere.* Edited by Stanley L. Engerman and Eugene D. Genovese. Princeton: Princeton University Press, 1975, 173–210.

Tandberg, Gerilyn G. "Field Hand Clothing in Louisiana and Mississippi during the Ante-Bellum Period." *Dress* 6 (1980): 89–103.

———, and Sally Graham Durand. "Dress-Up Clothes for Field Slaves of Ante-Bellum Louisiana and Mississippi." *Costume* 15 (1981): 40–48.

Taylor, Orville W. "Jumping the Broomstick: Slave Marriage and Mortality in Arkansas." *Arkansas Historical Quarterly* 17, no. 3 (Autumn 1958): 217–31.

Terborg-Penn, Rosalyn. "Black Women in Resistance: A Cross-Cultural Perspective." In *In Resistance: Studies in African, Caribbean and Afro-American History.* Edited by Gary Y. Okihiro. Amherst: University of Massachusetts Press, 1986, 188–209.

———. "Women and Slavery in the African Diaspora: A Cross-Cultural Approach to Historical Analysis." *Sage: A Scholarly Journal on Black Women* 3, no. 2 (Fall 1986): 11–15.

Thompson, Priscilla. "Harriet Tubman, Thomas Garrett, and the Underground Railroad." *Delaware History* 22, no. 1 (Spring–Summer 1986): 1–21.

Tilly, Louise A. "Gender, Women's History, and Social History." *Social Science History* 13 (Winter 1989): 439–62.

Trussel, James, and Richard Steckel. "The Age of Slaves at Menarche and Their First Birth." *Journal of Interdisciplinary History* 8, no. 3 (Winter 1978): 477–505.

Tuelon, Alan. "Nanny—Maroon Chieftainess." *Caribbean Quarterly* 19, no. 4 (December 1973): 20–27.

Vacha, John E. "The Case of Sara Lucy Bagby: A Late Gesture." *Ohio History* 76, no. 4 (Autumn 1967): 222–31.

Walker, Margaret. *Jubilee.* Boston: Houghton Mifflin, 1966.

Warner, Anne Bradford. "Harriet Jacobs's Modest Proposals: Revising Southern Hospitality." *Southern Quarterly* 30 (Winter–Spring 1992): 22–28.

Wertz, Dorothy C. "Women and Slavery: A Cross-Cultural Perspective." *International Journal of Women's Studies* 7, no. 4 (September–October 1984): 372–84.

Wetherell, Charles. "Slave Kinship: A Case Study of the South Carolina Good Hope Plantation, 1835–1856." *Journal of Family History* 6 (Fall 1981): 294–308.

White, Deborah Gray. *Ar'n't I a Woman? Female Slaves in the Plantation South.* New York: Norton, 1985.

———. "Female Slaves: Sex Roles and Status in the Antebellum Plantation South." *Journal of Family History* 8, no. 3 (Fall 1983): 248–61.

———. "The Lives of Slave Women." *Southern Exposure* 12, no. 6 (November–December 1984): 32–39.

Williams, Sherley Anne. *Dessa Rose.* New York: Morrow, 1986.

Wilson, Harriet E. *Our Nig; or, Sketches from the Life of a Free Black.* Introduction and notes by Henry Louis Gates, Jr. New York: Vintage, 1983. (First published in 1859.)

Winter, Kari J. *Subjects of Slavery, Agents of Change: Women and Power in Gothic Novels and Slave Narratives, 1790–1865.* Athens: University of Georgia Press, 1992.

Wood, Betty. "Some Aspects of Female Resistance to Chattel Slavery in Low Country Georgia, 1763–1815." *Historical Journal* 30, no. 3 (September 1987): 603–22.

———. "White Women, Black Slaves and the Law in Early National Georgia—The Sunbury Petition of 1791." *Historical Journal* 35, no. 3 (September 1992): 611–22.

Wood, Peter H. "'Liberty Is Sweet': African-American Freedom Struggles in the Years before White Independence." In *Beyond the American Revolution: Explorations in the History of American Radicalism.* Edited by Alfred F. Young. De Kalb: Northern Illinois University Press, 1993, 149–84.

Wright, Michelle D. "African-American Sisterhood: The Impact of the Female Slave Population on American Political Movements." *Western Journal of Black Studies* 15 (Spring 1991): 32–45.

Yellin, Jean Fagan. "The Text and Contexts of Harriet Jacobs' *Incidents in the Life of a Slave Girl: Written by Herself.*" In *The Slave's Narrative.* Edited by Charles T. Davis and Henry Louis Gates, Jr. Oxford: Oxford University Press, 1985, 262–82.

———. *Women and Sisters: The Anti-Slavery Feminists in American Culture.* New Haven, Conn.: Yale University Press, 1989.

———. "Written by Herself: Harriet Jacobs' Slave Narrative." *American Literature: A Journal of Literary History, Criticism and Bibliography* 53, no. 3 (November 1981): 479–486.

CONTRIBUTORS

Hilary Beckles is Professor of History and Dean of the Faculty of Arts and General Studies at the University of West Indies, Cave Hill, Barbados. Among his many publications are *White Servitude and Black Slavery in Barbados, 1627–1715* (1989); *Natural Rebels: A Social History of Enslaved Black Women in Barbados, 1640–1838* (1989); and *A History of Barbados: From Amerindian Settlement to Nation-State* (1990).

Barbara Bush has published several articles about slavery and slave women in the Caribbean. She is the author of *Slave Women in Caribbean Society, 1650–1838* (1990).

Cheryll Ann Cody is an independent researcher living in Houston, Texas. Among her publications are essays on naming practices and the familial lives of enslaved people and emancipated men and women in the *William and Mary Quarterly, American Historical Review*, and *Ethnohistory*. She is also the author of a forthcoming study of the demographic and family history of the Ball Family slaves.

David Barry Gaspar is Professor of History at Duke University. He has published articles on slavery and slave society in the Caribbean, and is the author of *Bondmen and Rebels: A Study of Master-Slave Relations in Antigua* (1985). He is also co-editor of the forthcoming *A Turbulent Time: The Greater Caribbean in the Age of the French and Haitian Revolutions* (Indiana University Press).

David P. Geggus is Professor of History at the University of Florida, Gainesville. He has published extensively on slavery, and the French and Haitian revolutions in the Caribbean, and is the author of *Slavery, War, and Revolution: The British Occupation on Saint Domingue 1793–1798* (1982). He is also co-editor of the forthcoming *A Turbulent Time: The Greater Caribbean in the Age of the French and Haitian Revolutions* (Indiana University Press).

L. Virginia Gould teaches at DeKalb College in Atlanta, Georgia. Her research focuses on slavery, slave women, and free women of color of the Gulf ports of New Orleans, Mobile, and Pensacola. Her book *In Full Enjoyment of Their Liberty: The Free Women of Color of the Gulf Ports of New Orleans, Mobile, and Pensacola, 1769–1860* is forthcoming.

Darlene Clark Hine is John A. Hannah Professor of American History at Michigan State University. She is the author of *Black Victory: The Rise and Fall of the White Primary in Texas* (1979); *When the Truth is Told: Black Women's*

Culture and Community in Indiana, 1875–1950 (1981); *Black Women in White: Racial Conflict and Cooperation in the Nursing Profession 1890–1950* (1989); and *Hine Sight: Black Women and the Re-Construction of American History* (1994). She is the editor of *The State of Afro-American History: Past, Present and Future* (1986); and co-editor of *Black Women in America: An Historical Encyclopedia* (1993).

Mary Karasch is Professor of History at Oakland University, Rochester, Michigan. She is the author of *Slave Life in Rio de Janeiro, 1808–1850* (1987) which won the Albert J. Beveridge Award of the American Historical Association. Her new book project is *Before Brasilia: Settlement Patterns and Population Change in Goiás, 1780–1890.*

Wilma King is Professor of History at Michigan State University. She is the editor of *A Northern Woman in the Plantation South: Letters of Tryphena Blanche Holder Fox, 1856–1876* (1993), and the author of *Stolen Childhood: Slave Youth in Nineteenth-Century America* (1995).

Bernard Moitt is Assistant Professor in the Department of History and Geography at Virginia Commonwealth University. His published work includes articles about enslaved women and children, and slave resistance, in Africa and the French Caribbean.

Celia E. Naylor-Ojurongbe is completing graduate studies in history at Duke University. She is Director of the Women's Center at Iowa State University.

Robert Olwell is Assistant Professor in the Department of History at the University of Texas at Austin. He is completing a book on slavery and social order in the South Carolina low country, 1739 to 1784.

Claire Robertson is Associate Professor of History and Women's Studies at Ohio State University. She is the author of *Sharing the Same Bowl: A Socioeconomic History of Women and Class in Accra, Ghana* (1984) which won the African Studies Association's Herskovits Book Award. She is also co-editor of *Women and Slavery in Africa* (1984) and *Women and Class in Africa* (1986).

Robert W. Slenes is Professor of History at the Universidade Estadual de Campinas, Brazil. Among his many publications are studies about the economic and social history of slavery in Brazil.

Susan M. Socolow is Professor of History at Emory University. She has written extensively on colonial Latin American social and demographic history, including *The Merchants of Viceregal Buenos Aires: Family and Commerce, 1778–1810* (1978). She is co-editor of *Cities & Society in Colonial Latin America* (1986).

Richard H. Steckel is Professor of Economics at Ohio State University and Research Associate of the National Bureau of Economic Research. He has published several articles on the demographic, medical, and social history of slavery in the United States, and is the author of *The Economics of U.S. Slave and Southern White Fertility* (1985), and *Stature and Living Standards in the United States* (1991).

Brenda E. Stevenson is Associate Professor of History at the University of California, Los Angeles. She is the editor of *Journals of Charlotte Forten Grimke* (1988), and author of several articles about enslaved women and the slave family in the United States. Her book *Life in Black and White: Family and Community in the Slave South* is forthcoming from Oxford University Press.

INDEX